BLACK THEATER IS BLACK LIFE

BLACK THEATER IS BLACK LIFE

AN ORAL HISTORY OF CHICAGO THEATER AND DANCE, 1970–2010

Harvey Young
and Queen Meccasia Zabriskie

NORTHWESTERN UNIVERSITY PRESS
EVANSTON, ILLINOIS

Northwestern University Press
www.nupress.northwestern.edu

This book has been published with the support of the Andrew W. Mellon Foundation.

Printed in the United States of America

10 9 8 7 6 5 4 3 2 1

LIBRARY OF CONGRESS CATALOGING-IN-PUBLICATION DATA

Young, Harvey, 1975–
    Black theater is Black life : an oral history of Chicago theater and dance, 1970–2010 / Harvey Young and Queen Meccasia Zabriskie.
        page cm.
    ISBN 978-0-8101-2942-9 (pbk. : alk. paper)
    1. African American theater—Illinois—Chicago—History—20th century. 2. African American theater—Illinois—Chicago—History—21st century. 3. African American dance—Illinois—Chicago—History—20th century. 4. African American dance—Illinois—Chicago—History—21st century. 5. African Americans in the performing arts—Illinois—Chicago—History—20th century. 6. African Americans in the performing arts—Illinois—Chicago—History—21st century. 7. African American theatrical producers and directors—illinois—Chicago—Interviews. 8. African American dancers—Illinois—Chicago—Interviews. I. Zabriskie, Queen Meccasia. II. Title.
PN2277.C42Y68 2013
792.08996077311—dc23
                                                                            2013016069

    ∞ The paper used in this publication meets the minimum requirements of the American National Standard for Information Sciences—Permanence of Paper for Printed Library Materials, ANSI Z39.48–1992.

CONTENTS

Photographs follow page 170.

ACKNOWLEDGMENTS

This book exists not only because twenty-two artists sat down and shared with us their experiences of working in the arts in Chicago but also because of the efforts of countless individuals who built the foundations on which those artists stand. These individuals collaborated with them—creating and sustaining theater and dance companies. As audience members, these same individuals supported their efforts. We thank them, the named and unnamed, for their commitment to and belief in the power of the arts to enrich a community, a city, and a nation.

We are greatly indebted to Tosha Alston, Babu Atiba, Alfred Baker, Darlene Blackburn, Sydney Chatman, Idy Ciss, Gloria Bond Clunie, Idella Reed-Davis, Joseph "Joel" Hall, Daniel "Brave Monk" Haywood, Kevin Iega Jeff, Najwa I, Ron O. J. Parson, Amaniyea Payne, Kathy A. Perkins, Kemati Porter, Derrick Sanders, Rashida Z. Shaw, Chuck Smith, Jackie Taylor, Geraldine Williams, and Jonathan Wilson for their significant contributions to Chicago's dance and theater scene and their willingness to share their stories with us and, by extension, with you.

Neither of us are native Chicagoans. Harvey arrived in 2002 and Meccasia in 2004. We are particularly grateful to the following people for their encouraging, welcoming embrace in the Chicago arts world and, in so doing, for gifting us with a vantage point to fully appreciate the local, regional, national, and international significance of the city's performing arts community: Vickie Casanova, David Catlin, Rives Collins, Imania Detry, Shawn Douglass, Wendell Etherly, Mashaune Hardy, Amanda Holman, Vaun Monroe, Sadira Muhammad, Sheelah Muhammad, Kimosha Murphy, Nicole Noland, Nakia Ocean, Clifton Robinson, Albirda Rose, Nahgeree Sutton-Silas, Ernest Perry Jr., Virgil C. Johnson, Willa Taylor, Andy White, and Albert Williams.

The Andrew W. Mellon Foundation, through a "Universities and Their Presses" grant, provided the core funding for this book. The grant, which provides for multiple publishing projects, was facilitated by co-project investigators E. Patrick Johnson and Donna Shear (and, later, Jane Bunker succeeding Shear) and was coauthored by several Northwestern faculty and staff, including Henry Godinez, E. Patrick Johnson, Susan Manning, Ramón Rivera-Servera, and Harvey Young. Alan Shefsky, Liz Luby, and Freda Love Smith processed expenses related to this grant. Gianna Mosser, the project manager for the grant, has been a steadfast ally and friend. Mike Levine, the acquisitions editor for this book, has impressed us with his patience and unwavering support for this project. Henry Bienen, former president of Northwestern University, and Barbara O'Keefe, dean of Northwestern's School of Communication, provided instrumental administrative and additional financial support that contributed to the success of the grant application.

In support of this project, numerous research assistants were employed. We are thankful for the efforts of Dawn Tracey Brandes, Dwayne Mann, Chris Eckels, Aurelia Clunie, Marco Minichiello, and Leah Kaplan. A Fellow Assistant Researcher Award grant, from Northwestern's Residential College Program, and research funds from Northwestern's School of Communication subsidized these research costs.

As may be evident from the names listed above, books are not created in a vacuum—untouched by the influence of others. In addition, we appreciate the casual advice, suggestions, and assistance of the following friends and colleagues: Kevin Douglas, Runako Jahi, D. Soyini Madison, Meida McNeal, Mary Pattillo, Sandra L. Richards, Billy Siegenfeld, and Wilhelmena Taylor.

The process of creating an oral history is time intensive. The interviews selected for inclusion in this book occurred over a three-year period. We greatly appreciate the support (and patience) of our families as we labored on and lived with this book over the past few years: Jerome Dais, Dolores Hartshorn, Mamadou Nguer, Heather Schoenfeld, Mark Ezekiel (Zeke) Young, Beverly Zabriskie, Hasan Zabriskie, and Queen Precious-Jewel Zabriskie.

This book is dedicated to every dance and theater artist in the city of Chicago. The work that you do is important, necessary, and vital. We appreciate you. We thank you for enriching our lives and preserving our history.

CHRONOLOGY

1905 Robert T. Motts opens the Pekin Theater; Robert S. Abbott founds the *Chicago Defender* newspaper.

1909 An interracial group of activists committed to racial justice establish The National Association for the Advancement of Colored People (NAACP).

1912 Heavyweight boxing champion Jack Johnson opens Café de Champion.

1914 Marcus Garvey establishes the Universal Negro Improvement Association (UNIA) in Jamaica, which has several chapters in Chicago by the 1920s.

1919 Race riots occur in Chicago; W. E. B. Du Bois organizes the First Pan-African Congress in Paris.

1922 Jazz trumpeter Louis Armstrong, at the age of twenty-one, moves to Chicago.

1924 Mary Bruce opens her dance studio at 58th and South Parkway (now King Drive).

1927 Savoy Ballroom opens at 47th Street and South Parkway; Bertha Moseley Lewis establishes the Masque Players, a Chicago-based black theater group.

1928 Regal Theater opens at 47th and Grand Avenue.

1929 Sadie Bruce opens her dancing school at 5419 S. Calumet Avenue; the Great Depression begins.

1930 Katherine Dunham forms a dance company called Ballet Négre.

1933 Sammy Dyer founds the Sammy Dyer School of Dancing (now the Sammy Dyer School of the Theatre); Katherine Dunham opens a dance school called the Negro Dance Group in Chicago; Katherine Dunham and Talley Beatty, along with other black dancers, perform in Ruth Page's ballet *La Guiablesse* at the 1933 Century of Progress World's Fair.

1934 The Club DeLisa, run by the four DeLisa brothers, opens; Elijah Muhammad, founder of the Nation of Islam, moves to Chicago.

1936 Parkway Community House founded by Good Shepherd Congregational Church; Author Richard Wright founds the South Side Writers' Group.

1937 *The Big White Fog* by Theodore Ward premieres at the Great Northern Theatre in a production by Chicago's Negro Unit of the Federal Theatre Project; Joe Louis beats James Braddock at Comiskey Park and wins heavyweight boxing championship.

1940 The American Negro Exposition takes place at the Chicago Coliseum (July 4–September 2); The South Side Community Art Center opens (December).

1941 Parkway Community House relocates to 5120 South Parkway (now King Drive).

1943 Johnson Publishing founds *Negro Digest* (later called *Black World*).

1945 World War II ends; Katherine Dunham opens the Katherine Dunham School of Arts and Research.

1947   Baseball player Jackie Robinson makes his first professional appearance in Chicago against the Chicago Cubs at Wrigley Field; Jimmy Payne Sr. moves to Chicago and teaches at a number of studios in the Loop before establishing the Jimmy Payne School of Dance.

1950   Sammy Dyer creates The Dyerettes, an all–African American female chorus line.

1954   The Supreme Court, in the *Brown v. Board of Education* case, decides that segregation in schools is unconstitutional.

1957   Tommy Sutton founds Mayfair Academy of Fine Arts; Ghana gets its independence from British colonial rule, becoming the first sub-Saharan African nation to achieve this goal.

1958   Club DeLisa closes in 1958 (reopening as "The Club" in 1966); Guinea gets its independence from French colonial rule and becomes the first French-ruled sub-Saharan African nation to do so.

1959   Les Ballets Africains, one of the national dance companies in Guinea, West Africa, goes on its first U.S. tour.

1960   Shirley Hall Bass becomes artistic director of Sammy Dyer School of Dance.

1961   Dr. Margaret Burroughs, along with other Chicagoans, establishes the DuSable Museum of African American History.

1962   Loop College (later renamed Harold Washington College) is founded.

1963   Darlene Blackburn establishes the Darlene Blackburn Dance Troupe; Neville Black and Maggie Kast cofound the Chicago Contemporary Dance Theatre.

1965 Malcolm X is assassinated; the Association for the Advancement of Creative Musicians is established in Chicago.

1966 Martin Luther King Jr. moves his family to Chicago's West Side; King names Jesse Jackson director of Operation Breadbasket in Chicago (which would become the Rainbow PUSH Coalition); Oscar Brown Jr.'s musical *Summer in the City* opens at Harper Theatre in Hyde Park; The Center for Inner City Studies at Northeastern University is established; President Léopold Sédar Senghor hosts the First World Festival of Black Arts and Culture in Senegal, which Katherine Dunham attends as a representative from the United States.

1967 The first "On the Beach" summer festival is held at 63rd and Lake Michigan, featuring Darlene Blackburn and Phil Cohran and the African Heritage Ensemble; the Affro-Arts Theater is established; Theodore Ward founds the South Side Center of the Performing Arts; the Organization of Black American Culture (OBAC) is established on the South Side.

1968 Kuumba Workshop is founded by Val Gray Ward; Jeff Donaldson, Wadsworth Jarrell, Elaine Jae Jarrell, Barbara Jones-Hogu, and Gerald Williams establish AFRICOBRA—African Commune of Bad Relevant Artists; Martin Luther King Jr. is assassinated.

1969 Shirley Mordine establishes the Dance Center of Columbia College Chicago; Fred Hampton and Mark Clark, two leaders in Chicago's Black Panther Party, are murdered by the Chicago police; Herzl Junior College is renamed Malcolm X College and moved to its current location on W. Van Buren Street.

1971 eta Creative Arts Foundation is incorporated; Northwestern Community Ensemble, a student gospel choir at Northwestern University, is founded; Julian Swain forms the Julian Swain Inner City Dance Theatre.

1972   Muntu Dance Theatre of Chicago is founded; X-BAG Theatre is founded and reopens theater at Parkway Community House.

1973   Playwright Useni Perkins founds the Black Theater Alliance; LaMont Zeno Community Theatre, Ebony Talent Associates, and Kusema Repertory Theatre are founded; Nubian Cultural Dance Theatre is founded.

1974   Joseph Holmes Dance Theatre and Victory Gardens Theater are founded; Joel Hall establishes a dance company as part of the Chicago City Theatre Company.

1977   FieldCrest, a performing arts center, is founded; Najwa I creates her dance company, Najwa Dance Corps; FESTAC, the Second World Black and Africa Festival of Arts and Culture is held in Lagos, Nigeria, consisting of 17,000 artists, including a 500-person U.S. delegation.

1978   Western Jamaica Folk Dance Company (later the West Indian Folk Dance Company) moves to Chicago; the *Chicago Tribune* hires theater critic Richard Christiansen.

1982   Phase II: Crosstown Crew, a legendary b-boy crew, is established.

1983   Harold Washington becomes first African American mayor of Chicago; Oprah Winfrey moves to Chicago and begins hosting a television talk show.

1984   The Chicago Bulls draft University of North Carolina–Chapel Hill college basketball player Michael Jordan; Tommy Gomez, a former member of the Katherine Dunham Dance Company, forms the Body Language Dance Company.

1985   ALYO Children's Dance Theatre is established by Kimosha P. Murphy.

1986 Khalidah Kali establishes Khalidah's North African Dance Experience.

1987 Columbia College Chicago establishes the Theodore Ward Prize for African American Playwriting.

1989 Richard M. Daley is elected mayor and will serve as mayor for next twenty-two years.

1990 MPAACT, Ma'at Production Association of Afrikan Centered Theatre, is founded; Lane Alexander and Kelly Michaels cofound the Chicago Human Rhythm Project; Homer Hans Bryant, a former principal dancer with the Dance Theatre of Harlem, establishes the Bryant Ballet School and Company (later changed to the Chicago Multi-Cultural Dance Center in 1997).

1991 Silimbo D'Adeane travels to Chicago from Dakar, Senegal to perform at a Black History Month celebration at the Chicago Cultural Center with Idy Ciss as one of the dancers in the company.

1993 K. Todd Freeman becomes the first black ensemble member of the Steppenwolf Theatre Company (founded in 1974).

1994 Meshach Silas and Nahgeree Sutton-Silas establish Minianka West Afrikan Drum and Dance Ensemble.

1995 Vincent Williams founds the Black Theater Alliance Awards to honor African Americans who achieve excellence in theater, dance, and all areas of the performing and technical arts in the Chicagoland area; Kevin Iega Jeff and Garry Abbott establish Deeply Rooted Dance Theater of Chicago; Idella Reed-Davis, Sharon Brushing, and Sarah Savelli establish Rhythm ISS; Laurie Goux forms Spirit Wing Dance Ensemble under the guidance of her mentors Tommy Gomez and Jimmy Payne Sr.

1996 Dennis Zacek creates a Playwrights Ensemble at Victory Gardens Theater.

1997 African American Arts Alliance of Chicago is created; The University of Hip-Hop (Healthy Independent People Helping Other People), a school of street arts that is multidisciplinary, is created.

1999 Derrick Sanders and Reginald Nelson cofound Congo Square Theatre Company.

2002 Le Bagatae West African Dance and Drum Ensemble is founded in Chicago.

2005 Sekou Conde creates Seneke West African Percussion Ensemble; Sydney Chatman founds the Tofu Chitlin' Circuit.

2007 J. Nicole Brooks, playwright and director, becomes the first black ensemble member of Lookingglass Theatre Company (founded in 1988); Ayodele Drum and Dance Company is established by seven women with Tosha "Ayo" Alston as the artistic director.

2008 Barack Obama, a former South Side community organizer, state legislator, and senator is elected president of the United States; Markeya Howard and Da'vid Braswell establish Mofindu African Drum and Dance Company; Vershawn Sanders creates Red Clay Dance, a contemporary dance company informed by the dance and culture of the African diaspora.

2010 Meida McNeal creates Honey Pot Performance, a woman-focused creative collaborative community and mixed-media performance company.

2011 "Black Theater Is Black Life" symposia series is held at Northwestern University and Chicago Cultural Center; Rahm Emanuel is elected as mayor of Chicago.

2012 President Barack Obama is reelected.

BLACK THEATER IS BLACK LIFE

INTRODUCTION
THEATER + DANCE = LIFE

On July 4, 1910, the attention of the nation focused on Reno, Nevada, where a boxing match was being staged. Jack Johnson, the defending heavyweight champion and the first African American to hold the title, competed against Jim Jeffries, the former champion who had retired undefeated and whose retirement allowed Johnson to compete for and win the heavyweight title. During his reign, Jeffries drew the "color line," thus ensuring that only a white man had an opportunity to become champion. Now, the latest and most prominent "Great White Hope," had reemerged from retirement in an attempt to reclaim the championship. At a time when racial segregation was legal, and lynchings of black men and women were rarely prosecuted, interest in the match ran high, with audiences viewing it as a battle for racial supremacy. Who would win? Black or white?

In Chicago, Johnson's mother "attended" the fight by going to the Pekin Theater, which was located on the South Side on 2700 S. State Street.[1] Joined by 2,000 fellow Chicagoans who "crammed" into the thousand-seat performing arts venue, she anxiously awaited the arrival and public reading of the "live" telegraph reports. The assembled crowd cheered whenever the announcer informed them of Johnson's successes. When Jack Johnson finally won, the audience applauded and roared its approval throughout the Pekin. Following the match, the crowd exited the theater and flooded the nearby and newly developed (and still developing) popular entertainment district, which would become known as "The Stroll," for dancing and merriment that would last into the early hours of the next day.

By 1910, the Pekin Theater had become the place on the South Side for both amusement and civic engagement. The community gathered there to consider matters concerning the race. Chicago politicians used the theater to deliver speeches to their constituents. Theater artists employed its stage to slowly revise popular stereotypes and caricatures of blackness. Chicagoans assembled there, as they did on this day, to receive current news updates on significant events occurring beyond the borders of the city. The popularity and varied uses of the Pekin signal the centrality of the performing arts (and arts venues) to African American civic life within the South Side and, more generally, Chicago. The very core of the black community centered on theater and dance. More than a century later, long after the Pekin permanently closed its doors, the performing arts maintain a vital presence within the lives of Black Chicago. This book spotlights the ongoing centrality of theater and dance by focusing on a rarely examined period in its history: 1970 to 2010.

Black Theater Is Black Life contributes to the literature on Black Chicago by focusing on the contemporary arts scene. The majority of scholarship on the lives and lifestyles of black folk in Chicago focuses on the period between 1930 and 1950, what has been called the Chicago Black Renaissance. St. Clair Drake and Horace Cayton's seminal sociological study *Black Metropolis* offers a glimpse into a number of social institutions within and the lifestyles of Black Chicago during those years.[2] Davarian Baldwin's engaging book *Chicago's New Negroes* examines the entertainment culture surrounding "The Stroll" during this period.[3] Other studies, such as Mike Rowe's *Chicago's Blues* and Jacqueline Stewart's *Migrating to the Movies*, cover Chicago's thriving film and music industries.[4] In scholarly studies of Chicago post-1954, scholars shift focus from the arts in favor of the economic and social welfare challenges facing the decreasingly populated and increasingly impoverished Black Belt neighborhoods.

Black Theater Is Black Life is an oral history of the African American dance and theater communities of Chicago, between 1970 and 2010. It centers on twenty-two individuals whose perspectives offer a first-person point of view into the recent history of the city's dynamic performing arts culture. The book documents the creation of new theater and dance companies in the waning years of the Black Arts Movement and the popular reemergence of black theater and dance in Chicago within the twenty-first century. In style, it resembles Timuel Black's two-volume history of Black Chicago, *Bridges of Memory,* a collection of interviews that, as its title suggests, connects present-day readers with community elders who share their memories of life in Chicago.[5] Similar to Black's absorbing study, *Black Theater Is Black Life* reminds us that history is made, written, and preserved through the efforts of individuals. This book introduces a range of folk who are the keepers of Chicago's performing arts memory.

Oral histories, the recollection and interpretation of everyday, lived experiences, offer the opportunity to learn from multiple perspectives on the past.[6] Through dialogue, interviewers and interviewees cocreate history through the process of selecting (and editing) past events for inclusion in a public record.[7] Oral histories grant the opportunity to witness the making of history through the eyes of another person. They also illustrate present-day social relations and the future aspirations of those engaged in the public act of remembering.[8] Through the interviews of these key individuals, readers experience the events leading to the creation of several of Chicago's most influential theater and dance companies, including eta Creative Arts, Black Ensemble Theater, Muntu Dance Theatre of Chicago, Congo Square Theatre, Najwa Dance Corps, and the Experimental Black Actors Guild (X-BAG). Prominent Chicagoans share their stories, experiences, and the strategies they used to navigate a shifting social, political, economic, and artistic landscape in the city. They remember their encounters with highly recognizable national figures, such as August Wilson, Katherine Dunham, Alvin Ailey, and Woodie King Jr., as well as important artistic innovators within the city whose legacy has faded following their deaths and risks being permanently forgotten, such as Theodore Ward, Lucille Ellis, Oscar Brown Jr., and Clarence Taylor.

The individuals featured in this book were given the opportunity to tell their own stories. As interviewers and conversation partners, our task was to listen as these artists mined their memories, shared their experiences, and, in the process, succeeded in writing history. Their accounts introduce the people whose efforts and contributions actively shaped contemporary theater and dance culture in Chicago. These notable figures spotlight turning points and events that contributed toward the current look of our society. This book is a collection of *their* stories, *their* memories, and *their* history. To keep the spotlight on the featured artists, we attempt, as much as possible, to fade into the background in the edited interviews. While our fingerprints exist all over this book—we recruited our subjects, sat in their presence as they journeyed down memory lane, asked questions to help jog their memory, and edited their words for inclusion in this volume, we respect the fact that the stories recounted belong to them. In the spirit of a folklore-inspired oral history, we do not seek to conarrate their stories or experiences. We also do not correct them. It is human nature to strongly, vividly recall certain details and to forget others. People occasionally misremember. Rather than establishing ourselves as the arbiters of truth, we have chosen instead to incorporate more voices and to give them the opportunity to speak at length. In their words, a more complex picture of the recent history of Chicago theater and dance emerges.

Tens of thousands of people could have been chosen for inclusion in this collection, with each of their accounts gifting the reader an important, privileged vantage point from which to observe a particular moment in the city's past. The individuals featured here were selected with the aim of offering not only a representative sampling but also a panoramic view of Chicago's black performing arts cultures and communities over the past four decades. They consist of producers, directors, choreographers, designers, actors, dancers, and audience members. They are men and women, gay and straight, teachers and students, elders and emerging artists, and native and adopted Chicagoans. In identifying subjects, we deliberately sought out people who frequently either assumed the lead in creating new theater and dance companies or sat in the front row and witnessed their development and subsequent performances. In light of the number of artists who could have been featured in this book, it is inevitable that some readers may feel that voices are missing. Indeed, voices are missing—tens of thousands of them—and they deserve to be heard. Books like this remind us that our shared history is embodied. To access history, we simply have to listen and learn from those around us.

It is our hope that readers may find inspiration to conduct their own oral histories. Only by working together will we record and preserve the past for the future.

A BRIEF HISTORY TO 1970

Although this book focuses on black theater and dance from 1970 to 2010, it is helpful, for the sake of historical orientation, to *briefly* consider the historical development of black artistic communities before 1970. Little is known about theater and dance in Chicago's black communities during the first decade of the twentieth century. Charles Gilpin, who would become the first black actor to headline a dramatic play on Broadway, in 1922, remembers that before the opening of the Pekin Theater in 1906, he would participate in play readings, along with twenty or thirty fellow actors.[9] These readings gave these actors an opportunity to perform serious dramatic roles that differed from the comic, musical, or vaudeville pieces that were popular during the period. Creating what could be considered an early black community theater or, more likely, an artistic salon, this group of professional actors read and performed pieces that were rarely produced by national theatrical syndicates or circuits. This theater was born from the need to see (and inhabit) a range of representations not available elsewhere.

The Pekin Theater, which is widely recognized as the first black-owned theater in Chicago, was founded by Robert T. Motts, who had profited from the "vice industry" and was rumored to be *the* "underworld boss" of the South Side. Despite the founder's unsavory reputation, A. N. Manners, a contemporary of Motts, remembers him as "a man of large stature, pleasing in manners, yet it could be discerned that he was very positive in character."[10] It is unclear why Motts elected to build a theater. Regardless of intent, his continual financial investments in building and expanding his theater reveals his active interest in the performing arts. The Pekin, which began as a space that was not much larger than "a wine room," was "remodeled and turned into a first-class theater" by 1909. It became a venue where integrated (but primarily black) audiences could attend an array of performances, from touring vaudeville productions to musical concerts to serious stage plays frequently presented by touring companies and artists. Its resident acting company, initially the Pekin

Stock Company, regularly performed, featuring Gilpin and eleven members of his "reading" group. Later the company was renamed the Jesse A. Shipp Stock Company.[11]

The Pekin, offering "high class entertainment at which a whole evening can be spent at the theater," quickly became the performing arts center of the South Side. Thousands of spectators regularly attended performances at the theater. Seating prices attempted to make the theater affordable to audiences with varying financial means: "Balcony 10–20 cents, main floor 20–30 cents. Boxes, 50 cents."[12] For those with greater disposable income and a desire for pre- or postshow drinking and dining, the Pekin featured a café.

> Above the theater was a finely appointed café, conducted in the highest order and catering to a high class patronage. Here could be found the season's delicacies, the choicest of meats, game and sea food [sic], as well as the finest liquors and wines. The tinkle of delicate glasses sparkling with champagne as members of parties eating leisurely the delectable and appetizing meat of broiled lobsters, to the accompaniment of an orchestra hidden behind palms, was a nightly occurrence. The setting was perfect; the cuisine, par excellence.[13]

The Pekin was *the* place for leisure and refinement for a mostly black clientele who resided on the South Side. During a period in which racist caricatures circulated widely and blackface minstrelsy remained en vogue, the theater offered respite from them. Even when minstrels appeared on the Pekin stage, the apparent differences between the representations onstage and the people in the audience were sufficient to challenge and subvert them.

The Pekin launched the careers of numerous types of performing artists: actors, vocalists, and dancers. Among the "Long List of Stars" who appeared at the Pekin, according to the *Chicago Defender*, were:

> Nettie Lewis Compton, Lottie Grady, Jennie Ringo, May White, Fanny Wise, May and Bobbie Kemp, J. Ed Green (director), Jerry Mills ("the old maestro"), Sam Lucas, Charles S. Gilpin, Lawrence Chenault, Harrison Stewart and Walter Crumley. Kinky Cooper, Oma Crosby, Effie King,

Ada Banks, Viola Stewart, Beulah White, Cornelia Triplett, Don Wormley, Lean Brooks, George White, Dick Cooper, DeKoven Thompson, Adolph Henderson, [and] John (Bass) Turner.[14]

The theater also advertised itself as a launching pad for future stars: "[E]very deserving and aspiring colored artists [sic] will, as always, find the Pekin a means to their chance to establish themselves in the profession of acting."[15]

In addition, the theater introduced a host of managers and producers. Henry Teenan Jones, a successful gambler like Motts who cohosted (with Motts) Jack Johnson's 1910 victory celebration, became a prominent producer of black theater in the opening decades of the twentieth century. The existence of the Pekin created management opportunities for prominent theater artists who had toured successfully during the previous decade. Jesse A. Shipp, who previously had achieved success working with Bert Williams and George Walker, would successfully oversee the acting company at the Pekin and, later, would return to Broadway—after having appeared in Williams's *Abysinnia* (1906)—as the Archangel in *Green Pastures* (1930). Sam Corker, who had been employed as an "advance agent" for Bob Cole and J. Rosamond Johnson, became the managing director at the Pekin.[16] Following Motts's death in 1911, Corker was identified, within the national black press, as a leading candidate to oversee operations at the theater.

The success of the Pekin inspired imitators. White entrepreneurs opened rival theaters and entertainment halls adjacent to the theater. Unlike the Pekin's, their theatrical programs were limited to vaudeville. The competition resulted in declining audiences and revenues for Motts's theater. The Pekin struggled financially and slowly began to amass debts. In an effort to turn the tide, Motts implemented several changes, including presenting more vaudeville acts, but none of these fixes successfully regained the audience numbers necessary to be profitable. When Motts died in 1911, the theater temporarily closed its doors. The Pekin would reopen but would never regain its former luster. In order to compete with nearby theaters, the new owner transformed the Pekin into an exclusively vaudeville house, no longer standing serious dramas. With the aim of capturing interest in the new phenomenon of motion pictures, projection equipment and a screen were installed. By 1918, the theatrical enterprise was abandoned. The seats were removed, and the space was converted into a dance hall. Two years later, it became a police station. In 1950, it was razed, alongside many surviving buildings of "The Stroll," to create space for a public housing complex, Dearborn Homes.

During the early part of the twentieth century, African Americans migrated primarily from southern rural to northern urban communities in massive numbers. Historian Ira Berlin states that between the beginning of World War I and the 1929 stock market crash, black men and women migrated at a rate of 500 people per day.[17] The arrival of tens of thousands of black families from the South into Chicago swelled the population of the city's black neighborhoods, particularly (but not exclusively) on the South Side. According to Berlin's estimates, this migration increased the size of the black population in Chicago from being 2 percent of the population in 1910 to 6 percent by 1930, 14 percent by 1950, and 33 percent by 1970.[18] The impact of this increase on black communities with limited housing stock, as a consequence of neighborhood segregation and discrimination within housing markets, is well documented. African Americans moved to the North searching for new employment opportunities, seeking to reconnect with family and community members, trying to escape Southern racism, and hoping for a better and more dignified way of life for themselves and future generations.[19] The *Chicago Defender*, started in 1905 by Robert S. Abbot, played a major role in encouraging the northern migration by running stories about the opportunities in the North and using an extensive network of "news dealers, black railway workers, traveling entertainers, barbershops, and churches" to deliver news about Chicago and, more generally, black culture and politics to Southern black communities.[20] Family and community members who already resided in Northern cities as well as a number of social service agencies helped new arrivals integrate into and navigate the new urban environment. During this same time period, black communities in Northern cities also continued to receive immigrants of African descent from other countries in the Caribbean and Europe, which added to the syncretic culture being created in urban communties.[21]

The "Great Migration" not only brought Southerners but also an infusion of Southern culture into the city. Southern migrants brought with them their distinctive tastes and myriad "lifestyle markers" that did not always fit in with the new urban environment.[22] Not only did these "markers" include various sensibilities around time, community, and self, but they also included practices related to everyday life, earning a living, and entertainment.[23] These decades were a time of immense artistic creativity. Jazz, which had been popularized as "novelty music" within vaudeville shows, quickly became entrenched in the city and a fixture alongside the dance clubs that populated "The Stroll." Southern musicians, particularly musicians from New Orleans, who did not travel with touring shows or find work in Southern establishments, migrated to Chicago in the 1920s and began to create the first jazz records as they adapted their style to the standards and environment of South Side cabarets.[24] The interactions that occurred between dancers, musicians, singers, and audiences also fostered the creation and development of new vernacular dance forms, like "jazz dance."[25] Before long, jazz, as well as the blues, would become synonymous with Chicago culture. The reception of jazz music and cabarets (as well as events like rent-parties) varied within Black Chicago communities, with upper-class, conservative, and more established blacks often expressing suspicion and dislike of the types of leisure activities and artistic forms associated with migrants and the lower class. Concerned with norms around "respectable" and acceptable behaviors, they thought these activities posed a threat to the "hard-won dignity of Chicago's 'Old Settlers.'"[26] However, for those involved in and supportive of these emerging art forms, the arts helped to forge a collective narrative, build racial solidarity, and illustrate the opportunities that northern urban environments afforded southern migrants.[27]

Cabarets, jazz, and rent-parties existed simultaneously with more "respectable" leisure activities like debutante balls, adding to the vibrant and dynamic mix of cultural and artistic activities in Black Chicago. Residents looking through local newspapers—like the *Chicago Defender*[28]—could find a number of ads for dances, fundraisers, and debutante balls sponsored by schools, businesses, women's clubs, membership clubs, and self-help organizations.[29] Nightclubs like the Apex, the Dreamland, the Sunset, and Lincoln Gardens offered spaces for audiences to view performances and for dancers to find work in revues or cabaret shows.[30] Additionally, dance halls like the Savoy Ballroom (1927) and theaters like the Regal Theatre (1928) provided Black Belt residents with spaces to create, perform, and watch many of the popular dances and performance idioms of that time.[31] As a result of the luxurious feel of both of these places and their policy of employing members of the local community, the Savoy Ballroom and Regal Theatre were seen as sources of pride for the Black Belt community.[32]

Sammy Dyer, who had a successful career in Washington D.C. and New York, came to Chicago in the 1920s and produced shows at a number of clubs in the city,[33] including the Sunset Café, which opened in 1921. Dyer performed both with a partner (e.g., a 1929 performance with Della Newcombe praised in the *Chicago Defender*) and choreographed performances for chorus lines and cabarets.[34] In 1929, Dyer began producing the cabaret show at the Regal Theatre. There he developed a group called the Regalettes who won acclaim for their "novel ideas and stunts."[35] By 1931, he owned a well-known studio in the loop, and he taught students in a South Side studio.[36] In 1933, Sammy Dyer created his own dance school, the Sammy Dyer School of the Theatre.[37] His school trained countless youth for careers as professional artists by teaching tap, acrobatics, ballet, and vernacular dances. In 1941, he became the producer of the stage show at the famous Club DeLisa.[38] He would later create a professional female dance group called the Dyerettes, in 1950, which consisted of five students from his school: Muriel Foster, Shirley Hall, Clarice White, Vera Mann, and Gloria Broussard.[39] This group performed a "class act" and toured all over the United States and Canada.[40] When Dyer died of a stroke in 1960s, one of the Dyerettes, Shirley Hall, directed the school.[41] The school still exists and continues to train dancers in tap and a variety of other genres.

In the 1920s, black concert dance traditions began to develop as African American dancers sought to distance themselves from the "neo-minstrel forms associated with vaudeville and musical theater."[42] Similar to other Harlem Renaissance artists, many black concert dancers believed that the arts and culture were important for uplifting the race and achieving equality with whites. Chicago dancers like Mary Bruce and Katherine Dunham were a part of the development of this black concert dance tradition through the performances they staged and the dance schools they opened.

Mary Bruce was at the center of a pioneering movement to forge a black balletic and interpretive dance tradition that could go alongside existing dance forms popularly associated with African Americans. The dance studio that she opened in 1924 provided a place for blacks to train in various dance techniques at a time when the doors of many contemporary concert dance studios were closed to black students.[43] At its height, the school boasted 300 or more "scholars" participating in its classes and performances.[44] Reviews of some of these performances reveal that Bruce's shows contained a mixture of chorus-line numbers, tap dance, interpretive dance, classical ballet, and plantation dances.[45] That she appropriated the term "classics" and described her students as "scholars" indicates that she was actively engaged in challenging the "color line" in dance as well as stereotypes of black dance that devalued the artistry of black practitioners.[46] Bruce was extremely successful in Chicago, and the annual shows of her students often received positive reviews in newspapers. In 1935, her students performed their annual revue downtown at the Goodman Theatre.[47] After her sister, Sadie Bruce, opened up a competing school in 1930 only a few blocks away, Mary Bruce left Chicago and opened up the Mary Bruce School of Dance in Harlem in 1938, where she became an important pillar of the black community.[48]

In 1928, Katherine Dunham moved to Chicago to live with her brother Albert Dunham, and she attended the University of Chicago. Upon her arrival, she was pulled into a group called the Cube Theatre, which had succeeded an amateur black theater group connected to the Little Theatre Movement called Masque.[49] An interracial theater troupe, the Cube performed a number of plays about the African American experience and served as an important locus of activity for many black youths getting involved in leftist politics at the time.[50] The troupe lasted from 1929 through the mid-1930s.

Dunham, who studied briefly with Mary Bruce, began working with Mark Turbyfill in 1929 to start a black ballet company.[51] They were able to rent space from Adolph Bolm,[52] one of Turbyfill's teachers, on Michigan Avenue, where they attracted a steady stream of students. However, they had to move the studio when a manager in the building told Bolm that he did not approve of blacks attending Turbyfill's classes.[53] They opened up a studio next to the University of Chicago at 1547 E. 57th Street, The South Side Ballet Studio,[54] but they were unable to attract the number of students that enrolled in their classes at the downtown location. In his diary, Turbyfill writes that he was "mortified to discover it was the novelty of their access to a Michigan Avenue studio" that blacks were attracted to and valued the most.[55] Additionally, some of the white neighbors in the area let Turbyfill know that they were not particularly pleased to see blacks in that part of the South Side.[56] The neighborhood was rapidly shifting due to the expansion of the black community as an increasing number of migrants arrived in Chicago from the South, and this expansion fomented racial tensions in that area.[57] Dunham and Turbyfill engaged in a number of activities, including holding tea party fundraisers at the dance studio, to build support for their "Race Ballet" and patronage for their dance studio within upper-class social circles.[58] Despite all of their efforts, Turbyfill and Dunham were unable to attract enough students or sponsors, and they were forced to close the studio because they could not pay their bills.[59]

After the failure of this project, Katherine Dunham began studying ballet, modern dance, and ethnic dance with Ludmilla Speranzeva.[60] In 1932, she and her dance troupe, who were being trained by Turbyfill and Speranzeva, were able to successfully put on a piece at the Steven Hotel Beaux Arts Ball, *Fantasie Negre in E Minor,* which was choreographed by Speranzeva and accompanied by pianist Margaret Bonds.[61] An article in the *Chicago Defender* titled "Modern Dancers Praised at Stevens Hall" lauds the piece as a significant achievement for black dance and a pioneering effort.[62] In 1933, Ruth Page invited Dunham to perform with her in *La Guiablesse,* a piece based on a Martinique folk tale.[63] Dunham also worked with five other choreographers—Hazel Thompson Davis, Sadie Bruce, Cardebel Plummer, Prince Modupe, and Sammy Dyer—to set pieces on children performing in the play *Oh, Sing A New Song.*[64] During this same year, Dunham and her dancers appeared in Hall Johnson's *Run, Little Chillun,* a successful Broadway play that was being reproduced at the Harris Theatre.[65]

Beginning in the 1930s and continuing through the 1940s, Chicago's black community experienced a period of considerable artistic and creative production and experimentation known as the Chicago Black Renaissance. Occurring alongside the Great Depression, this period witnessed a number of shifts within Chicago's black artistic communities as individuals and businesses attempted to navigate the economic, political, and cultural climate of Chicago at that time. As unemployment increased and individuals had less money to spend on leisure activities, smaller local entertainment businesses—including local nightclubs, dance halls, and other after-hour joints—closed down.[66] Surviving larger businesses and theaters scaled down their services, started bringing in more traveling troupes rather than employing large numbers of local artists, or shifted their policies in other ways to navigate the depressed economy.[67]

Despite this bleak reality, new arts patrons and sponsors—including the U.S. government as part of the New Deal—helped sustain artists and facilitate an increase in creative output.[68] One important new arts sponsor during these depression years was the Julius Rosenwald Fund, which by "supporting creative individuals and providing seed money to build community institutions constituted an absolutely necessary, if not sufficient, conditioning for the flowering of the Chicago Black Renaissance."[69] Dunham received a fellowship from the Rosenwald Fund in 1935 to study folk dances in the Caribbean for one year for her master's thesis. After completing two manuscripts on her fieldwork, Dunham received her master's degree and left academia to concentrate on her artistic career. She began working with the Federal Writers Project, where she conducted research on the relationship between deprivation and cult formation in Chicago. Upon completing that research, she was hired to work with the Federal Theatre Project. Chicago's "Negro unit" of the Federal Theatre Project brought together leading artists such as playwright Theodore Ward, whose production of *Big White Fog* (1938) employed scores of black artists in the city. The impact of these New Deal–era arts programs are evident in a production photograph of *The Mikado* that appears in an October 1938 edition of the *Chicago Defender*.[70] At least twenty-five dancers appear in the production photograph—thus offering a hint at how Depression-era arts funding fostered the growth of artistic culture in the city in the late 1930s.

Beginning in 1937, Dunham and her dancers performed material from her field research in the Caribbean, as well as modern dance and ballet pieces, in various venues on both the South and North Sides of Chicago.[71] In 1938, through the dance unit of the Federal Theatre Project, Dunham and her dancers participated in a performance of *Ballet Fedré* with two other choreographers at the Great Northern Theatre. During this performance, Dunham staged her celebrated piece based on her fieldwork in Martinique, *L'Ag'Ya*.[72] Dunham continued to perform with her company and train youth throughout the Chicago area for the next couple of years.[73] In 1938 and 1939, Dunham and her dancers participated in the

Art Institute's dance series at the Goodman Theatre.[74] In 1939, the youth with whom she worked performed at the Abraham Lincoln Center, and, later that year, she worked with youth at DuSable High School, creating dances for the Children's Theatre Group's performance of *Pinocchio*.[75]

By the 1940s, Dunham and her company relocated to New York to begin performing in a number of plays there. After relocating, her company's national and international profile took off, and Dunham became highly regarded. Dunham's technique and anthropological approach to dance continued to have an impact on the Chicago area through the presence of a number of former members of her company—including Tommy Gomez, Carmencita Romero, Wilbert Bradley, and Lucille Ellis—as well as her frequent visits to the city. Not only did Dunham challenge the "color line" through her technique and performance practice, but she also continued to protest and challenge various inequalities throughout her career as a dancer, scholar, and community activist. Her approach and technique shifted what both black and white audiences thought was possible for black dance.

During the Chicago Black Renaissance, the city became the center of an exchange between African American activists and artists and organizers within American leftist communities.[76] Like the Federal Arts Projects and the Rosenwald Fund, leftist communities generated important activity that inspired, depended on, and supported African American artists and cultural production.[77] Though Bill V. Mullen states that African Americans in Chicago were exceptional in their response to American Communism since the founding of the Communist Party USA in 1919, the shift toward and emphasis on the "cultural front" in the American Communist Party's policy in 1935 and the establishment of the National Negro Congress in 1936 marked important moments in the development of a progressive black radical tradition.[78] The establishment of the National Negro Congress was a manifestation of the "Popular Front" ideology of the Communist party that "sought to build a multi-prolonged 'Negro People's Front' against white supremacy and worker exploitation by consolidating black freedom struggles and activist networks along economic, political, and cultural lines."[79] Moreover, as dance historian Susan Manning shows, leftist dance networks offered important sources of patronage and cultural advocacy against discrimination for black dance artists and cultural workers.[80] Edith Segal, one of the pioneers of the leftist dance movement who was based in New York City, performed at the first National Negro Congress that took place in Chicago in 1936.[81] Katherine Dunham created choreography for a play, *Pins and Needles,* produced in New York by the Labor Stage, which was affiliated with the International Ladies Garment Workers Union.[82] However, as Manning notes, this relationship was tenuous because of stereotypes within leftist communities that limited the participation of black dancers. Black dancers usually required alternative performance outlets and audiences to support their artistic work.[83] The Negro People's Theatre, which was organized by leftist artists trained within the practices of the Little Theatre Movement, was also a source of "Popular Front" activity in Chicago. Established in 1938 with Fanny McConnell as its executive director, the company sought to "create opportunities for black actors and directors and to combat the stereotypes of the stage Negro."[84]

The South Side Community Arts Center was founded in 1940 through the Community Arts Program funded by the Works Progress Administration (WPA) and the work of cultural workers like Margaret Burroughs, Bernard Gross, Peter Pollack, and Charles White. The center stood as an important cultural institution for the interracial, cross-class alliances and activities within Negro People's Front activism and cultural productions in Chicago.[85] Through workshops, exhibitions, and artistic events, the South Side Community Arts Center influenced the development of black radical cultural and artistic productions during the Chicago Black Renaissance and provided support for cultural workers. Their annual Artists and Models Ball, which started in 1937 as a fundraiser for the creation of the center and lasted until the 1990s, helped finance the center and served as an annual meeting for many prominent Chicago cultural workers. The ball often featured a number of highly regarded theater and dance artists like Katherine Dunham, Lester Goodman, Katherine Flowers, Julian Swain, Jimmy Payne and the Negro People's Theatre. The Abraham Lincoln Center served as another cultural institution that supported communist activity within the South Side. Jenkin Lloyd Jones created it in 1905, and the center maintained a close relationship with the South Side Community Arts Center.[86]

Toward the end of the 1930s, the Parkway Community House, a South Side community center originally located in the basement of Good Shepherd Church and under the directorship of Horace Cayton, emerged as one of the premiere venues for staging black artistic expression, along with the George Cleveland Hall Public Library (founded in 1932). Over the next half-century, Parkway would move several times, become a "center," and ally with the Jane Addams Hull House Association. What remained consistent was the center's role in supporting and nurturing black artistry. The Parkway hosted its own resident theater company, the Skyloft Players, who performed in the Skyloft Theatre. Arguably their most significant achievement, as measured by newspaper coverage, was their 1942 world premiere production of Langston Hughes's *The Sun Do Move* starring Brunetta Mouzon and Clifton McLin. With Marva Louis, the wife of the reigning heavyweight champion, and Hughes in attendance on opening night, the production was the arts-related society event of the year for Black Belt Chicago.[87] Six years later, the Skyloft Players were still thriving under the artistic directorship of Helen Spaulding, a doctoral student in drama at the University of Wisconsin who had developed a series of theater training programs. Classes were in demand as a result of the "sudden boom of opportunities in professional theatre on Broadway" for black theater and dance artists.[88] In addition, the Skyloft Players at Parkway regularly sponsored public lectures on the arts for the South Side community. For example, a lecture featuring singer and Broadway star Etta Moten, who achieved the distinction of being the first black theater and film star to be invited to perform at the White House, attracted an audience consisting of "100 theatre directors and actors."[89] The following year, when Spaulding unexpectedly resigned as artistic director and then died, the Skyloft Players suffered from their loss of artistic leadership and slowly disbanded. The Center Aisle Players filled the void as a repertory theater company that performed at the YMCA on 38th Street and Wabash Avenue. They would become the most popular South Side theater company in the late 1940s and early 1950s.

The 1940s began with the American Negro Cultural Exposition (1940), which signaled Chicago's importance as a site of African American cultural production.[90] Led by attorney Truman Gibson Jr. as its executive director, the exposition marked the seventy-fifth anniversary of the Emancipation Proclamation and celebrated African American achievement. With racism and discrimination still a major problem in the United States, the exhibition also aimed to promote understanding between blacks and whites as well as highlight the contributions of African Americans.[91] During the exposition, Sammy Dyer produced a revue show, and Katherine Dunham organized an exhibit and performed with her company.[92]

In 1941, choreographer Sadie Bruce collaborated with the National Negro Opera Guild, which was founded by Mary Cardwell Dawson, on a production of *Aida*.[93] Mary Cardwell Dawson was an artist and activist who worked to challenge barriers for professionally trained black opera singers. Working with communities in Pittsburgh, Washington D.C., Chicago, and New York, Dawson sought to bring opera to black communities with the hopes of racial uplift and cultural development.[94] Bruce and the National Negro Opera Guild performed a preview performance in 1941 at Wendell Phillips High School before performing the full production in 1942 and 1943 at the Chicago Civic Opera House.[95] The performance signified the first all-black performance of Giuseppe Verdi's *Aida*, and it successfully showcased the rich musical talent within the black community on a stage that belonged to the city's artistic mainstream.[96] Lester Goodman, who mentored Joseph Holmes and helped him found the Joseph Holmes Dance Theatre, participated in this production. In 1948, Bruce began working with Willa Saunders Jones on the production of *Passion Play* at Chicago Civic Opera House.[97] After engaging in extensive research on Hebrew dances, Bruce created an interpretive dance that audiences received well.[98] In 1949, she also began to use the opera house, among other venues, to stage her students' performances.[99] By this time, her school, which opened in 1930 at 54th and Calumet on the South Side, was one of the oldest dance schools in Chicago, and she was one of the most prominent dance teachers in the black community.[100]

With the beginning of World War II, the focus of many government initiatives shifted toward national defense and unity. Artists participated in the wartime efforts through their cultural productions and performances. In his 1941 Director's Report for WPA Illinois District 3, Peter Pollack lauded the South Side Community Art Center's success and outlined a "defense of culture" theme (drawing on wartime ideology) that talked about the important role that the arts could play in unifying and uplifting the population.[101] In 1943, the South Side Community Arts Center organized a special tribute to women working in wartime industries by crowning one of nine "Negro Girl War Workers" Mrs. Victory at its Artists and Models Ball.[102] Additionally, the center used the proceeds from this event, which usually went toward operating expenses, to buy war bonds.

The prolonged war caused the government to search for additional revenue, and one new source was the 1943-instituted "federal cabaret tax." This newly levied tax greatly impacted the artistic workforce because it forced many nightclubs, theaters, and hotels to stop using live entertainment and dance in order to avoid having to pay it.[103] It also caused customers who could not afford the 30 percent increase in their bill to stop frequenting establishments that had live stage performances. The government reduced the tax to 10 percent in 1960 in order to generate employment and activity within the performance sector, but by then it was too late for many entertainment businesses and professionals. Many of the institutions that helped to develop and sustain the formerly vibrant professional performing arts community no longer existed.[104] Those that did weather the storm could not employ the overabundance of talented performers without work.

A number of events occurred in the 1950s that impacted the lives of black artists and their employment opportunities. As a result of the decline in what Clovis E. Semmes calls "commercial segregation," the black consumer market—which was highly concentrated as a result of residential segregation and other Jim Crow laws and practices—began to disperse as blacks had access to new venues previously closed off to them.[105] This decline in commercial segregation did not mean a decline in residential segregation, social segregation, or racism within Chicago's political system; it only meant that whites developed a heightened recognition of the purchasing power of black consumers.[106] The opening up of the marketplace meant that black entrepreneurs no longer had a concentrated and segregated audience to which they could market their products; yet, they continued to face inequality because of limited access and opportunities. The shift in musical tastes within the black community—from large, "big" bands to solo performers and, later, to the emergent rhythm and blues music—also caused a contraction of the market and performance opportunities for large "jazz/dance bands."[107] Additionally, technological developments—such as the increasing popularity of film, radio, and television—caused Black Belt residents to decrease their participation in live arts and entertainment, a trend that was mirrored in the wider American population.[108]

The 1950s also witnessed the rise of the civil rights movement, which continued and expanded the work against racism and inequality that African American activists, artists, and communities were engaged in. Not only did artists participate in the movement by joining protests, performing for activists, and challenging Jim Crow segregation laws in the theaters and performance venues they visited, but they also created works that were inspired by the movement and used the arts to teach about and question racial injustice and inequality. For example, as a result of the *Brown v. Board of Education* decision, Tommy Sutton worked with a number of artists to form the Stage Arts Theatre Group in 1956. The group performed integrated ballets in the hopes of shifting audience perceptions about race relations and promoting racial understanding.[109] Sutton, a Chicago native who was famous for his tap dance routines and organizing debutante balls, also formed the Mayfair Academy in 1957 to address the lack of dance training facilities opened to blacks.

The turbulent 1960s, during which Martin Luther King Jr. and Malcolm X were assassinated, witnessed a reemergence and, arguably, a new renaissance of artistic creativity. As the civil rights movement advanced and shifted in response to various wins, losses, and events, artist, activists, and local communities continued to join the movement and agitate for equality. The Black Power Movement, which grew out of the civil rights movement in the sixties, expanded and developed the various activities that African Americans and their allies engaged in to initiate social change. Moreover, anticolonial and independence movements in Africa happening at this time (which can be traced back to before World War II) bolstered the Pan-Africanist consciousness of many black Chicagoans as they advocated for social justice, human rights, and self-determination for people of African descent locally and globally. This consciousness has its roots in earlier movements, organizations, and events that helped to create connections and a sense of "linked fate" between populations of African descent around the world like Marcus Garvey's United Negro Improvement Association and the Pan-African Congresses that Du Bois helped to organize. Black newspapers and publications like *Black World*, originally published as *Negro Digest* by the Johnson Publishing Company in 1943, also helped to create these connections by printing articles about and by black folks living in different parts of the globe. Cultural and artistic productions and activites associated with the Black

Arts Movement, the cultural counterpart to the Black Power Movement that fostered the creation of a number of community-based arts initiatives in Chicago, could also be viewed from the pages of publications like *Black World*. Organizations like AFRICOBRA (African Commune of Bad Relevant Artists) and the Organization of Black American Culture (OBAC) were at the center of this heightened period of creativity in Black Chicago. Within the dance community, artists such as Darlene Blackburn traveled to the African continent, learned indigenous performance practices, and brought that knowledge back to Chicago to share with fellow artists. Chicago-based artists such as Katherine Dunham and Jimmy Payne, who specialized in Afro-Cuban, calypso, and other African Caribbean traditions, had already introduced African and African diasporic cultural material into the Chicago community. Moreover, others like Julian Swain studied with African dance artists like Asadata Dafora, who lived in New York. However, Blackburn's movements around the globe and within Chicago would spark a heightened level of activity and interest in researching and learning West African cultural and artistic material. Within the theater, this heightened Pan-Africanist consciousness inspired the incorporation of African rituals and storytelling practices onto the stage. Blackburn, in collaboration with jazz musician Phil Cohran, created Affro-Arts Theater, with "'Af' for Africa and 'Fro' for 'from out of.'"[110] Val Gray Ward's Kuumba Professional Theatre Company was founded in 1968, initially as an itinerant theater company before eventually moving to the South Side Community Arts Center, then to a warehouse on South Michigan in downtown Chicago's "Loop," and finally to Malcolm X College on the West Side, where it closed in 1996.[111] In 1971, eta Creative Arts Foundation was established. It was (and still is) dedicated to the "the preservation, perpetuation and promulgation of the African American aesthetic in the City of Chicago."[112]

In the early 1970s, "a group of artists, activists and community leaders," lead by playwright Useni Perkins, joined forces to create the Black Theater Alliance.[113] The purpose of the alliance was to "to raise public awareness of African American artistic achievement and impact in Illinois."[114] The Black Theater Alliance advocated for the power of black theater and dance—inspired by a Black Arts Movement philosophy that the arts exist as an ideal form to engage issues of social life and politics and by nostalgia about the declining presence of live performing arts as a unifying force in Chicago's Black Belt. One of its first and most visible and enduring creations was "Black Theater Week," which debuted in 1974 with the theme "Black Theater Is Black Life."[115] The music, theater, and dance performances that occurred during that week demonstrated the power of the performing arts to capture and relay experiences, forge bonds of community, and elevate the spirit. In 1997, the African American Arts Alliance of Chicago was established with the mission to "[expand] the scope of the Black Theater Alliance to include all artistic media."[116] This new "alliance" annually sponsors and promotes Black Arts Month every October.

IN THIS COLLECTION

The oral histories in this collection intersect with and continue the previously outlined history. They speak of a continued struggle of black artists to earn a living through their artistry, empower youth and adults through dance and performance, and position black theater and dance forms on equal footing with other performance media.

Chuck Smith, a native Chicagoan, talks about how he joined the theater community in the early 1970s after having served oversees in the Marines. He recalls the founding of a series of prominent theater companies, including the Experimental Black Actors Guild, Amistad, and the Chicago Theatre Company, and remembers conversations with theatrical innovators Clarence Taylor and Theodore Ward among others. Arriving in Chicago in the late 1960s, Kemati J. Porter remembers the early days of eta Creative Arts and reflects upon the community-based theater's long history and continued efforts to serve emerging black artists throughout Chicago. Gloria Bond Clunie, founder of Fleetwood-Jourdain Theatre in Evanston, vividly recalls the revolutionary spirit of the early 1970s on Northwestern University's campus, where she was an undergraduate theater major, and shares her perspective attending Northwestern and making theater during these years and, later, founding Fleetwood-Jourdain and joining Victory Gardens Theater Company's esteemed playwriting ensemble.

Jackie Taylor, who was raised in the Cabrini–Green public housing development in Chicago, talks about the building of the Black Ensemble Theater only weeks before the grand opening of her theater company's new, multimillion dollar facility. Jonathan Wilson shares his memories directing the work of August Wilson on Chicago's stages and the special relationship that he forged with the esteemed playwright. Ron O. J. Parson remembers his experiences working with his theater company, Onyx, and directing within the city's Tony Award–winning regional theaters. Kathy A. Perkins also reflects on the early days of Onyx. In addition, she talks about the unique challenges facing contemporary black designers, specifically black female designers, within professional theater.

Derrick Sanders, a cofounder of Congo Square Theatre, pulls back the curtain and reveals the process and unique challenges of creating a theater company. He also discusses the active role that August Wilson played in supporting his company. Rashida Z. Shaw, a theater scholar, offers the perspective of an audience member with a sharp ethnographic eye in her reflections on attending dozens of touring urban entertainment theater or "Chitlin' Circuit" performances in the city. Sydney Chatman talks about her twenty-first-century community arts and education initiative, the Tofu Chitlin' Circuit, and how it seeks to entertain and engage South Side audiences with the aim of bolstering community support for the performing arts. The theater section ends with a cross-generational conversation between Chuck Smith and Sydney Chatman in which they talk about the unique challenges currently facing black theater.

The dance section begins with Najwa I, who enjoyed a successful career dancing in chorus lines and revue shows on the commercial stage before moving to the concert stage in the late 1960s. Her interview offers an overview of the development of the Julian Swain Inner City Dance Theatre and the creation of her own dance company, Najwa Dance Corps. Darlene Blackburn discusses her experience as an interpretive dancer during the Black Arts Movement and the Darlene Blackburn Dance Troupe. In her interview, she talks about her travels to Ghana and Nigeria and traces the development of West African dance and drum practices in Chicago. Babu Atiba, who was born and raised in Chicago, provides a history of the development of Muntu Dance Theatre of Chicago, one of the oldest dance companies in the city focusing on African and African American dance. Idella Reed-Davis discusses her involvement with the Sammy Dyer School of the Theatre in the 1970s and the development of two all-female tap groups, Rhythm Women and, later, Rhythm ISS. Her interview also addresses some of the specific concerns that women face within the tap dance field. Joel Hall discusses his own experience developing a jazz dance company as a student at Northeastern Illinois University and talks about his attempts to challenge the lack of performance opportunities for black artists on the North Side of Chicago through his work with the Chicago City Theatre Company/ Joel Hall Dancers.

Geraldine Williams, a certified Dunham Technique instructor, recalls her own involvement with Dunham's technique through Williams's relationship with her mentor, Ms. Lucille Ellis, who danced in Dunham's company, and her participation in the Katherine Dunham Technique Seminar. Williams also discusses her work with youth, which employs dance as a tool for empowerment, as a public school teacher and dance instructor with eta Creative Arts Foundation.

Fred Baker, originally from Montego Bay, Jamaica, shares memories of his career as an international dancer and the circumstances that led him to relocate his dance company, the West Indian Folk Dance Company, to Chicago. His presence speaks to the continuation of a Caribbean Dance tradition in Chicago, which begins in the 1930s and 1940s with individuals like Katherine Dunham and Jimmy Payne. Amaniyea Payne, who relocated to Chicago from New York, reflects on her work with Muntu Dance Theatre of Chicago and the impact of this company on Chicago. Idy Ciss, also with Muntu Dance Theatre of Chicago, reflects on his experience migrating from Senegal to Chicago to continue his professional dance career and the strategies he used to navigate the city when he first arrived. Kevin Iega Jeff, who relocated from New York City to direct the Joseph Holmes Chicago Dance Theatre before transforming the company into Deeply Rooted Dance Theatre of Chicago, shares his experiences of trying to navigate the racial politics of the city, secure funding, and thrive as a black artist. Tosha Alston, who is also originally from New York, discusses the experiences that led her to establish a multicultural all-female West African drum and dance ensemble, Ayodele Drum & Dance Ensemble. As an emerging artist, Alston provides insight into some of the contemporary shifts taking place within the African Dance field in Chicago. Lastly, Brave Monk recounts the development of the hip-hop dance scene in Chicago and the multiple traditions that impact this dance form. His narrative, like many of the other stories shared in this collection, discusses the role that the arts and culture can play in educating and empowering youth.

d26 NOTES

NOTES

1. Lerone Bennett, "Jack Johnson and the Great White Hope," *Ebony*, February 2005, 92.

2. St. Clair Drake and Horace Cayton, *Black Metropolis: A Study of Negro Life in Northern City* (Chicago: University of Chicago Press, 1993).

3. Davarian Baldwin, *Chicago's New Negroes: Modernity, the Great Migration, and Black Urban Life* (Chapel Hill: The University of North Carolina Press, 2007).

4. Mike Rowe, *Chicago's Blues: The City and the Music* (New York: Da Capo Press, 1981); Jacqueline Stewart, *Migrating to the Movies: Cinema and Black Urban Modernity* (Berkeley: University of California Press, 2005).

5. Timuel D. Black Jr., *Bridges of Memory: Chicago's First Wave of Black Migration* (Evanston, Ill.: Northwestern University Press, 2003).

6. C. A. Hamilton, "Ideology and Oral Traditions: Listening to the Voices 'From Below,'" *History in Africa*, vol. 14 (1987), 67–86; Paul Thompson, *The Voices of the Past: Oral History* (New York: Oxford University Press, 2000); Luise White, "True Stories: Narrative, Event, History, and Blood in the Lake Victoria Basin" in *African Words, African Voices: Critical Practices in Oral History*, edited by Luise White, Stephen F. Miescher, and David William Cohen (Bloomington and Indianapolis: Indiana University Press, 2001), 281–99.

7. Della Pollock, "Introduction: Remembering" in *Remembering: Oral History Performance*, edited by Della Pollock (New York: Palgrave Macmillan, 2005); Justin Willis, "Two Lives of Mpamizo: Understanding Dissonance in Oral History," *History in Africa*, vol. 23 (1996), 319–32.

8. Bayo Holsey, *Routes of Remembrance: Refashioning the Slave Trade in Ghana* (Chicago: University of Chicago Press, 2008); Della Pollock, "Introduction: Remembering"; Justin Willis, "Two Lives of Mpamizo."

9. Quoted in Edward A. Robinson's "The Pekin: The Genesis of American Black Theater," *Black American Literature Forum*, vol. 16.4 (1982), 137.

10. "Theatrical Stars of Early Chicago," *Chicago Defender*, May 27, 1933, 11. National Edition.

11. Bernard Peterson, *The African American Theatre Directory: 1816–1960* (Westport, Conn.: Greenwood Publishing Group, 1997), 181.

12. "The Pekin Theater," *Chicago Defender*, April 15, 1911, 6. National Edition.

13. "Theatrical Stars . . ."

14. Ibid.

15. "The Pekin Theater," *Chicago Defender*, May 13, 1911, 4. National Edition.

16. "Cole and Johnson's 'Shoo-Fly Regiment,'" *The Freeman*, February 8, 1908, 5.

17. Ira Berlin, *The Making of African America: The Four Great Migrations* (London: Penguin Books, 2010), 154.

18. Berlin, *The Making of African America*, 157.

19. Berlin, *The Making of African America*, 152–200; Robert Bone and Richard A. Courage, *The Muse in Bronzeville: African American Creative Expression in Chicago, 1932–1950* (New Brunswick, N.J.: Rutgers University Press, 2011), 61–64.

20. Bone and Courage, *The Muse in Bronzeville*, 38–39.

21. Michael Gomez, *Reversing Sail: A History of the African Diaspora* (Cambridge and New York: Cambridge University Press), 162–68.

22. Drake and Cayton, *Black Metropolis*, 73–76. Mary Pattillo, *Black on the Block: The Politics of Race and Class in the City* (Chicago: University of Chicago Press, 2007), 11. Drawing on Max Weber's work, Pattillo uses the term *lifestyle* to talk about the class and status markers that

are used to connote difference and distinction within the urban black community that she studies in Chicago. She prefers the term *lifestyle* to *culture* because of the biological and moral overtones that scholars have attached to the term *culture*. We follow Pattillo's lead in order to highlight the connection between the creation of artistic distinctions and social order.

23. Drake and Cayton, *Black Metropolis*, 75; Katrina Hazzard-Gordon, *Jookin': the Rise of Social Dance Formations in African-American Culture* (Philadelphia: Temple University Press, 1990).

24. Bone and Courage, *The Muse in Bronzeville*, 64–65.

25. Marshall Stearns and Jean Stearns, *Jazz Dance: The Story of American Vernacular Dance* (New York: Da Capo Press), xvi. In their book *Jazz Dance,* Stearns and Stearns show in detail the connection between the development of jazz dance and the development of jazz music in the United States. See also Jacqui Malone, *Steppin' on the Blues: The Visible Rhythms of African American Dance* (Urbana and Chicago: University of Illinois Press, 1996), 83–90.

26. Bone and Courage, *The Muse in Bronzeville*, 68.

27. Bone and Courage, *The Muse in Bronzeville*, 69; Katrina Hazzard Gordon, *Jookin': The Rise of Social Dance Formations in African-American Culture.*

28. Drake and Cayton, *Black Metropolis*, 398–412. Drake and Cayton state that five weekly newspapers were published in Bronzeville before World War II: the *Chicago Defender,* the *Chicago Bee,* the *Chicago World,* the *Metropolitan Post,* and the *News-Ledger.* The *Chicago Defender* had the largest number of papers in circulation. Drake and Cayton also state that these institutions were extremely important for shaping and reflecting public opinion in Bronzeville at the time.

29. For an example, see "Children to Benefit from Charity Ball: Society Dances La Fete des Nations," *Chicago Defender,* June 15, 1929. National Edition.

30. Bone and Courage, *The Muse in Bronzeville.*

31. Clovis E. Semmes, *The Regal Theatre and Black Culture,* 21–26. A few additional theaters serving Chicago's black community at that time, which are mentioned in Semmes's book, include the Metropolitan, the Vendome, the Apollo Theatre, the Grand Theatre, and the Willard Theater.

32. Ibid.

33. "Young Ballet Master Makes Good Record," *Chicago Defender,* July 26, 1930. National Edition.

34. "Hot Dancers at Sunset," *Chicago Defender,* February 16, 1929. National Edition.

35. "Young Ballet Master Makes Good Record," *Chicago Defender,* July 26, 1930. National Edition.

36. Clifford W. MacKay, "Going Back Stage with the Scribe: Bessie Smith Answers," *Chicago Defender,* June 6, 1931. National Edition.

37. http://www.sammydyerschoolofthetheatre.com/#Legacy.

38. "Death of Sammy Dyer Created Vacancy Not Likely to Be Filled," *Chicago Defender,* September 10, 1960.

39. http://www.sammydyerschoolofthetheatre.com/#Legacy; "Dyerettes Train Successors: Pros Adopt Young Chorus Line," *Ebony,* April 1961, http://books.google.com/books?id=fK y4uNR5ThsC&lpg=PA35&ots=JqaNRSW3jO&dq=dyerettes&pg=PA35#v=onepage&q=d yerettes&f=true.

40. "Dyerettes Train Successors: Pros Adopt Young Chorus Line," *Ebony,* April 1961, http://books.google.com/books?id=fKy4uNR5ThsC&lpg=PA35&ots=JqaNRSW3jO&dq= dyerettes&pg=PA35#v=onepage&q=dyerettes&f=true.

41. http://www.sammydyerschoolofthetheatre.com/#/Legacy; According to the website for the Sammy Dyer School of the Theatre, which still exists today, Hall directed the school until 1998.

42. Lynne Fauley Emery, *Black Dance: From 1619 to Today* (New Hampshire: Ayer Company Publishers, Inc.), 241–71; John O. Perpener III, *African American Concert Dance: The Harlem Renaissance and Beyond* (Urbana: University of Illinois Press).

43. Perpener III, *African-American Concert Dance.*

44. "Mary Bruce Presents Her Dancers in Annual Classic," *Chicago Defender,* May 30, 1931. National Edition.

45. Ibid.

46. Perpener III, *African American Concert Dance.*

47. "In Mary Bruce 'Classic,'" *Chicago Defender,* June 1, 1935. National Edition.

48. "Mary Bruce Takes Action: Seeks to Block Sister, Sadie, from Opening School Here in 'Unfair' Competition," *New York Amsterdam News,* June 17, 1939. In New York, Bruce continued to have a successful career and positively impact the black community by working with both youth and adults. Bruce died in New York in 1995 at the age of 95.

49. Bone and Courage, *The Muse in Bronzeville,* 80–81.

50. Ibid.

51. Bone and Courage, *The Muse in Bronzeville,* 81; Jennifer Dunning, "Harlem Legend Saluted," *The New York Times,* August 12, 1987.

52. Bolm is credited as being one of the pioneers in the creation of the ballet dance scene in Chicago. He is a part of a wave of Russian ballet teachers who immigrated to the United States after the Russian revolution and helped to establish ballet companies there. For more on this history, see Jack Anderson, *Ballet and Modern Dance: A Concise History* (New Jersey: Princeton Book Company, 1977), 143.

53. Vèvè A. Clark and Sara E. Johnson, eds., *Kaiso! Writings by and about Katherine Dunham* (Madison: University of Wisconsin Press, 2005).

54. "Chicago Will Witness First Race Ballet," *Chicago Defender,* June 28, 1930.

55. Clark and Johnson, *Kaiso!,* 183.

56. Ibid., 184.

57. Drake and Cayton, *Black Metropolis.*

58. "Chicago Will Witness First Race Ballet," *Chicago Defender,* June 29, 1930. National Edition.

59. Clark and Johnson, *Kaiso!*

60. Bone and Courage, *The Muse in Bronzeville,* 81.

61. Ibid.

62. "Modern Dancers Praised at Stevens," *Chicago Defender,* December 24, 1932. The article said that they chose the music because *Fantasie Negre* won the Wanamaker Prize in 1932 for its composition. Katherine Dunham was accompanied by five other dancers—Dorothy Jackson, Ruth Cromer, Frances Dunham, Jessie Anderson, and Beatrice Betts—in the performance that evening.

63. Ruth Page played the lead role in the original piece. "Composer Here for Showing of La Guiablesse: Katherine Dunham in Main Dance Role," *Chicago Defender,* December 8, 1934. National Edition.

64. John R. Dewey, "O, Sing A New Song Is Triumph of Race: 60,000 in Stadium to Witness Huge Music Pageant," *Chicago Defender,* September 1, 1934, 1.

65. Rob Roy, "*Run, Little Chillun'* Pleases First-Nighters: Producer Takes Local Talent Through Broadway Trip," *Chicago Defender,* November 3, 1934.

66. Semmes, *The Regal Theatre and Black Culture.*

67. Ibid., 69–73.

68. Ibid., 85.

69. Bone and Courage, *The Muse in Bronzeville,* 85.

70. "Women in Federal Theatre's 'The Mikado,'" *Chicago Defender,* October 1, 1938, 19. National Edition.

71. "In Dance Concert," *Chicago Defender,* June 5, 1937. National Edition.

72. Cecil Smith. "Federal Dance Project Gives First Program," *Chicago Daily Tribune,* January 28, 1938; "Katherine Dunham to Open with Ballet Fedré in Loop," *Chicago Defender,* January 29, 1938; "Ballet Fedré Is Fine WPA Theatre Production." *Chicago Defender,* February 5, 1938. National Edition.

73. Cecil Smith, "Othello Opens Opera Season Next Saturday," *Chicago Daily Tribune,* October 23, 1938.

74. "Katherine Dunham to Dance 3 Days," *Chicago Defender,* October 29, 1938. National Edition; "Katherine Dunham's Group in Dance Series," *Chicago Defender,* November 25, 1939.

75. "Katherine Dunham's Dancing Darlings Give Show," *Chicago Defender,* July 8, 1939. National Edition; "Children's Theatre Group in Play December 16." *Chicago Defender,* December 9, 1939. National Edition.

76. Bone and Courage, *The Muse in Bronzeville,* 85.

77. Ibid.

78. Bill V. Mullen, *Popular Fronts: Chicago and African-American Cultural Politics, 1935–46* (Urbana and Chicago: University of Illinois Press, 1999), 5.

79. Michelle Yvonne Gordon, *Black Literature of Revolutionary Protest from Chicago's South Side: A Local Literary History, 1931–1959* (PhD dissertation, University of Wisconsin–Madison, 2008), 50.

80. Susan Manning, *Modern Dance, Negro Dance: Race in Motion* (Minneapolis, Minn.: University of Minnesota Press, 2004), 59.

81. Julia L. Foulkes, *Modern Bodies: Dance and American Modernism from Martha Graham to Alvin Ailey* (Chapel Hill: University of North Carolina Press, 2002), 119; Susan Manning, *Modern Dance, Negro Dance,* 68.

82. Susan Manning, *Modern Dance, Negro Dance,* 61.

83. Ibid., 59.

84. Melissa Barton, "'Speaking a Mutual Language': The Negro People's Theatre in Chicago," *TDR: The Drama Review,* vol. 54.3 (2010), 54–70.

85. Bill V. Mullen, *Popular Fronts.*

86. Bone and Courage, *The Muse in Bronzeville*; Mullen, *Popular Fronts.*

87. "Enjoy Performance," *Chicago Defender,* May, 9, 1942, 10. National Edition.

88. Ibid.

89. "Helen Spaulding Back After Theatre Survey," *Chicago Defender,* June 19, 1948, 8. National Edition.

90. Adam Gree, *Selling the Race: Culture, Community, and Black Chicago, 1940–1955* (Chicago and London: University of Chicago Press), 24; Bill V. Mullen, *Popular Fronts,* 25.

91. Green, *Selling the Race,* 28.

92. Green, *Selling the Race,* 30.

93. "Opera Dream Comes True before 2000: Local Artists Praised for Performance of Bit from 'Aida.'" *Chicago Defender,* August 16, 1941.

94. Karen M. Bryan, "Radiating a Hope: Mary Cardwell Dawson as Educator and Activist," *Journal of Historical Research in Music Education,* vol. 25.1 (2003), 34.

95. "Opera Dream Comes True before 2000: Local Artists Praised for Performance of Bit from 'Aida,'" *Chicago Defender,* August 16, 1941; "All-Negro Cast to Present 'Aida' at Opera House: All Except One Singer Are Chicagoans," *Chicago Daily Tribune,* October 4, 1942; "All Negro 'Aida' a Triumph for Cast, Directors: Rewarded by Appreciation of Good Sized Audience," *Chicago Daily Tribune,* October 11, 1942; Grace W. Tompkins, "Opera Guild Scores a Triumph with Aida: Reah's Title Role Lauded by All Critics," *Chicago Defender,* October 17, 1942; Grace W. Tompkins, "Critics Acclaim 'Aida' for a Second Time," *Chicago Defender,* March 6, 1943.

96. "All Negro 'Aida' a Triumph for Cast, Directors: Rewarded by Appreciation of Good Sized Audience," *Chicago Daily Tribune,* October 11, 1942.

97. "Cast Rehearses 19th Annual 'Passion Play,'" *Chicago Defender,* March 20, 1948.

98. "Sadie Bruce's Dancers Rehearse 'Passion Play,'" *Chicago Defender,* March 27, 1948.

99. "Sadie Bruce Dancers at Opera House Dec. 8," *Chicago Defender,* December 3, 1949; "Sadie Bruce Is Back with Fine Frame Show," *Chicago Defender,* May 19, 1951; "Sadie Bruce Classic to Opera House May 4," *Chicago Defender,* May 1, 1958.

100. Semmes, *The Regal Theatre and Black Culture.*

101. Mullen, *Popular Fronts,* 99.

102. "Artists, Models Ball to Choose 'Miss Victory': Negro Girl War Workers to Vie for Crown," *Chicago Daily Tribune,* October 17, 1943.

103. Jacqui Malone, *Steppin' on the Blues,* 114.

104. Ibid.

105. Semmes, *The Regal Theatre and Black Culture,* 140–42.

106. Drake and Cayton, *Black Metropolis*; Semmes. *The Regal Theatre and Black Culture.*

107. Ibid.

108. Ibid.

109. Roi Otley, "Negroes Form Stage Arts Group: Promoting Dance Is Aim," *Chicago Daily Tribune,* June 16, 1957.

110. George E. Lewis, *A Power Stronger than Itself: The AACM and American Experimental Music* (Chicago, Ill.: University of Chicago Press, 2008), 165.

111. S. Brandi Barnes, "Kuumba Theater's Comeback," *Chicago Reader,* October 31, 1996.

112. "About eta-History," eta Creative Arts website. Web. Accessed March 9, 2012.

113. "About Us," African American Arts Alliance website. Web. Accessed March 9, 2012.

114. Ibid.

115. "Black Theater Alliance Sets Theater Week," *Chicago Defender,* May 14, 1975, 24. National Edition.

116. African American Arts Alliance, "About Us," http://www.africanamerucanartsallian cechicago.org/aboutus.html.

Theater

CHUCK SMITH

Chuck Smith is Goodman Theatre's resident director. He served as dramaturg for the world-premiere production of August Wilson's Gem of the Ocean. *At Columbia College, he was for twenty years contest facilitator of the Theodore Ward Prize for African American Playwriting. He was a founding member of the Chicago Theatre Company, where he served as artistic director for four seasons and directed the Jeff Award–winning musical* Po'. *His Chicago-area directing credits include eta Creative Arts, Black Ensemble Theater, Northlight Theatre, MPAACT, Congo Square Theatre Company, New Regal Theater, Kuumba Theatre Company, Fleetwood-Jourdain Theatre, and Pegasus Players. He was inducted into the Chicago State University Gwendolyn Brooks Center's Literary Hall of Fame and named 2001 Chicago Tribune Chicagoan of the Year.*

In this interview, conducted in June 2011, Chuck Smith reflects on his life in the theater, including his experiences working with Dramatic Arts Guild, X-BAG, the Chicago Theatre Company, Victory Gardens Theater, and the Goodman Theatre. Interspersed among his reflections are Smith's comments on a range of contemporary issues: the challenges facing black theater companies, diversity initiatives by large regional theaters, and whether major newspapers should employ black theater critics.

What events led to you becoming a resident director at the Goodman Theatre?

It was the 1970–71 season. I auditioned for a play that they were doing here called *The Night Thoreau Spent in Jail* and I got the role of—I didn't get the role but I got the understudy part [of Henry Williams], a runaway slave. Ira Rogers, who was probably at the time one of the main go-to guys—this is the seventies, completely different picture of theater than today in Chicago—got the role. When they needed a black actor, they would go to Ira Rogers. But Ira Rogers hated the role. Every chance he got, he would duck out. He would get sick and let me play the role.

And then was he fired? Or did he just . . .

No. No. No. He didn't get fired. He actually told them, "Look, I can't do the such and such matinee," so I was always on certain matinees. I only had two scenes but they were great scenes. The play was about Henry David Thoreau and some of his experiences at Walden Pond. He comes across this runaway slave and a conversation gets going and then he moves on his way. That part [Thoreau] was played by Christopher Walken. This was before he returned to New York. That's how I was introduced to the Goodman Theatre. It was such a wonderful experience. Not just being onstage. It was how fair they treated you, how they made you feel. While you're here, you actually feel as though you're at home. On the night the show closed, there was a closing night party and I was extremely sad and I made a vow to myself. I said, "One of these days, I'm going to be on staff here and I'll say goodbye to the actors and I'll be able to stay." That's been my focus from 1971 until I joined the staff here in '92: to work here at the Goodman Theatre.

What was the first play that you directed for the Goodman?

My first assignment was to be an assistant to Steve Scott on *A Christmas Carol.* That was in 1992. In 1993, I directed *A Christmas Carol,* and again in 1994 and 1995.

How did you go from being an assistant director to a member of the artistic staff?

Assistant directing was my assignment. Back in the old days, that was the way you got familiar with directing here. You learned how the Goodman works by directing *A Christmas Carol.* That's why I had it for three years. It took me three years just to get this system under foot because this is a big operation. There's more to the Goodman than directing plays. There are many various engagements and meetings. There's so much going on here, like at any large operation. You've got to learn everything else in order to function efficiently. After three years I said, "OK, I'm ready."

Who approached you about assistant directing A Christmas Carol*?*

How I got on at the Goodman was strictly my own initiative. At the time, I was working with the Chicago Theatre Company. I was with the Chicago Theatre Company from 1984 through 1990. Part of it was as artistic director and then it was as associate director. At that time, I was associate director. I applied for an Arts Midwest Minority Administrative Fellowship, which would take artists who were at a certain point in their careers and give them the skills to move up to the next step. I was at that point where I had learned all I could learn in terms of working with the Chicago Theatre Company, and I wanted to know how to work in a larger space like the Goodman. And I also wanted to learn how to take a show on the road. I applied for this fellowship. Bam! I got it. I was assigned to work with Cornerstone Theatre Company starting in the fall of 1990. At the time, they were a company that did nothing but take shows on the road. So I worked with Cornerstone and helped them put together their national tour. That was the first half of the fellowship. For the second half of the fellowship, I went to St. Paul, Minnesota, and worked with an organization called The Great American History Theatre, now known as The History Theatre in St. Paul, Minnesota. They have a beautiful six-hundred-seat space. Working with them, I learned how to program space. While I was away, I submitted my resignation to the Chicago Theatre Company. And that way, there was no flak. I was away from Chicago. When I came back, I was no longer part of the Chicago Theatre Company. There was no press. No "Chuck Smith leaves Chicago." None of that gossip news. Smooth as silk. The very first thing I did was apply to the Goodman Theatre. I put a proposal together, got it in the hands of the people over here at the Goodman Theatre. They read it, brought me in for an interview. I got hired.

What was the proposal?

Basically, "Hey you looking for black people to sit in your seats aren't you? I think I know how to do it. I can help you with that." That's the basic crux of the proposal.

In terms of getting black people in the seats at the Goodman, how would you characterize your contribution to the Goodman in the years that you have been on staff?

Well, the very first contribution I made, as far as I'm concerned, and satisfying what I said I was going to do in the proposal, was a production of *Ma Rainey's Black Bottom* [2001]. At that time, *Ma Rainey's Black Bottom* was the only show of August Wilson's that the Goodman hadn't done. I directed it here at the old theater and that show set a box office record. Part of the reason why it set a box office record is because a lot of black folks came to see it. Bingo!

In response, did the Goodman adjust its programming or give you more opportunities to direct on the main stage? What was the response to the success of Ma Rainey?

I can't say because of *Ma Rainey* things have worked out better for me. I can say that what *Ma Rainey* did was solidify that Chuck Smith belongs here. That's all it did was verify that Chuck Smith, he knows what he's doing. Bingo.

And prior to that, was there ever a moment when people were questioning whether you should be at the Goodman Theatre?

Yes, of course. Like any job, until you prove yourself. "What's he gonna do. Is he using the Goodman to move on to someplace else? Is he trying to go to New York?" I think everyone knows that Chuck Smith is a Chicagoan and plans to stay in Chicago. And is very, very happy at the Goodman Theatre and has no intention of leaving the Goodman Theatre. I'm embedded as far as I'm concerned.

When it comes to deciding where to direct, I'm assuming your first choice is the Goodman.

Yes. There have been very few seasons that I have not directed, not been a part of the season. Last season, was one. I requested not to be a part of the season because I had so much going on outside. Bob [Robert Falls] gave me a pass so I didn't have to work onstage, here at the Goodman. But just because I don't direct doesn't mean that I'm not here functioning in other capacities.

If there's a piece that you want to direct, does the first pass go to the Goodman? Here, I'm thinking about your [2011] production of The Gospel According to James *at Victory Gardens. What is the conversation like in terms of you directing—working—outside of the Goodman?*

Bob knew about *The Gospel According to James* from its early conception, but there was no way it was going to be staged at the Goodman. Charles Smith, who wrote the piece, is a part of the Victory Gardens writing ensemble. So, they naturally had first dibs on it after Indiana Repertory Company, who commissioned the work. If anything had happened that Victory Gardens decided not to do it, Goodman would have been my first choice.

And you directed the Indiana Repertory production?

Yes, I was a part of it from . . . not from its inception but early on. Janet Allen, the artistic director of Indiana Repertory Company commissioned Charles Smith to write the play. Charles has a history with Indiana Repertory. It's the third commission that he's done for them. She commissioned that play as part of their "Indiana series." They put in for a grant to help develop the work with the Joyce Foundation. The Joyce Foundation said they would help and suggested having a Chicago director tied with the work. Charles called me and asked if I would be interested in being part of the team. I said, "Yes, of course."

How do you know Charles Smith?

There's a cute little story about Charles and I. Charles was a young writer out of either Iowa University or Iowa State, I forget which one. But, he came to work at Victory Gardens. He's from Chicago, Chicago's South Side like me. When he got out of college, he went to work at Victory Gardens Theater. He was working in the office and he would pick up the phone and say, "Victory Gardens Theater, Charles Smith speaking," and the person on the other end would say, "Charles, hey I know you. I know your work," and he would have to clarify, he would say, "No, no, no, I'm Charles Smith, a writer; you're talking about Chuck Smith, the director." So this goes on for a long time. One night at a social event, Charles pulled me to the side and said, "Look, man, I'm getting sick and tired of people mistaking me for you." He said, "I vow to you one day somebody gonna mistake you for me." And from that point on, I've been a fan of Charles Smith. And lo and behold, not too many years later, someone called me and thought I was him. And the first thing I did was call him and say, "Hey, man, guess what happened." Charles and I worked together on a television project called *Fast Break to Glory* [1988] about DuSable High, the first black Chicago high school basketball team to make it all the way downstate to the finals. It was based on the DuSable Panthers in 1954. I was in high school at the time. The game was televised. I watched the game as a big, huge fan of the DuSable Panthers. I didn't go to DuSable but everybody in the South Side community was saying, "Hey DuSable, they're gonna do it." They [the referees] would not let those brothers win that game. And you could see it. I mean they just stole the game from them.

Calling fouls left and right?

Yes. Fouls, traveling, no basket—all that kind of stuff. It was right there on television for everybody to see. I said, "One of these days, I'm gonna do something about that. Gotta do something." Years later, I told that story to Charles. We put up a screenplay together and we did it on local television, channel 5, won Emmys, all kind of stuff. That was the first time we worked together. The second time we worked together was at Victory Gardens eleven years ago now, with *Knock Me a Kiss* [2000]. [*Knock Me*] is about W. E. B. Du Bois's daughter and her marriage to Countee Cullen and her relationship with the bandleader Jimmie Lunceford. Based on truth. It's in the history books, you can read it. We worked together on that one. It was a world premiere at Victory Gardens. Recently [2010], we took it to New York to the New Federal Theatre. A little showcase production and it went wonderfully well. I'm raising money now for a Broadway production. That's sort of the history of Charles and I. Charles is a very, very good friend of mine.

Can you tell me about the beginnings of the Chicago Theatre Company?

The beginnings are simple; its roots are with another company called X-BAG, the Experimental Black Actors Guild, which I joined in 1972. It was what I could consider my first real experience in black theater. Before that, I had been doing theater—what we now consider basic community theater—with the Dramatic Arts Guild at Michael Reese Hospital. That's where I started off in theater. It was an integrated group and we did all kinds of plays. And the basic reason, the mission of the organization was to do plays for the patients at Michael Reese Hospital. To give them some diversion, some way to keep their minds off their illness. We would put a play up and we would do it for a couple of nights, maybe a Friday and a Saturday. When I came on board, I asked, "Why don't we do it on a Sunday and invite the public, invite our friends." That became a policy and, after that, we would say, well, we do it for the patients and then we'll just run it for a while and let not just our friends but the general public come and see. So that was Dramatic Arts Guild. One of the Dramatic Arts Guild members joined this group called X-BAG, which was located at the Parkway Community House at 500 E. 67th Street on the South Side. A good friend of mine named Lynn Logan was doing a show. She was in it with another Dramatic Arts Guild member—Richard Umbra, one of the guys who got me into the theater—he was directing it. It was wonderful. It was a black play, [Ron Milner's] *Who's Got His Own* [1973]. Three characters. I said, "They got a real theater, not an auditorium, so I'm going to see if I can join this group," and I did. I became quite a mainstay at X-BAG. I became their resident stage manager and worked with X-BAG close to four years. At X-BAG was Douglas Alan Mann, who recently passed in May [2011]. Doug was one of the other actors in *Who's Got His Own,* [a] wonderful actor. Doug was sort of the resident actor and I was like the resident stage manager. We were pretty much involved in just about everything that went on down there under Clarence Taylor who, at the time, was the executive director. He called all the shots. He made all the decisions and his basic thing was "I'm the H.N.I.C" ["Head Negro in Charge"]. You know what that means?

I get it. [*Laughing*]

"That's what I am, I am the H.N.I.C." So Clarence's philosophy was black theater for black people in the black community. That was his philosophy. And he preached that to Doug and me. We would have long sessions after rehearsals and performances and Clarence would just sit us down and talk about our obligation to the black community. All that resonated. I loved my time at X-BAG. While I was at X-BAG, Clarence introduced me to playwright Theodore Ward, who was a good friend of his. We were going to do a play by Theodore Ward and Clarence wanted me to direct it. It was a play called *The Daubers,* a political play. So, I directed *The Daubers* [1974] and Ted Ward really liked what I did with it. Ted and I became good friends. I was very fortunate because Ted had this friend—his lady friend lived—in the same South Commons building that I was living in. I was on the thirteenth floor and they were down on the tenth floor. After the rehearsals or performances of whatever, I'd go down and talk to Ted. Ted would sit me down and school me about ways to go, which were not completely different from Clarence. While Clarence said stay in the black community, Ted said go out, learn and bring it back. Or, just expand it. Expand your knowledge and then apply your knowledge to the black community. That was the difference and that made even more sense to me. So that's the philosophy that I use today. I'm still loyal to the black community, no if[s], ands, or buts about it. There is nothing wrong with using what's here at the Goodman to give back to the black community and to help expose the black community to more stuff. Bigger stuff. Nothing wrong with that at all. I left X-BAG thinking about what Ted said: "Look man, you've got some college. You've worked at the Goodman already. You don't have to stay in a small space down in X-BAG to do that. You should finish school and expand, expand." So, I went back to school. I went back to school, got my degree, and that's why I left X-BAG. I left X-BAG to get my degree. While I was gone, X-BAG folded. A few years later, I was working with the group that Ernest Perry put together called Amistad. We were doing equity showcases, professional theater under union contracts but under the showcase code where you didn't have to pay the actors. It was cheaper. We didn't have any money and most of us by this time were in the union [Actors Equity] so we had to do union work. So that is what was available to us. We did a lot of stuff. After one of these showcases, a musical called *Po'* about poor people, Douglas Alan Mann was at the show and he said, "Chuck, why don't we just go back to Parkway and get something going?" And that was the beginning of the Chicago Theatre Company. The closing night of *Po'* was the beginning of the Chicago Theatre Company.

What happened to Amistad?

Amistad just drifted away. You get a group: it's a family, and your family gets together and grows, and then they sort of drift away. You're always a family but you're not that unit anymore. That's what happened. Bonnie DeShong was a part of that and Michael Perkins. Michael Perkins came over with me with the Chicago Theatre Company. He was one of the original founding members of Chicago Theatre Company.

And when was this?

Early eighties, 1983 to 1984.

When you announced and you launched the Chicago Theatre Company, what was the reception like from the community?

Huge, huge. *Po'*, the same show that I did under Amistad, was the first show I did with the Chicago Theatre Company. I knew it worked. So Bingo! That thing ran for about four months to full houses. It was big, received Jeff [Joseph Jefferson Award] nominations. We won one of the Jeffs for music direction. My very first show at Chicago Theatre Company. The second show also was nominated. Ernest Perry was in it. Ernest Perry and the late Vince Viverito [Sr.], both of them got nominated. Two guys—one black guy, one white guy—stuck in an elevator. It was called *Suspenders* [1984], a beautiful little play. So that was the start of the season. From that point on, Chicago Theatre Company was a mainstay in the black community. It was the very first black company to start under an equity contract. We didn't grow into an equity contract; we started with an equity contract. That's our history. And it lasted for years. Again, this is mid-eighties, and I stuck with the company for five years more or less until, like I was saying, '90/'91 when I submitted my resignation while I was on the fellowship. I wanted the company to expand. I had already worked at Parkway and the Chicago Theatre Company was at Parkway. Ted Ward said, "Look, you don't have to stay here at Parkway." And my philosophy was, "If you don't grow, you die." In this environment, people aren't going to continue to give you money to do the same thing. You got to have plans to move on. You got to have plans to grow. If you don't have plans to grow then they're going to stop giving you money. They are going to give the money to someone else who has plans to grow. That's not how they saw it. They said, "We're on the Clarence Taylor philosophy, we want to stay right here, we wanna do this here—we do good work. Everybody knows we do good work. We're gonna do it here." Well, after a while, the funding dried up and they're not around anymore. In 2005, they disappeared. That's too bad but I predicted it.

When you came back and worked at the Goodman, was there any pushback that you experienced for not working on the South Side?

No, no, no. None of that, not at all. Fortunately, the way I left Chicago was quiet and clean. Plus, I was no longer the artistic director. Even before I left Chicago Theatre Company, I realized that sooner or later I was going to have to leave. Months prior, I prepared my exit. I said, "You run the company. You be the artistic director, I'll help you do whatever you want to do. I'll assist. I'll stage manage," which I did. "I'll direct, I'll do anything." Just to help the company move along. But I was no longer calling the shots because I knew I was going to have to leave. So that was my experience with Chicago Theatre. Great days, great experiences. I can say working with Doug and Michael were some of the best years of my life.

Could you paint a picture of the South Side theater scene during the time that you worked with X-BAG and Chicago Theatre Company?

I would say that the heyday of the black theater scene was in the seventies. Late seventies, early eighties. In 1972, when I got to X-BAG, there were a lot of companies around. There was Lamont Zeno on the West Side. That was part of the Better Boys Foundation. Useni Eugene Perkins was in charge of the Better Boys Foundation. In that space, they had a theater where Pemon Rami was running the theater. It was about that time that Useni said that we needed an umbrella organization and that he put together the Black Theater Alliance of Chicago. All the companies would meet once a month. I was with X-BAG and Clarence Taylor would assign me—because I was the resident stage manager and he hated meetings—to go. I don't know why he hated meetings. I just know he was a public school teacher, taught art, wonderful set designer, and he would send me to the meetings. That's how I got involved and got to know all these other theater companies that were around. Like today, the fact that Chicago is so full of theater doesn't mean that I go to all these other theaters because I'm working. And resident stage manager means I'm working. So I couldn't go to all of the other theater companies and see all of what they were doing. But they were there, like Kuumba and Zeno and New Concepts, Black Heritage, Kusema, Ebony Talent School; there were many, many companies. It was a rich scene. The beautiful thing about the Black Theater Alliance is that it kept us in touch with each other. Otherwise, I would have never known there was so much going on out of the Washington Park Fieldhouse and stuff like that. There were groups all over the place. If you want to put them in a category: community theater. But, these were artists who knew their crafts. They could not work in the legitimate theater scene at the time because they were black. And that had a lot to do with the bitterness that Clarence Taylor had, in terms of staying here [on the South Side], "do your thing here" . . . because he'd been rejected. C.T., as we called him, this man was beautiful—visual artist, set designer, director, producer. The contributions that he could have made to Chicago theater at-large back in the sixties (if they had let him) are immense but nobody paid any attention to black theater in those days. It was black theater and it was white theater. They were separated. Fortunately, Richard Christiansen started taking note of what was going on and started reviewing black companies when the Parkway Community House was part of The Hull House organization. And when they [Hull House] expanded, they put theaters in all their locations such as the Parkway Community House on 67th Street, and the space that Jackie Taylor's in right now [Uptown Center] on Beacon Street. The home base was the place on Belmont [Broadway and Belmont], 3212 on N. Broadway. When Steppenwolf came in from the suburbs. They moved into that space. That's where the blooming of Steppenwolf occurred. When those companies started, Clarence Taylor and the original X-BAGers were out of the Hull House organization that was at Parkway. They would tell me about when 60 percent of the audience was white people who were coming to see the shows and 40 percent black people. And after Hull House shut it down or whatever they did, Clarence Taylor went back to get things going again, but not under Hull House. They got the 40 percent black people but the 60 percent white people were gone and never returned.

How did you become a director?

Ted Ward. I was thinking that I was an actor, but Ted Ward said, "No, you got other skills. You got skills that can really be much more useful to you and to the community at-large than your acting skills." He said, "You are only a mediocre actor," and he was right. He says, "You can get work, but you're a damn good director and you're a good stage manager and you got a good head on your shoulder so you can do other stuff." He was absolutely right. I have never not worked. Back then, I turned down work, in stage managing and directing. The point is Ted Ward was right. There were no black directors in the professional scene at the time. There was one fine actor/director Bob Curry but Bob Curry had some serious problems which we won't discuss. According to the [*Chicago*] *Tribune,* I was the first black guy to direct on Chicago's union off-Loop theater scene. It was a play called *Eden* at Victory Gardens in 1978. How I got the job was initiated by Ted Ward. He taught me. He said, "This is how you do it. You do this. You do this, and then you do this." I did exactly what he told me and it worked. That's how I got the job at Victory Gardens. They brought me back for seven consecutive seasons to direct on their main stage and that pushed me off on my directing career. People know who Chuck Smith is because of that.

How were black theater artists prevented from working in the city's profesional theater before the mid-1970s?

From my own point of view, there was a racial line that nobody would cross. It was sort of known that if you went to one of the white companies then the kind of roles that you would play was going to be a maid or something like that. Or a slave, like I was in the *The Night Thoreau Spent in Jail*. Those are the kind of roles that were offered. One of the things that happened was that all of a sudden more theater companies jumped into the Chicago theater scene. More theater companies but the funding money was still the same. Still the same pie with more people eating off [it]. In Chuck Smith's opinion, they started looking for another source of income. And then, they saw all these black people in all these theaters outside of their circle. How can we get these black people into our seats, because, as always happens in theater whether black or white, there is a certain group of people who go to the theater. Usually, they have some disposable income. Most are of a certain age and, unfortunately, they pass on. How do you replace these people? Who do you replace them with? "OK, whoa, let's try this." That's what happened. There was even— years later in the early '90s—a huge grant called the Lila Wallace [Lila Wallace–Reader's Digest Fund, 1991] Audience Development Fund that was available to certain larger institutions to do programming to get black people in their seats. The black community was furious. "Why can't we get some of that money?" "How come we can't apply, we've been doing this for years? You want to know how to do it, give us some money and we'll show you how to do it." Lila Wallace folks didn't do it that way, they just gave the money to people like the Goodman, which by the way, is how I knew that money was there and available. Still, I don't thank Lila Wallace because I don't think what they did was right. That was the wrong way to go.

For denying money to black theater companies?

Yes. Give some of that money to those people.

In the seventies, you'd go to these Black Theater Alliance meetings and you would see a lot of black theater companies represented? What happened? Why are there so few black theater companies in Chicago today?

You can't blame it all on the Wallace grant. To be honest and frank, after a while you can run your organization just on art but you really got to have your business together. Also, you must have vision and I think the same thing that happened with the Chicago Theatre Company happened to all of those other companies. The lack of vision. Don't just think about what shows you're going to put on. Think about how you're going to expand, how you're going to make your organization better and stronger. It's not all about the plays. Theater is a business. It's art and it's business. The African American community has always, always been able to put up good art. No if[s], ands or buts about it. But the artists have got to get in closer communication with the business community. "People in the business community—this is what we, theater artists, do and we need your help. We can help you do this. You can help us do this." There has to be some kind of partnership, which has never been formed. Even today, it is what's lacking. You know, at the Goodman, that Bob Falls is the artistic director but you also know that Roche [Schulfer] is the manager. And Roche, like a rock, has been here from the get-go. He started here working in the box office, fresh out of college. The Goodman is the only place he's ever worked and now, he's running the place. Get it? That's what the black community, black theater needs. More people like Roche, not just artists. We've got all the artists we need. In other words, we got all these bullets and ain't got no guns. You see it's as simple as that. I can't say it's as simple as that but that's always been the case. In my many years of being involved in theater, African American theater, this is always what I've discovered. Companies go under not because of their art; it's because of their business.

I have a question about location. Can the South Side support a major regional black theater?

Yes. Yes. Yes. Location is key. I have always said that if you're going to do something on the South Side, do it in Hyde Park. The Court Theatre is located in Hyde Park. Court Theatre has been there forever. The University of Chicago used to perform Shakespeare outside, in Mandel Hall court, every summer. All of this is to say that Hyde Park is an area where all people feel safe. Yes, it could work, if you were smart enough. There's another spot where it could work: the old South Shore Cultural Center. It would be a wonderful place to go and do theater. I live in South Shore and I was part of an organization called Coalition to Save South Shore Country Club Park. They were going to tear that beautiful structure down. We did save it. I was mainly involved because I was proposing that we put a theater, a legitimate theater, in there. Unfortunately, once the organization saved the building, the first thing that got scratched was the theater. I still believe it is a perfect spot for a larger theater. There is parking. It is scenic. There's a Metra stop and the #6 CTA bus from downtown. Perfect!

It is said that there are two hundred, almost three hundred producing theater companies in Chicago. Of these, there aren't that many that are black or urban theaters for people of color.

No. The Latino companies are starting to pop up. I think they're going to continue to increase and are going to do quite well. Unfortunately, again, it's the black companies that still haven't got that knack for . . . Jackie Taylor has been able to survive and grow. Smart woman. Smart lady from the get-go, smart. Learned how to play the game and plays it well. And building her own theater right now. And don't forget eta [Creative Arts]. eta is still planning to do the same thing, but they've been planning to do this for many, many years now. Jackie Taylor jumped in there, bam, bam, bam, and got her stuff together and flew. It is knowing how to play the game. It's political—yes. But, it's also being smart. You got to have the ability to go with the flow. "Oh, this ain't working, let me slide over here." How to shift those sands to get to your destination rather than "No it's gonna be done our way or no way. If we can't get it this way, we'll just wait."

You'll wait a long time.

A long time. You'll wait a long time. [*Laughing*]

Does Chicago need to have a black critic writing for one of the major papers,
Chicago Tribune *or* Chicago Sun-Times?

That's not going solve the problem. The fact that [those papers] review
the shows, the black shows, means that the readers get the information
that the show is going on and what the reviewer's opinion of the show
is. Just because you got a black critic—or even a black critic giving you
a good review—is not going to make those readers come and see your
show. I think what has to be developed more than anything else is a
strong relationship with a good reviewer or a respected theater person in
a major black newspaper like the *Defender.* Consistency where people say,
"OK, what's going on in black theater." Pick up the *Defender* and read
what so and so says. One should know exactly where to find the black
theater information on any given day rather than [relying on] a critic in
one of these other papers. We do have a community that does have some
disposable income. We have people my age, senior citizens, who look
for places to go. They have friends coming into the city and they want
to take them somewhere. A lot of the time when they come, that's who
goes to the theater because it's a novelty. They say, "Hey let's go to the
theater," and, fortunately, there's always black theater here in the city
because of Jackie Taylor and eta. And the fact that the theater scene is so
rich, there is usually something black going on even if it's not at Jackie's
or eta. You can usually find a black play or . . . a play that represents the
community in some kind of way or a good black person in the play or
something like that. Black people love to see themselves onstage, like
anybody else. There's nothing wrong with that. That's part of the game.
Go over to Steppenwolf right now. There's Ora Jones and Alana Arenas
onstage right now. Chicago Shakespeare, they have good black actors in
those shows over there. You can go to almost any show in Chicago and
see black folks now onstage.

How did you first meet Ernest Perry Jr.?

Ernest was getting Amistad together and a good friend of mine, Wanda
Christine, was a friend of Ernest and she brought him by my house.
Ernest said, "This is my plan: we're gonna do showcase shows since we
don't have any money. We will go to these community centers or some

place that is OK with the code and put on a play. We'll get the best actors in the city, some of the black actors in the city and do some shows." And I said, "Sure." I was all for it. Unfortunately for me, the meetings were set to be on Wednesday nights and on Wednesday nights during those times, my daughter was with me. That was the night I had my daughter so I couldn't go to the meetings, but the few I went to were electric. Ideas. "Should we do this show, or we should do a show this way?" It was just a wonderful time. There was an energy that led to a different way of thinking in terms of doing shows and producing shows which fit my energy. If nobody else is hiring me, then I should be able to hire myself. I can't just sit around and wait for somebody else to put me to work. I should be able to figure out a way to make work for myself. Even if it doesn't pay, it will help me as an artist. That's the kind of thing that came out of Amistad. Ernest and Amistad were right before Chicago Theatre Company. Ernest's Amistad did two one-act plays down at the Parkway Community House about two years before the Chicago Theatre Company took it over, and that was the very first equity show that was done there. It must have been around 1982. And then Amistad worked with Loop College right before that.

Which college?

Loop Junior, Loop City College, which is now Harold Washington. Loop College was located at 64 E. Lake Street, right across the street, east of the new Harold Washington College on Lake. They changed the address, but that is where I went to junior college working under a brother named Sydney Daniels, who is a wonderful set designer, fine director, and an original member of the Jeff committee. Ernest, myself, and Vince Viverito, we mounted the production of *Suspenders,* the second show of the Chicago Theatre Company, there. Daniels designed a beautiful set for us, and one of the reasons why we did that show in that space was to bring attention to the community-at-large that Harold Washington, the new building, did not have a theater and you would not see this kind of work in that space. That was an Amistad-Loop production and that's the kind of stuff we did. We did fine work. Ernest is from Evanston. He took me to a student production years ago, *Witness for the Prosecution,* just to show me the kind of program that he came out of. I was sitting there in that audience, totally forgot I was watching a high school show, got totally engrossed in it, and I know the play but they did it for me. A strong program. He's from a serious background. Ernest got so popular here at the Goodman—first through *A Christmas Carol* and then through other productions—he was once number one, Goodman's most hired actor. I'm not saying that right now he has got more theater productions than any other actor in this city—he hasn't worked in quite a few years—but he's close. For a while, Ernest was onstage here [at the Goodman] every season and more than one show. Now, he's maybe not number one, but he's ranked, you know what I mean. And I always say, "You don't have to win. Just be sure you're playing the game. Play the game, play it well."

How did the Theodore Ward playwriting prize competition come into being?

I'm not a founder, I took over the contest in its third season. The founders are Paul Carter Harrison, he was on staff at Columbia College; Sheldon Patinkin, the chairman of the department; and Dean Lya Dym Rosenblum, dean of Columbia College at the time. I would imagine that Paul initiated the idea that there be a contest of plays that would come through the college. Paul and Sheldon went throughout the black community and asked what would be a good name for this contest. The community universally responded "Ted Ward" because he's sort of a spiritual leader. At the time everybody knew Ted Ward so that's how the name came about. There were two seasons of contest winners before I took it on. In the third season I was on staff at Columbia College, they asked me if I would take over the contest, and I said yes. I had it for about twenty years. I was responsible for coming up with the top five. I would read them all, and I had other people reading, not just me. I had a series of readers. People who I knew who liked to read. Not so much reading plays but just liked to read, people who liked to read [and] who knew a good story. I had about ten people—"you read these, you read these"—and then I'd come up with these five. I would send them out to the community, all over, not just the black community but all over, to anybody who could produce these plays or might be interested in producing a play. "Here, tell me which one of these you think is best." And they would. I would tally the votes and that's how I would select the winner. That was the beauty of the contest. Not so much the winners but just exposing these plays to producers. Unfortunately, after I left Columbia College, a new chairman decided to eliminate the contest, so it's no more. But it had a wonderful run. It's gone and now it's up to the community to come up with something else. We knew that worked so you know, I'm hoping the community will come up with something else. I dream that one of the historically black colleges will see its necessity and take it on.

Who are some of the people who emerged through the Theodore Ward competition?

Lydia Diamond, Gloria Bond Clunie. Those are the two main ones I can say; Charles Smith, his play was a second-place winner once. Wow, those are the three writers that just pop off right away. I wouldn't be surprised if Darren Canady, this guy who wrote *Brothers of the Dust* (2011), succeeds. He's got a nice flow. He's got a nice touch to his writing. But [the contest] it's gone now, unfortunately. Who else is in there? Shepsu or Reggie Lawrence, another good writer, a very fine writer. He won twice. Gloria Bond Clunie won twice. Those are some of the Chicago people who I think, as writers, we will hear from. They're still writing and they're still doing good stuff.

The competition lasted for twenty-three years?

I was over there at least twenty-three, twenty-four, closer to twenty-five years. It would be wonderful if I could say it was institutionalized, but you know such is not the case.

How did you become interested in theater?

I'm an ex-Marine. In 1964, I was getting ready to go back in the Marine Corps when I met these guys that took me to this theater company, and they wanted me to be a part of the company. I was reluctant at first, but they said "come on," so I went in there and it worked. It was Dramatic Arts Guild and they worked out of this small auditorium—maybe seventy seats. I walked in there . . . I can say when I walked into that room my life changed. It took me ages to figure it out. The initial attraction was that there's lots of girls down there and I was single, but I walked in the room and it wasn't the girls, it was just something about being in that room that worked for me, and it took me years to figure that out. I walked in and everybody was busy. It was during tech week. People over here doing something, people over there doing something, and everybody was doing something to put on this show. Everybody was working. And, I figured it out that that was the first time that I had been in a situation that reminded me—that I felt comfortable in because—of my relationship with the Marine Corps. Everybody working to complete a mission. And I walked in the room and everybody was on it. I was at home. Psychologically, I identified with that. It took me years to figure that out—that's exactly what we do in the Marine Corps. These guys are working and everybody's working to accomplish the mission. Everybody was working to put on this play and that's when I said, "Oh wow, I get it." That's what it was. I walked in the room and there I was, I was at home. Now, if I had walked in the room and everybody was just sitting around, kicking back, it would have been a whole different thing. And to this day, the process of theater that I love the best is tech. Most people hate tech but I love it.

What do you think someone would say was Chuck Smith's most successful production in Chicago?

I don't know. Fortunately, they come back and say a lot of different plays. A lot of people like *Proof* (2004). I take a lot of pride with *Proof* because a lot of people don't realize *Proof* wasn't a black play. It wasn't about the black community, but it worked with black actors. *Proof* sort of sticks out. *Black Bottom* is still my own personal favorite because of what it means to me and my relationship to August Wilson. If *Ma Rainey* hadn't been such a . . . well, *Ma Rainey* was huge and because it was huge, "Chuck is good now." [*Laughing*] Another play that I'm really, really happy with was my production of *A Raisin in the Sun*.

Was that staged at the Goodman?

Yes, in 2000. Everybody who saw it had seen *A Raisin in the Sun* before. I mean how many people—especially theatergoers—haven't seen *A Raisin in the Sun*? They came back to me and said, "I've seen *A Raisin in the*

Sun so many times but there was something about your show that was different." What was it? And I say, you know—I know exactly what it is myself. It's a Chicago play for one thing. It takes place on the South Side of Chicago where I'm born and raised. Travis, the little boy, is the one character in theater that I identify with and can say that's me onstage. That kid is Chuck Smith, I can say that. I know exactly what that kid is going through. I know exactly what's happening with that kid. I was that kid. Regardless of all of that, what it was—I think—is that I used all Chicago actors in roles Chicago actors needed to be in. It was an all-Chicago cast. Harry Lennix born and raised in Chicago, T'Keyah Keymah born and raised in the city of Chicago. Celeste Williams born and raised in the city of Chicago. All those characters needed to be born and raised in Chicago. Irma Hall played Mama. She, just like the character, was born someplace else but came to Chicago. Everybody fit the roles perfectly because of who they were. That's all it was. It's a Chicago play, and I made it a Chicago play by using Chicago actors, who were not only good actors. They had to be good actors but good actors from Chicago who understood the environment. They didn't have to do research. They didn't have to try to be like Chicago. They were Chicago.

They had it in them.

It's there. It's in them and that's all it was. Plus, it was a good show, a very good show. Chicagoans who saw that play saw themselves without a doubt. They didn't see actors who were trying to be Chicagoans. And somebody said, "What is it, what's so Chicago? How can you tell it's Chicago? How can you tell it's Chicago?" I can't, but I can tell when it's not. Before I got into theater I saw *A Raisin in the Sun,* the movie, with Sydney Poitier. I love Sydney Poitier. I'm a Sydney Poitier man. I took this lady to see the movie. *A Raisin in the Sun.* I was like, "That was great, that was great." She didn't like it, and I said, "Why?" and she said, "Sydney Poitier." "Chuck, you from Chicago, aren't you?" "Yes." "You were born and raised in Chicago, right?" "Yeah." "Tell me one person you know who talks like Sydney Poitier. Tell me one person you know." And I was like, "You don't know what you're talking about." But, I get it. I get it now that I am into theater. I am not knocking that brother's performance, but she had a point. She had a point. What if I had done a

Harlem play and used Chicago actors who had nothing to do with Harlem? I would have gotten nailed. You get me? If I went to New York with a play about Harlem with Chicago actors who don't know anything about Harlem. Man, I'd get murdered, you see.

Because if you don't feel it, it can't sound real.

Yeah. And if you don't know it, you can't be real.

What was it like growing up in Chicago? What was life like in Chicago before you left for the Marine Corps?

I had a wonderful childhood. I've never had any problems basically. I was blessed with a family that's close knit, just straight working people, nothing fancy. Grandfather—stockyards. Mother and Father split up when I was a kid living in Ida B. Wells [a public housing project], but Mom took me over to Grandma's house, and there are my uncles. They're my dads, the men who I look up to, the cats who I still try to be like.

Where did they work?

Uncle Abe moved to New York after World War II and worked as a postal worker. Warren was a steelworker, and my younger uncle was a lab technician. He was the first one that graduated college, and he graduated from Roosevelt and became a lab technician, but just working people. They would not let me mess up. They made sure that I did what I was supposed to do. They gave me the tough love that all children need. So all that's cool. We lived in Bronzeville until they decided to build Lake Meadows and Prairie Shores [high-rise apartment developments]. My grandparents were on 32nd and Vernon. They bought a place over in Hyde Park, so when I was in seventh grade, I moved to Hyde Park. It was predominately Jewish over there, and I never had an ounce of trouble with those guys. I wish I could find them now. We were tight. Seventh and eighth grade, I graduated from Kozminski on 53rd and Ingleside and was the first black guy to become a class officer out of Kozminski. I was vice president of the graduating class.

Went to Hyde Park [for high school] and that's when things started getting crazy because I was friends with my guys from Kozminski and the black kids coming in didn't like the idea, couldn't relate to me having lunch with these guys. So they would confront me, "How come you eating lunch them?" I would say, "Oh, those are my friends." They would say "No, you supposed to come over here and have lunch with us." I said, "No, I eat lunch with who I want to eat lunch with. You can't tell me who to eat lunch with. Matter of fact, I'm inviting you to come over and have lunch with us." And he said, "No, we don't eat with those white people." "That's your choice." I was getting in fights with the black kids because of that. So this went on for a semester and my mother—she had moved into another neighborhood—said, "Instead of living with your grandmother, come on and live with me in Park Manor," and then I went to Parker High School. The trouble was at Hyde Park High. The following year, in 1953, I went to Parker High School as a sophomore and then merged into the black community and that was it until I joined the Marine Corps.

Now, certain things happened when I was in the Marine Corps that changed—not changed, but made Chuck Smith who Chuck Smith is. When I joined the Marine Corps, I had no military training whatsoever, none whatsoever. When I got out of boot camp, the Marine Corps' Boot Camp, some of the toughest training there ever was in the world, they gave me a stripe. I thought, "I can do this." Like *Ma Rainey's Black Bottom,* I can do this. Bam! That was the first thing I ever did on my own that I was consciously proud of.

A year later, I'm in the Philippines, stationed there as an MP, military policeman, guarding the base at Subic Bay. Me and a bunch of guys out there in town partying, having a good time, a real good time. We were supposed to be back on the base at midnight. We didn't make it. Ten after twelve we pull up in our little jitney and the guys said, "Hey look, don't go through the gate, let's jump the fence." So one jumped, there were seven of us, and the other five they jumped the fence. I went through the gate. "Man, you late. I got to write you up, man." I'm in there [main gate office], they're writing me up for coming in late, and as I'm walking out, the guard is bringing all these six brothers in that got caught. "We caught these guys jumping the fence." A week later, we had to go in front of the commanding officers and we all got wrote up. They got wrote up for being late and jumping the fence. I got wrote up for being late. All six of them—one at a time—went before me. They got really bad sentences. I went in and the officers, "Rah, rah, you don't be jumping no fences, what have you got to say for yourself?" "Sergeant, I didn't jump the fence." "You were with them, weren't you?" "Yeah, I was with them." "You didn't go over?" I said, "No, they jumped the fence, I came through the gate." He checked the charge sheet, took a long look at me and said, "Don't ever come back in here for anything. Never let me see you in this office again." That's it. Boom. Next thing I know, I got a promotion, a better job, everything—I didn't ask for none of this. I was up for promotion, but usually you have to wait—it comes to the officer's desk and a couple of weeks later you get your answer. One day after I was up, I got my stripes. Two days later, I was transferred to a choice assignment with the section running the brig [jail]. All because I came through the gate and didn't jump the fence. That taught me a lesson.

The third thing that happened, which is negative, one of the negative things that happened. It was not because of the Marine Corps. I had reenlisted and was going through some training, to be a mechanic, aircraft mechanic to get a better job in the Marine Corps and go back to Japan, which I loved. I was in Memphis, 1959, winter. I was going to see this movie that was downtown, had my uniform on. Went down there, went downtown, put my money on the counter—lady couldn't sell me a ticket. She was embarrassed. She knew it was wrong. It showed all over her face. I had my uniform on but because I was a brother, I couldn't . . . you know. Segregated South. That hit me. That's the only time that it had been thrown in my face like that. You, a black man. You can't do this. And I got my uniform on. So I know what that's like. Hit me right in the face. Now the civil rights workers they were there all the time, but me, it was just that once but that once is enough. I get it and that has affected me in the kind of work that I do because I know what it's like. A lot of people don't know what it's like, I do.

The last thing that happened in the Marine Corps was what I call "Chicago calling." In 1963, I was back in Japan. I had it made, living large, had a little car, a place of my own. Had the duty section [job] I wanted. The new job was cool because every fourth night I had to stay on the base but the other three nights I was out there on the town and it was a regular job, a sweet job in Japan. I was going to reenlist and I was telling everybody, "The Marine Corps is the best thing. You ought to think about keeping the Marine Corps as your career like I'm going to." This is 1963. Jazz was big in the Tokyo area, that's where we were stationed—that's where I was stationed at, in Tokyo. In Tokyo there's a suburb called Shinjuku, and Shinjuku played a lot of jazz and I was a jazz fanatic in those days. I still love jazz but in those days I lived for it. Art Blakely and Jazz Masters would come over every year and everybody, the Japanese loved jazz musicians. We'd go to Shinjuku—me and this Japanese friend of mine—and get over like fat rats. My Japanese partner, he was a taxi cab driver. One night, either he would drive or I would drive. I didn't have the car one night and his cab had broken down so we had to take the train from Yokohama to Tokyo. This is when those new trains had just come out, those bullet trains. So, we jumped on the bullet train and boom got to Tokyo in no time. And that fascinated this taxi driver, my buddy, and that's all he was talking about—"This train, this train, this train." And we are in this joint man and the ladies are looking good. He's [still] talking and I said, "Man, forget that train, we come in here to party," and he would say something, and I'd say, "They got trains all over the world, man. Chicago got trains." This led to a Chicago–Tokyo debate. Chicago, Tokyo, Chicago, Tokyo, Chicago, Tokyo, and this cat knew me well. He knew I was getting ready to reenlist to stay in Tokyo so he said, "I got one for you"—because every time he said something about Tokyo, I'd say something about Chicago and he got frustrated—"If you like Chicago so much, why the hell you going to reenlist to stay in Tokyo?" I had no answer for him. I kept thinking about that: "Why am I staying here, if I love Chicago so much?" And the first sergeant kept bugging me: "Smitty, are you gonna [reenlist]?" They called me Smitty. "If you are going to reenlist, you got to do it soon because otherwise you're gonna have to go back, reenlist there and then come back, but you reenlist now, you can stay right here and everything will be cool." Then after a couple weeks—"Smitty, this is your last chance, what you gonna do?"—I said, "I'm going home." That's when I decided to get out of the Marine Corps because I got homesick thinking about Chicago. I got out, came home, checked it out, and was getting ready to go back in to the Marine Corps when I walked into that theater. Nine months later, my organization that I was with in Japan was now in Da Nang, Vietnam.

That would have been me. Now, I'm not saying my life wouldn't be as good as it is right now. I'm not saying what would have happened. All I'm saying is that it would be different, and I know that I like my life now. But it haunts me. That's one of the things that haunts me, because they went to Da Nang and a lot of them got wasted over there. My partners, they would write me, "Why didn't you tell us, you knew something otherwise you wouldn't have gotten out." "You were the one that was telling us that this is the way to go." It still bugs me, yep. I didn't know nothing. All I knew is I got homesick. That's all I knew. If I had to do it over, I wouldn't change my decision. I would do the same thing, but it still bugs me that I got out and a lot of them stayed in because I sort of talked them in and got wasted, because I'm telling them they should stay in the Marine Corps. That's one of those things I think about. But there is not a day in my life that I don't think about them.

KEMATI J. PORTER

Kemati J. Porter is a producer, director, actor, and arts administrator with eta Creative Arts Foundation. She resides in Chicago and holds a BA in writing from Columbia College Chicago and an MFA in directing from DePaul University.

In this interview, conducted in December 2011, Porter recounts her journey in the community and professional theater worlds and speaks passionately about eta Creative Arts Foundation's role in assisting artists of color in entering the world of professional theater.

What brought you to Chicago?

I was running away from home, I mean literally running away from home, but I was old enough to be leaving home. I'm Southern born and reared. At eighteen, I was coming through the throes of the civil rights movement in Memphis. I was very much active for Martin Luther King's "I Am a Man" campaign for the sanitation workers and had spent the summer (1968) in Washington D.C. living in the poor people's camp on the mall. Watching people like Harry Belafonte and Sidney Poitier empty garbage and assist organizers. They would come down and volunteer. I decided that I wasn't quite ready to go to school and didn't want to go to school. I met this very interesting group of people from Chicago, and they said, "Why don't you come to Chicago?" A friend of mine and I, we did. We packed our trunks and suitcases and bought tickets. I had the money to buy an airline ticket. And it was quite a disruptive moment in my family life because as a young Southern girl, you just didn't leave home; you either went to school or you got married, and I was not doing either one of those things. [*Laughing*] It caused some discomfort, but it's the turning point. I now realize, at this point in my life, if I had not made that decision, I would not be on the path that I'm on. So, I'm grateful for that. My mother and I and my father, we all got past the departure. He was very encouraging and she, of course, was reticent. I thought that was really interesting since she allowed me to go to D.C. and spend the summer living in a wood hut. "Why can't I go to Chicago?" So, I did. I came [to Chicago]. My whole mantra was that I didn't want to go to school, but within two months I was enrolled in Loop Junior College, the YMCA college downtown, and I did enjoy school. I apparently just needed that break from high school to do something else. And interestingly, at that time, people like Useni Eugene Perkins were teaching at that college. I wasn't taking drama per se, but I was keeping busy and working and being a good girl.

What were you studying?

Liberal arts, general studies. It had not settled on me really what I was going to do. One of the things that stayed with me . . . my freshman year in high school, my homeroom teacher was Miss McClain, English teacher. It's always the English teacher. She also taught drama and she was also the kind of person who watched over and noticed certain children. One day, I was having a very, very difficult day. I can't even remember what . . . I was just so out of sorts about, but she picked up on it and she pulled me over to the side and she said to me, "Janice," because that's what they called me, she says, "What's the problem?" I couldn't articulate what was wrong, but it was like in that teenage moment, nothing was right; nothing was right. She said to me, "What you need to realize, just today, just realize that this is just one moment in your life. As you get older and grow up, you're going to meet people who do the things you want to do." She said, "It's going to be OK. You're going to find your tribe," so to speak. I didn't quite put it all together, but it did calm me down and got me through the rest of the day, but somehow I did understand that it was OK to be me, whatever that was, and I wasn't sure what it was at that little teenage angst moment either, so I just kinda worked with this. But it got me all the way through high school. It allowed me to make decisions about who I was and what I wanted to do and what I wanted to try to be and stuff like that. I still didn't know it was anything to do with arts, but I got here, went to school.

When I was really looking at a university, a four-year school, to go to, I was not really happy with what I saw, so I got a Peterson's guide out one day and flipped through it. What's art? What's art? What's art? And I came across Columbia College. Back in the day, Columbia College used to be around the bend, right there at the corner of Lake Shore Drive and Ohio. It was in a warehouse. You would go through the dock—climb up the dock—to go to class. I don't know why this appealed to me, but it did. So I went there. I started taking liberal arts classes. I took writing but I also took drama and dance. My drama class was taught by a couple of really interesting people. One was Michael Cullen who came out of the Art Institute-Goodman School of Drama before that became The Theatre School of DePaul University. It was probably one of the most fertile educations I felt I had ever had the chance to fall into, and I did feel like I fell into it because it's very avant-garde. It was very raggedy. It wasn't this whole structured thing. It wasn't like that. It was very open and it was very free. One day we were told to go to the zoo and study an animal and bring that animal back to class. I went to the zoo. I studied the sloth which barely moves but by the time I did my investigation and came into the class and got on the dance bar and did that sloth, Michael looked and said, "I know exactly what you are." Part of that, though, was still the fear and the intimidation of being an artist because even back in the sixties it was not the best thing you could be, and everybody still challenged you about it. "An artist. What you going to do with that? How are you going to make a living with that?" I didn't know, so I started [taking] marketing and advertising [classes] just to have something to fall back on so I could go get a job. I did finish Columbia College about 1976, '77. At that time commercials running on [the radio], WVON or whatever, were announcing this new black arts company that started on the South Side. It happened to be eta [Creative Arts]. They were housed in the 63rd Street Y. I got my young daughter and myself, after work one day, and we went in and we both enrolled in classes. We have been a part of this theater company off and on from then . . . I say from that time on because I've always gone and come back. I studied acting, stage management, directing, all of it. We worked in little classrooms. We took dance on Tuesdays. It wasn't about being a commercial actor; it was more about working on things that were liberating, that spoke to what was going on in our communities, reading African American playwrights, which is something that had been out of reach for a while. That's the great thing about growing up in the South, particularly with your teachers being African American, was that they would bring the extra work to class. We did Langston Hughes. We did all of that. That was not a part of what they were supposed to teach us, but they knew to teach us that. To come back and be immersed in reading these plays now, I was like, "Wow." We did a lot of new works. A lot of local playwrights in Chicago were submitting stuff we were working on.

Who was submitting work at that time?

Useni was submitting work. Oscar Brown Jr. had work. We were doing all of that. And I continued to grow with eta. I always say my daughter grew up in eta. I worked here as an administrator, as a director, a stage manager, and an actor for years, for years. I later went to school, went to DePaul to get my master's, but all that time I was juggling, [going] back and forth at eta working and developing programs for the community and exploring what it meant to be an artist. I [remember] working with Abena Joan Brown. I was the stage manager for . . . oh my gosh, what was the show? We would be sitting on little wood hard benches over there in the gallery, and she would just lean over and give me her notes. I need you to do this. I need you to do that. I'd go out and get the costumes. Everything, you would just do everything. So when I see how people isolate stuff now, particularly with the younger [artists] . . . well, I don't know. We used to go buy the props. We used to go buy the costumes. We used to make the stuff. The other great thing that happened here in this environment for us is that we were able to attract some of the major directors who were working in New York. Woodie [King Jr.] would come here almost every other year and direct a play. When he was here, he was then able to educate all of us. We would learn so much by just watching a master work. Vantile Whitfield was like the cream of the crop. He had done just about everything that there was to do in theater. When we would think that we couldn't do something or couldn't make something, he would say, "Oh no, no, no, we got it. I saw some stuff back there." He was doing a play—it was called *The MF in the Tree*—and there had to be an upside-down piano onstage and of course we were like "that's never gonna happen." He said, "Oh no?" He went out to the junkyard. He found an old piano, took the guts out, really walked everybody through how you string this upside down and it was done. It was done. He was a scenic designer. He was a builder. We learned so much about working with masters like that. Oscar Brown Jr. would come in here for his show, and there was just a professionalism. You know what I mean? What it meant to be a working artist, to do your work was what was important. To work. To do your work, always to do your work.

When did you begin directing at eta?

I started directing in 1990. By '91, I think I was doing my first production, a children's play, *The Legend of Deadwood Dick,* and I moved up to doing what we called our mainstage productions or evening productions. Shortly after that, I went to grad school and pursued the MFA in directing. There was an interesting turn of events. One of my professors suggested to me that I do an internship, and I'm like, "I'm too old for an internship." It was enough that I came into grad school and the first assignment I got was *Charlie and the Chocolate Factory.* I was so beyond *Charlie.* And when she said that I was like, "I don't think so." We were looking at this particular application and it was for the McCarter Theatre [Center] in Princeton. I applied, got the letter and stuff together, and I was accepted via a phone interview with Emily Mann and Mara Isaacs. So off I was, an advanced intern. That was another experience that really opened my eyes to another side of the business: producing. I went in as an artistic associate, and it was stuff that I had been doing for a long time, although it was very informative because you got to work in the room with some really great directors. I worked in the room with Gary Griffin; Emily Mann, I worked on a piece with her; Michael Unger. And those kinds of experiences are so informative—just in watching process and understanding and affirming that what you know is right, is good, and you can use it anywhere you go and that there are challenges in every process. You think the greats don't have any challenges; yes, they do. Yes, they do. So it was really affirming to see things go wrong and then get fixed. I was working with Mara Isaacs who was the producing director there and I had come to the end of my internship and a funny thing happened. We were doing *My Fair Lady* [2004] that Gary Griffin had directed and it needed to go to Hartford Stage and it was quite apparent that Gary was not going to be able to take the show. They looked at me, because I was the assistant. "Do you think you could consider?" I said, "Yes, I will. I'll take the show to Hartford until he's able to get there." And so we did. As I was preparing to leave [McCarter]—actually, I had gotten all the way back to Chicago—I got a call from Emily and Mara saying, "We have this TCG application that we want to do and it's for a New Generations Fellowship, is there anything that you'd like to come back to McCarter Theater and try your hand at?" Because at my exit interview with them from the internship, they said, "What would you do differently if you could do it again?" and I said, "If I could do it differently and if I had known what this experience was going to be, I would have come in wanting to be the assistant to the producing director because I would want to look at producing." When the TCG application came through, we applied together and it was approved. So I went back to McCarter Theater as an associate producer for Mara Isaacs and stayed there for over two years. That got me on the road to producing. When I came back here, Abena and I sat down and she said, "What do you want to do now?" I said, "I want to be the producing director." She said, "We don't have a producing director." "But that's what I want to be because we need a producing director." And we went through all the things that a producing director does. She said, "OK, all right, that's what it is." I have not set foot onstage as an actor, but actively being a producing director and directing has been very rewarding and satisfying at this particular point.

Why has it been satisfying to you?

Well, because two things are happening. One, there's a responsibility to cultivate playwrights and artists and designers for this work. A lot of time on the East Coast was spent in New York and Philadelphia following people's work, following certain playwrights, seeing what they are doing. It became clear to me that [that was] what we had been doing here. I thought we just needed to step it up a bit more. You know what I'm saying? When we look at new works, really look at the body of work, [we need to] really give ourselves the time to develop the work. But most importantly, have a relationship with the artist. That was essential. McCarter had long-term relationships with artists. Coming back, that's something that I started. We need long-term relationships with artists, not only the writers but designers. We're a facility of first chance. I believe deeply in what we do. I always say to people who work with us for the first time, "This is a place where you can fail successfully and it's not going to cost you your career. We're going to help you, we're gonna get on you, we're going to counsel you, but it's not going to mean your career's over if it doesn't go perfectly. Here you can actually train toward that level of perfection or performance that you feel that you need." We have done that. We have really nurtured and cultivated a host of actors and directors, but it's still very hard for African American directors to get positions, very hard to get a leg in somewhere. And I'm proud that we're able to provide that, and I think that's the learning that comes through the process of becoming an artist. You understand the needs of other artists and what they're seeking to do. When you know that, I think it helps you to assist in the process, where to bring them in, where to sit down and have a conversation, and that's a large part of what I do, particularly with the young artists whether they're stage managers, technicians, actors, or directors.

What would you say is the mission of eta? Has that mission changed since you first signed up for classes?

The mission has really not changed. It is to preserve and to promulgate the African aesthetic in this community, in this city, in this nation. Too often, we can be convinced that that's frivolous. When I look at where we are not, I see that it is very necessary. When I see the opportunities that are not there for our artists, it is very necessary. Training is crucial. Training is crucial. We've started some touring shows this year [2011] and, of course, we have to take our technicians and our support staff with us. We just did a piece at Governors State [University]. As a result of our technicians being there, they've been invited back to do independent gigs. And they're both female. That has opened a whole 'nother door for them because in that facility, which is advanced technologically and space-wise, they're learning new things. If we had not stepped out, if we had not brought them along, they wouldn't have been in the position to get the invitation.

They never would have had the opportunity.

That's what it is . . . it's really about being where you can be invited. You know what I'm saying? You have to be around and that can be hard for us. It was hard leaving Chicago and going to the East Coast and coming out of my community. Most people don't want to put themselves in that position. They really just do not. It's too strenuous. Yes, our mission has been maintained. I think we're embracing it even more now.

When you first came to Chicago, did you attend theater? If so, where did you go?

I used to go to Kuumba all the time. I did. I used to go to things on the North Side. I'm an adventurous spirit. A lot of times I wind up . . . I'm the only person sitting in the audience who looks like me. I would go down to Old Town. Jackie Taylor used to do a piece down there called *AC/DC*. Sometimes I didn't know what I was going to, but it was just a whole experience. My English teacher, my drama teacher, really taught us that theater was something that was exciting. I loved seeing it . . . I used to . . . I would dance and I knew what it meant to be a part of a community, a collective of artists doing something, so I would just venture out and try to see whatever I could see. But Kuumba was really big. I would go to the Goodman when it was in the old space. I would go down to Old Town just to hang out. And I would come here [eta], because we would always do pieces over at 63rd when we were in there . . . in a room, just in a room. There was no black box; it was just a room with fluorescent lights so you can imagine, hard theater. Hard theater. Hard . . . theater. I was much more of a theatergoer than I was a concertgoer. Some people like to go to big concerts and stuff. I did more theatergoing.

Who were your favorite directors in this period of time?

Well, I don't know about [that] period of time. I like Shirley Jo Finney. I've always liked her work. I don't know if she's one of the first black women who directed at the Goodman, but I first saw her work at the Goodman. I was like, "Wow, really good." And I had the chance to work with her at McCarter because she directed *Stick Fly* there. I loved Vantile Whitfield. He's old school. He's not with us today, but I learned so much from him. I always considered him my mentor, my real mentor in directing because he taught me how to keep it simple, to really go for it but to keep it simple. He was part of the Black Repertory Company. He started that in D.C. and it's defunct now. Jay Stewart came out of that.

How did you meet him?

I met him here. We brought him in to do something. He was a colleague and a friend of Abena's. We started doing the playwright's discovery initiative, bringing in really seasoned directors and writers from across the country to talk about their work. He was a part of that. Plus he had been a NEA [National Endowment for the Arts] reviewer. He worked with NEA and he would come to Chicago.

I like Ron O. J. [Parson]. I think up and coming: Aaron Todd [Douglas]. If you can ever get a chance to see anything that Cheryl Lynn Bruce directs. Everybody sees her as an actor, but I saw the most amazing production of *From the Mississippi Delta* [that she directed].

How would you describe Cheryl Lynn Bruce's process as a director?

I think what's great about her and I think any young actor would benefit from being in the room and at the table with Cheryl, under her tutelage as a director, because she's very text driven in getting underneath what's there. The process is not about jumping up and running around until you know what you're doing or what you're trying to accomplish as that character. She's very exacting and very helpful in terms of challenging pedestrian acting. And I think that is her most strong point. She does her work. She does her research. She goes line by line. She gets the story out. She gets the story out and she always is there; because she has such a heavy tool bag, she's able to bring a lot to the table. And she knows how to communicate with an actor, which is a key thing.

What circumstances led to your first encounter with Abena Joan Brown?

When I heard that WVON commercial and took myself down to 63rd and Cottage Grove to the Harris Y, there she was. That was the beginning of the eta. I think they'd been working since 1971. Who's still around as part of that process? Darryl Goodman among our staff here has been a part of eta the longest, then Runako [Jahi] and then on and on and on. And even our new president, Phil [Thomas] has been part of Abena's and eta's life for a long time. He worked here as an administrator and now he's back as the president.

What in your understanding was the motivating energy to create eta?

The motivating energy to create eta was they [the founders] needed to develop work for themselves because they could not get work anywhere in this city as actors. That's what it was for.

As you understand it, was race playing a role in terms of them not being able to get cast, get roles? What were the limits?

Oh, I'm sure. If you go back and look at the history, during that time probably in the early seventies and late sixties and you looked at theater history in Chicago, I don't think you'd see much being offered to African American actors. So there it is. But these people were trained and well trained and had nowhere to practice. When that happens, you do your own thing. That's why a lot of solo actors become solo performers: because there's no one knocking down the door to use them. Daniel Beaty is a wonderful example. Will Power is another wonderful example. Will is well-rounded. He wasn't getting what he needed so he started developing his own work and now he is a solo artist. That's what you do. That's the cultural imperative: to keep yourself alive. You have to take responsibility for it. So, we keep the doors open.

In your opinion, can the South Side support and sustain a large-scale, professional regional theater?

If someone decides to do it. Yes, that's all it takes.

Why hasn't that happened yet?

Because no one has taken the risk.

You would think in a theater town like Chicago . . .

No one has taken the risk. Certainly, there's politics and all other kinds of stuff in it, but someone has to be willing to take the risk . . . to take the hit for it. The question always comes to us: "Why don't you guys go do this or do that?" Well, because we know what we're here to do. We're here to train. There are people ready to go if anyone does the next step. They're ready to go. Jackie's on the North Side—so I understand what you're saying. It's not something that's impossible. Someone has to sacrifice. That's what it's always going to be about. You're going to have to sacrifice your career so that others can work. You're going to have to commit your money so that others will bring theirs. That's what it takes.

Chuck Smith told me that there needs to be more producers of black theaters.

I would agree to that, but that's not what people have been trained to be. See? There it is. I went back to McCarter and I went, "Oh, this is something I should be doing. I should be producing. I should be trying to figure out how to get a number of things going at one time." Some of that's happening to a degree [now] in New York with this new black money that's coming in from the stars. They're going, "We need to support theater." And I'm glad that they are because the fact that they are means that Broadway now has shows it never would have had before. The other part of that education is getting the audiences in and [developing a] marketing arm. Education is key. We always say that we've developed our audiences over years, over years.

What advice would you offer a person who is aspiring to become a producer?

Get into a theater and work with someone who's doing it. Volunteering is great. I don't care what anyone says. At this point in my life when I look back, I cannot believe how much time I spent at this theater, worked a job, and raised a family. Unbelievable. With no money. I was not paid.

And we joke about that today, those of us who have been around for a while. We were working nine to five, raising a family, and we'd spend our whole evening here at this theater. I always would say my daughter would get a pillow and her snacks because she was generally asleep by the time we finished in the theater. We'd pick her up and go home. Her birthday parties were here, some of them. But that's how much of a family [we are] . . . and I just . . . volunteer. Find someone you want to work with, someone who's doing what you want to do and get with that person. I love to mentor. The essential thing that I think we learned at eta, the old heads of us, was that when we came here, we had to work. We did it. We couldn't pick up the phone and call somebody, "Can you come over here and put this together?" No, we had to get the hammers and the nails and the paint can and everything else. We had to do it. And I am looking for those people myself who want to do it under some guidance. So my advice is volunteer. Find a place you want to be. Find a theater home if you can. Get in the door. Pass out the programs. Do whatever you got to do but let people know what it is you are interested in. Find someone who is doing what you want to do and work with that person.

What's the next step for eta Creative Arts, in terms of going into the future?

Our plan is pretty steady. Everyone is trying to manage the economy. The thing is to survive it. We're not just surviving it, we're looking at new programming. Like I said, we're going back to touring. We're look-ing at creating a presence on the West Side, which is a cultural desert, a theater desert. This morning, that's where we were. Westinghouse [Col-lege Prep High School] is a part of this initiative through the Chicago Community Trust to bring live theater back to the West Side. Lamont Zeno and theaters used to be there, but they're not there anymore. That's a big push for us, if we can have a presence on the West Side. Shows here that go there, or shows that we can develop specifically for a site there. That's what we're aiming to do but it's a part of our long-range plans. It's also to look at provid[ing] deeper training in things that we have not been able to do in the past: voice, speech. Sometimes we joke about it, but I always say, when we're having meetings, my goal is to have a guerrilla MFA program here. People can't afford MFAs. I have one. I know what it costs. [*Laughing*] I get a bill every month so I know what it costs. I said, "There's enough of us who have paid or are paying for those MFAs, we should just go ahead and teach the MFA programs." Because that's a part of our mission. I want to do a guerrilla MFA program to really have a well-rounded school for theater here. When people have [money], they give. That much we know. People don't give when they don't have as much. If we can get back to a level in the economy where people have more, can give more, then I think we'll be well on the road to constructing that new space.

If you were to write a history of black theater in Chicago, who are the people who you feel would have to be in that history?

It would certainly be Abena and Val [Gray Ward] and Okoro Johnson. Some of them are dead now. Oscar Brown Jr. They really put in the dues. Organizations like the Center Aisle Players. Jackie [Taylor]. They really laid down the foundations and in very different ways and that's what's so interesting. Val was downtown. She had a theater downtown, smack dab on Wabash in the middle of the Loop. She made that work for years, for years. I think they're major people . . . they're major, major people. And then you have your next . . . Chuck Smith, Paul Carter Harrison, Jonathan Wilson. And so on. Then you get into the Ron O.J.s, the Runakos [Runako Jahi] and myself and Cheryl Lynn, Mignon Stewart, Aaron Todd Douglas, Derrick Sanders. And in an interesting way, Regina Taylor because she did a lot of her early work here in Chicago. Julian Swain; he's gone now, but he was one of the most wonderful choreographers. Jimmy Payne, all those people.

GLORIA BOND CLUNIE

Gloria Bond Clunie is a playwright, director, and creative drama specialist. Her play North Star *premiered at Victory Gardens Theater in Chicago and won the 1995 Joseph Jefferson Chicago Theatre Award for Best New Work/ Adaptation and the 1994 Theodore Ward African-American Playwriting Award. Other produced works include* Shoes; Living Green; Sweet Water Taste; Secrets; Sing! Malindy, Sing!; Dream: A Tribute to Dr. Martin Luther King Jr.; *and the children's play* A Basket of Wishes, A Bucket of Dreams. *Clunie is founder of the Fleetwood-Jourdain Theatre in Evanston, Illinois, where she served as artistic director for eight years and directed over twenty-five productions.*

In this interview, conducted in September 2011, Clunie reflects on her experience as a student and young actress in Chicago in the 1970s and early 1980s, the founding of the Fleetwood-Jourdain Theatre, and the importance of community theater.

How did you become a member of the Victory Gardens Playwriting Ensemble?

I wrote a play called *North Star,* and it won the Ted Ward Prize at Columbia College. It had a production there, and the Goodman and Victory Gardens and several other groups came to have a look. Chuck Smith directed it at Columbia. Sandy Shinner [of Victory Gardens] said, "I'd like to direct it." She loved the coming-of-age story that was in there. At the time, both of our daughters were about the same age—they were about eleven. We hit it off.

And when was this?

I think it was 1995.

Prior to that had you ever worked with Victory Gardens?

To be honest with you, I have a very strong connection with Victory Gardens. When I graduated from Northwestern, as an undergraduate, I went out into the theater world and the educational drama world. I was looking at theater and I was seeing perfect theater. Visually, it was exciting and interesting and it seemed like every line was in place. It wasn't moving me. I'm talking about going to some of the bigger theaters in Chicago and just seeing a lot of theater. And I'm saying, "It's not hitting my heart." I remember going to Victory Gardens, and it might have been a Steve Carter play, and feeling, "Wow, this theater is talking to me." Because at one point [earlier], I was wondering, "Why did I major in theater?" I wish I could remember the production, but I know it was at Victory Gardens—early on. Victory Gardens started in the seventies. I saw the production, and it helped me feel that theater was very much alive. I also started to see other works by some of the newer theaters like Organic and Steppenwolf. At that time, they were burgeoning theaters. Also, Chuck Smith was there [at Victory Gardens].

He was directing a lot of Steve Carter's plays and this was at the time that I was auditioning and acting and stuff. So, I saw Steve Carter's work. I talked to Chuck. I knew Chuck. He made a very instrumental comment that was the impetus for Fleetwood-Jourdain Theatre. He said, "Go direct any place." So, I went some place and started directing. Those kind of connections were there before. I was not in the space all the time, but it had inspired me a great deal. When Sandy asked, I was very excited that they were gonna do the production and that she directed it.

How does one become a member of the Playwriting Ensemble?

You get a little badge with a jacket. No, no, that's not true. *North Star* went on to get a Jeff. It was my first equity production as a playwright. It won a Jeff. I had directed and produced quite a few other pieces at Fleetwood, but now one that I had written got a Jeff. At that point, Dennis [Zacek] was forming a playwriting ensemble, and he wanted twelve writers. He simply called up and said, "I would like to invite you into the Playwriting Ensemble." The agreement was word of mouth, basically saying, "We would really love to see when you've written something, you know, first take." There was Jim Sherman, Jeffrey Sweet, Kristine Thatcher, Steve Carter, Doug Post, Nicholas Patricca, Charles Smith, Dean Corrin, John Logan, and Lonnie Carter. It was a combination of people who had worked with Victory Gardens from the very beginning plus obviously somebody who was just beginning to work with them. Racial balance, female balance, gay/lesbian balance, that kind of strong mix of playwrights in the group. Claudia Allen is a wonderful playwright who is a part of the group. That's how I became part of the ensemble. Actually, it stayed those twelve playwrights up until . . . and you'd have to kind of look this up . . . until Nilo Cruz and Joel Drake Johnson.

I didn't know Nilo Cruz was in the playwriting ensemble.

Yes, he is. Before he won the Pulitzer [in 2003], Dennis had already made arrangements for *Anna in the Tropics* to be in the season. It was in the season and it won the Pulitzer and he was invited in.

Are there Playwrights Ensemble member parties? Is there a social component to it? Do you ever interact with one another and have a chance to talk about each other's work?

We're not all from Chicago. It wasn't designed like Chicago Dramatists, where I imagine playwrights are sitting at a table, sharing a piece with all of the other playwrights, and evaluating it. We have, let's say, an informal connection. One of the things that we used to do—and did for quite a few years—was what was called "play slam." We would all come in. Jeffrey and Lonnie Carter, they would fly in. So, everybody. People were not away. They would all come in and, for one night, we would read excerpts from something new that we were working on. It was literally a play slam. There would be a wheel of fortune. Dennis would spin it and we'd all have a number and whoever's number came up, that's who read. So, you didn't know what order it would be. And you would get up and you read. It was in the original Victory Gardens space, and it would be to an invited audience. Once a year for a number of years, four or five years, we had play slams. That was the time when we all got together. One of the big party times was the Tony Awards [in 2001] because we got that call that said we're getting a Regional Tony Award and we want all of the playwrights to come out. That was pretty exciting. We all ended up meeting and they flew us out. We met in New York and we all went to the Tonys and that was a really neat time to all be together. I remember when my feet got tired, I kicked off my shoes, and I was walking around New York. That was an exciting time. If you're doing a show and one of the playwrights is in town, they will come and sit in or might give comments and support and that kind of thing. Charles Smith came in from Ohio to dramaturg *Shoes* [2005]. That was great because I knew Charles from before the ensemble. That kind of support.

What is the future of the playwriting ensemble with Dennis Zacek no longer being artistic director?

I think that's being resolved now. I really do. I think it has to be redefined and I think that's an in-process type thing. This is the first season [with Chay Yew as the new artistic director].

What brought you to Chicago?

I came to Northwestern for the first time as a Cherub, as a high school student. The Cherub program was a summer program in theater. So I came up. The sun was shining. It was gorgeous. I thought it was a wonderful place. In 1971, I came back as a freshman. I'm from North Carolina. I went to Chatham Hall, a boarding school in Virginia, a girl's boarding school. Wonderful school. Do you know who's coming this year? Gloria Steinem. A two-hundred-person high school. The year before it was Judith Jamison. Back then, it was a really strong, wonderful school. I originally grew up in Henderson, North Carolina. Henderson was on the cusp of integration. There was one black kindergarten, Adams Kindergarten, which was right behind our house in a Quonset hut with something built on it. It looked like an old woman's shoe. Adams had a very strong tradition of theater. Literally, you're five years old and you're onstage and that's their graduation performance. You onstage. And then I went to Eaton-Johnson Elementary School in Henderson. In doing some research for *North Star,* it came to my knowledge that that was a brand new school when I was in it. I knew it as a glorious place with a wonderful stage. Every grade was responsible for a play every year there. Then integration came; it comes to different places at different times. It was 1954 when it happened . . . when *Brown v. Board of Education* happened, but some people had to listen later. Eaton-Johnson was a wonderful school; it was an African American school. As I started high school, I went to an integrated high school in Henderson. There were concerns for my brother as far as the type of education [he was receiving]. I ended up at Chatham Hall in Virginia. All of this is to say [it was a] great boarding school that created opportunities for all the students. So, I was involved in drama and they said, "Between your junior and senior year, how would you like to do this program?" I was one of two black girls who were at Chatham. I ended up coming up here [to Chicago] because I was involved in drama and it was basically arranged through Chatham Hall. They said this was a great program. When I first saw Evanston Township [High School] I thought that it was Northwestern because it was so big. And then when I saw Northwestern, I was like, this is a really big place. And it was warm. Great program, long tradition of the Cherub program. We ended up doing *Trojan Women* and I was Hecuba. A lot of good training. In applying to schools, I applied to a lot on the East Coast and it may have been that I knew this school. I had been here in the summer. And I got accepted to all the schools, but it was like, which one do you choose and, "Oh, I know Northwestern."

Then I got up here and it was cold as the dickens and I wanted to go home for a period of time. It snowed. They suck you in with that Cherub program. Les Hinderyckx was the chair [of the theater department] at the time. There was also Black Folks Theater which had just begun . . . again . . . I didn't realize it was just beginning until retrospectively looking back and realizing it. Black Folks Theater was through the Black House and was dedicated to doing black theater. When I think about it, it was a great opportunity because not knowing it, it was teaching you how to make theater from scratch when you don't have the facilities. That's how I got to Chicago and also got that foundation for creating independent theater from Black Folks Theater. In the theater department, there weren't that many African Americans. Eileen Cherry was a student here then and she was responsible for gathering us up and going down to places like Kuumba Theatre Workshop. That's how I became familiar with Chicago theater. She would go to Les and ask him to sponsor [an independent study] because you had to have a faculty sponsor who was "teaching." We would have these wonderful forays into black theater. It was through Black Folks Theater that I was exposed to what was happening in the country, who Ed Bullins is and . . . how to direct. You didn't have faculty. It was all student run. All student directed. My first directing shows were through Black Folks Theater.

What professional theater did you see as a student at Northwestern in the early 1970s? Which companies influenced you?

Well, particularly Kuumba Workshop. You didn't get off campus that much. Going to the city was a big deal. As I said, Eileen would gather us up. A lot of Kuumba Theatre Workshop. It wasn't like there were a lot of theaters that we could go to. At that point Kuumba Theatre was . . . I don't want to say it was it [the only black theater], because it probably wasn't. They had the concept of ritual-based theater. They would take one of Gwendolyn Brooks's works and then devise it into a theater piece. It would be very ritualistic theater. They would use poetry and music to create a production. It was something—ritualistic theater—that became a touchstone there.

At Northwestern, ritual theater fed into Black Folks Theater. There was a ritual every year, at the very beginning of the year. I think it's still done. I've heard that it's changed somewhat. At the time—this was the early 1970s—'71 through '75 (and '68 was when the bursar's office was taken over), you had a sense, particularly in the first year all over campus, of revolution. You had the Vietnam War, etc. There were rallies and strikes and all kinds of things. They [Black Folks Theater] were doing pieces like *El Hajj Malik*. Besides the ritual, very politically based theater. The echo of Kuumba influenced Black Folks Theater and then even the starting of Fleetwood. There's a thread of family in making theater.

You noted that you founded Fleetwood before you joined the Playwrights Ensemble at Victory Gardens. How did Fleetwood-Jourdain come about?

I had graduated from Northwestern, and I was doing some auditioning but I've always taught. I've taught since . . . except, say for two years, pretty much taught since I graduated. So I'm juggling these two things.

I'd been auditioning but also wanted to do more directing. I directed here, I directed in high school. And I wanted to do more directing. It wasn't necessarily saying that I wanted to go into ethnic background theater, I just knew I wanted to do more directing. I auditioned for something for Chuck Smith and he said, "Go direct anywhere." Sometimes things people say go in one ear and go out the other but this became my mantra. Literally, the next day I started calling places in Evanston to ask if they were interested in either theater classes or directing. I called up Fleetwood first. I called up Robert Crown [Center] next. Robert Crown was going to see me in three days, and I think another community theater was going to see me early that week because they were really interested. And then Fleetwood said, "I'll see you the next day." Mr. Evans said come on over. I think God takes you where you need to go. I didn't have a certain mission but that was exactly where I needed to go based on my history, based on a very strong commitment to an Afro-centric focused theater. First, we were talking about classes and then it became, "Why don't we do a play that could get people interested and maybe possibly have classes later?" I had seen *What the Wine-Sellers Buy,* I think at the Shubert here [in 1975] and it was touring. It had been on Broadway. It has two endings. It's about a rough neighborhood. There's a pimp involved—this is not necessarily why but I was really drawn to the story. Young people were being influenced by it. In the Broadway version, the pimp lives. When I read it, the resolution in the second ending, with the pimp dying, fit more with the community. The play had a large cast. It was on "a wing and a prayer." It turned out that a lot of things aligned.

There were not a lot of people when we had auditions . . . so I started going into the gym and pulling some people out of the weight room. I went to Wisdom Bridge on Howard Street. I'd seen a show there— one of their something *Macbeth*s—and met two students. They were two older high school students who were taking classes at the Goodman. They were there and I was talking about *Winesellers* at intermission, and they became very excited and they lived on the South Side. They came to audition and they were really good and they traveled every day because there wasn't that much black theater available. eta [Creative Arts] definitely was going then. X-BAG was probably in process at that particular point. Fleetwood—we were in the community center. It had a small stage, like an elementary school stage. We built it out some. We had six performances and they sold out. Literally, we set up chairs and I guess maybe had a 150–200 people all the way back. The community turned out. It was a large audience, a lot of people from the community. There was a range of true talent [in the cast], and we took a long time to rehearse. We weren't trying to get a show up in three weeks. I think our rehearsal process was generally six to eight weeks. The reason was that you're blending communities so you weren't rehearsing every night and training was very much involved in the process.

One memorable moment . . . [the center] was all filled up, except for the back seats. I love this theater. People just . . . we are home. A woman took one of the last seats of the last row and proceeded up to the front to put it in front of somebody. And someone gently let her know, all these people were here, you're going to have to put the seat back. But it was the fact that there was a great deal of enthusiasm about it. I remember, there was this kid at intermission. This is not a children's show. You got a pimp in it, you got drugs. This kid was maybe seven, maybe eight or nine, and he was in the third or fourth row back. And we hadn't gotten to intermission. He came to the back—got to the point that if you went a little bit further you would reach the bathrooms. He was just standing there. You could tell this kid needed to go to the bathroom. I told him, "It's [the bathroom is] around there." And he said, "No, I can't. I want to see what happens!" And I swear, I thought the kid was going to pee himself. And finally intermission came, he went running. The whole idea of community theater is something that I had grown up with from those kindergarten days, when the community came out to see our kindergarten plays. And the point was to make it an event of who we are.

What are the challenges of creating a community theater?

Well, you don't know that you're doing it at the time [*Laughing*] . . . because we weren't starting out to create . . . We were creating an event. The event of *What the Wine-Sellers Buy* led to the community saying, we need a theater. It was Foster Community Theater because it was Foster Community Center at that time. This was in 1979, I just smiled and realized why it was 1979 . . . it was the year I got married. It wasn't setting out to create a community theater. It evolved into a community theater after *What the Wine-Sellers Buy*.

The next show that we did was a senior show. There was a senior's club, still is. There were wonderful women who wanted to do a show. Their ages ranged from seventy-five to ninety. One of the women was a WPA [Works Progress Administration] theater actress. She was wonderful, fantastic, kept everybody on task. I was in my twenties. It was really wonderful and they were listening to me. It was, "OK, Gloria, what are [we] doing?" Then, we did a children's piece and a talent show. I'm not a talent show person but that was one of the things. And then we evolved that year: "Let's do a theater season." We went into *Tambourines to Glory*, which was a big musical. We ended up extending it three times because it sold out, and sold out, and sold out, and we only had runs of like two weeks and then people were like, "We didn't see it."

Yes, you have to keep running it . . .

. . . when you have somebody's grandmother saying, "You all need to do that play again. My church didn't come and so-and-so's church did come." There was a wonderful board. Bo Price was on the board. Just a wonderful board that began to push for a physical space other than the center. They made that happen with consultation from me, but the workings of going to the city and petitioning was really the community and the board saying, "We want this." So we ended up moving into the space next door with *Raisin* as our opening musical there. At that point, Mamie Smith had come and for over twenty-some years she was the director of the center. She was from Detroit, very strong, powerful, and wonderful woman, and we were about . . . she may be a couple of years older—so we're in the same age range—and had worked in theater. Fleetwood had started. It was a really good, functional space. I directed over twenty-five productions: *Raisin, Purlie Victorious.* Shirley Hardy's work, Charles Michael Moore's plays. It was learning as you go. I had not set out to be an artistic director . . . I did not start out to be one but there was a need. Which is frequently why I've written plays. Some of the plays that I wrote were because . . . "I haven't found a comedy": *Secrets.* The first musical—*Sing! Malindy, Sing!*—that I wrote was because we needed a musical, and I wanted *Arms Too Short to Box with God* and could not get it, and could not get it because they had never set it down. I had seen [it] in New York. They had never set down all of the music. You couldn't physically put your hands on it. They knew it. The script was down, but you couldn't get the rights. Things like that. A lot of black theaters were working that way. In the sense of, "We've got a season, we've got this up, we've done the production. It's a new play but have we actually disseminated it to other people?" That's definitely gotten better over the years.

JACKIE TAYLOR

Jackie Taylor was born in Chicago and was raised in the Cabrini–Green housing development. She is the founder of Black Ensemble Theater and the author/producer of more than 100 plays. She previously served as the artistic director of the New Regal Theater and vice president of the League of Chicago Theaters. Named one of Chicago's 100 Most Powerful Women by the Chicago Sun-Times, *she is the recipient of numerous awards, including a League of Chicago Theater Lifetime Achievement Award.*

In August 2011, when this interview was conducted, Taylor and Black Ensemble Theater were still headquartered in the Uptown Theatre, a former Hull-House building, and were preparing to move into a newly constructed building of their own. She reflects on her lifelong mission to eradicate racism, recalls her meetings with Mayor Richard Daley and actor Sidney Poitier, and offers advice for anyone interested in becoming a producer of theater.

How did your new building come into being?

Black Ensemble is thirty-five years old. About fifteen years ago, I started thinking about institutionalizing the organization, not that I was planning on just leaving. I had been doing everything—writing the scripts, starring in the shows, raising the money, managing the company, everything—and I did not want Black Ensemble to die if for any unforeseen reason I would not be around. That's the reality of the situation. That started me to thinking, "You know, you are not going to live forever." "What? I don't believe that." "But it's true." And that really started me thinking, "I really have to stop this one-woman whirlwind and figure how to solidify this organization so that it can run without me." That was about fifteen years ago. The first thing that I did was to get a stronger board [of directors] who could help me think through this process and what it would mean and what it would cost and how we would raise the money for it. I started with the staff. Instead of Jackie Taylor doing everything, I really needed to create a staff who could actually raise the funds and manage the company and so forth and so on. I wanted a strong inward foundation and then I had to raise the profile of the company. We weren't doing bad. We've been pretty controversial since we started because our mission is to eradicate racism, and I don't know of any other theater where that's their specific mission. So, we have always been controversial, and we have always done controversial pieces. I wanted to create excitement so I said, "We're going to start producing productions that people respond to in a totally different way." That's when I came up with *Elvis Presley Was a Black Man* [1999]. That was the first production where we said, "Let's get people to talking," and nothing does it like a show called *Elvis Presley Was a Black Man*. That helped the company to get a much wider audience.

We always had a diverse audience, but it just increased. So, the foundation was coming together. In the foundation coming together, again the board had to change because those people had those kinds of skills, and they really helped me through that process, but I needed another skill set of people because that's when I started talking about "now we need to institutionalize." It took about five years. We need assets and we need a foundation. Right now, we are renters, and that means we are dependent on our landlord, and tomorrow if the landlord said, "I don't want this building anymore, I'm going to tear it down," what are we going to do? So, that's when I started talking about having to build our own building and owning our home and having this strong asset as a foundation. And it . . . cost twenty million dollars when we looked into it. It was twenty million dollars. We did a feasibility study. We paid fifty thousand dollars for [it] to tell us that we couldn't do it. [*Laughing*] I said, "We're going to do it." I got the right people that I needed to surround the organization, and we started working on looking for property, looking for resources because I was definitely going to have a building, and I didn't care what the feasibility study said. It didn't matter. And I got people who believed in me and who supported that dream and said, "OK, it [the study] says it's impossible, but if you think it's going to work, then let's go." Those folks gathered around and we started working on finding property, and we found a property that was not for sale. I did a very good job of convincing this multimillionaire that he really needed to do something for black people. I was actually trying to get him to donate the building, but he said, "You are good but you are not that good. I will sell it to you." So he sold us the building, and I got the former Mayor Daley and some other high political figures to help, and I was able to purchase the building, and then we pulled together a capital campaign team. I'm a good beggar, a very good beggar, and I begged a lot of people. We're still raising money. We're still three million dollars short, but I'm not worried about that because we've raised almost seventeen million dollars now [October 2011].

How long did it take to raise that amount?

We started in 2007 and then we were hit by the recession, the worst financial market in the world in '08 and '09, but that didn't stop us. We just kept going. My philosophy: somebody got some money. All we have to do is find out who they are and ask them to give it to us. That's it. Somebody got some. We got the building. We started fundraising and we're still fundraising. I have another board around me that was needed for this part here. Now the building is about 65 percent done, and we're going to be opening November 18 [2011]. We're in transition again because now, we've transitioned into the Black Ensemble Theater Cultural Center. We have a twenty-million-dollar facility and that's a whole lot of building. [*Laughing*] We have to have a board that can support this facility. So, we're transitioning our board again so that when we move into the new facility we will have a board that will help us with operations but also will be a funding board. It will be their job to raise a significant amount of money each year to keep Black Ensemble Theater Cultural Center going.

What's your plan for the transition from theater to center? In your vision, what is the expansion?

It's a 300-seat theater, not 100 . . . well actually it's a 299-seat theater. We're 299 and we have a 150-seat theater. It's a black box. Black Ensemble is known for its formula of producing historical productions, all musicals that reflect a part of our history in terms of a time period or reflect a person, and they all have to be uplifting. They all have to be cross-cultural. People always talk about how I always want a happy ending. I say, "You're absolutely right. If you want an unhappy ending, you've got a whole lot of choices. Pick up the newspaper, turn on the TV, you've got fifty million channels to go to. You can turn on the news on ten stations at one time. You want an unhappy ending? I understand. You go get it." For the cultural center, we're going to do something different, but we'll have our [brand]. I liken it to McDonald's because to me McDonald's is the greatest marketing firm in the world. The 150-seat theater is going to be different than our 299-seat and our 299-seat will keep our McDonald's hamburger, because that's what everybody buys. But McDonald's throws in a McRib or an Irish shake or an apple parfait. They throw in little stuff and that's what Black Ensemble is going to do. In our small theater, we're going to experiment. We're going to have all kinds of different productions that are not going to fit the mold of the McDonald's hamburger. It's going to be totally different. First of all, it's going to be age specific because we're trying to build that twenty- to forty-year-old audience. So, the first production in that theater is going to be the story of Tupac Shakur. Then, we're going to do a hip-hop opera and we're going to do different kinds of things and we're going to do some dramas in there. The dramas, some of them won't have [happy endings], "Oh it's the end. Yay!" but they won't depress you. Why pay fifty to fifty-five dollars to feel bad? That's like paying to get your hair dyed and it all comes out. We ain't doing that.

Has uplift always been part of your mission as a playwright?

Yes, yes. Because that's my philosophy of life, yes. I mean I've done some things as an actress. I played Medea. There's nothing that you can uplift about Medea. She killed her kids. I could only play her for two weeks, because I just couldn't take myself through that reality. I just couldn't do it and I just pulled out of the show. We were experimenting trying to see what would cross over. Are the classics it? It's just who I am and it's just my belief and it's my philosophy. If I'm going to put the time and the money and the work into doing this, I want people to feel good about it. Both the small and large theaters will utilize live music, period. Even if it's not a musical, it will still have live musicians who will accent what's going on, kind of like in the [early film] talkies. That's exactly what we're going to do with the smaller theater. And then we have a dance studio, we'll utilize that. We'll allow the community to utilize that. I want to bring in different cultural performances, special performances. One night you might find a kabuki performance or you might find an African, an East African something or you might find an Indian something. I want to continually . . . maybe twice a year, you will walk in and all these Japanese people are there. They're coming into our world and seeing the history of the Black Ensemble or mingling with the other people coming out and it sparks an interaction and you never know what can happen from that interaction. In that sense, that's why it's a cultural center because it's going to bring all kind of cultures into the facility and those cultures will interact, mingle, and talk and share. The Black Ensemble is an educational tool at essence. All of our productions are educational. You are going to walk out of there knowing something that you did not know before, and that's on purpose. We don't tout that because people think they know everything and they don't want to learn anything; they just want to go and have fun. So, we let them have fun and then when they come out, they go, "You know, I didn't know that." So, that will remain a part of our essence.

In 1976, when you formed this company, was eradicating racism your goal?

Yes.

One thing I've noticed in looking at a lot of larger theaters in the city is that diversity is something that comes along pretty late in their histories. It's once they cross the thirty-year mark, then they take an active interest in diversifying their ensembles. In 1976, what was the theater climate like?

It was very racist, same as it is now. It hasn't changed. It's still very racist. However, in the cultural community in theater, it was not racist. It was very open in terms of producing. We all worked together.

By "cultural community," are you talking about in the arts in general?

No, theater. I don't know the arts in general. Theater is what I do; that's what I know. But it was very all-encompassing. We were all like Roche Schulfer and the people who started the St. Nicholas [Theatre]; I can't quite remember their names now. I know Patricia Cox was one of those folks, Stuart Oken. There were a lot of young upstarts. We were all in our early twenties and we all had great dreams and goals. In the theater world at that time, it was just all-encompassing, and it was young people who didn't buy into the racist thing. They just didn't buy into . . . they weren't even thinking on that level. It was about creating theater, maintaining theater, whether it was a black theater or Spanish theater or a white theater. It just really didn't matter. It was about coming together and making it a solid community. And that's how it was. It was like that for theater, in general, and then it was like that for the African American community. We had a strong theater community. We didn't think of ourselves as competition. We didn't think, "We're not going to let you get up there," like crabs in a barrel—like some people say we are. We were never like that. We had a very strong political foundation in terms of let's work together, let's stay together, let's focus on what our similarities are and build that and let's keep moving forward. That's the kind of foundation in the arts and theater that we had at that time.

When I came out with the Black Ensemble Theater, I was chastised because it was on the North Side and not on the South Side. It was just an image—that was not true—that everything black was on the South Side. I grew up on the North Side. I grew up in Cabrini–Green. I didn't even know black people were on the South Side for a long time until I got out of my little world and somebody said . . . when somebody said, "We're going down south," they meant, "We're going down south; we're going to Mississippi or Alabama." That's where everybody was from. I didn't even know . . . I knew there were black people on the West Side because we had come from the West Side when I was five. That's where I lived then. But the South Side, it took getting into high school, where people were from everywhere, that I learned, "Oh, there's black people on the South Side." I put my theater on the side of town that I knew. I didn't know the South Side. I just didn't know it. North Side it was. It made all the sense to me and since my mission was to eradicate racism, I said, "We need to be somewhere where all the races can come."

The mission of eradicating racism was not a popular mission. I was told that it was too lofty and it's impossible and my response was, "When the Wright brothers said to somebody, 'You know I want to make a machine that flies through the air like a bird,' I'm sure people looked at them like 'Are you out of your mind? That's impossible. That's crazy.' But it takes somebody to see it and to believe it and to make it happen." It's not even a goal that is going to happen in my lifetime, for sure, but the seed is planted. I have no idea what a world without racism would even look like. I have no concept, but somebody will, and somebody will take this [seed] and water it. Heaven only knows what it needs in order to grow. So somebody will figure that out and they'll spray it. It's just going to happen. Those two things for a long, long time were my biggest challenges: (1) getting people to accept [that] no, I'm not on the South Side and I'm not going to be on the South Side, and (2) that the mission of the organization is to eradicate racism. It's not to have diversity. In fact, diversity . . . that term didn't even exist at that time. It was to eradicate racism; take it away, destroy it. Those were the two biggest issues when I started.

How did you go about creating your company in 1976?

I had done a lot by that time. I had my degree in theater. I was trained by Dennis Zacek. That was a remarkable training, remarkable. He trained us and he said at the time, "If you guys want to start a theater, you'll be able to." And I was like, "Who wants to start a theater?" I wanted to get the first Academy Award as the first African American [leading lady]. I didn't want to start a theater. But before I graduated, I was hired by Patrick Henry who was a visionary and a real descendent of the Patrick Henry who created Free Street Theater. Free Street was a theater that went into a community that had never seen black people and performed. Then, we went to black communities that had never ventured out of their community and all these white people came in to perform. This was

Patrick's dream. Two months before I was to graduate, I was cast in that and I talked to Dennis, and he said, "Mail your assignments in. Go do this. Mail them in, complete your work, but this is what you went to school for, so go do it." So, I went on tour with them for two years, and then I was a major actress everywhere. I played the Goodman, Organic Theater, and Victory Gardens Theater and almost every African American production that was produced; if they had a female part that fit me, I was the person that did it. And then I made a major motion picture right after that. I went into—well, that was after having a daughter—but I went into [the film] *Coolie High* [1975], and that propelled me to a whole 'nother level. And then my goal was to act. It wasn't to produce, it was to act, but I naively thought that, like *Coolie High*, I was going to have the opportunity to play somebody in a film that had a positive statement. I wanted my roles to be positive. I didn't believe in guns or violence and that movie was against all of that. It had a great message. I thought, "Well, this is what I want to do," but the reality was that *Coolie High* was a fluke. A lot of producers tried to stop it from being made because it didn't fit the black exploitation mold. Black people, we're not stupid. We're not a stupid people. We're not a violent people. We have some deficiencies, but so does everybody else, so get over it. They were making money exploiting this image. I was under contract to do that stuff and I said, "No, I don't want to do that. I ain't doing that period. I'm not doing it." I didn't care about the money. It wasn't important. It just wasn't important. I had been an educator during this time too, and I was thinking about all the kids I've taught about "no violence" and "no guns" and "you can rise above." Just because you live in the projects doesn't mean you're not worth anything. I'm just thinking about all this stuff and then they're going to look up at the screen and say, "Oh, look at Miss Taylor. She told us, 'You can rise above.' That ain't true." I couldn't do that. I decided that I couldn't just walk away and not be a part of the solution. As Malcolm X taught us, you are either part of the problem or part of the solution. I was like, "I can't be part of the problem. I'm going to have to be part of the solution. I'm going to have to do something." I decided I couldn't do anything in film because it was 1976. How many black people do you know from that time, except for Melvin Van Peebles, who had broken through and done their own thing? He did his thing. For a woman? No, it just wasn't happening.

I decided, "I'm going to start a theater and that's how I'm going to make a difference. The purpose of that theater is going to be to eradicate racism." I was in the bathtub and literally, I said, "I'm going to start a theater. I'm going to call it Black Ensemble after the Negro Ensemble [Company]." I'm in a different time period, where we dance to James Brown: "I'm black and I'm proud, hey." So, I had to name it Black Ensemble. It was a tribute to the Negro Ensemble, except it was in Chicago. And that's how I literally started it. I had some money left from my film, and then I found a theater. I went into Old Town, which was a couple of blocks from where I lived. I had to find a theater. I walked around. I got to Wells Street, which was two blocks from my house, and there was this big sign that said, THEATER FOR RENT. I went in and I talked to the guy, Paul. I told him that I wanted the theater and what I wanted to do and the mission and everything. And he said, "I'll rent you the theater for this much, and I'll rent you the lights for this much, and I'll rent you the sound for this much, and that comes to blah, blah, blah, and this is what you will have to pay monthly." I said, "This theater is empty. I'm going to pay you two hundred dollars a month. The lights and sound, that's all included." You don't go into a home and say I'll rent you the kitchen for five dollars and I'll rent you . . . I said, "Come on now. That's not happening. I'll give you two hundred dollars, or I'll just keep looking." He said "OK" with a smile on his face and gave me the theater. I went to get a loan from the bank because I needed more money after I had tried to figure out what my monthly costs were going to be and what show I was going to put up. I told them how much I needed and he asked me all those questions. Then the last question was, "What are you going to do with the money? We think we can do this." I said, "I'm going to start a theater. He said, "I'm sorry. We don't. That's not collateral for us. That's very risky. Theater businesses don't make money. No one goes to the theater. No, we can't do that." I asked, "What will you give me the money for?" He said, "Well, let's say you want to buy furniture for your house; that's good collateral." He said, "You want to buy a car or something." I thanked him and then I went across the street [to another bank], and I went through the same process, and I answered all the questions. We went through all the checking, everything. Exactly the same. Then again, the same question at the end: "Well, what are you going to do with the money?" I said, "I'm going to buy furniture for my house." He said, "Yes, we can handle that." And that was it. I got the money and that started the Black Ensemble Theater.

Do you remember your first production?

The Other Cinderella, of course, I remember that one. I had written it.

Was this the first play you had written?

No, I've been writing plays since I was like four years old. I had been writing plays even though I didn't know how to write. I still was writing. I would put the name of the person down and it would look like little scratch but in my mind, I was writing. Then, I would read it and act out all the parts. So, I've always, always written and I've always written in play form.

What was The Other Cinderella *about?*

The other Cinderella. Cinderella was from the projects. The stepsisters didn't do anything. The fairy godmamma was from Jamaica. Brothers were from the 'hood and there was a king, queen, and prince, and everybody had soul. It was a Cinderella story except in this story, the shoe fit the stepsister before it fit Cinderella and the fairy godmamma had to resolve all of that. I had written that with my kids [students] because they wanted to do a play. Walt Disney had just [rereleased] *Cinderella* at that time. They [my students] were so crazy and I was a new teacher, and I just didn't know yet how to impact or get them to where I could teach. So, I said, "What do you all want to do because you don't want to do this work? What do you want to do?" And they said, "We want to do a play." No, they didn't say "a play." They said, "We want to do *Cinderella*," or something like that. They had seen *Cinderella*. I said, "OK, we're going to do Cinderella, but we're going to do the other Cinderella," and I wrote this story. In writing it, I incorporated the things that I needed to teach them: math and English and vocabulary. We did *The Other Cinderella*, and they also learned their reading, their math, their history, and their scores went up. So, I got to do what I needed to do and they got to do what they wanted to do, which set me on another path in terms of education and understanding what you really need in order to be a teacher, not what they taught us in school. It's totally different. Now, I'm actually in graduate school. I waited forty years to go back for my master's. Now, they're trying to talk about social skills and the need for social skills and why they're important. But I was teaching it. I call it developmental skills because that's what they are. I've been teaching them since 1973. So, I'm like, "Y'all got to catch up with me because this is some old stuff." After I wrote that, I decided, "This could be a show, a real show." I wrote the music and starred as Cinderella and it ran for two years.

In the same theater?

Yes. As I'm thinking, that wasn't the first play. The first play was *Miss Ann Is Still Alive* by Oscar Griffin. That was about a Southern couple. The white woman makes him make love to her and how the couple deals with it. There was a writer—he still is a writer, Gary Houston—he worked for the *Sun Times*. He saw it and he just went crazy over the play. He thought it was the greatest thing in the world and this new theater company and this new talent, and he really pushed us out into the public. After that is when I produced *The Other Cinderella*. That was the second play.

How did you get word out?

I'm really good at picking up the phone. I called people. I called Irv Kupcinet. He wrote "Kup's Column" for the [*Chicago*] *Sun Times*. He was the person in terms of marketing. If you got your name in "Kup's Column" . . . So, I called Kup and I pretended like I was my manager, and I was telling him all about me and what I had done and how I was innovative and it's the only theater company, blah, blah, blah, and "She would like to talk to you." And he said, "Well, just tell her to call me." I said, "OK, no problem. Then I hung up the phone [and quickly redialed]. "Kup, this is Jackie Taylor." He, in turn, did an item, and I got my name in the paper a lot. I made it visible. I made it be seen. I did it all kind of different ways. Sometimes they needed controversy, so I would create controversy. Whatever it took to market, to get the name out there, that's what I did and then I went to stars. I was trying to get stars involved, to get them connected with the theater—to get more publicity. I asked Kup did he know Sidney Portier and he said yes. I said, "Well, I think he should donate to the theater to help us." He said, "I'll talk to him." Two days later, my phone at home rings and I said, "Hello," and he said [*imitating Sidney Poitier's voice*], "Miss Taylor?" I said, "Yes?" He said, "This is Sidney Portier." I said, "OK, who is this 'cause this ain't no Sidney Portier? Who is this and why you . . . don't do this." And he said, "No, dear, this is Sidney Portier. Kup asked that I call you. He told me about your mission, and I'd like to talk to you. I'm in Chicago and I want you to come down to the set." That's when they, him and Bill Cosby, were doing those movies [*A Piece of the Action,* 1977; etc.]. And I went down to the set and *everybody* was on the set, everybody who was anybody in Chicago was down there. I went down there and I was standing outside and Kup saw me. I don't know how he knew who I was or if he just said I bet that's her and he said, "Miss Taylor? Miss Jackie Taylor?" I said yes. He said, "Come, come." He gave me this big ole hug and then he took me in [Sidney Poitier's] trailer and I talked about the Black Ensemble, what I wanted to do. He wrote me a check right then for ten thousand dollars. At that time, that was a lot of money. Kup wrote about that and other people grabbed onto it. You just have to keep the ball going and that's what I did. I never let the ball drop. If I thought we hadn't had any press in a while, I would think, "I'm going to produce this and get somebody's attention. They'll write about this." That's how I kept the theater going. I didn't know what those skills were at that time. I was just innately doing what I needed to be done to keep the theater alive, but it was marketing. It was marketing, it was publicity, and it was fundraising. That's how it all started in 1976.

How long did you balance teaching and running the theater?

I'm still teaching. [*Laughing*] I'm trying to get out of teaching, but it doesn't work. I don't do classroom teaching full-time, not anymore. I'm still in the classroom, but I teach theater as a learning facilitator, so that schools develop my system and then they integrate it so that it changes the climate of the school and the climate of the classroom. It's called strengthening the school through theater arts. The teacher must be the actor and a director. Or the kids are the actors and directors—and they're running you; you're not running them. And the skills that you need for theater are the same skills that you need to learn [in school]: focus, concentration, observation, control of emotion. I love teaching. I love it. I didn't want to just leave it, but I did not have the time, so I developed a program that would allow me to be in the school, to make a difference in the school, to transform the school and then move on. And now that program is about thirty years old. Now, I teach artists how to deliver the program. I just didn't want it to be Jackie Taylor and then no more Jackie Taylor, no more program. So, I taught and I still teach artists how to deliver my program.

In terms of your playwriting formula, how did you develop it?

Well, really by accident. Like I said, I had always written plays. One of my first major plays that I wrote and finished was called *The Swinging Wizard of Oz*. This was before *The Wiz*. I think I still have that script somewhere, it was handwritten. It's going to be worth a lot of money someday. I've always written scripts, it was just something I did for fun. I never thought it would make me money someday. I was trying to produce plays that would have a cross-cultural interest because I wanted to bring a mixed group into the theater and then I figured once we get them there, at least they're there together and they have that experience and something can grow from just that happening. I tried different things. I tried the classics like *Julius Caesar* and *Medea*. And then I tried classics like Tennessee Williams because I love Tennessee Williams, so I starred as Blanche DuBois in *A Streetcar Named Desire*. I did a whole ten years of different stuff. It was like nothing was working. It was just a hit and [a] miss, hit and miss, hit and miss. I'm like, "There's something missing that we just have not captured yet." Jimmy Tillman—he used to be my music director, he's not now—brought me a script based on the life of Muddy Waters. I didn't care much for the script. I said, "Let's rewrite this script." He said, "I know your mission and I know you're trying to get a mixed crowd in the door, and the blues is very mixed. A lot of white folks love the blues." He said, "This might work for you." I said, "Let's give it a try." Almost overnight, the audience was fifty–fifty. It was very mixed. We ran that a long time. I said, "Let's try that again. Let's do Otis Redding," because I liked Otis Redding. Put up Otis Redding. Boom,

JACKIE TAYLOR ❊ 95

there it was again. I was like, "Oh my God. There's something to this cross-cultural music. That's the key. There's something to this." And it made sense because music already crosses cultural boundaries. It already does, so it's like let's keep this music as the core of what we do and let's put everything else around the music. Let's put the messages, let's put the history, let's do everything around the music and make the music the magnet, and it worked. Everything that we did, it just worked. We had a consistent audience. They supported it. They knew they were going to have a good time. They knew they were going to hear some great music. They knew they were going to learn something, and that became our formula.

In thinking about my process, I decided to develop a Black Playwrights' Initiative, a BPI, and it would be the focus of the BPI to write plays for the Black Ensemble Theater, but I had to teach the formula because we have to keep that. I had to add some incentives for people who didn't write musicals or who weren't interested in our kind of theater, so I started developing playwrights and helping them to get their product out if it didn't fit Black Ensemble Theater. We still do readings and we still do productions, we have a black playwrights' festival and we have a summer festival to get playwrights' work out, in general. But the core of it is to ensure that Black Ensemble Theater has a steady stream of productions and a steady stream of people who continually write those productions so that our product continues. We're not going to run out of people, we're not going to run out of product, we're not going to run out of music. It's going to keep going no matter what. It might have to change and adapt, but there's a whole bunch of stuff still out there. We just need the people to sustain it, and that's what we did with the BPI.

How many plays have you yourself written?

Over one hundred, I can tell you that. I stopped counting a long time ago. I used to count and then I was like, you know what? This is ridiculous.

What is your process? Do you get the music first and then listen to it?

My process changes with every single production. Sometimes I start with a scene and it grows out from there. Sometimes I start with the ending.

I'll think of this great ending and then ask, "What can go before this that will make this ending work?" Or sometimes, I hear a great piece of music and I say, "I want to write a play around this music." Or, it could be a person like Rick Stone. Rick works for me. He was in *Coolie High*. He played Stone and we grew up together. I create titles first because you got to have something that's going to attract people's attention, so I always create titles and then I figure out from there what's going to happen. I created [the title] *Message Is in the Music* and said, "This is in our season," but who knew what *Message [Is] in the Music* was about. I certainly didn't. Ricky's one of our actors, and he's very popular. He played Muddy Waters. He played Howlin' Wolf. He played Rufus Thomas. He played all of these characters. *Message [Is] in the Music* was coming up and the BPI had given me some scripts and I was like, "I don't like these. They're not hitting me. They're not saying anything." I was going to star Ricky, but none of the scripts worked, and I was walking down the hall and I said, "I got Ricky, I got a *Message Is in the Music*," and I said, "Why not make Ricky God and call this script, *God Is a Black Man Named Ricky, the Message Is in the Music,* and then figure out what music fits within this story?" I said, "I'm just going to keep this story simple: heaven and hell, they at it again." I created this story around Ricky who was God and he sang Curtis Mayfield and "It's All Right to Have a Good Time" and "I'm So Proud of Being Loved by You." He sang that to She; that's his wife. And it became this wonderful love story. It just came from that title and "this was my star" and it was three weeks from the opening of the show and I still didn't have a script. And that's how that script was done. Every script . . . I don't know how it's going to happen. I just know it's going to happen. But I have the same fears that all playwrights have. You put the title on the page and you go, "What am I going to do? I don't know what to do." And you spend the first two minutes going crazy, then you get down to work. But I never know how it's going to come out.

What percentage of the plays are now written by the BPI?

Fifty percent, at least 50 percent, and we're growing it (to make it more) so that if I want to write a script, I can but if Jackie don't feel like it, I don't have to.

You grew up in Cabrini–Green, a public housing development. What is the legacy of Cabrini–Green on the performing arts in Chicago?

Well, Jerry Butler, Curtis Mayfield, Gene Chandler, Major Lance. Cabrini–Green, or any project, is a big place. There's a lot of people there. At that time, the arts were fed. We had Seward Park where we had a drama teacher, a voice teacher, a tap teacher, a dance teacher. After school, you'd go to Seward Park. You could sing or you could dance or you could act. Kids had choices. I think this is still part of the racism that exists all over . . . the parks were taken away, people were taken out of the parks. They stopped having things for the kids to do. It's not rocket science. If you have a poor neighborhood where there's a lot of violence, put a center in there. Put a basketball center where they can go play basketball, where they can play volleyball, where they can do tap. Put something there. Cabrini had a lot of resources and you didn't have to be a crook, you didn't have to be a drug dealer, you could be an artist. You had choices. We grew up and we had choices. Some people chose, like Jerry Butler, who's the commissioner of the city, to sing. I chose to be in the drama department, you know, act. We were fed. We were fed. There were more choices. Cabrini happened to get a name in the seventies because of the policemen being killed at that time and the publicity that that drew. It became the worst thing in the world after that, when really it was just three kids, and they were kids, and they were stupid. But it gave us this notoriety that stood out from the other projects. You could go anywhere. You could go to the Robert Taylor Homes, you could go to the Ickes, you could go anywhere and you can trace back very famous people who grew up in these areas.

The Cabrini buildings are down now.

Oh, it's all gone.

What advice would you offer people looking to create their own theater company?

They either have to have certain skills or they have to be smart enough to make sure that the people that they pull in have the skills. If you want to be a producer, you have to be able to raise money, plain and simple;

you have to be able to raise money. You have to be able to market. And you have to be creative. You have to be a leader. You have to be strong, and you cannot be afraid to fail because you are going to fail. We all do. When you get knocked down, be dizzy for a minute and then get yourself back together and keep going. And learn the business. Learn it. Learn what it means to be a producer, what it means to market, what it means to fundraise. What does that mean? Basically, it means go get the money. Where is the money? What do I need to get it? You answer the basic questions and then you put together some kind of plan and it can be something as simple as, "OK, I want to start a theater company, I need some money, these people have money, I'm going to go to them and ask them for it," or whatever. Then you find that in order to do that you need some background material, you need to incorporate yourself. You need to decide, "Am I going to be for profit or not for profit?" and what that means. It's about educating yourself in understanding business because it's a business. It might be art, but that means nothing. It has to be a business for the art to exist. You have to know business. If you don't know business, then don't get into it because you can do theater in your house and you'll be fine. Invite some people over and go right ahead.

You mentioned that Mayor Daley was involved in the new building. What role did he or City Hall play in supporting the development of Black Ensemble Theater?

When you talk about Mayor Daley, you have to talk about Maggie Daley [his wife]. Maggie Daley is a very strong art supporter, and she understands the business of art. She understands that art creates jobs, creates money, creates tourism, creates business, and it's a great investment in a city. Mayor Daley had a great partner and still does in Maggie Daley, because Mayor Daley is strong in different areas and Maggie Daley is strong in other areas. I think Maggie Daley had a great deal to do with the mayor's view of what the advantages of supporting the arts could do for the city. The mayor has always been interested in the city and what could make this city the greatest city in the country. And Maggie saw the advantages that the arts have and that they play. So, yes, Mayor Daley was very supportive of the arts, very supportive, more supportive than any mayor that I've known. I set up a meeting with Mayor Daley and talked to him about the Black Ensemble Theater. I mean after all, I have a little name for myself. I've been here a long time. The mayor knew about the Black Ensemble Theater.

When was this?

It was like in 2005 when I wanted to build the Black Ensemble Theater. It's my philosophy to go to the people that can make it happen. They're only people. I don't care what their title is. Call them up. That's what I did. I called him up. They gave me an appointment and I went down and I used my fifteen minutes, and I told him everything about Black Ensemble, why I started it and blah, blah, blah, and I told him that I needed his help and that I wanted him to be my partner in this and that he had made such great things happen for the city and that this would be a very wonderful thing for the city, the state, the total community and diversity. He, in turn, became a very strong advocate.

How did you become involved with the New Regal Theatre?

I got a call from Mr. [Edward] Gardner who had opened the theater at that time and we were talking about how to make the Regal work. I was running *The Other Cinderella* here and it runs for a long time when I put it up. So, he asked me to come down and help him with the Regal and I did. The Regal has its place in history, of course. It was a dream of the Gardners [Edward and Bettianne], and they made their dream come true. Again, theater is a business. It's a business, and the Regal had a difficult job, because it wasn't big enough for the touring companies and it was too big for the regular companies. You have to find programming that's going to fit into that 2,000-seat theater. How many 2,000-seat theaters do we have that stand alone in this city? We don't. We have churches that have large theaters, but they're churches and their membership feeds into those theaters. This 2,000-seat theater stood alone. How can you make it work? In order for it to work, a lot of money has to be invested and it takes time. You can't put up a theater and expect that it's going to turn a profit within a year. You have to plan so that OK this year it's going to lose this much, this year it loses a little less, this year a little less. By the time we get to year five, people are really going to start getting accustomed and used to us and we can break even this year, so that's a strategic plan of action. The Regal never had that. I think there was an expectation that the Regal was going to be built and they will come, but it doesn't work like that.

You were a vice president of the League of Chicago Theatres. What is the connection between the League and Black Ensemble Theater?

The League, in the beginning, was called OLPAC, Off-Loop Producers Association of Chicago, and it was a group of producers who were working together to create a contract we could all work under. That was our initial purpose and then it built itself into the League of Chicago Theaters, and Roche Schulfer was the president for many years and then I was vice president and then Chuck [Smith] was vice president. We stayed involved because it's a resource and it's a strong resource. Black Ensemble Cultural Center will be a member but Black Ensemble Theater wasn't a member because it wasn't advantageous to us. Theaters that have a lot of empty seats, they can benefit a great deal from the League. You get promotion, you get marketing. You get all of these perks. You get into Hot Tix [discount ticketing service]. But Black Ensemble never needed that. We don't have empty seats, and if we do have empty seats, we give them to the community. We give them to disenfranchised communities like veterans who are disabled and people coming out of addiction. We have a philosophy that we adhere to, so they get those tickets. But we don't have a lot of free tickets or half-price tickets. I never bought into the [idea that] Hot Tix will develop new audiences. I never bought into that. I don't think it develops new audiences. I think it gives discounted tickets to audiences that are going to come to your theater anyway but they're going to go there to get their discount. I never saw how is it building a new audience. That's my dilemma. I can't, I don't, I can't jump on the Hot Tix wagon. When they first started Hot Tix, it was mandatory that all the theaters give a certain amount of tickets to be given away for Hot Tix. "No, I ain't doing it. No, my tickets are going to sell for what they are and that's going to be it." And Black Ensemble, we have a strong reputation. We're very visible. We just didn't need Hot Tix. We didn't need the League. Now it's different. It is not mandatory—you don't have to do Hot Tix. I'm very political and I think that it's important to be involved in our associations. I think it's important for Black Ensemble to be a part of the League of Chicago Theaters because it's the League of Chicago Theaters, and we're one of the theaters, so we should definitely be involved, but it would also be good for the League for the Black Ensemble to be a part of it because now it looks lily white and they need some diversity. They've reached out. They've done their due diligence and now it's a good time. When we transition, yes; we're going to become members of the League.

If you were to write a history of black theater in the city, who were influential artists who should be remembered?

Charles Taylor, X-BAG. Oscar Brown. Of course, Chuck Smith, Val Gray Ward, Pemon Rami, Masequa Myers, John Bellamy, Philip Walker—I think Phil is in Philadelphia. Jonathan Wilson. Paul Carter Harrison. Runako [Jahi]. Leroy Jones. I think from my perspective that would kind of cover it for me.

JONATHAN WILSON

Jonathan Wilson is a professor of theater and drama at Loyola University–Chicago, where he has directed more than forty university productions. His Chicago-area directing credits include TimeLine Theatre, Steppenwolf Theatre Company, Goodman Theatre, and Court Theatre. For excellence in professional directing, he has won two Joseph Jefferson (Jeff) Awards.

In this interview, conducted in November 2009, Wilson fondly recalls Chicago's emerging theater scene in the 1970s and 1980s and reflects on his personal experiences with playwright August Wilson.

When you arrived in Chicago in 1976, what was the theater community like?

One of the oldest black theater companies in the United States going at that time in Chicago was called Kuumba. It was run by a woman named Val Gray Ward. She was very instrumental in getting a lot of veteran black actors work. She was well-known and respected. Jackie Taylor was just getting underway with the Chicago Black Ensemble [Theater]. And, perhaps the most influential black theater artist in the city at that time was a woman by the name of Abena Joan Brown, who was running a community theater on the South Side called eta [Creative Arts]. That was pretty much the extent of it. There wasn't a great deal going on. There had clearly been a history of some rather significant black productions, black directed, all-black casts, and so on, but they were few and far between. As a matter of fact, Chicago theater at that time was chiefly made up of just a few equity houses. The Goodman Theatre was going, the Court Theatre on the South Side was going, Victory Gardens had just gotten started with Dennis Zacek. Dennis, at the time when I came in '76, was a full-time faculty member at Loyola University–Chicago. So there wasn't a great deal going on. The Steppenwolf was not even heard of. In fact, the Chicago theater scene did not really get rolling until Steppenwolf (at the time housed in a suburban garage) began to gather a lot of public attention, enough so that the newspaper critics went to see their work and to give their productions high praise. There were also other signs of growth. Many small theaters were launched. During the 1980s, I had a chance to actually observe and be a part of a theatrical renaissance in Chicago. In 1981, I remember I took a leave of absence from Loyola to do another degree program in play direction at Northwestern University. I took an acting class that was taught by Bud Beyer and I got to know many of the students in his class. Some of those students in the class became the originators of what is now the distinguished Lookingglass Theatre Company. These young companies were developing. Steppenwolf, the gem of this group, started as a result of some disgruntled theater graduate students at Illinois State. Their work ultimately became so explosive that Steppenwolf quickly became one of the most experimental theaters in America. Chicago, as a second city, exploded with theatrical activity. And as more young theater companies developed and matured, students from schools all over the country started coming to Chicago for work. I remember in 1989, I was working at the Pegasus Players Theatre Company. Richard Christiansen, a former critic for the *Chicago Tribune* who had seen August Wilson's *Ma Rainey's Black Bottom* in New York, thought that Wilson was this significant up-and-coming playwright. Mr. Christiansen recommended that Chicago should do August Wilson's play to Arlene Crewdson, the artistic director of the Pegasus Theatre Company. Arlene asked me if I would direct *Ma Rainey* and I agreed. So that was my first introduction to doing August Wilson. We started out in a loft church on the corner of Kenmore and Bryn Mawr. It was scheduled to be a three-week run. The play and production were highly successful. Audiences fell in love with it. The production ended up having a six-month run. In the last couple of months, we moved it from the church to the main theater at Truman College where Pegasus is housed. The casting of *Ma Rainey's Black Bottom* presented a major challenge. The play requires four actors who play musical instruments. I didn't know much about the New York production and didn't know that the music had been recorded. So I went about the business of trying to find four actors who could play instruments. And I found them. Most of them had learned their instruments in high school. So it took a lot of practice and work to get them to the point where they could play. But they did. One of them was Harry Lennix who subsequently became a big television/movie star. Arlene was basking in the fact that she had a major hit going on at Pegasus and wanted me to direct something else the following season. "No, Arlene, no, no, no, no, no." "Yes, Jonathan, yes." "I know what I'll do to get her off my back. I will give her something that she will definitely say no to." And so I offered Howard Sackler's *The Great White Hope*, a powerful, large-cast production about the life of the first black heavyweight champion of the world, Jack Johnson. Arlene said, "Yes, yes, yes." Oh no! And so it came to pass. I think I saw nearly four hundred actors over a two-weekend audition process. And I eventually wound up with a cast of thirty. Twenty-eight of them were MFAs in acting who had just recently come into Chicago. It was incredible.

What was the first professional production you directed in Chicago. Was it Ma Rainey?

No. It was with a small theater company called the Commons Theatre. It was a brand new play called *A Two-Story House*. The Commons Theatre was housed in a small loft just down the street from Loyola University on Sheridan Road. The staff of the theater asked me direct and I accepted. When I came to Chicago in 1976, I had two degrees in play direction; a BFA from Rosary Hill College in my home town of Buffalo, New York, and a master's from the University of Cincinnati. I had also done extensive doctoral work (all but dissertation) at the University of Wisconsin–Madison. During my time in college, the focus of my work was chiefly the study of European dramatists, European directors and designers. So during my educational journey, what knowledge I gained about black theater in America I acquired on my own. I got hired at Loyola as a faculty member in both the Theater Department and the African American Studies Program. In the Theater Department, I was allowed to direct essentially anything that I wanted. For the African

American Studies Program, I was asked to annually direct what was called the Black Theater Workshop. There were some 120 theater majors at Loyola at that time when I came in 1976. I'd say close to 35 percent of them were African American. In one semester, I was able to direct a play by an African American dramatist, and then in the second semester a play for the department that ranged from Shakespeare to Edward Albee to Harold Pinter. I mean, you name it. I had the best of both worlds. And I was very content. I was not even interested in directing in the professional theater. One day however I got a call from the Steppenwolf Theatre saying that one of my recent graduates had recommended me to direct in their high school program. It was a production of Lorraine Hansberry's *A Raisin in the Sun*. It was an important moment in my career as a director because the success of the work at Steppenwolf sent my name around the city to other theaters. Ironically, however, they were not black theaters. They were white theaters. After the success of *Ma Rainey* in '88, and *The Great White Hope* in '89, I remember getting a call from Russell Vandenbroucke, the artistic director at Evanston's Northlight Theatre. Having heard of my work at Steppenwolf, Russell asked me if I might be interested in working on a play by Dr. Endesha Ida Mae Holland. The play was a series of monologues that outlines her journey from growing up on the Mississippi Delta, being raped at nine years old by a white man, becoming a prostitute at eleven, actively participating in the civil rights movement, and acquiring her PhD in American Studies at the University of Minnesota. *From the Mississippi Delta* captures Dr. Holland's autobiographical journey. After acquiring her doctoral degree, Endesha accepted an appointment in the American Studies Department at the University of Buffalo. In Buffalo, a workshop production of the play turned it from a one-woman play to a three-women. This was the script I received at Northlight. But as I said, it was all monologues. So I began working on it to find a way of giving it some type of stage business that my three actresses could play. Originally the production was scheduled to have a one-weekend run of previews and a three-weekend run of performances. However the run of this production eventually turned into a two-year journey traveling from Northlight to the Studio Theatre at the Goodman, and then on to the Arena Stage in Washington, the Hartford Stage in Connecticut, and culminating with a six-month run at the Circle in the Square Theatre off Broadway. *From the Mississippi*

Delta became the breakthrough play for me opening up opportunities for me to direct in equity houses around the country. After *Delta*, I had the opportunity to direct Wole Soyinka's *The Lion and the Jewel* [1991] for the Court Theatre at the University of Chicago, Athol Fugard's *Playland* [1994] for the Steppenwolf Theatre Company, and August Wilson's *Joe Turner's Come and Gone* [1991] for the Goodman Theatre.

I met August Wilson for the first time in 1991, when the Goodman brought him to see the production. This was the beginning of a seventeen-year relationship with August Wilson. Over the course of this relationship, August taught me how to help my actors develop their characters truthfully. He taught me about the relationship between African Americans and their African ancestry. In 1998, August assisted me in the casting of his play *Seven Guitars* for the Seattle Repertory Theatre in Washington and the Alley Theatre in Houston, Texas. In 2002, I directed his play *Jitney* also at the Alley Theatre. In 2005 I directed his *Ma Rainey's Black Bottom* at the Seattle Repertory Theatre and *Two Trains Running* for the Pegasus Players Theatre Company in Chicago and won the city's Jeff Award for Best Director. Finally, in 2007, I directed August's play *Fences* in a three-city tour across the country. The production began in Hartford, Connecticut, for the Hartford Stage Company and then moved on to the Dallas Theatre Center in Texas and the Portland Stage Company in Oregon. I learned from some close theater friends that August Wilson had never forgotten my production of *Joe Turner's Come and Gone* at the Goodman. When I directed it, the theater brought him in for it. He came and he saw a run-through one night before we opened. He was quite pleased. August demanded that I pay strict attention to having the actors play his characters truthfully onstage. And yet, at the same time, there was another side to him. I will never forget him at the Alley Theatre in Houston one night. We were celebrating the opening of his play *Jitney* and also the reopening of a studio theater. At the reception for the studio theater I looked around at one point and August had disappeared. So I went outside and there he was all by himself. He was smoking a cigar. And I said to him, "August, I want to ask you a favor." I said, "I've always wanted to direct something in Europe, and I would love to have the opportunity, if it ever presents itself, to direct one of your plays with your permission there." He said, "Sure, I'd be happy to help make that happen." I believe it was either November or December of 2004, only months before his death in October of 2005. When August asked me to direct *Ma Rainey's Black Bottom* (2005) for him again at Seattle [Rep], I did. He was very busy at the time trying to get financing for one of his shows. It was his last play.

Was it Radio Golf, *or was it the one-man show?*

It was *Radio Golf.* He was very tired from having acted in his one-man show, [*How I Learned What I Learned*], and trying to get money to take *Radio Golf* to New York. He was also a little bit peeved with Seattle Rep because they had not given him the kind of publicity that he wanted [for] his one-man show. But he gave them *Ma Rainey.* Anyway, he was so busy that he didn't have time to give attention to *Ma Rainey* being mounted in Seattle. And thank God he wasn't because *Ma Rainey* is a rather larger-cast play. August did not have the time to help me with it. I didn't know that he was ill. Ironically, during the course of the rehearsal process, by the time that we opened, only three of the ten actors that had originally cast in it were still there. The production unto itself was a comedy of errors. People were leaving the cast for all sorts of reasons. One actor had a heart attack. Another actor, the actress playing Ma Rainey, learned her brother was killed in a car accident while she was in rehearsal. I mean, it was just one thing after the next. Things got so bad that we had to cancel a sold-out preview in order to be able to have the time to continue to rehearse. When we finally opened, we had four new actors in the cast. Consequently it was a very rocky opening. Nevertheless, August was there. He was very grateful for our efforts. After the performance, he sat in the lobby and greeted patrons. I'm told he was not feeling well. It was the last time that I saw August Wilson. But my relationship with him lasted for seventeen years. So I am very grateful that I had the opportunity to be a part of his history and legacy. I'm now at that point where things are beginning to quiet down for me. I'm in what I think is the twilight of my career. I am now getting ready to go into rehearsal for Athol Fugard's *Master Harold . . . and the Boys* (2009) at the TimeLine Theatre Company. I am excited about it. One of the actors [Alfred Wilson] who I have cast as one of the lead roles in it, can only do the January–February run but can't do March. So I am going to do March. I have not acted in a long time, and I know I am going to be nervous. But I am really looking forward to the experience.

What are your thoughts on color-blind casting and the debate about whether white directors should (or can) direct "black plays"?

I am tired of dealing with this question of color-blind casting. I think that there are plays like Lorraine Hansberry's *A Raisin in the Sun* set on the South Side of Chicago that is indigenously African American, and I think that it should be cast with African American actors. But in plays that are not culturally specific such as Shakespeare's *As You Like It,* Jean Paul Sartre's *No Exit,* or Beckett's *Waiting for Godot,* the director can cast anyone who best portrays the story of the play. It is as simple as that. If a white director takes on the challenge of directing an African American play, then he or she must be prepared to study the African American culture as Hansberry gives us in the play. If an African American director takes on the responsibility of directing Shakespeare's *As You Like It,* then he or she must also study the culture within the play. This is what color-blind casting means to me. The art of acting, the art of play direction, the art of the theater is a study in culture. I believe that if a director is willing to do the research and work that needs to be done regardless of what their own cultural background is, the concept of color-blind casting no longer becomes an issue and thus warrants no debate. I believe that a director, regardless of what their own cultural background may be, must commit themselves to doing the work. Do your work, and do so without apology.

RON O. J. PARSON

Ron O. J. Parson is a resident artist at the Court Theatre. He is the cofounder and former artistic director of the Onyx Theatre Ensemble of Chicago. His Chicago-area directing credits include Chicago Theatre Company, Victory Gardens, Goodman Theatre, Steppenwolf, Chicago Dramatists, Northlight, Court, Black Ensemble Theater, eta Creative Arts Foundation, and Writers' Theatre.

In this interview, conducted in November 2009, Ron O. J. Parson shares his experience breaking into Chicago theater, talks about the founding of Onyx Theatre Ensemble, and offers compelling advice and important survival skills for young artists.

I'm from Buffalo, New York. I won a scholarship at the age of twelve to a theater there called the Studio Arena Theatre, which is now gone. The founder of that theater actually came into the "ghetto" just to give some kids an opportunity. I know people knock affirmative action, but that is what it was. He wanted to go into the community and find some talented kids and see if he could change some lives. *Day of Absence* came to my school. It was crazy. Kids were throwing stuff and laughing. I was watching. It changed my life. I went to [the University of] Michigan as a journalism major. I was a sports writer and an athlete. I played football and baseball [in high school] and was coming to college to do that, and ended up playing rugby at the University of Michigan. We beat Northwestern. I came to Michigan as a journalism major, but I had always [been doing] theater [from] a young age. When I got to Michigan and my sports stuff fell through and I didn't know what I wanted to do, I was walking in the theater building, where we have our theater program called the Frieze Building, which is gone now, and I heard a play being rehearsed. *Day of Absence*. It's a reverse minstrel show by Douglas Turner Ward of the Negro Ensemble Company. He put people in whiteface. The play is about how one day, all the black people in town disappeared. Now, the black people did all the cooking, the cleaning, the washing, the working, and everything. For that one day, there weren't any black people. The play showed how the town couldn't function. There's a movie that came out a few years ago. And it's the same idea—only it's Mexicans. They disappear and the town is in chaos. That play was being rehearsed, and I knew that play. I walked into the theater room, the class, in rehearsal, and they happened to need an actor. I said, "I can do that. I did that when I was a kid." Long story short, I changed my major. I started directing.

I started a little company called the Back Alley Players in school with David Alan Grier. He is pretty famous now. We started it together. I actually got him into it. He was a musician. He was a music major but he decided to change majors, and the rest is history. Through my years at Michigan, having my own company allowed me to direct. Even without the training of the directing program, I was doing it. And because they were letting us use the theater a lot, the director of the program said, "Ron, there's complaints about you using the theater space." I don't know how it works in school now, but you need[ed] to be in the program to use the space for rehearsal and this and that. And I wasn't technically in the directing program and people were complaining. "Why is this guy allowed to use the theater?" So he said, "Ron, you need to, even though your shows are doing great, you need to get in the program." So I got in the program. And one thing led to another. I started directing. I started acting.

When I got out of school, I then came to . . . well, actually I went to New York. It's funny because I didn't even know Chicago theater. I didn't know Steppenwolf. I didn't know Goodman. I didn't know anything. I just knew New York. I was from Buffalo and we used to go to New York a lot. I tell actors now to start in Chicago. Get your feet wet here before going to New York or L.A. Because this [Chicago] is a mecca of theater. There's no doubt. I got out and moved to New York. Didn't work, didn't work out really. I got involved in some things I shouldn't have been involved in because of the business and how it ate me up. I'm honest with that, that it can eat you up. If you go to every audition and you think, "Oh, I didn't get that part, what am I doing wrong?" It stresses you out. It can eat you up, especially New York. So that's another thing about Chicago. There's not that much pressure. It's not the same kind of pressure. This business is really hard on you. And you need to have that attitude of "OK, I am going to do the best I can. I did the best I can. I didn't get it. It's not because it's me. It's not personal. They just went somewhere else. They went a different way."

Leaving New York let me try something else. Let me try a different place. Let me get out of that environment that was taking me away from my focus. Onyx Theatre Ensemble is what got me going here: being able to do my own plays and show talent without having to deal with the pressure of another person telling me what to do. A friend of mine who went to Michigan started Onyx with me. He had moved here. He worked his way up from telemarketer to becoming a marketing director at the Goodman for about ten years in the '80s. I think he left in the '80s. That was Alfred Wilson, he's an actor too. He said, "Man, I am in Chicago now and I am at the Goodman." I didn't google Goodman, I couldn't google. There was no Google. But I found out about the Goodman. So I moved here. Well, actually, I didn't move here. I came here to audition. I told my girlfriend at the time, I said, "I'm going to Chicago to audition for a play. If I get in that play, I am going to stay, I'm gonna move there. So, do you want to come? I'm gonna move." And she's like "Yeah, yeah, sure." I know she's thinking, "What luck? Never been to Chicago, this and that." She had two kids and I was ready to do that, I was ready to make that move. I got cast. I called her, I said, "Yeah, I got cast. You ready? Can you get your stuff together?" "I can't move to Chicago. That's crazy." Long story short, I moved here. Alfred and I decided to start that company. I got my first play audition and my first film audition. I said to myself, I think I need to be in Chicago. It was [the film] *Primal Fear* (1996), and it was [with] Richard Gere and all of that. So I was like, whoa, this is exciting. So anyway, I moved here.

When you came to Chicago, were you thinking about starting a theater company?

No, I came here really just to relocate, get my head together, get out of the New York mentality, the "New York State of Mind." That's a song. And I said, "Wow, this is the place to be." Alfred actually brought up the idea: "Let's start a company." Because we had already done that in other places. I had been doing it since school. David, David Allen Grier, was already a bit successful by then. He sent me some bucks and we got some stuff going. One thing led to another.

Now I did set a goal for myself as a director. I told myself, "If I am going to be serious about this, I want to have directed at Steppenwolf and Goodman within five years." Four years later, I was directing two shows at the same time, one at Steppenwolf and one in the Goodman. And it was just a miracle that the City Lit show was rehearsed in the evening, and *Let Me Live* [1998] at the Goodman in the daytime. One thing led to another. I only had to [hustle] for one year, I sold group sales at the Goodman, and I temped for a little bit, for about a year, 1996–1997. I could quit because I was getting directing work. And acting. Voiceovers. That's the most lucrative part of this business right now. That's how I got to Chicago.

Let's go back to Onyx. When artistic directors approach potential donors, they have to pitch their vision of their company and say how their theater contributes to the arts in Chicago. Why did Chicago need Onyx?

Unfortunately, at that time, there weren't a lot of theater groups doing the kind of work we were planning to do. Segueing a little bit to Derrick [Sanders]. I met Derrick and Javon [Johnson], and I directed them in their MFA project at the University of Pittsburgh. They were thinking about starting a theater, and I said, "Well, Chicago. It's ripe for it right now." And the rest is history. They moved here, they started it [Congo Square]. They were able to prevent making some of the mistakes that we made because, to answer your question, we had no foundation. We had no fundraising. We didn't have grant writers. We didn't . . . we were just guys who said, "Let's do a play." We basically got the money ourselves. I borrowed a couple thousand from my father, a couple thousand from David, a couple . . . just so we could produce this first show. Now, we didn't know what was going to happen after that, that was the thing. It was just like, "Let's do this show and see what happens." Now technically, we should have done it the other way. We should have had the organization. Get your 501c3 [nonprofit certification], get your board, get your . . . before you do a play. The play was so successful it was like,

"Wow, what do we do now? How can we top that? Now we need to raise the money, and now we need to get the board." We had a good product, we just didn't have the infrastructure. Congo Square came in, they had more of an infrastructure. They had August Wilson behind them. They had a lot of influential people. And they had me directing their first show. So that helped. No, actually, they had asked somebody else to do it, and he couldn't do it, so I kind of got in there. Half of my work, more than half of my work is from people who can't do something, and then my name comes up because they google. They google "directors in Chicago." Boom, my name comes up. And that's how, that's how it happens. There's a lot of luck involved.

What was the first show that you directed with Onyx?

East Texas Hot Links (1996). It takes place in 1955. It's a love story. I look at every play I direct as a love story, whether it's love of people, love of country, love of culture, love of family. Even if you're doing crazy, crazy plays with a lot of violence. A lot of times, people are doing all of that stuff because of love of something—obsessions or whatever. So, we did that, and then we followed with a play called *Flyin' West* (1996) which is a Pearl Cleage play. I also did it at Court too. I am actually trying to do a lot of those plays that I did with Onyx because we didn't have any money [then]. I am trying to [re-stage] them at Court because now we can put more money in and we can achieve more of the vision that I had in the first place.

We [Onyx] were around for five years. We did a coproduction with the Goodman called *Let Me Live* which was a really, really compelling show. And if you google these plays, you will see the impact they had in the city. So, to answer your question, there was a need for it then. Now, there's more diversity. Back then there wasn't the diversity that there is now. Goodman was doing some. Victory Gardens (Dennis Zacek) had been pioneering diverse theater for a long time. For the most part, there was a void of Latino plays, Asian plays. I mean, now you have Asian theater companies, a Native American company, some black theater companies. There is a lot of diversity. There still could be more. Theaters are opening up to nontraditional casting more. That's a controversial subject. I have thoughts on that. It's good to see what Steppenwolf is doing now:

the plays they are doing and the actors that they have in their ensemble. It's just . . . it's a good thing. *East Texas Hot Links*. That was the answer to your question.

What are your thoughts on nontraditional casting?

It's really not that controversial. I did *Wait Until Dark* (2009), a play that is not necessarily about black, white, or whatever. It is about this blind lady in Greenwich Village. The Village in 1965 was very diverse. I used to go there with my cousin. My cousin was a "hippie." I was just a kid, a little kid. He used to play with [Jimi] Hendrix, and Richie Havens, and those guys. And I used to see all that, and I was like, "Man, that's more color than I've seen." Because I was from a "black neighborhood." So anyway, when I got to do the play and it took place in that era, I said, "Well, let's do it that way." The blind woman was Asian. Her husband was Puerto Rican. Her neighbor was Latino. One cop was Italian, one cop was black. I look at that as nontraditional casting. It's not the traditional way you see it [in the theater]. That's different than blind casting. Sometimes blind casting is just indiscriminately putting any race in any play. Sometimes race is important to what the play is about. It's about a particular group of people. If you're doing *Juno and the Peacock,* it's about Irish people. If you're doing a play like *A Raisin in the Sun,* it's about these black people in this neighborhood. There are plays that you can do nontraditionally. I just saw a production of *Death of a Salesman* that was a little bit diverse and it didn't take away from the story. Sometimes blind casting takes away from the story for me. That's just my opinion. There's enough plays out there that aren't about what race the people are that they could be any race. So that's what I mean. I say controversial because there's the thought that anybody can be in any play. I don't agree with that. In some plays, race is specific to the story that the writer was trying to tell.

In terms of the development of your directing career, who were some of the people who assisted you along the way?

That's a good question. One of my biggest mentors is a guy named Stephen McKinley Henderson, who does a lot of August Wilson. He is the person that really got my career going again. A lot of actors get to New York or they get to L.A., and they don't get the roles that they got in school. That happened to me in New York. I got a job as an artistic director of a small community theater in Flint, Michigan. That helped me a little bit. But then I got fired from that because of Reaganomics. [President Ronald] Reagan had cut back the [federal] arts budget. And my job suffered from that. Me and the dance director got fired. I went back to New York and tried again and I was, again, hanging with the wrong crowd. Focus was gone. I needed a break. I went back to Buffalo, got out of the business. I called myself retired. And I was still young. I'm still young now, actually. It's [age is] just a state of mind. I had to regroup. When I went back to Buffalo, Stephen McKinley Henderson, at the University of Buffalo, got me in the production of *A Raisin in the Sun* as the moving man. And, I eventually got my career going. I am actually in the book of the revival of that show because I was in the play then. And, he said this is what you are supposed to be doing. I started gradually doing theater in Buffalo, small theaters. And one thing led to another. I went to help him. I assisted him on a play he was directing. Ironically, he acts more than he directs. He's good at it [directing]. He had to go do a production somewhere else and left me at this theater to direct. And it just came back to me. One thing led to another. Paul Carter Harrison who was at the Negro Ensemble Company, one of the founding people. Here in town, Martha Lavey [artistic director of Steppenwolf Theatre]. Anna Shapiro was very supportive of what I was trying to do. When I was really young, there was a guy named Robert McKee, who is now one of the premiere consultants on screenplays. He has a book called *On Screenwriting*. He was a teacher during my freshman year of college. And I saw the book on the Internet—I went to RobertMcKee.com or whatever—and I wrote, "I think your name is the name of the teacher I had at the University of Michigan and we did this movie together," and this and that, and it was him. I told him how he changed my life. I had his class in acting. I did some scene work and he took me to the side and he said, "Look, is this what you want to do? I mean, are you serious about this?" And I said, "Man, I don't know." And, he said, "Well, get serious about it." And, I got serious about it. And I started taking him to heart. He went on and did his thing and I went on and did my thing. It was nice to be able to write him and let him know how he affected my life. He was a big influence. But, I would have to say Stephen McKinley Henderson because he picked me up from my bootstraps. He's a genius. A brilliant actor, director. He does a lot of stuff everywhere, a lot of the August Wilson series. I've now directed eighteen productions of Wilson's plays. Well, actually acted in or directed eighteen productions of August Wilson's work.

The Stratford Festival. In fifty-five years, they had never had an African American director, male or female. They had a Canadian, I don't know what you say—Canadian African, African Canadian woman, black woman in Canada—direct one. I didn't even think about that [being the first] when I was going up there. But a woman from Montreal saw me at a bar having a drink. She said, "What are you doing here?" And I said, well, "I'm here directing this play." And she was like, "Really? I've been coming here for thirty years. I've never . . . let me look that up." And she went through the whole history of the theater and she came back to the bar the next night and said, "You're the first African American to direct here." And I was like, "Wow, OK, that's cool." But then the news services picked up on that. It was in *American Theater* magazine and a couple other places. So, that helped. Because working up there, it's an international theater. I'm just beginning to branch out a little bit more.

Let's talk about the 2003 production of Wedding Band *that you directed at Steppenwolf. Was that the first show that you directed at Steppenwolf?*

Wedding Band was actually not the first show I directed at Steppenwolf, but it was the first on their main stage. I did *The Horn* (1998) in their studio space now it's the Upstairs Theater. It was a jazz piece about a guy like Charlie Parker. He was a famous jazz musician, during the bebop era. When Onyx Theatre Ensemble did *East Texas Hot Links,* a coproduction with City Lit Theatre. Martha Lavey came to see it. And, the conversation with Steppenwolf began. I had just moved to Chicago. I moved here in 1994, but the theater directing thing started happening in '95 because I came here to act. Going to *Wedding Band.* It's Alice Childress, a famous black writer. If you know the TV show *Amos and Andy,* her husband [Alvin Childress] played Amos. That's a little trivia fact. *Wedding Band* was very controversial, even at Steppenwolf. Now, Steppenwolf has several black ensemble members but their whole history had been that they didn't. They didn't do anything with black people, they didn't do anything black. People were actually telling me, "Why do you want to go over there?" And I said, "Well, how else are you going to change something? How else are you going to start something if you don't pursue it?" Plus, I was from out of town. So I wasn't jaded by the history of Chicago theater. Congo Square Theatre Company, which is a company that is still around today, was pretty new then.

Martha and Congo Square were looking for a coproduction. It took us a good while to figure out a play that we could do that had white people and black people, and use their [Steppenwolf's] ensemble and use Congo Square's ensemble. Javon Johnson, who was a member of Congo Square had written a play *Breathe* specifically for this collaboration, but it wasn't ready yet. So we went to the drawing board, and we read about twenty plays. I suggested *Wedding Band*. It's a famous play. It used to be done quite a lot, but now it's not done much. I felt that it fit the whole collaboration thing. It takes place in 1918 and is about an interracial couple. And it's the interracial couple the other way. I say the "other way" because most of the time it's a black guy and a white woman. This time it was a white guy and black woman. And it's a love story. I usually go into every, just about every, play that I do and I find the angle that makes it a love story. Because most plays are about love. Whether they are about two people being in love, the love of family, love of land, love of nature, love of culture. So, for me, that's the starting point: to find the love in the play. And that one particularly, because I think a lot of the youth of today really take interracial society and stuff for granted. I mean, back in 1918, she literally could have been lynched. And he was, if you read the play or saw the play. Every director is different. I tried to pull out a lot of the emotion—I mean take it, find it, and bring it to the stage. We did that. Did you see *August: Osage County* [2007]? Well, the woman who played the matriarch in that, Deanna Dunagan, played the mother in *Wedding Band*. And she could have won all the stuff she's winning now for that. Because she really, she really pulled it out. I felt *Wedding Band* would be good for Steppenwolf to do if they were embarking on a new attitude of diversity. I think that probably was the beginning of them seeing theater as a way of bringing together different people of color and telling story lines that are relevant to today.

Even though it took place in 1918, the play is still relevant. There is still a lot of hatred. There is still a lot of racism when people see interracial couples. Back then there was no such thing as biracial. I'm biracial. I like to educate and entertain at the same time, which is what the play does. It educated a lot of people about the stupidity of racism. The play had a lot of characters. It was very diverse. And I just think that it fit what we were trying to do. It's a good story. It's a really, really good love story. And it got mixed reviews to be honest. Some people weren't ready for it—to be honest—for Steppenwolf to be doing something like that. Congo Square was a very new company then. They had some fine actors. They still do. It opened up a lot of eyes. It helped me with my career. Court Theatre saw productions, a couple of productions of mine. That's a whole other story how I got in there. But, anyway, that's the story behind *Wedding Band* and how it happened.

What are the challenges specific to working on a collaboration project like Wedding Band *compared with a single-company production?*

Whenever you are dealing with two institutions, in which one is a major institution, there will be issues of ego. There will be issues of who is going to take the upper hand, who is in charge, what happens with the money, the tickets, things like that. Unless you have two equal, level companies, it's an issue. Because, the one [smaller] company doesn't want to feel like, "Oh, they are just bringing us in here"—which was kind of the case in *Wedding Band.* There was the thought of "Somebody is try-ing to get something out of this, and maybe they are not really involved in wanting to do something." So those issues came about. Yeah, there are challenges to that. Not every time, but in a lot of cases. Steppenwolf and Goodman are machines. It is different to work in that environment than, for instance, Court, which is a smaller theater. It is more of a family atmosphere. And I think Steppenwolf tries to have that atmosphere with the corporate atmosphere. I felt comfortable at Steppenwolf and Good-man, but a lot of people don't. I just adapt to wherever I am. And Court is such a family-oriented theater. It's like you know everybody, you know the crew, you know the designers. You know the production people. At some of the bigger theaters, you don't know them. It's kind of like com-ing into a corporation. So, there are those challenges.

Is there a difference between Court and Steppenwolf audiences?

When I first got to Court, no, there wasn't. They're about the same. The theater audience at that level is pretty old and pretty white. One of the things at Court that I am trying to do is to bring in more people of color and more young people. I'm big on going into the community and getting—like at the University of Chicago—classes to come. And the casting director is also the education director. And he goes into the schools. And I'm not just talking about the inner city. I am talking about suburbs. Everybody. Get young people excited about theater so once the old people are too old to go, those young people will fill in the void. And I think that's why a lot of theaters are suffering because young people aren't coming to the theater. I mean, who has eighty dollars to see a play? Nobody. Even the people who have it don't really have it, but they want to see it. That's what I am trying to do. I go out and I talk at different places about theater and what we're doing at Court. In the last few years, the audience at Court has changed. I like to say that the plays that I have been doing there are getting a different audience and a new young audience. Like the one they didn't want me to do, *Wait Until Dark*. Everybody was like, "What kind of classic is that?" It was the suspense genre. That's what the kids are into. They're into suspense and blood and cutting and stuff. So we did *Wait Until Dark*. I don't know if you know the play. It's totally black onstage. We did that. Again, they weren't sure how it was going to go over. And I said, "Let's wait and see." The audience was very young and people were coming to see it. Even the parents who saw the original were bringing their kids because they wanted them to experience what they experienced. So that, that was a good thing. The audience has changed. It's gone from about 5 percent people of color to 30. They are the people who live right down the street from Court and didn't even know it was there. They had no interest in going. Yes, I love the classics. You need to know and learn them. But there's a lot of other stuff out there that you need to learn.

How would you describe your process as a director?

Well, it's very organic. I've been in situations where directors come and they want you off book. And they are going to tell you everywhere to go and stand. And, granted, some directors may be in that framework, that's the way they work. It's even taught. I mean, some people teach that way—tell you everything. "You are going to stand here, sit here, say this like this here." And I just, personally, as an actor, didn't like that. I never wanted to be told what my character was about until we discussed it.

I have an interesting Stratford story. My style or technique is very emotional. I don't know if you read the *Time Out* [magazine] issue about three or four years ago. But one of the writers sat in the rehearsal and watched me and then wrote about it. And I didn't know he was going to listen and write. I have this thing, it's called "The Motherfucker Technique." Basically, it's your emotions. That word [motherfucker] is used when you are calling somebody something, or you are saying something about somebody. You want [to] use that kind of emotion mentally but not audibly so that it comes out in the performance. An example: if you are mad at somebody and you say, "What you want me to do, motherfucker?" That's an attitude. So if I say, "What you want me to do?" and I'm feeling it but it's [motherfucker's] not coming out, then it's getting at the emotion that the character needs to have in that moment. And it's funny because he wrote it, and a lawyer friend of mine said I need to copyright it, because other directors are doing that.

Even as a young director, fifteen, sixteen years old, I knew that I couldn't tell everybody what to do. I didn't know everything. It doesn't bother me, when somebody asks me a question, to say, "I don't know. Let's see what happens. Let's keep working at it. What do you think?" Sometimes I'll ask an actor, "What are you feeling here? But don't tell me. I don't need to know it, let me see it. Let me see what you feel." Coming from Michigan, we had Stanislavski, Meisner, and then I studied with William Esper for a bit at Rutgers. You don't need to use just one style. That's what I put into my technique—using all of them. I believe that the major plays are told in between the lines. You're saying what you say but you're feeling what you feel. And that's a whole other story. I worked with William Esper. He recruited me to Rutgers. And, so, I worked with him for a little bit. Then he got his own private thing going. So when I got outside, when I was out of school living in New York, I went back to him. The Rutgers program wasn't what I expected it to be. Avery Brooks was supposed to be there teaching. I don't know if you remember him. He used to be on a TV show, *Spenser: For Hire.* A big black guy, bald headed. He was a detective. But he wasn't there when I got there. Then, some issues came up with my family. So I just left the program and moved to New York.

As a director, what advice would you give to people who are interested in becoming directors?

I think for directors who have had some experience acting, it helps. Not to say that you have to be the greatest actor. You should do it to experience it from the other side. It makes you a more understanding director. That's why you get some actors who will say, "Oh, he's an actor's director." That's very true because you understand. I understand my actors. The other thing I would say is to direct any opportunity you get in the beginning. You know? I directed before I got here [Chicago], in Buffalo. This and that. But when I got here I understood that I had to start over. So I was doing little things, Chicago Dramatist readings, new companies that want to do a reading. Plays that friends had written. Things like that. I did get to a point where I was asked to direct a show here at a theater. And I said, well, how much do you pay your actors? And they said, well, we don't pay them anything. And I said, well, I can't direct them. I can't direct a show where nobody is getting paid. Not even a stipend, gas money, or whatever. In college, maybe, but not out here. Because I didn't want that pressure on the actor to be hustling. Give them something to make them feel valued. If they are getting a stipend, fifty dollars, a hundred dollars, or whatever, for the entire run or whatever, it just makes it a better environment to work in. So I didn't do that. Just take any little job you can. Intern, assist.

My last assistant was assisting to break in. And she met people. For me, it's not like, "Could you get me some coffee?" and this and that. She had worked at the Goodman with a director who had her doing that. You know, "Go get me copies, get me coffee," this and that. So the first thing she said to me: "Can I get you some coffee?" I said, "No, I'll get my own coffee. I don't drink coffee, but I'll get it if I need it. No, I need you to sit here and help me. We're doing this thing here." And she appreciated that. And from then on, we had a really good relationship. If I was the type to have her go get coffee, she would have done that and then took in and learned what she could learn in that way. But now she learned even more because she was in on the conversations. I would ask her, "What do you think?" And she was like, "Me?" "Yeah. Everybody has an opinion." It can be a group think that helps the product. That's just how I am. Everybody is not like that. Everybody is different.

What advice would you give an actor starting out today?

Take every opportunity that you have. Chicago Dramatists is a good place because you can go do readings and you meet directors. When I first got here I did the Bailiwick's Director Festival. That was good, getting a project in that and getting your name out there. I would write letters. As an actor you want to write, send e-mails to people and invite them to see your work. Directors too. If you send out a hundred invites and two people come, that's good. It establishes you, makes you recognizable. If you keep doing the work and get the word out there that it's happening, eventually good things happen.

What are your thoughts on the appeal or draw of Broadway?

I love New York, and I love working there. It's just a fun place to be. Eventually, you got to go to New York. I know actors who stay here and do it all here. But you're going to want to go to New York, Broadway and all that. That's what we're striving for. Once you get there, it's a rude awakening. But you do want to get there. [*Laughing*] I was in my dressing room on Broadway, there were mice there. I was like, "Wow, OK, this is Broadway." It is because it's so old. Some of those theaters are just ancient. But it's a beautiful thing. It's like, "Wow, I made it." My parents, my mother actually, died before I made it, but I bought her a ticket because she was still alive to me. I bought her a ticket and I left that seat empty so I saw it. It was very emotional. Broadway. It's a big thing, but it's just another part of what we do. Just keep your eye on the prize, which is the work that you're doing at the time you're doing it. On my résumé, I have eta [Creative Arts], which is a community theater on the South Side. Now, I have had a bit of success, but I went back to eta to do something. People were like, "Why are you going back there?" Because, we are doing the same thing there as we do anywhere else.

KATHY A. PERKINS

Kathy A. Perkins, a professional lighting designer, is a professor in the Department of Dramatic Art at the University of North Carolina–Chapel Hill. Previously, she taught at Smith College and the University of Illinois at Urbana-Champaign. Her extensive Chicago-area design credits include Goodman Theatre, Steppenwolf Theatre Company, eta Creative Arts, Congo Square Theatre, and Court Theatre. She is the editor of six play anthologies concerning black women theater artists.

In a June 2011 interview, Kathy A. Perkins recalls her early experiences as a lighting designer, her collaborations with director Ron O. J. Parson, working in the Chicago theater scene, and the need for greater diversity in professional theater.

How did you become involved in theater?

I grew up in Mobile, Alabama, born in 1954, the year of *Brown v. Board of Education*. I was always involved in music—playing piano, choir, theater—as far back as I can remember. When I got to junior high school and high school, I became more involved in theater. This was during the civil rights era with some of the civil rights groups in my community. We did theater as a way of educating people. For me, theater has always been about the arts educating people. When I decided to go to college, I knew I wanted to perform because that's what I had been doing. And I went to Howard University for my undergraduate degree thinking that I wanted to be an actress. This was 1972. My best friend, who was a sophomore at the time, was in communications and pursuing lighting design, and I'll never forget, we were backstage, I was helping him do something with lighting, and he said, "What are you going to do with a degree in acting as a black woman with so few roles for you?" and I had never really thought about it. And he said, "Why don't you go into technical theater, like lighting? He said, "I think you'd be good in it." At that time in Washington D.C., there were so many shows going on—this was before they had production firms and production companies. If an entertainer needed a lighting person, they would just call a lighting person, not a lighting company. And he said, "There's just so much work out here." And so, at the end of my freshman year, I decided, "OK, I'll switch over to lighting design," and it was the best decision I ever made. As an undergrad, I worked on campus and off campus. We had a big roadhouse on campus, and I met people like Stevie Wonder, Earth Wind and Fire, Chaka Khan, Patti LaBelle. You name it. All of these people were coming through D.C. By the time I finished Howard, I had a résumé with all of these incredible people that I had worked with. I went on to graduate school. My sister convinced me—my sister was ahead of me in college—to go to grad school. There were so many times that I was ready to just drop out of school because a group would come through and say, "Hey you're great, we're gonna take you on the road with us and maybe a world tour . . ." My sister said, "Those shows will always be there; just go to grad school." And I did. I went to Michigan and got my MFA, and that's where I met Ron Parson. He was an undergrad, an older undergrad. That was quite an experience coming from Howard to Michigan. That was a good experience. Before I went to Michigan, I knew that I would be lacking some things like theory because we didn't really focus on theory in terms of design. At Howard, you did it. When I got to Michigan, I knew that I was farther ahead of my classmates in terms of the practical aspect and the business aspect. When I was in D.C., my mentor who ran the roadhouse was the president of the IATSE [International Alliance of Theatre Stage Employees] union in D.C. It was still segregated then but I learned a lot about the business from him. By the time I got to grad school, I was way ahead of my classmates, but I lacked certain things like drafting, or whatever.

You mentioned that there weren't opportunities for an actress, for a black actress, when you were in college.

In college, but not professionally. This was around 1972. There were certain roles for black women. If you were light skinned, you played the Halle Berry roles. If you were dark skinned, you played the prostitute or the mammy. If you were brown skinned, you played the prostitute. So, there were not a lot of substantial roles for black women once they left college. Yes, black theater was taking off. It was still part of the Black Theater Movement—so there were a lot of opportunities there. But it wasn't really until *for colored girls* came along that there were roles. Just about all of my classmates who were actresses, they all worked on *for colored girls*, like a gazillion road companies of *for colored girls*. And then all of the big musicals came along: *The Wiz* and *Bubbling Brown Sugar*. So, if you were in musical theater . . . I couldn't dance, I couldn't sing. I wouldn't have worked anyway.

How does race operate, if at all . . .

If at all?

. . . as a designer in terms of your opportunities to work professionally within the theater?

It makes a big difference. It's a very racist business. And it hasn't changed. This is 2011. I'm still working in theaters and hearing, "Oh, you're the first black person we've ever had design here." What was really interesting, while I was developing my career, was that I would send my résumé to places. "Kathy Perkins." People see that as a white name 'cause I don't have a typical—what people would think would be a typical—Negro name. I would send résumés to people and they'd say, "Oh yeah, come on in," and "You look good," and blah, blah, blah. I'd walk in and it's like, "Oh . . . OK." Then all of the sudden, I didn't have the job. I had so many experiences like that.

And why was that? What was the assumption?

This is not something black people do. And not only black people . . . women. There are fewer women designing big shows. There was a big article on that on Broadway. There are very few women designers on Broadway, be it lighting, scenery, or anything. It's still a very white, male-dominated field, even though most of the major designers in lighting were women. So, yeah, race still plays into it. I'm not going to complain much because I probably worked more than any black lighting designer, female lighting designer, not that there's a million of us out here. In February, I get called for about a thousand . . .

I can believe that.

I will usually tell people, "Yes, OK, that's fine. I enjoy doing black theater, but think about another show during the season. I can do something else." I always have to remind people of that. It's very difficult. A lot of people have left the business because they can't work. So, yes, race plays into it a lot.

Was there ever a moment when you thought about leaving the business and doing something else?

No. No. No. I knew that this was something I was always passionate about. I never wanted to leave the business because I could always do so many different things. After I left Michigan, I got my first show working with a dance company in New York, Dianne McIntyre, *Sounds in Motion.* I worked with Dianne in New York for like six months. I've always been very fortunate; things just come up. Something comes up. It's always a matter of being in the right place at the right time. I was with her for six months. We were on the road. I was a lighting designer, stage manager, sound person, you name it. But it was a great experience, and it was a job that I knew I could do because of my senior year at Howard. My senior year, I had a chance to work with Roberta Flack. I know I'm going way back. I had the chance to work with Roberta Flack for a whole week in D.C., and just before the summer started, the end of my senior year, I get this call out of the blue: "Hi, this is Jim Lucas." And I said, "Oh yeah, I remember you." He said, "Yeah, I'm Roberta's production manager. We are ready to take a tour, a world tour, but every summer I do this job with the Smithsonian. It's called the Folk Life Festival. It's a wonderful festival. What they do is bring in different groups from all over the world, and they perform at the mall in D.C." This year was going to be extremely special because it was 1976; it was the bicentennial of the U.S. And he said, "This year it's going to be very special because they're bringing in every country to celebrate the U.S. birthday." And he said, "I've been assigned to work with the country Jamaica." And he said, "We're going to be on the mall for three weeks, and we're going to tour for a month all around the country." And then he says, "I can't do it. I really enjoy the way you work, how you work with people, you're very personable." And he said that they needed someone who can do lighting and can do stage management and know sound. And he said, "I'd like to recommend you to do the job. Would you take it?" And I said, "Of course, I'll take it." It was great. It was a really good experience. It was [also] very, very stressful, because I was dealing with a lot of money. This was before ATM machines, and . . . cell phones and whatever. It was like, "You've got to keep at least $800 on you at all times in case something happens, someone's guitar breaks or whatever. You got to be able to just jump in a cab and go and do this." It taught me. When I worked for the dance company, that was a piece of cake after what I had gone through that summer. I was with Dianne for five or six months, because I finished in August, my program at Michigan. In August, I worked with her from August through December. What happened in December? She lost her grant, and she felt bad: "I don't have money to keep you." But as fate would have it, another job came up out of the blue. It's like, "Oh, they're taking a production of *Raisin* to Europe, and they're going to be based in Switzerland, and they're taking another production . . ."

The musical or the play?

The musical. They were going to produce a production over there, but they were using some of the original cast members from the first *Raisin,* some of the understudies, not the stars. And then, they were taking another production called *Sound of Soul* by Owen Dodson. I went as a designer for that show and as the assistant designer for *Raisin.* That was six months overseas, just a wonderful experience. When I came back, this was '79; I came back that April, I worked in New York. I had the chance to work with Woodie King and then, all of a sudden, another job came up out of the blue. Smith College had a position open for a lighting person, and the chair of the department contacted me. She says, "I've been following your career and I remember when you were an [exchange] student here, and I thought you were really great, you had a lot of potential. Would you apply for the job?" So, I said sure, why not. Not that I was dying to teach, but I applied and I got the job. I was there for five years and then I left and went to Los Angeles because another job came up out of the blue. They had just opened up the Los Angeles Theater Center (LATC). I went there to be a resident designer. The LATC had four theaters and their goal, Bill Bushnell['s goal], was to have an international theater. We did plays from all over the world. It was theater, it was dance, it was performance art. I had never done performance art before. Music concerts. It was just a great experience. I was with them for two years. I [freelanced] with the Japanese American Theatre housed in the Japanese American Center.

Then, I became interested in museum lighting. I volunteered at the California Afro American Museum because I wanted to learn about lighting exhibitions. While I was there, I worked with the visual artist, Linzetta Lefalle Collins, I was working with her. I told her that I did research, and I was doing research on black people. She says, "Oh, well we have a new history curator and he's looking for someone with some research experience, and would you be interested in talking to him?" For four years, I worked as a curatorial assistant with Lonnie Bunch. He also got me projects for PBS and other local stations as a researcher. So, when you asked, did I ever want to leave lighting, the answer is no because I could do a lot of things. And then, I got a call to come to Illinois. It was like, "We're looking for a lighting person." That's my career path in a nutshell.

When you joined the Illinois faculty twenty-two years ago, in 1989, did you live in the Urbana–Champaign area or Chicago?

No, I've always lived right there in Champaign. There was a period when I worked a lot in Chicago, but my design work takes me everywhere. Not just in the U.S. I've done a lot of projects in South Africa. So, it's wherever. I was here when—I'm sure, O. J. [Ron Parson] talked to you about Onyx—when Onyx was going. It felt like I was living here.

What do you remember as being your first production in Chicago?

I was thinking about that on the way, saying, "I know he's going to ask me that." I'm trying to think if it was at Victory Gardens. It may have been at Victory Gardens. I can't remember if it was the Goodman or Victory Gardens. It may have been Victory Gardens with Sandy Shinner. And it was a nonblack show, which I'm seldom offered, which is kind of interesting. That was one of my earlier shows, and then I did something at the Goodman. And then I worked with Ina Marlowe at the Organic Theater. And these weren't black shows either. So, early in Chicago, I was doing a range of things that weren't necessarily black shows. When Ron got together Onyx, I was really excited about that. I brought my students with me. It was like, "We're going to Chicago." And a lot of students came. Ron is responsible for a lot of my students moving on with their careers, technically. Well, not only technical but acting students too.

What was Onyx like?

It was Ron's vision. Well, not just Ron, Ron and Alfred Wilson. I can't remember whose idea, but it was the two of them; it was their vision. They wanted a theater. They wanted a different type of black theater. I think the focus was on history or classics. It was either history or classics. He wanted theater with heart, which it was. And he had no money but everybody was committed, and we did quality productions. You don't have to have a lot of money to do good theater. Talk about people doing it on a shoestring budget. We had no budget for the most part. I would come in. I would do the lights, and I would bring my students with me, and we would borrow gels and stuff from Illinois, and we would just get the show done. Lydia Diamond came through Onyx. A lot of young kids . . . there were so many. The idea was to try to develop talent, black talent. My goal was to try and develop . . . not just black talent but people of color. My focus has always been on women of color. There was a young woman Christine Pascual—she's worked all over Chicago now—came through Onyx. She was a student of mine and she is a costume designer.

There was another young lady, Lori Fong, who was a set designer. She did a lot of stuff through Onyx. I would bring students, regardless of color. We did a lot of work there. And again, it was quality work. It was very professional. We did amazing things with twenty-five lights. And he had good actors. Onyx was the type of theater where people were knocking down the doors to come and work with us, because the work was so good. We were a ninety-seat house. It was a small house. The stage was about the size of this room [an office]. I just remember this one show we did called *East Texas Hot Links*. I'm sure Ron talked about that.

He did. He said that it was the first show.

That was our first show, and it was the best show and we did it again. People just packed in to see that one show. Another show that we did was one of my favorites: Pearl Cleage's piece *Flyin' West*. And Pearl's a friend of mine, and she was very gracious because that year, everybody wanted to do *Flyin' West,* and I think the Goodman had competed for it, and she gave it to Onyx. We were like, "What?" She let us do the show, and we did that show forever, and then we took it to Theater on the Lake. What they do is pick the best shows of Chicago . . .

. . . from the year, and remount them.

Yes, so we remounted it there. Those were the two that really stand out, *East Texas* and *Flyin' West.* Ron would direct several of the shows. That's when I spent a lot of time in Chicago. And then when Congo Square took off in the early years, I would work with them a lot. Those are University of Illinois students, not all of them. They're U of I and Howard students. Reggie Nelson had gone to Howard and ended up coming to Illinois. Derrick Sanders went to Howard . . . They had this vision of theater, of a black theater in Chicago. So, yes, I worked with them early on. I'm like a consultant to them. So, those two groups have kept me in and out of Chicago quite a bit.

What is it about those two groups or about the need in Chicago in that moment that would allow these two start-up theater companies to thrive out of the gate?

Quality. What stood out about these two companies? I think what made Congo Square and Onyx so unique was, not only did we have superb acting, but the technical aspect was good. And I think that's unfortunately what's missing with a lot of black theater companies. They put so much focus on the acting that they don't think about the scenery, the costumes, and lighting. All of that makes for a good show. That was one.

Why do you think that they were so attentive to the technical aspects?

Because I was there. [*Laughing*] No, I'm not being facetious . . . that's one of the reasons why Ron had me come. I'm working with eta Creative Arts. That's been one of the missing links for a lot of the black theaters. They just don't . . . they just sort of . . . not ignore, but they don't put as much emphasis on the technical aspect as they do the acting. Financial resources have also been a factor.

Are there differences among eta Creative Arts, Onyx, and Congo Square audiences?

Yes. Well, Onyx was . . . I forget which part of town it was in. It was based on the neighborhood. Like, the people that go to eta are a lot of people from the South Side. Congo Square . . . it's sort of a mixed audience. It's really hard to say, but I think it's people more in that particular area. But then, a lot of other theater artists will come. I see that more at Congo Square and Onyx than I did at eta. And Ron also has a following in Chicago. He has quite a diverse audience that will come. Everybody used to come and see the Onyx shows. And there was also a period where everybody wanted to coproduce with him. He probably told you that. From the Goodman to . . . we did a Steppenwolf show, which I'm sure he talked about it.

Wedding Band.

Yes. Everybody said, "Oh, we want to coproduce with you." But then what happened [to Onyx]? Money. The rent went up at the place. I think it had to do with the rent, we just couldn't afford it. And you can't make a fortune off of ninety-nine seats. That was unfortunate. Onyx was around for four years. We did wonderful theater. Like I said, no one got paid and people were very passionate about what they did. They helped promote a lot of young artists' careers behind the scenes. We did some great work. And Ron is really good to work with. He's so passionate, and that passion is sort of contagious. He's so passionate about the work, and he's going to get everybody all psyched up to do the shows. I enjoyed working with him. We've known each other since Michigan, since about 1976; that's a long time.

And how was he at Michigan?

The same. The same. He had lots of blood in his shows. He can always find a reason to have blood in his shows. No, he was great. I worked with him. I think one of his first productions was *The Toilet*. Did he ever talk about it?

No.

Do you know *The Toilet*? He said, "This is a realistic production of *The Toilet*. We're supposed to be in a men's bathroom, and we're supposed to smell the urine." I was like, "Oh my gosh." It was quite an experience. At that time, David Alan Grier was a student with us and a guy named Reginald Cathey, so it was a really good group of actors. I've always enjoyed working with Ron.

And you were in the graduate program and they were undergraduates?

Yes. David Alan Grier was an undergraduate. Yes, because he went and got his degree from Yale, right? So, yes. They needed a lighting designer, and I was the only black person around. I said, "Sure, OK, whatever." And it was great working with him.

Outside of Onyx, where else have you worked in Chicago?

In Chicago . . . I've done shows at the Goodman. Like I said, I worked there a couple of times. Victory Gardens. I just finished a show there called the *Gospel According to James* (2011) [by Charles Smith, directed by

Chuck Smith]. Steppenwolf. Court Theatre. Organic eta, I've developed a relationship with eta and am working with them. Congo Square. That's about it. Basically, those theaters.

How is working at a place like the Goodman or Steppenwolf different than working at one of the smaller theaters?

They have great resources and all the lights I need, so that's not an issue. I don't have to worry about budget. I don't have to run my own board. It's resources. That's the difference. A lot of times people think that because you have more resources, the play is better. Like I said, we did incredible shows at Onyx with no money. The shows had so much heart and so much passion. You saw it onstage. You could see the people weren't method acting. The thing at the Goodman and the Steppenwolf, you had the resources. That's the big thing.

It has been interesting, to me, to watch those larger houses, those Tony Award–winning regional houses making a push to actually reach black audiences.

Well, they don't have a choice. Their audiences are dying out. They're not stupid. The demographics are changing, so they have to do that. They don't have a choice. The subscriptions are dwindling, the numbers are dwindling, and people are trying to figure out [how to survive]. Stop and think about it. When you look at the Court Theatre . . . I don't know if Ron told you the story about the Court Theatre. They had never done a black show before *Fences*, although they had done an African play years ago. They had never done a black play, and when it was produced, it was done in the shortest slot of the season. I think they said they were expecting maybe 30 percent, maybe 40 percent capacity. It sold out. I mean, it packed the house. I mean, there were people literally sitting in the aisles. It wasn't just black people coming to the theater. It was people of all races and backgrounds. People said this is wonderful, why haven't you been doing this. The next year, they did two black shows. I think they did *Raisin* and then they did *Flyin' West*. I didn't see Raisin. They're doing *Porgy and Bess* this year. So, now they do two black shows a year, and those are their big sellers. What these theaters are doing . . . they understand that there is an audience. When a white theater wants to sell a lot of tickets, what do they do? They do *Crowns*. Arena Stage has done *Crowns* about three times.

That play, Crowns *by Regina Taylor, was the most produced play by regional theaters a few years ago.*

It still brings in houses. It brings busloads of churches, people in. They realize that there's an audience. It's like, "Oh yeah, black people come to the theater." It's not just black people, you know, white people want to come hear black church music or whatever. It's really interesting. I was in London last week, and I was talking to one of the artistic directors of the black theater there. She was saying the same thing is happening. She says now all of a sudden the major theaters see that there's a market in doing plays by black artists. Right now, there's a huge Nigerian community in London, so everybody's like, "Oh, let's do Nigerian plays." They're doing festivals and stuff. There's a market. They're doing it because there's a market. Years ago, they had the Lila Wallace [Lila Wallace–Reader's Digest Fund] money. It was like "[If you] do plays, diversity plays, you get funded." And some of the theaters are really committed to them. There's some you can tell that aren't. It's like as the money runs out, that's it. I think most of the theaters realize that the demographics are changing. They have to do something if they're going to fill seats.

What are some of the theaters that are rightly committed to reaching diverse audiences?

I really think that the Goodman is. I always thought Victory Garden was. Dennis Zacek. I've always liked him. I think he's committed. I think the theaters are committed when it comes to certain things involving diversity. Yes, they will do certain black playwrights. My big concern with a lot of these theaters, and because a lot of my focus is on black women, is that they don't bring in black women directors. That's the problem that I have with a lot of these theaters. I can't remember the last time Goodman had a black female director. I mean, I'm not talking about Regina Taylor, aside from Regina. This is what black women are lamenting. We just aren't working. We just don't work. And not that they have to direct a play by a black women, but they're just not directing anything. Sandra Richards and I wrote an article about this for . . .

In Theatre Journal [*2010*]. *Yes, with alternating voices.*

She had to tell me to tone it down. I was like, "What are you worried about?" I'm on the production end and I see this. It's becoming, it's a real issue. I will hear playwrights talk about this. It's like, "Well I had to do this show, but I got to have this white female director." That's the trend now. If it's a black woman writer or even if it's a black man, if you don't get a white director, the show ain't won't get produced. Have you read the book titled, *Outrageous* . . . ?

Fortune. *Todd London, right?*

Yes. He talks about that. If you're not associated with a white person, more than likely your show's not going to get done. And that's a real issue. And I've heard—I'm not going to mention any names because this is taped—I had a very prominent playwright sit in my kitchen and say this. She was getting ready to have a play produced, and she said, "The first thing my agent said was, 'Do not take this to a black theater. Make sure you put this in the hands of a white theater and a white director or a black male director that the white establishment trusts.'" This is what's happening. So this means there are fewer and fewer black women directors out there working at the larger theaters. I don't know of any black women directors who've been at Steppenwolf. Years ago, there was Shirley [Jo] Finney. She was at the Goodman. She used to do Regina Taylor's work years ago. One of the few prominent black female directors. Now, I think she's directing in Africa. She's doing something over there. But they just aren't working. How many black women are the head of any major theaters? I think there's this fear of black women maybe being too demanding. Well, I guess when black women are assertive or demanding, we're bitches, but if it's a white man who's doing it, oh he's just being assertive or whatever. It's a real dilemma. You just aren't seeing black women in those roles—artistic directors, directors—in any of the major theaters being brought in. To me, that's real problematic.

So what advice would you tell a female college student who's interested in pursuing a career in the theater?

As a director?

Interested in becoming an actress.

Well, I don't have any advice for an actress.

When you meet college students in a theater department—when they first walk through the door in their first year—more often than not they are thinking about becoming actors.

If they ask my personal view, I would just say there are too many actors. I mean, of course, they may be the next Angela Bassett or Denzel Washington. I will never forget. I know Lydia [Diamond]'s mother. I remember years ago she said, "I want you to meet my daughter. She's in high school and she wants to go into theater. Is that a good idea?" I said, "If that's what she's passionate about, but tell her she better learn how to do something else." I always tell actors, "If you're going to go into the acting field, make sure you know how to hang some lights, run sound, or make sure you have something else to back it up, because everybody wants to act."

Would you steer that person toward directing as a career path?

As a career path, I don't know. I think if people are very passionate about something, they're going to do it anyway. They're not going to give up. They're going to find a way to work. I was passionate about lighting. But I was also told by my mentor at Howard and even my professors, "You're going into a field that's very white male–dominated. You're going to catch a lot of BS, flack and you have to . . . if you're prepared to deal with this, then go ahead." I said this was something I really want to do; I'll deal with it. And so, I've always gone in with that mentality. I mean, I've been in situations where people have tried to humiliate me. I will never forget—which is why I am not impressed with working on Broadway—the first time I assisted on a Broadway show. I went in because I had to start focusing lighting for the show. It was Shirley Prendergast, who I was assisting. I walked in. The crew, IATSE, it's a brotherhood, they stick up for each other. They don't care who you are. They're going to stick up for each other. I walked in, and one guy looked at me and said, "I'm not working with her," and he left. What that meant was I couldn't focus my show because the law requires that if I have a ladder onstage, there has to be four people, one person on each end of the ladder and somebody going up top. So, this guy left. No one said anything. They just sort of laughed. It's like, "We need to wait to call somebody else to come in." So, they had to call some guy who was coming all the way from Long Island. So, I wasted like an hour and a half, and I just played it cool. I haven't had a lot of situations like that, but I have been in situations where I walk in and it's like, "I'm supposed to work with you?" Not a lot, but now it's sort of subtle. Or else, I will go into places and people just are delighted to see, "Wow this is something different; let's see if she knows what she's doing." It's a tough business, and I always try to take my students with me. A lot of times people, the guys, it's usually guys, they will test you to see if you know what you're doing or how much BS can you take. I've always seen it as a challenge. I'm always trying to encourage, again, my big thing is encouraging minorities to go into this field. When I was talking to the artistic director in London, we were saying the same thing. She says, "I don't know why young black kids don't go into this field," and I think a lot of it has to do with exposure. It's that they don't know it exists, so . . . I never knew about it until I got to Howard. I did, but I didn't know you could make a career in this, you could make a living doing this, until I started doing it. I always tell people that the lighting designer . . . I know this sounds awful. I don't want to say I'm the most important designer onstage, but I can make or break a whole show. I determine what you see, how you see it, when you see it, what duration. I can destroy a costume. I can destroy your scenery. I have to tie that whole production together. Everybody's role is important, but I'm crucial because I have to work closely with everybody, the costume people. I'm working with a design that's not tangible. When I sit down and talk to Ron, I can talk to him about lighting, but he can't see it. So, that's the thing, directors really have to trust their lighting person to know, "OK, you understand exactly what I want," but I have to be in touch with the costume person early on, the set designer, particularly the set designer. I always like to come in at the beginning before there's a set even created. Some directors feel like we have to deal with the set first, and lights will come last. Let's do the sets and the costumes and then lights will come on. I like to work with the set designer because, a lot of times, I will have ideas about how the lighting could work better with the set. I like to come in [from the] ground up. I need to know hair colors. Lighting affects everything. Am I working with a set of all pale white males with bald heads, or is it a mixed race cast, because that determines what colors I put on them. I create the mood. Again, I have to tie this whole show together, which is really important.

In terms of Chicago designers and directors, who do you believe are the active contributors to the theater scene?

What's really unfortunate is that there are very few black designers in Chicago. I was really shocked when I came here. There are a couple in New York, which is to be expected. There are a few in L.A. Directors, there's Ron O. J. Parson, who I work with a lot. He's great. There's Chuck Smith. There's Ilysa Davis. She's at Chicago Dramatist. There's Tiffany Trent. She designs smaller scale shows, but I think she's good right now. She runs the program at Trinity Church, the one that [Barack] Obama was going to. They have a whole drama program there. Tiffany's good. McKinley Johnson. He's a director. He's also a playwright. Young guy. He's also a costume designer. I don't know who's at Jackie Taylor's place, but these are the ones that I've encountered. Then you've got the group at Congo Square, there's Derrick Sanders, there's Aaron Todd Douglas, and Daniel Beaty. Congo Square's cultivating a whole new group of directors. And I don't know who's at MPAACT, the directors there. There's not enough black directors in Chicago. eta, there's Kemati Porter. She works over there, directs a lot of their shows. Cheryl Lynn Bruce, people know her as an actor, but she's also a director. I'll probably think of some more later, but those are the ones that stand out and people that I've worked with. But we need more designers and production managers. I don't know who the black production managers are in town other than the ones at eta.

DERRICK SANDERS

Derrick Sanders is the founding artistic director of Congo Square Theatre. Widely considered to be one of the foremost interpreters of August Wilson's works, he has directed Chicago-area productions at Congo Square, Steppenwolf, and Chicago Children's Theatre.

In this interview, conducted in November 2009, Derrick Sanders talks about the creation of Congo Square, shares his perceptions on what it takes not only to build a theater company but also to become a successful artist, and reflects on the special influence that playwright August Wilson had on his life and career.

As a graduate student, you attended a lecture by August Wilson. Afterwards, you approached him and asked him a question. How did his response impact your career?

I went to South Africa. I should move back [start earlier]. How did I get to that moment? I went to Howard University, majored in acting. In 1996, I was graduating. August wrote "The Ground on Which I Stand," and it caused a big ruckus between him and all the legit regional theaters. There were town hall meetings with him and [Robert Brustein]. It caused this big upheaval [because] August said we don't necessarily need to play the butlers or to cross-culturally cast. We don't necessarily need that. We need you to develop our playwrights. We need you to develop our theaters. He felt that the majority of American theater was a white table, an old white male table. In order to get at what it truly means to be

American and to express all the ideas of America, the only way to do that is to support theaters of color. At the time, I was coming out of school, and I was going to grad school, and I was trying to figure out exactly what I wanted my career to look like, and this speech spoke to my soul, and I decided then that I knew enough talented people to create my own theater. Like Steppenwolf, like Lookingglass [Theatre Company], like a lot of ensemble theaters start. And I started to ponder how do I create that. Exactly how do I make that happen? And I read his speech and I was inspired by him. I started to really get to know his work.

I went to grad school at the University of Pittsburgh. During my time at the University of Pittsburgh, I started a small theater company. It was an educational thing. We did one-act plays and we would tour them around the schools to [make] some money as grad students. We got an opportunity to go to South Africa, and I wrote a research grant to go out there. It was an Arts and Science research grant. We got to travel to South Africa and be a part of the Grahamstown Theater Festival. Javon Johnson, who wrote the plays, ended up getting an invitation to go to the O'Neill [Eugene O'Neill Theater Center]. We not only had to revamp our whole casting and what we were going to do with the shows, but also we [had to take] some different people with us to the Grahamstown Theater Festival.

It was an amazing experience going to South Africa. When I got there, I opened up this big program book, and I found out that August was speaking there. I was like, "This is fantastic. I'm going to get a chance to meet him. I'm going to go and I'm going to sit up front." To my surprise, when I got there, there were maybe twenty people. I sat right up front and was in his face. Afterwards, people were around taking pictures, talking to him and such. I took that opportunity and I said, "Hey, I would love to talk to you about some of the ideas that I have about creating a theater company." He said, "Fine. Let's do it now. You want to grab some coffee?" We went downstairs and I told him about my ideas in theater, and I told him what I wanted to build and how his speech really inspired me. And at the end of the conversation, it may have been a two-and-a-half-hour conversation, he said, "Well, that sounds like a great idea, Derrick. If you're going to do something, let me know and I'll support it. I think it's a great idea." As far as I was concerned, I was done. August Wilson said I had a great idea. Nobody else can stop me.

I went away and I talked to my partner, Reginald Nelson, who started the company with me, and I told him, "August says this is a great idea. I think we should look into this. How can we do it?" I started researching cities. New York. I looked at D.C. I looked at Atlanta and I looked at Dallas. They all had large African American populations. Chicago was the only place that had, at the time, five African American theater companies with year-round seasons. I was like, "Well, if we go to Chicago, all we gotta do is be the best." So, I decided let's move to Chicago and start the company.

We were going for a specific niche. Our niche was . . . I often say that my generation represents the first generation outside of Jim Crow, the first generation that had the benefit of going with white, black, Hispanic, Asian. My friends reflected that. It was more about the way in which to tell a story and the quality of the work. A lot of theaters at the time grew up, came out of the Black Power movement and they were black theater for black sake for black people. What I was trying to do was establish a national theater for artists of color ultimately, meaning from Asian and Hispanic and [every group] about how we cross-pollinate and what we share that's similar. What do we share that is alike? Starting with the work that I knew the best and branching out to bigger things as the company grew and became an institution. I wanted to do that through an ensemble theater like the Negro Ensemble in New York. A lot of great actors came through there: Denzel [Washington], Samuel L. [Jackson], Phylicia Rashad, Debbie Allen, all these great actors. Samuel L. Jackson, his wife [LaTanya Richardson], came out of the Negro Ensemble. If there was a Negro Ensemble still around, I probably would have went there. But there was nothing like that around—actor-based that benefited from and used a powerful work to tell of the African diaspora.

The idea of an ensemble was built on that. We ended up getting some people, friends from our grad schools, University of Pittsburgh and the University of Illinois, and we asked them to join once we had gotten our 501c3 and stuff like that. When I told August that I was going to start in Chicago, one of the first things he said, "Well, you going to Chicago? Talk to Chuck Smith. Chuck is a friend of mine." So, I went to Chicago and I said, "Chuck, I would love to meet with you." I met with Chuck and I said, "Chuck, August told me to come and talk to you. I'm starting this new theater company. It's going to be an ensemble . . . We're trying to pick our season and I'm trying to figure out . . . what should I do?" And he said—the best advice Chuck ever gave me—"New company, new play, new space, bad idea." I knew August was coming into town to do *King Hedley* at the Goodman. Around the same time, we wanted to start our season in November of 2000. It may have been '99. Anyway, he was doing *King Hedley* at the Goodman. I said, "Well, why don't we do August Wilson. Nobody in the city does that kind of work. They don't know us, but they know August. They might not know who we are, but they know Chicago Dramatists." We chose Chicago Dramatists [as the place to stage the play]. And all I gotta do is convince August to come. I gotta get August to come there. We decided to do *Piano Lesson,* as it best reflected our ensemble at the time, and it was something I felt like we could knock out of the park. We got an opportunity on the Goodman's dollar to get August to come and see our production. He came to the very last performance and he was wowed. He was amazed at the work that we had done, and he, from then on, became one of our strongest advocates and one of my deepest mentors and friends. He enjoyed the work.

Ron O. J. [Parson] directed the first production. We got him to direct. We had a thesis production in our master's program. They were going to do *Cat on a Hot Tin Roof,* but they didn't know how to divide us because we had about four or five black people in the class. They didn't know what they were going to do with the casting. So I told them, "Hey, why don't you all do *Cat on a Hot Tin Roof.* Let us do a play in the studio for our thesis. Let us pick the play and let us pick the director." So, they were like, "Oh, great, that solves our problem. Derrick and Javon, you all go do that." I knew I was moving to Chicago, so I came up here and Ron at the time had Onyx Theatre. He was doing a show at the Goodman, *Let Me Live,* and he was also doing a show at the Steppenwolf with City Lit, and it was at the Steppenwolf Studio. I asked Ron to direct. I wanted somebody to know us in Chicago. So, I was like, "Come here, direct, come talk to my people. They'll hook you up." Ron directed us in *Before It Hits Home* by Cheryl West. After that, I went to Philly for a summer to work at Freedom Theatre in their education program. After that, I packed up my stuff and moved to Chicago and started it from here. Usually people in ensemble theaters start a show and then say, "Oh, let's incorporate." But we didn't want to do it that way. We got our logo together. We got our mission statement together. We got our 501c3. We had our board together, and we took a year to get all that stuff together. And then we came out and it looked like we had been here for five years.

It sounds like you had people who were willing to welcome you into the city.

Yes. It was partly strategic and partly just the hustle of it. Strategic in that some people who were friends from the University of Illinois had been here already and working in the system. The connections that we got were from people who were already in the system. I became kind of a known entity just because of the fact that they had already worked with certain people in our ensemble and . . . August opened some doors for me and Chuck opened some doors for me. That made it relatively easy. I guess it was easier than coming up here by myself and not knowing anybody. I had some "ins." And my "ins" were more national "ins" than they were local "ins," but the ensemble that we created had some "ins" in the city that made us relatively known quickly.

How has your ensemble changed over the years?

Well, we've grown. I think we're at fifteen now, sixteen . . . sixteen now. As we get older, the dynamic has to change. The time that people have to put in at the start of their careers is totally different ten years later. Ten years later, [you are] a totally different actor, totally different professional. In my career, I've made some hard choices. I had to stay here and do this stuff and turn certain things down. Some sacrifices are just simply made for the bigger idea of the institution. The bigger idea of the company.

Looking forward, how does Derrick Sanders, the director, exist alongside Derrick Sanders, the artistic director?

Wow . . . you speak to the heart of where I am. I think it's important first and foremost that I'm an artist. And as the artistic director, it is important as an artist that I [remain] vital as a component of the arts nationally and locally. What that sometimes means is I have to, sometimes, pick when I'm going to take the next step in my career. That also reflects back on the company. The work that I do in the company. And it's a difficult balance. It's a difficult balance, institution building. I know some artistic directors who stay there [as artistic directors] pretty much forever and pigeonhole the company in some ways. It is their baby, and they don't want to grow above them. They want to keep it because this is the only thing they have. I've never wanted to do that to Congo Square. I've always wanted it to be a home for a multitude of artists and, at the same time, put it on a track where I felt it was going.

I also need to explore different things. As an artist, I think I'm getting interested in different mediums and different ways of telling stories. At Congo Square, I like to say, we make the Whopper. We flame broil our burger. If you want to go and fry a burger, you gotta go somewhere else. We flame broil. That's what we do. And that goes for me too. And things that I want to do at other places, they're not necessarily right for Congo Square, but they're right for me as an artist and for me to grow as an artist. I've dedicated ten years to [Congo Square], but right now I'm at a crossroads, to think about what's next.

Ten years is a point when you mark and reflect. What are Congo Square's achievements over those years?

Looking back on the ten years, it's quite amazing the level of exposure that Congo Square has achieved and the level of artistry that we have gotten because of collaboration, of working together and knowing each other. A lot of people nationally think we are bigger than we are, just because of our rep. The thing about rep is it can go either way. It could be good one day. You could say, "Oh, well, I heard of Congo Square, you all are great." And you go, "Have you ever seen the show." They go, "No, but I've heard." And then you say, "Oh, that's dangerous." Just like you hear something is good, you can hear something is bad. The proof is in the pudding. The proof is on the stage and the proof is to actually experience the work. Marion McClinton used to tell me, "There's only one thing that's true in theater and that's what the audience feels." Everything else is dust. That's the only thing that's truthful, it's what I feel and what I experience. The most important thing is to go and experience it for yourself and decide for yourself. I think we've done an amazing job at changing not only the landscape of American theater but also the Chicago landscape. We came in gang busters and people had to deal with us in a different way than they had ever had to deal with an artist. Not only because we were young and hungry and we were talented. But also, we had these big national connections and the big national support that believed that this was necessary. This was needed. It still is very important. When August wrote "The Ground on Which I Stand," fifteen or sixteen years ago, there was one LORT [dedicated to telling stories reflecting the experiences of people of color]. The League of Resident Theatres. They are all the major theater institutions, the major regionals of America. And at the time, there was one . . . Crossroads Theatre and now, there are zero of color. In some ways we've gone back and in some ways we've moved forward. The need and the warmth for the kind of work that we've done . . . Congo Square has definitely made a mark even at ten years. It takes some theaters thirty years to do what we've done in ten and I'm proud of that.

Were there any obstacles or pushback in the development of Congo Square Theatre?

Yes, there's always pushback. I would say that one of the major things that we're still dealing with is educating the audience about the need for these stories. I don't know if you noticed that the majority of people who came to see August Wilson [were white]. You could go to the South Side of Chicago and August Wilson could slap somebody and they wouldn't know who he was. It's educating people about the level of world-class art on a theater platform as well as telling them this is not something separate for you, this is for you. Even though we don't have the resources or the time that a Goodman or Steppenwolf or Lookingglass have, we are often compared to them. We have fewer resources, less time, and we have to still produce on the same level of art. That's one of the reasons I came to Chicago, though. If you had a good production in New York, there is no way you're going to be on the same page as Lincoln Center. *The New York Times,* you're not going to get that. You'll be lucky if you get in the *Village Voice.* But Chicago, if you knock it out of the park, you will have an article right beside Steppenwolf or Goodman, just as big and sometimes maybe bigger. I thought that opportunity there to have a national platform gave us a clear opportunity here. It evened the playing field for us some. Good work would be recommended as good work.

That's always the hope. No matter where you are, that your work will be perceived as on the same level, regardless of how much money you have. It's the heart that's put into it that gets recognized.

Tell me about your interactions with Hope Abelson.

Hope was a great lady. Astounding. I've learned so much from the meetings that I have had with her. August was coming to town on one occasion. The League of Chicago Theaters was honoring two people. They were offering August an award and they were offering Hope Abelson an award. I went to the event just so I could meet up with August afterwards, hopefully, and speak to him a little bit. When I saw him, he was like, "Derrick, you gotta meet this lady. You gotta meet her. You gotta get to know her." I was like, "Who is she?" So then I had to research who she was. She was a producer of *A Raisin in the Sun* on Broadway. She was a Broadway producer. She gave start-up money to Steppenwolf. The Court Theatre space is named after her. She gave a million dollars to Goodman for their new space. She's just an amazing lady who has done so much for Chicago theater. I got to meet her in her later life. I said, "Hope, I would love for you to come to see one of our shows." She would come see our shows. I would sit her right up front. Give her the brown copper treatment—whatever we had. I think she appreciated the work. One time I went up to her house and she had a beautiful penthouse on Lake Shore Drive. I sat up there and I said, "Hope, I'm hoping that you will be able to contribute to us. I know you've done so much for Steppenwolf and I know you've done so much for Court Theatre, and we're the institution that's next, I believe." She sat down and told me a story about producing *A Raisin in the Sun* and what it took to do that. She talked about how [John] Malkovich and [Gary] Sinise were sitting in the same chairs saying the same things [as] me. She liked us and she wanted to give us a donation. Now, these things take time. And when I started to get to know Hope, that's not something that, unfortunately, she had. That year, she said she was going to give us something, she did. She gave us $200. But when she passed away, we were the first recipient of the HOPE [Award] and we got $25,000, which was very, very kind. For her, in her death to think about us. August didn't do that but chose three organizations to donate to, in lieu of flowers, when he passed away. We were the only theater in the nation that he chose. We've had great icons believe in us and have supported the organization in a great way. It's very special.

When did you first realize that your new theater company might succeed in Chicago?

I would say it was our very first review. Chris Jones wasn't the top reviewer when we first started.

Richard Christiansen?

Yes, it was Richard Christiansen. We couldn't get Richard Christiansen to come. We couldn't get [*Chicago Sun-Times* reviewer] Hedy Weiss to come. But we were persistent. And Richard didn't come, but he sent Chris. Chris wrote a review that was . . . a slam dunk for us. That's when we got calls from other people. "Oh, I want to come and review this. Oh, I need to come and review this." That's when I started to go, "Oh, OK, this might work." This actually might work. Then when August came at the end of *Piano Lesson*, it was like, "This is one of the best regional productions I've even seen of this show," and that was also a very proud moment. So, I would say then, that's when I saw the tide turn. When people started to understand. With our first show, they understood what we were going for and the niche that we were filling. I would say it was early on.

How did the Steppenwolf–Congo Square coproduction of Wedding Band *come together?*

The funny story is, when we came to Chicago, Javon Johnson and I went [to] the major theaters. It was like, "We want to go to Steppenwolf." We went there, we go up there and we were like, "Hey, we want to see the casting director." They were like, "Who is this?" "Derrick Sanders, Javon Johnson." They were like, "OK." She came out and she was like, "Hello, can I help you?" I say, "Yes, we're new to the city. Blah, blah, blah. We want to let you know that we're in town. If you want to have us audition for stuff, we're available." And she was like, "You should go out and do some things and let me come see that and I'll call you based on that." I was like, "Oh, OK, all right. Fine." Three years later, we were coming back in the office and we were sitting there waiting for Martha Lavey, and I said, "Remember they told us to come back. They told us to come back once we'd done something. Here we are at the table, now they want to do something with us." We did our first coproduction on Steppenwolf's main stage. It was *Wedding Band*. Originally, we were going to do a new piece. Steppenwolf was trying to reach out. They were trying to diversify because that became a moniker of theirs. They weren't diverse at all, so they were trying to reach out. We tried several new plays and those didn't work out, and finally we kind of relented to *Wedding Band* just because of the age of their ensemble and the age of our ensemble. That's what we ended up doing.

Have you coproduced anything with Steppenwolf since?

No, that was it. At some point, we had to ask, "Is this really serving us?" I know we're going in and we're being very diverse for [Steppenwolf], and these guys look great for bringing in diversity. We're getting some exposure, but is any of that audience transferring [to] us? You could probably start a very successful business on the side by just going in and doing coproductions with white theaters and diversifying them. You could probably make some good money at that. But we weren't interested in that. And once we did the Steppenwolf coproduction, everybody else wanted to do coproductions with us and we were just like, "Hold up, hold up, hold up. We don't want to be known as the coproduction kings. We want to be selective."

What is your approach to directing?

It starts with the words. It starts with the story, even though I translate things into a visual medium. I get my impulses from actors, and I get my impulses from the words. And I believe if you have a great piece of work, it is in there. It's up to you to figure out how to make it work and to connect the human fabric in it. If you got a great piece of work, all the answers are in there and from there, can spring forth all kinds of things. Some people have an idea and they come in like, "I want to put *King Lear* in World War II because I think it does this, this, and this." My ideas come from the opposite way. Not visually or socially. I'll read a text and there will be a phrase, something in a play, that will make me go, "That's just like Hitler's Nazi Germany, that part right there," and then from there, it will go out until the fabric of that life lives.

I had a special kind of education in August Wilson. Not only was I able to be an assistant director to sit there at the table and watch the way they [Marion McClinton and August Wilson] worked with [*Gem of the Ocean*], I also was a part of the closed-door meetings with the director and the playwright as they were talking about the text. I got a chance to see how painstakingly each word was put in there. People tend to correct August Wilson. Like, "Oh, that's not correct grammar. I'll go in and . . ." and it was like, "No, you're not correcting my words. I meant she *ain't* seen this. I meant that." And because of that, the rhythm of it is bop, bop, bop, bop, ba, da, da, da, da, da. And when you look at the thing, it's a paragraph and then you kind of realize the rhythm of the poetry of what he's writing, the rhythm of the poetry, the ideas open up in August. Mamet does it really well. Of course, Shakespeare does it well. Tennessee Williams does it well with the lyrical quality of the Southern dialect. There are some playwrights . . . once you understand the rhythm, the text opens up in a different way if you're not there trying to correct what they've done. That's why I think it all starts from there. And then from there [the words], I get a whole bunch of visual ideas.

I love to be a collaborator, too. I like, if it's thoughtful, what you've brought to the table, because it may get me to think a different way about it, and I might open up to a whole new way of thinking about a situation and a scene and what the dichotomy is of the character in that scene. All of it is based on the words. It's called audience because there are more receptors in your ear than there are in your eye. So what you hear is much stronger than what you can see. You hear nuance in a voice. The emotional life in what you hear, from the way you say your words and the way they come out and their relationships, is what you gather from a scene and that ultimately is what affects us. That's why music is so immediate. It's rhythm and it's lyrical and it's immediate to our souls. Words do the same thing, if they're crafted right. My job is to get the lyrical and the emotional quality of the speech and translate that into a visual medium that explains the story on a much bigger level. That's my process.

What advice would you give people who want to start their own company?

There's two things. One of my professors used to say, "It's business show." It's a business first. Respect that level of it. Everyone has artistic impulses, on some level. Look at the landscape of wherever you are going to be, whether it be Chicago, New York or D.C. or San Francisco. What is missing in the context of the landscape of the theater work? I think that's an important decision. Lookingglass offers something unique. Goodman does a certain thing, they do it the best. Steppenwolf is the mother of ensemble theaters. Everybody does their own specific kind of thing to highlight the work that they do and it's accessible and, at the same time, very specific. In a land of over 200 theaters, that's what you have to know. What am I bringing that's unique to the table? Am I passionate about that? Because it's going to take a whole lot of pain. It takes a whole lot of pain. It takes a whole lot of tears. But at the end of the day, if you can achieve it, there's no greater satisfaction in the world, besides the birth of my son. I think that you have to know that it is a business and know your impulses to get together and create a certain kind of work. If there's nothing else out there like it or you feel like you can do it better, then that's what you should aim to do. And you have to do it and you have to stand on that. You have to be unique and passionate about what you're bringing to the table and think around the conventional way of doing. Be OK with "no." Be OK with "no," sometimes. Perseverance. I don't calculate my hours. They say you got a forty-hour week. I don't even do that [calculate my hours] because I'm scared to do it. I don't actually want to know how much time I'm spending on it. The time that I give, I give willingly of my heart. And it's because I have a bigger vision and a bigger idea of what should be achieved. And if you have a collective of people, you have some people willing to support that idea, then you should definitely put it out there. August used to always say and I keep this in mind, "You have a right to the work but not to the reward." You have a right, just like anybody, to sit down and write a play and write down words, characters, but you don't have the right to win three Jeffs and you don't have the right to be at the Tonys and you don't have the right to all that stuff. At the end of the day, that means very little. That means very little. It's great to be recognized and it's an honor to be recognized. But at the end of the day, it's just you and your play or you and your company members and you and the work. You want people to feel something. You want people to, even if they hate it, you want them to feel it. So, one, you have [to] know that it's a business, and two, know what you are adding to the landscape.

Even though I knew August, it never came easy to me. The reason that I was able to assist on Broadway was because I made that happen. I did write August and say, "I would love to assist." He said, "I'm not the director [Marion McClinton], you gotta talk to the director." I wrote the director and said, "Hey, I would love to assist, to see the process in which you develop plays." And he was, like, "Yes, great. I would love for you to do that." Two weeks before the start of production at the Goodman, he hadn't called me. So what did I do? I went, bought a ticket, flew up to Minneapolis and knocked on his door. His home door. I called him when I got in Minneapolis. I didn't have a place to stay. I was like, "Hey, man, I happen to be in the neighborhood. You know, we should sit down and talk about doing this thing. I hadn't heard anything from any . . ." I went and met him. Stayed up all night talking to him at his house. He had gone and hired somebody else. People don't know this: Marion paid for me himself to be there sitting at the table. Then it went to Los Angeles. The same thing happened because they had assigned an assistant from Yale to go all the way with him. They had started rehearsal. I bought a one-way ticket to L.A., and I just sat in rehearsal and I was just there. They didn't kick me out because Marion said I could be there and they hadn't paid me anything. It had gotten to three or four weeks before August and Marion had found out from the producers that I wasn't getting paid, and they thought that was unfair and BAM . . . now I got a way back home . . . but it never came easy for me. I always sought it. It's not like August gave it to me. I always hustled for it. The same year, I got a chance to work with Peter Brook [*Hamlet* at Chicago Shakespeare Theater, 2002] and that's because Peter Brook liked me. Who else can say they had a chance to work with August Wilson and Peter Brook in the same breath? I have that unique experience, but that's because I went after it.

RASHIDA Z. SHAW

Originally from St. Croix, Rashida Z. Shaw is an actress and scholar whose research centers on theater history, performance and aesthetic theory, musical theater, and dramatic literature with a special interest in African Diaspora and African American theater. A graduate of Northwestern University's doctoral program in theater and drama, she wrote her dissertation on contemporary African American musicals, also known as "Chitlin' Circuit" plays in Chicago.

In this July 2011 interview, Dr. Shaw shares her observations as a researcher, ethnographer, and audience member who has attended urban entertainment theater productions in Chicago.

What was the first Chitlin' Circuit play that you attended in Chicago?

It wasn't by a big playwright. I actually can't remember who it was, but I do remember it was by an entertainment company, Marvelous Entertainment Company or something. I remember I bought the ticket on Ticketmaster, and I remember being amazed that it was about forty or fifty dollars. I sat in the mainstage area at the Arie Crown which is huge, almost five thousand seats. I was way up in the double-alphabet row on the left side. It was my first time in the Arie Crown at McCormick Place. I remember being amazed that there were elevators to take people to the other seating areas of the theater. I was sort of overwhelmed by everything that was going on. There was a lot of music everywhere in the lobby. There was a lot of music and talking and laughter throughout. The people with whom I was sitting were very talkative. It was this amazing experience—where I had never been in a theater space where people were talking, people were laughing, and the play to me seemed to be very predictable, but everyone was laughing and involved in it. The other thing that was striking to me was that I wasn't laughing at everything that they were laughing at, and I realized pretty quickly that I was sort of out of my cultural comfort zone for some of the things. And I remember thinking to myself, "Is this Southern black American culture, is this Chicago culture? What is this?" I wish I could remember more about the play. It was in spring of 2005.

How many plays of that type of play have you seen since?

At least twenty-five or thirty.

All in Chicago?

Yes, in Chicago. I saw one play, one Tyler Perry play, about four times in Indianapolis. I would go to see every play in Chicago. Before I got grant money to pay for tickets, I wrote for *Time Out Chicago.* They would get comp tickets for me, and I wouldn't have to pay.

How did you first hear about these plays?

I would listen to the radio in Chicago. I forget the radio station, but I would hear it on the radio. And interestingly enough, I didn't have cable, so I would see commercials on the local stations, like channel 9, WGN. So, either TV commercials or the radio. When I started going more frequently, there would always be people passing out flyers, little laminated flyers—at the event before you walk into the main auditorium—advertising not only Chitlin' Circuit plays but also upcoming gospel concerts, upcoming R&B concerts. I would collect those. Later, when I started looking at websites, I would find out when people were touring because their websites would list their next tour stop: Chicago or Peoria, etc.

Were all, or the majority, of the performances at the Arie Crown Theater?

Yes.

Where is the Arie Crown?

The Arie Crown is near the Magnificent Mile or Michigan Avenue in downtown Chicago. It is almost the furthest thing before you hit the South Side. It's really a convention center, which is a nontraditional space, for a theater. When I first went, I couldn't find the Arie Crown because McCormick Place is huge. I didn't have a car in Chicago, so I took the bus down, and I got dropped off where the bus dropped me off. I got lost and I kept asking security guards, and I would go into these cavernous spaces where it would be dark and ask, "Where's this theater? Where's this theater?" And finally, I found it. At first sight, it reminded me of a movie theater. It had sort of a movie marquis and digital titles that were running across the marquis that were advertising the play. The first play I went to, it wasn't a Tyler Perry play, so it was actually advertising the celebrities that were in it. As the electronic words kept running, it would advertise the next event that was coming to the Arie Crown. It was interesting because what I realized that first time, even though I bought my ticket on Ticketmaster, was that many people ["walk-ups"] were at the box office buying tickets. One time I went afterwards, I went with a friend who had a car, and I found out that the parking at the Arie Crown was something like twenty or twenty-five dollars. Many of the people that I saw seemed to be on dates. I kept thinking: fifty dollars per ticket for two people plus twenty-five dollars for parking; this is easily an over hundred dollars event not including food and drinks and beverages and programs, etc. But the Arie Crown, it's a weird theater space.

And for the plays that you've seen there, what percentage to capacity was the theater?

They were all packed. They've been all packed. And when I really started doing the research for the dissertation, I would purposely buy tickets or seats in different locations. So, I wouldn't always sit in the first row or second row. There were nights when I would sit all the way up in the balcony. A few years ago, I noticed that for some productions they would sell binoculars for audience members, so I bought my own binoculars on Amazon because it was cheaper. I would be up there in the balcony. I think it's like the fourth floor or the fifth floor up there, and the stage is tiny, and I was the only one with binoculars. It was perplexing for a while. They really cannot even see what's going on onstage. The stage looked so small, but the actors are amplified, and it was also curious to me that many people didn't buy programs. It didn't operate the way that I see traditional theater where I want to read the actors' bios before I go or while I'm there while the house lights are on. It didn't seem to be like that. And then, because I had a program, there would be people around me asking to borrow my program. My program would get passed around all over the place and I would hope that it would come back. But it was interesting to see that it was just different. I think part of it was driven by people are laughing at the jokes, singing along with the songs, and less about space recognition and sort of the way, in the theater world, we think about how good acting is. People were really excited to see someone like Morris Chestnut or Malik Yoba onstage. They could identify those people from afar, but it wasn't the same for the details. I don't know if that was the researcher side of me or the audiencegoer side of me, but I like to be able to see what's onstage really well.

Have you seen any productions at eta Creative Arts or Black Ensemble Theater or Congo Square?

I've seen Congo Square, but I have not seen eta or Black Ensemble Theater. Part of that, actually, was because they were so expensive, and I couldn't get transportation there, so I didn't. I run across people who, when I tell them about my research, say, "You should go to eta, you should go to Black Ensemble." I did not. The only comparable black theater event that I went to was a church on the South Side. This was when I started to work with *Time Out Chicago*. They [*Time Out*] got invited to a preview of a production that this church on the South Side was doing. And they were advertising it as the Real Urban Theater, the real Chitlin' Circuit Theater. There was press—and a space for the press and important people in the community. There was actually a formal dinner before the event and then we [were] led into the auditorium. I think the play was called something like, I have it written down somewhere, but it was something like, *What the Church Folks Do* or *What the Church Folks Don't Do*. I got in for free but the tickets were going to be fifty to fifty-five dollars. It was in a theater, and it seemed to be an old theater that had been redone. It was . . . I hate to say typical, but it was a play about stereotypical representations of black church folks: the nosy church woman, you had the church woman who was sanctified and trying to save everyone. It was a comedy. Before the play began, the pastor, on the mic, said, "This is the real black gospel theater. Don't go up to the North Side." It was interesting that the Arie Crown at that point was the North Side. Like, don't go up to the North Side. Come here. We have the real gospel theater.

How was it different than productions at the Arie Crown? What made it more real?

I don't know if I would say it was more real. These people were not necessarily trained in theater. Someone wrote the script, probably wrote the script, but the length of time was shorter [than in the professional theater]. It didn't have a lot of depth. It was very flat, which is interesting when I say that because I do think that the urban theater plays get pigeonholed as not being that complicated or complex. It was pretty simple [musically]; I think there was a church organ. There were some songs, but there wasn't what I would say is the more complex arrangements in the urban theater that I saw at the Arie Crown for the most part. There wasn't an interplay of different types of black music, different types of narrative. There wasn't really a plot in this South Side play. You know what it was, the title was *Talking about Church Folks*. There wasn't a story line. People would just walk onstage and have a little dialogue with each other and then walk off, if that makes any sense.

Going back to the Arie Crown and those urban entertainment, Chitlin' Circuit productions, how would you broadly characterize or describe those who attended the plays?

I would say that they ranged from—and this is a combination of my observation and people with whom I actually spoke—working to middle class, black American. I hesitate to say solely Chicagoans because I did meet people who came from other parts of the Chicago area and Indianapolis to see these plays. They ranged in age tremendously, so you definitely had a lot of older black people, I would say in the senior citizen category, and then you had . . . I would say the majority of people were probably between the ages of late twenties to fifty. Many of the women, which is interesting because I think the Circuit gets pigeonholed as being something that black women primarily are interested in. Many of those women, the majority of those women were with men. And then there was another smaller segment of teenagers to twenty-year-olds. Then a lot of families. Women—I don't know if they were women on their own or with men—would bring their babies and/or toddlers or seven-year-olds, which I thought was amazing, because they would have to pay for a seat for a seven-year-old, I'm sure, equally as costly. So, it was a wide, wide range, but for the most part, I think these plays seemed to operate as a date night.

In your conversations with people who attended these productions, did you talk to anyone about why they elected to go to see that production as opposed to one at Congo Square or the Goodman?

Yes. One woman who seemed to be about my age (in her thirties), for example, said that she wasn't a theatergoer. She didn't like plays. Her comment struck me. I tried to push her a little bit more and she said, "I'm coming to see Malik Yoba," or Morris Chestnut or Leon from *Waiting to Exhale.* For her, yes, this was a play, but these are film people, and this is more exciting than plays. She was like, "I wasn't exposed to plays." And so, with her and some other people, it seemed to me that they were more willing to go to other plays if given the opportunity, if it seemed to be in the same sort of content [as film], but they also stressed to me how much of a social experience this was. I saw this and people told me about this. It seemed like everyone knew everyone. I don't know if that was because I knew no one or everyone knew everyone. So, it was this sort of neighborhood feel. I'd be talking to people and they'd say hi to somebody else, and then somebody else would come over. It was good for me in a way because they would say, "She's doing this study at school and you should talk to her." I would sort of get passed around in that way.

There seems to be this social component like this was the place to be. It was not only the place to be, it was the place to be and to be seen attending, which I don't think . . . if I put on my researcher hat, that these other black theater spaces in Chicago, for these people at least, have yet to be places where [they] want to go and be seen. The interactions that they have with each other are so much greater than traditional theater. These plays would start at eight o'clock, and I realized that I would have to start getting there by six because people would be there that early, and people would be eating. The Arie Crown would allow vendors in the lobby to sell food. JJ Robinson's Rib Shack Company, they're big on the South Side. JJ would be there. They would have a stand. There would be a pretzel stand. At JJ Robinson's, they would set up tables with tablecloths, and so people would actually have dinner before the play right outside of the doors. There was this huge social component that I think made it more like hanging out, gathering, family, and then you get entertained.

To follow up on the idea of people "going to be seen," what were the markers of being there to be seen that were noticeable to you?

That's a tricky question. At first, I was taken aback. I was like, "Oh my gosh, people are dressed really nicely." Fur coats and heels and lots of matching outfits for couples, lots of matching outfits, which I was like, "OK, this must be regional or something."

What do you mean by matching outfits?

This is the island in me coming out. This is my island perspective. For example, men would be dressed in blue suits, a blue suit with a hat and a matching scabbard around the hat and these amazing alligator shoes and their companion would be wearing a blue dress that was the same fabric of that suit. And I would see this in different colors, different fabrics and what was striking was when I started to see it in younger couples. When I say younger, I mean like early twenties, and for me that was striking because I wondered why they just didn't wear fancy jeans or something. It was interesting. It was like, "OK, this is really an event." Now I say that, but at the same time, when I would go to the Goodman when there would be an August Wilson play and I would go to the preview nights, and there would be a lot of black people in the audience and they would also be wearing fur coats and stuff, so I hesitate to say that it's remarkably different than what was happening at the Goodman, but I do think on a whole, the Arie Crown spectators reminded me more of black church-goers as opposed to . . . black churchgoers or this sort of very unique regional black Chicagoan style of dress that I wasn't familiar with hav-ing lived in New York and the Virgin Islands. Because the Arie Crown space in the McCormick is so huge, there was a wing in which there was an impromptu promenade that was created where people would be. The older black women would be sitting on folding chairs—this is before the theater doors would open—and there would actually be a parading of people and outfits, just sort of impromptu. The outfits would definitely get seen. Not only was there food there, but there's the shoe shining stand that was there and those guys would have music playing from their radio. There was music everywhere. It was a very interesting place. It was fun.

What language do you use to describe these plays? Are you referring to them as urban entertainment? Do you refer to them as Chitlin' Circuit?

I prefer to put them under the category of African American musicals, but for the purposes of my research and dissertation I have been referring to them as the Chitlin' Circuit theater because that is the way it is most identifiable. When I speak to the practitioners, they do not like the term Chitlin' Circuit, and they prefer to use the term urban theater or urban plays. As a person studying this, I have to grapple with which term to use because I want to respect how the practitioners are feeling about this theater. What they have expressed to me is that the term "Chitlin' Cir-cuit" has negative connotations for them and they feel that urban theater better defines what they're doing.

Of the artists with whom you've spoken, how many of them originate from Chicago?

The ones that I have spoken to . . . none, but I have seen plays where Chi-cago actors have been in the production and that has been announced at the curtain call, they announce that, or it's in the program. So there have been a few actors from Chicago who were born and bred and who have managed to find their way on the stage. Now some of them are not there solely for their acting. For example, there were a few *American Idol* finalists who happened to be from Chicago, but they're really on the stage because of their *American Idol* affiliation. These plays try to localize their performances as much as possible when they're in a particular city. And I know this because of the DVDs. The DVDs that actually get distributed and sold are taped at a particular city. For example, if it's Washington D.C. where the production is taking place, you'll have all these D.C. references in the play, but when I would see it in Chicago, they would have all these Chicago references. I could imagine that the actors who belong to a particular city, they [would] get more attention from the producer in front of the audience so they [could] have more of a connection.

What are some examples of Chicago references, or localized references, that you have noticed in these plays?

Street references, building references, radio station references. If the play has a particular radio station or a TV station is being listed it's usually a local channel or a local radio station, a local DJ name. Those are the ones that really stood out to me. I'm trying to think if there are any others. Those were the most apparent.

In the curtain call, how was the Chicago background for a person recognized?

At all of these plays, at least at the Arie Crown, there is an orchestra pit already built into the auditorium section, so that was where the live band is playing for these productions. There's a person who the audience can't see who has a microphone, and he announces the person as they run out on the stage and bow. So, they might say, "Chicago's own such-and-such," you know, fill in the blank. They'll say that or they'll say something like, "the South Side's own" or "the West Side's own" or they'll say a neighborhood. That happens. One play . . . I saw five or six runs of this play and it was by Je'Caryous Johnson and Gary Guidry. The first two nights, they had the pastors, and their wives, of the major black churches sitting in the audience in the first row and the playwright actually sat with them. It's rare, but I was kind of lucky when I was doing this research that at least one night out of every visit, the playwright himself would be there that night and he would come up onstage. And so this night Je'Caryous was there and he came up onstage, after the actors were introduced, and he identified these pastors and their wives. He asked them to stand up. Pastors, wives, deacons. I would say the entire first row stood up. I was sitting like three rows from them. "Oh my God. I had no idea." That was an amazing moment to witness. It was validation.

How was it validating?

It was validation for me. It validated how I was thinking about how these plays relate to the black religious community in Chicago. My hypothesis was that this connection was being made. These plays for these black spectators, these plays had the potential to—not necessarily be a substitute—but really to be another way of going to church, of getting religious instruction. They're validating and validated entertainment. So much so that their pastors are here. And Je'Caryous actually . . . he's from Houston, Texas . . . as he would introduce these people, he had his own sort of personal connection that he would share. He would say, "Pastor (such and such), I've known him for X number of years and he has counseled me about this and that." It was clear, and it seemed sincere so I don't want to say that it was an engineered audience engagement ploy, but he definitely was also showing, despite not being from Chicago, that he not only had a Chicago connection but [also] a religious connection; he himself was religious. So, it was amazing actually to see. I wish I could have talked to them. The one night that I saw Tyler Perry there I actually was sitting two rows away from him and I didn't know. Then one of the actresses who is on his TV sitcom and who is also in his plays a lot, she was sitting in the row behind me, and I didn't know until he said, "Can you stand up." I didn't have the *Time Out Chicago* pass, I had no reason . . . I could not get backstage, but I really tried. I really tried. I was like, "Oh my God, he's here." Moments like that would happen.

Moments like?

Tyler Perry and Je'Caryous Johnson and David Talbert. You go to their plays. These men become people who you don't actually see. You see them on TV, you see them in print, but you don't actually [see them]. You

never are actually there when they're there, and these plays are their creations. So, moments when they would actually emerge as real people are
fascinating. And, of course, the audience would stand up and they would
give applause. What these plays already have in place, which is different
than traditional plays that I've gone to at the Goodman or in New York,
is that the celebrity actors come out after the play is over. They would
come out in the lobby and sign autographs and take pictures. Sherman
Helmsley would be there, Boris Kodjoe, Leon. That's where you would
see that there were a lot of black women there because there would be
this mass of black woman in front of these guys trying to get them to
take pictures and sign their books. That ability to get close with a celebrity would happen with the actors, and it seemed to be another part of
the whole production of the night. When those rare moments happened
when you would see the playwright himself, that would be interesting. In
my mind I'm always wondering if they actually travel to every city and do
this sort of random pop-up. I've never been able to find that out; maybe
in the future.

SYDNEY CHATMAN

Sydney Chatman is a director, educator, producer, and founder of The Tofu Chitlin' Circuit, located in the Bronzeville district of Chicago. She is a former artistic associate with Congo Square Theatre and is the performing arts instructor at University of Chicago Charter School.

In this May 2011 interview, Sydney Chatman reveals how she came to Chicago and talks about the formation of The Tofu Chitlin' Circuit.

What events brought you to Chicago and led to the creation of Tofu Chitlin' Circuit?

I went to Indiana University, studied there. There were no black teachers, there were no black professors, there was no one but me. And I had this very thick regional accent, so I got made fun of a lot because I wasn't like everyone else at the school. I was frustrated with not being able to see plays with people like me. I put myself on the ninth floor of the library where all of the black plays were in just this one section. I read all the August Wilson, every black play. That's what I was doing at IU. I was a stage manager as well. As I was leaving, I sent out my résumé and a letter to every black theater company in the country—to everybody. Congo Square was one of the theaters that called me and said, "Hey, we have a job. We need you to be an assistant stage manager." And this is how I met Chuck Smith. My first show in Chicago, I worked with an emerging theater company and Chuck Smith. "Come in like Flynn." So that's how I started.

What was the show?

Playboy of the West Indies (2002). I was the assistant stage manager. I ended up having to understudy, to actually play a role, perform, and I also found the props and things. I would set pieces and things like that. So that's a short, truncated version of where I've been. While I was at school I was a directing major so I studied directing, but also stage management because I figured it would be a fallback. Just in case I don't get that directing job, I can stage manage. But then I hated it because that's not something that I really wanted to do—but I was really good at it. Really good at it. Fast-forward to working with Congo Square. I think I did about four seasons with them, with Congo Square.

When did you start?

I left school in 2001, so it's between 2001 and 2004-ish, something like that. I was working with them around that time and was really excited. I had heard about eta and that was pretty much all I knew about black theater in Chicago. I'm from Gary, Indiana. It was really like a come up. My first show I worked in Chicago was three hundred dollars, and I was the assistant stage manager, the props girl, and an understudy. So I was excited. Around 2003 Chuck told me about the Goodman's stage management internship. He's like, "You should do this." It was with August Wilson. *What!? Gem of the Ocean,* his second-to-last show, which was exciting. I had a chance to see him work, see Marion McClinton . . . who else was there? . . . Kenny Leon, Yvette Ganier . . . a bunch of people. I also worked with Ernest Perry. So that was nice to be a part of this with—not the 'ol heads, like old in a bad way, but—the people who forged their way in the community first. I was in the middle of that, and I just knew I was going to do contemporary black theater and that was it . . . until I went to New York and had the wonderful fortune of working at the Director's Lab at Lincoln Center. And there were seventy directors from around the country . . . the world, actually, and I was one of five black directors. And I was the only [one carrying] this flag of black theater. And I was challenged with the notion of black theater: What does that mean? What are you saying? Are you trying to alienate? And it was a good challenge because I wasn't quite sure who I was at the time or where I was as a director or what I wanted to say as a human being. I read a lot of books at that time, watched a lot of film. The Performing Arts Library in New York is fantastic, you can see absolutely anything, any show. I watched a lot of footage and was really frustrated with where theater was going. I loved the traditional theater, but I didn't like this new sort of Chitlin' Circuit that was sort of pushing out traditional values. It was irritating me. I just got in a conversation with a friend of mine about the Chitlin' Circuit—"I'm so tired of this Chitlin' Circuit, why won't they just . . ." We were playing with the name "Chitlin' Circuit," and he was like, "What about Greens and Chitlins or Ham Hocks and Chitlins?" And we were just playing around. And he said Tofu Chitlins. I was like, "Can I have that?" Thank you—trademark. I took the name and it became . . . initially it was supposed to [be] a company; it was supposed to be a theater company with an ensemble, with a bunch of directors, playwrights, but the more and more I was thinking about the structure of things, what I realized was lacking in our community, in the black community, was that no one was teaching anymore. I learned from Chuck because I was around, I was hungry, I wanted to be a part of it. I learned from the old guards because I was interested. But people don't really do that anymore. You see these shows all the time. They just aren't really good. I'm not really knocking it, but they're really not good because of the structure of things. So I was like, "Well, what if it's a company that's focused on teaching?" And the conservatory idea came about. I transitioned from thinking of a theater company, from a fringe festival ensemble base to a school, and that was about 2006. My tagline is "Fighting stereotypical theater since 2006 . . . WE'RE THE CHIT!" Get it? The Tofu Chitlin' Circuit is all the things that traditional theater maybe is, and then some. We are sexy with bad hair. We're this dichotomy of really cool things, but it still has an understanding of the tradition, an understanding of the foundation of what we have been taught, what we have learned, and just trying to make it accessible to the people, to the community. This is a for-profit company. I want to make money. It's not not-for-profit. But it's also about teaching. It's really educating the community in order for them to be able to tell their stories and freak the system. So you start off with, "Oh, I know that this is a play structure; I know that this is a beginning and an end structure, or I know this is how you would probably do things, but let me change it up. Let me flip it over a little bit to create a new genre, just something that we really don't have in the black community." We have, "This is a traditional play," and that's it. And those very small pockets of people or artists or companies doing something that's avant-garde or different or weird. So that's the Tofu Chitlin' Circuit. The way that I structured it, initially, I didn't have an audience. I didn't know anyone. I knew Chuck and I knew people from Congo Square but I didn't have an audience. And I didn't read a "How to Start a Theater Company" book. I read all the other books, though. I didn't have a plan in mind. I just knew that if I was going to do this, it had to include the audience and it had to be genuine. I noticed that a lot of theater companies include the audience in rehearsals or talk-backs, and I was like, "This is interesting," because this is stuff that I had been thinking about. We have monthly conversations about theater, and those are called "A La Cartes," and the A La Cartes have food attached to them because people love to eat and talk. So every A La Carte is a month and it has a theme. So the first one we did was black-eyed peas, of course, for the New Year, January, and then it just sort of trickles down to collard greens, yams, all soul food/comfort food. And the conversations were wrapped around issues: about directing, things about playwriting, the audience. How do you get them to come? What were some other things? The one that you came to was about should a white director direct a black play. And it was really fiery because right at that time August Wilson's play was in New York [with a white director, Bartlet Sher]. A lot of people were really upset about it. And they should have been—rightfully so. But it's not so much should they direct it, but how do we as persons of color, black people, get into those theaters to be able to direct that type of work. Those are the types of panel discussions we had. I also interviewed theater practitioners, emerging and established, to get their [perspectives]. It's really more focused on the directing side, which is what I'm mostly interested in. Allowing the directors to tell their side of the story. How do you set up a play? How do you do these things? The "how to's." What else did we do? We still have plays. We still direct plays, we still produce work. It's just that the focus at the beginning was to get the audience to be a part of the discussions, to get them coming in, to get them to sit and talk, to get them to see how work happens earlier as opposed to later so that they have a say-so in the structure of things. They now become the board. They now become the artistic board. They now become the money board.

CHUCK SMITH AND SYDNEY CHATMAN: IN CONVERSATION

In this May 2011 interview, which occurred at the Chicago: Theatre Capital of America *symposium at Columbia College Chicago, community arts advocate Sydney Chatman and director Chuck Smith talk about the current state of Chicago theater.*

What are the significant issues facing artists of color, specifically black artists, in Chicago today?

Chuck Smith: At this moment in time there's just not enough African American people producing plays. That's what I see. As an African American community, we're always looking outside of our community for somebody to do our work when we should figure out a way to do our work ourselves. In the Chicago theater community, the League of Chicago Theatres has about three hundred [theater companies]. How many of them are black? A handful. A handful out of three hundred. That's the issue if you ask me. That's the problem. It's been that way, and unless more people like Sydney come along to start theater companies and learn how to produce plays, it's not gonna change.

Sydney Chatman: I think it takes a different type of person to do that. You're an actor, you get into a university setting, they tell you this is how you audition for plays, "This is the next step." They don't really give you that class on, "If this next step doesn't work, there's something else. There's an alternative to it." A lot of these actors come out, a lot of directors come out, and they say, "I'm gonna just go and work at the Goodman or I'll work at MPAACT or I'll work at Victory Gardens. I'll work at these major houses." They become equity and then they're without any sort of work. It takes a very strong person who doesn't have an ego to say, "I'm going to sacrifice two years of my career, three years of my career, to put something up to make it work." That is the challenge.

CS: We need more producers. That's the bottom line. We just need more producers. We have the talent, the onstage talent. We've got directors, we've got tons of actors . . .

SC: Writers.

CS: We've got writers, we've got everything else, but we . . . No, we still need some set designers. There's not that many black set designers and lighting designers. They're kind of rare. But they are out there. But the producers, that's what we need. We need more black producers.

SC: There's a lot of black millionaires in Chicago, and they're not invited in the same way that the larger white companies are inviting them. The Goodman has a black female women's board who make change over there and say, "What we're looking for and the types of plays that we want to see"—you know, cause a ruckus when there are shows like [Thomas Bradshaw's] *Mary* onstage and, the Wooster Group's piece [*Emperor Jones*].

CS: It's nothing new. It's nothing new. I've been saying it since I was in Sydney's shoes years ago that there's a disconnect between the black artists and the black business community. There's a huge disconnect. They [members of the black business community] have no idea what we do and they don't . . . I'm not saying they don't care, but they just don't know. Until that bridge is spanned, we will have this discussion fifty years from now.

How can we bridge that gap?

SC: The Tofu Chitlin' Circuit. [*Laughing*] No, really, because I know every black business owner in my neighborhood. They all know me. And not because I have cool hair. I introduce myself and say, "This is what I'm doing; hey, come see this play." Or, "Can I use your space to have a read-ing?" Or, "I'm gonna bring people here . . ." And that's the other thing that we do. We do this thing called the Tuxedo Junction, and I get people to come and meet up at a particular restaurant or place, and we just eat, we share, we talk. I get to know more about "the Circuiteers"—that's what I call them, the audience members that come to see the work. And not only am I getting to meet people, but I'm also supporting these busi-nesses that are in my neighborhood and which I'm trying to serve. That's how I've been bridging my community and the theater. And I want to preface that it's not community theater by any means because I want to be equity as well. I want to make money. But it's like I have had to sacrifice my directing in order to be able to do this, but I really believe in it. I think the only way that you can actually get art in these businesses and get people to support it is if you're in their face and you're saying, "Hey . . ." (*snap*) ". . . your space, it's open, right? After six? Can I use it?" That type of thing.

CS: We need more of this. That's all I'm saying.

SC: [*seductive voice, joking*] You'll never get . . . this. [*Laughing*]

How do you balance being a director or actor and being (or recruiting) a producer?

CS: Chuck Smith doesn't see it. I've gotten to the point now that I'm a senior citizen. I have to admit, I'm laid back . . .

SC: You still look good, Chuck.

CS: Yeah. [*Laughing*] I've been working at it for all this time, and now I just do what I do. I talk to the people on the board of the Goodman and try to get them involved in everything I do. And I do work. I work at MPAACT, a small theater company on Lincoln Avenue. I work with them. I'll work with anybody.

SC: I think people are afraid to do something like this with no money. I'm broke and rich at the same time. How am I gonna make it if I have a negative balance but I have a job, like a full-time job? That just doesn't make any sense. But I still love what I'm doing. I love . . . I'm passionate about it. And I think there are small pockets of people like that.

CS: Yes, there are.

SC: There's something that you [Chuck Smith] mentioned—that you work at the Goodman but you also work at MPAACT. I think the biggest challenge with the community in general is just being a community. I listened to Pemon Rami and his wife Masequa, and they were from this era of the sixties . . .

CS: Higher.

SC: . . . seventies, eighties, and they were saying how they'd have a play up north and then someone else would have something on the South Side, and they would all travel to go see it, even if it was at the end of the play. It's just that camaraderie, that support. Now what's happened is that because so many larger theaters are doing our types of plays, black plays, we're split up. It's not where you have this community that started out of frustration and out of anger and out of revolution. Now it's like, "I have a master's degree, I'm gonna go get that job at the Goodman." And somebody else has a master's too, and we're both vying for the same job, so there's this sort of tension that happens. I have the Tofu Chitlin' Circuit, but I still want to work. I can come back and still feel like I contributed to the community in that way. You know, it takes a strong person to do that.

CS: Yes, that is true, but it's a different time now. Once before, right after the civil rights movement, it was much easier to connect with everybody in the black community. Once integration was cool, everybody split up. Things are not the same and they'll never be the same again. When I grew up, black people had to stick together, because if you didn't stick together, you were dead. Real simple. So we had to stick together. We had to communicate.

SC: I think that the technology age has sort of brought people back together.

CS: I hope so.

SC: No, it has. I mean, you're on Facebook. I was like, "Maannn! Chuck Smith is on Facebook." I'm good about going to the Internet to find somebody. You want to find out something, you Google it, and then you find the person and you ask them. Also, it can't just be about black anymore, it can't be this is just a black theater, this is just a Latino theater, this is just an Asian theater, it has to be inclusive in order for you to be able to get those producers and to get people of like minds to come together.

Chuck Smith

Kemati J. Porter

Gloria Bond Clunie

Jackie Taylor

Jonathan Wilson

Kathy A. Perkins

Ron O. J. Parson

Derrick Sanders

Rashida Z. Shaw

Tofu Chitlin' Circuit Members, including Gloria Bond Clunie (*back left*) and Sydney Chatman (*center, kneeling*)

Najwa I (Arnell Pugh) in a 1972 performance of *The Fire Dance* at Dunbar Auditorium in Chicago, Illinois

Najwa Dance Corps in a 1979 performance of *April in Paris,* with show girls Bocezeon Bush, Patricia Walker, Pam Watson, Beverly Henderson, and Sheila Walker

Darlene Blackburn

Darlene Blackburn Dance Troupe in 1969:
Melveda Blackman, Darlene Blackburn, Gwen Barnes,
Harold "Atu" Murray, and Donna Morgan

Queen Meccasia Zabriskie, Geraldine Williams, Alfred Baker,
Darlene Blackburn, and Najwa I at the "Black Theater Is Black Life"
Symposium held at Northwestern University in 2011

Idella Reed-Davis

Idella Reed-Davis and Ted Levy

Babu Atiba in a 1999 Muntu Dance Theatre of Chicago concert,
"Celebrating Humanity," at Kennedy-King College, Chicago

Joel Hall

Alfred Baker presents Clifton Robinson the Rex Nettleford Award for
Outstanding Dedication to the Cultural Performing Arts in Music,
awarded at the First Annual Caribbean Heritage Month Gala in
Hillside, Illinois, in 2011.

KWABENA SHABU

Amaniyea Payne in a 1997 performance of "Fat Tuesday and
All that Jazz" for Muntu's Twenty-Fifth Anniversary Concert at
Kennedy-King College, Chicago

Idy Ciss at the 2012 Kakoly Fifth Annual Drum and Dance Project
Guest Artist Performance, Heart of Beast Theatre
in Minneapolis, Minnesota

Kevin Iega Jeff

The Ayodele Drum and Dance Community in a 2012 performance of *No Mirrors in My Nana's House* at the Bruce K. Hayden at Malcolm X College, Chicago: Iman Martin, Naomi Kinslow, Maria Estes Hall, Khadyijah Harper, Tosha "Ayo" Alston, Michelle Ouellette, and Sherice Grant

Daniel "Brave Monk" Haywood

Dance

NAJWA I

A gifted choreographer and dance historian, Najwa I (Arnell Pugh) is the founder and artistic director of Najwa Dance Corps. She has traveled and performed nationally and internationally, from Harlem to New Zealand. She is the recipient of numerous awards, including the Paul Robeson Award from the Black Theater Alliance (Chicago).

In interviews conducted in May and June 2011, Najwa I talks about her career as a chorus line dancer and the development of her company, Najwa Dance Corps. Najwa also talks about her transition from "commercial" to "concert" dance as the political climate shifted within the black community during the 1960s. She discusses the development of interest in West African folklore, dance, and drum culture in Chicago as a result of the Black Power Movement.

I am the artistic director of Najwa Dance Corps. I am the director of the dance company and the dance studio at Malcolm X College. I've been in the business of dance for over fifty years. I'm an Enstooled Elder of The Bolozi Wazee Council of Elders. I'm also the Chief Elder of Dance Africa Chicago. I am presently working on a documentary titled, *The Vision of Najwa I: Najwa Dance Corps.*

Are you originally from Chicago?

I was born in Clarksdale, Mississippi, but I've been here most of my life. I'm from the Mississippi Delta. I don't know of any relatives down there anymore. I was raised on the West Side of Chicago.

How did you begin dancing?

I remember my first dance classes were at the Marcy-Newberry Center. I think it was on Newberry and Maxwell. That was a long time ago. Then the next dance classes I really remember were classes at the Douglas Park Field House. My favorite teachers there were Jane Dixon and Miss Luigi. Those were my young days, and that's where I had tap, jazz, and ballet. It seems like all of my friends danced, and so we had dance classes in the neighborhood in everyone's basements. Later, I went to Jimmy Payne's dance studio, Sammy Dyer's dance studio, Sadie Bruce's dance studio, Mayfair Academy with Tommy Sutton, and Stone-Camryn School of Ballet. Those were my teachers.

You said that everybody was having dance classes in their basements in your neighborhood?

We had dance classes in the backyard [and] in the basement. At my house, we had classes under the porch. We used to go under the porch, and it had a little concrete area there. That was like our dance studio. We had our dance classes and our little shows there. And, with my friends from across the street, we also used their backyards for our shows and some classes. It was like that up and down the block on 16th Street and Central Park where I grew up. Our dance material for our shows came from dance classes that some of the children were attending and from movies.

For whom did you perform? Was it mostly for family and community?

Yes, we performed mostly for our families, each other, and the neighborhood kids. We charged a nickel or whatever we could charge the neighborhood kids. All of us went to dance classes at Douglas Park Field House. We all knew some of the same steps and techniques.

Were those classes at the park district free at that time?

Yes, they were free at that time. I took dancing but I was basically an athlete. I loved sports. Today, I still have the heart of an athlete.

What sport did you play?

Track and field. I did all sports—volleyball, basketball, baseball, and ten-nis—but track was my favorite. I probably would have gone into sports later if I hadn't gotten into dance so heavily. Around the neighborhood, everyone knew me as a dancer. In the neighborhood you have those you know as athletes and those you know as singers. We had all of that in our neighborhood. I was with the group known as "dancers." That's how I got pushed into dance. People would come around the neighborhood and get kids to perform for them. See, at that time, you could do that. Somebody would come into the neighborhood and say they wanted us to dance or sing, and we could go do it outside of the neighborhood. They would take us in their cars to wherever they wanted us to perform.

Were these professional musicians or artists? What kind of gigs were they?

One particular man that I remember put on shows for different organiza-tions. He use to come and get us. He would take us to a lot of events for Jewish organizations. My sister and I used to do these events because we lived in a mostly all-Jewish neighborhood. I went to Howland Elemen-tary School at that time, and we had to do the pledge of allegiance, face the front for the American National Anthem, and to the east for the Jewish National Anthem in Hebrew. Then, we would turn to the front again and do the Black National Anthem. When we would go to these affairs, people would say those little girls standing there are singing the Jewish National Anthem in Hebrew. That was a big thing and everybody at those events loved us. We used to love to go with him. I don't remem-ber his name. We didn't even ask my mother or father if we could go. He used to just take [us]. Everybody knew when he came in the neighbor-hood he was coming to get the kids to do a show. We, and other people in the neighborhood, would just go. That's how we got a chance to do some shows outside of the neighborhood.

And these were community organizations?

I don't know, but the events were downtown in the big ballrooms in different hotels. I hate to think about what costumes we wore, and how they accepted whatever we had on. We were kids getting this together ourselves. It might have been what we wore in classes or the costumes might have been something we had from the classes from the park district. I just don't remember. I danced and ran track straight through elementary school and high school. When I graduated from high school [Harrison High School in 1954], I was taking dance classes with Jimmy Payne. I met some dancers and other girls there my age, and I guess we were like sixteen/seventeen. We did shows with Jimmy Payne. When I went to him, I could dance already because I had been doing little shows. He would put four or five girls together to form a group, and we would go out and do performances.

What kind of dancing were you doing with Jimmy Payne?

With Jimmy Payne, I did Caribbean, Afro-Cuban, West Indian dance styles, and some African dance—a little African—mostly Caribbean and Afro-Cuban.

And where were some of the places that you performed with him?

I performed in many places with Jimmy Payne during the years I was with him. We used to do a "West Indian Carnival" tour to colleges and universities throughout the Midwest. It was more than the Midwest because we were up in Canada and the Black Hills of North Dakota, through Yellowstone Park, the Rocky Mountains, Wyoming, and trips to many Indian reservations. We toured and performed in places most people at that time did not get to see or visit. I performed with Jimmy Payne before and after I went abroad, performed in various countries, and toured through the USA.

What were some of the dances that you performed?

We had basic dances that we did like the limbo, the basket dance, and all of the dances that you would see on the islands at that time. I think

Jimmy himself was from Panama or Barbados, one of those islands. He was really great with Caribbean dance. Later, when I went to join a show in the Bahamas, I could just jump right in. Freddie Munnings, an impresario in the Bahamas, brought black people from all over the world to the Bahamas to dance in his productions. He said he did that because he knew that he was going to get the same thing once the dancers were put together, and he did. We all performed together and looked alike. We had dancers and choreographers from Jamaica, dancers and choreographers from Trinidad, and dancers and choreographers from the United States. It was just a beautiful experience. I stayed there four years.

What year was this?

It was in the sixties, I remember Kennedy being president. We were over there when he got shot [1963]. I was in the Bahamas four years but would come back home in between [tourist seasons] to visit. I have a son, Herman Cedric Collins. One time I came back, and I brought my son back to the Bahamas. He went to school there. The season started in late October, but I had to get back early in September for my son to start school. The Bahamas was very nice. It was lots of fun. I had a lot of friends and dancing buddies, dancing buddies from all over the islands. We learned a lot from each other. When I was over there I learned, from a Haitian girl who worked with us, how to eat fire. When I came back home, fire eating became a part of my dance act.

Back to my very early days when I danced with Jimmy Payne, this was in the late fifties, my friend Betty Frazier—[Betty] Comeaux at the time—came into town. She had been on tour with Larry Steele, in a big revue called, "Larry Steele's Smart Affairs." She came to Chicago because she was in between gigs. Jimmy had asked us to go to Milwaukee to perform. Larry Steele was looking for dancers to go to Australia with his show. Betty had invited him to see the show because she thought he might be able to use a few of us. He was looking for dancers from all over the country. He came to our show, and the next day his wife called and asked if I wanted to go. They were leaving right away. She said that Larry had seen the show and wanted to know if I would join his show in Australia. Of course, I was excited! I wanted to do it. But, when I asked my mother, oh, she had a fit. My whole family had a fit. My aunts came over and said, "Your father would not have approved of your going away to join a show." My father had been a minister. My mother wouldn't want you to go to the next block. Anywhere was too far for her children to travel. "No, no, no," was her answer. She got my sisters together to agree that I should not go. They were supposed to be talking me out of it. Anyway, I ended up going. I was supposed to go back to college that September, but I put that on the back burner.

What finally convinced them to let you go?

Nothing convinced them. I just went.

How long did you stay in Australia?

Actually, it was eleven months in Australia and two months in New Zealand. I'll never forget my stay there. When I first got there, I saw that the girls had on eyelashes and makeup. I was seventeen. All of the dancers had bangs and a ponytail and a lot of makeup on. I wondered how in the world was I ever going to put on that much makeup. I didn't wear makeup. A few people were from Chicago, and what they thought about the West Side at that time was that the people lived in the "sticks." They asked, "Who is that little girl from the West Side? Let me meet her. I want to see her." When I got to them, I know they must have thought, "You got a long way to go now," with my clothes and everything. [*Laughing*] Basically, I only had my school clothes. My cousin had given me a coat, she said, "Take my coat. I want you to look really nice." She had a pretty coat with batwing sleeves, and she let me take her coat. Other than that, I had young girl clothes. They [the other dancers] were all in fancy clothes, shoes, jewelry, and everything. I met my best friend there, Julian Swain. Have you ever heard of Julian?

Yes, I have.

When I got there, he said to this one girl, "Where is she?" I came in, and he said, "Oh, I wanted to meet you." He said, "My name is Julian Swain. I live on the West Side. Where do you live?" I said, "Central Park and 16th." He said he lived on 13th and Sawyer, and we were friends and buddies from that moment on. You heard me mention the name Betty? Betty, the one who told Larry Steele about me and brought him to see the show in Milwaukee, was my roommate when I got there. So, my friends there were Julian and Betty. We had another buddy from Chicago, Jackie Greenwood. She didn't hang with me as much as Julian and Betty and I hung together. We were buddies all through Australia, all though our lives after that. Isn't that something? Julian took me up under his wings. [He] helped me learn how to dance right and understand line technique, formations, and everything. For the past fifty-something years, he was my friend, my buddy, my teacher, my mentor, my everything. I danced in his company too. I worked in his company as an assistant director.

When I came back home from Australia, [there] was no getting back to school. There was no getting back to track [sports] and all that kind of stuff. I had new friends, which prevented me from reconnecting with things I did before I left. When I got back, everyone knew me and knew who I had toured with, and people referred me to others who wanted dancers. Before I knew it, I was on the road all the time for years. I was just always going, doing a show here, there, and everywhere.

What are some of the groups that you performed or danced with when you came back from Australia? Were you working freelance?

Not groups. We were doing revues, shows.

In Chicago?

No.

They were traveling shows?

Yeah, they were.

What were some of the revues?

The Idlewild Revue [created by Arthur Braggs in Idlewild, a Michigan resort town]. There were so many names. I can't start remembering everything that had a name, but this is what I did for years. I wasn't with a company until Julian formed his company in the late sixties. Other than that, it was like working in groups and joining shows. There were many different revues and shows.

What was the difference?

Well, the revues were bigger, more acts. A show could be one person performing or many, but when you say revue, you expect a big production. I did revues and shows at the Regal and Tivoli in Chicago and the Apollo Theatre in New York. I worked at the Apollo with Dinah Washington. It was the Dinah Washington Show.

Was most of this chorus line dancing? What kind of dancing were you doing?

Well, we had enough to say a chorus. When you're touring like that, they were trying to keep the cost down. It was four of us. I don't think we had a guy with us, even when I toured with Dinah Washington. I think it was just four girls. Prince of the Step Brothers used to choreograph for us. Being a part of the four dancers, we toured as a chorus line. Four or more is considered a line. When a line was wanted, they [producers] wanted to keep it [its size] down. They had to keep it to at least four to say [they] had a chorus line. Everybody liked to see a chorus line. Everybody wanted to see the girls and their dances. Men wanted to see the girls. The women wanted to see the girls. Everyone wanted to see the show, especially if it had a line. People would ask, "Do they have a line?" If yes, they would say, "Oh great! We are going to go to the show." I don't know what happened, but they cut down on shows. Performers, meaning big acts, started touring just by themselves, and they weren't in a big package of acts but with maybe just one other act. Something happened in the sixties. I don't know when they stopped using a lot of chorus lines. At the same time, others started creating dance companies.

Did things open up for black people? Or was the chorus line the only way that blacks could tour and could dance?

No, people had their dance acts. There was the commercial stage, and then there was the concert stage for dance. In the sixties, I was on a commercial stage. My dance company today is on the concert stage, you understand? On a commercial stage, people got to hustle to make their living. But, there were dance acts [and] dance teams. I did my own act. I performed by myself as well as with other groups. There were plenty of places to work because in between dance shows, I could go and do lots of other commercial gigs and dancing gigs at different places. I remember—I guess this must have been in the sixties or seventies—when I'd come back to Chicago, and in between shows I could work every night. Every afternoon there was go-go dancing. I would get up and put on my go-go boots and my little skirt and go downtown to dance. Dancers used to go to the restaurants on Rush Street in the afternoon during lunch hour, and dancers could make $100 for that time. Some places would pay like $75. I would work during that hour dancing with people who wanted to learn how to do the twist and the mashed potato. Do you remember those dances that were popular then? We would dance all the popular dances. Dancers could just go and walk in and just tell the man that they were there to dance and dance for the lunch hour. I danced with the customers who wanted to learn how to do the twist. Usually in the evening, I did go-go dancing or something else. At night I just did my dance act. Dancers had ways that they could make money. They did all kinds of dancing and had all kinds of acts. I had my fire dance act also.

What were some of the acts that you performed when you went out on your own?

I mostly danced with fire, and I danced with Julian a lot. Before he created his company, I worked with him a lot in the late fifties. I worked here in Chicago at the Club DeLisa. I could work there as long as I wanted. I worked at Roberts Show Lounge too. I just worked anywhere at that time. Dancers with skills could join the line or join a group. Some dancers are talented enough to do that now, such as tap dancers. They make a way. They find their way from show to show. It just seems like there were just so many more shows at that time.

Then it shifted in the sixties?

I don't even know if it was the sixties or seventies. Maybe it was the sixties. Somewhere in there things kind of shifted. By then, there were a lot of clubs, ballrooms, auditoriums, and theaters. There was the Regal Theater here in Chicago and the Tivoli Theater. There was the theater circuit that went across the country. I worked a lot with Count Basie and Duke Ellington here in Chicago. Say, for instance, Julian Swain might have the gig. He was a choreographer, and choreographers liked to work with certain dancers. They would call them for their shows. Julian was called all the time for Count Basie and Duke Ellington shows. Then, there was Shirley Hall. I've worked with her but not with the Dyerettes. Shirley Hall was one of the Dyerettes. She had lots of connections. When different people would come into town, they would call her. She would call me when she needed dancers. I worked with her at the Regal when she did the show with Duke Ellington. Also, I worked there when Julian did a show with Billy Eckstine. It was just like that. Performers were coming into town, and I was able to be a part of their shows. They would come into town for a show at the Regal. They would call the dancers here in Chicago to be a part of their shows. They didn't have to bring dancers with them. They would bring their bands, but they would add musicians from here. They didn't have to travel with thirty musicians. They would travel with twenty-five performers and pick up the others, dancers and musicians, when they got here. So performers called people in Chicago like Julian Swain or Shirley Hall or Sammy Dyer to get their dancers. It was mostly big bands and jazz. At the time, Count Basie would have a tune, his new record, and he would want some choreography to go with it so he'd send the music ahead of time. Julian would choreograph the material and work it out with his dancers. Count Basie would come in to town a day or two early, and the dancers would rehearse one day and maybe the next day have a little rehearsal before the show and then do the show for whatever length of time they were here performing. I don't remember how long they stayed at the Regal, maybe a week or more.

And then what happened?

I think all of that changed with the Black Power Movement. All of that came in and everything just went in a different direction. All we really wanted to do was relate to Africa. We changed. We were trying to relate to Africa, and we started getting into different kinds of dances, more African dances, and trying to research African dance. Darlene Blackburn went to Ghana in the sixties. I think she went with Dr. Margaret Burroughs. She went there and studied African dance, and, boy, she came back and had some authentic African dances. I always say she brought African dance to Chicago. So, we all got it. We all wanted to get into African dance and study African dance.

What were the "African dances" that you were doing before she went?

Before we just had steps. Later, after studying, we started putting names to African dance. When Darlene Blackburn went to Africa, she came back with dances with some names. That was good. Before that, we were doing . . . I guess African. We didn't have it in any kind of real context. The steps that we had been doing for years and things we had picked up from years ago were a part of our African dancing. Julian danced with Asadata Dafora—I mean he studied with him. We studied African dance, but the things we are doing now with African dance is more in depth. I am not saying that we did not always do it because when I was a little kid we just knew we were doing some African dance. [*Laughing*]

And it was just based on what you thought was African dance?

No, what we had learned from different people. We always had those dance numbers. They used to call them, like in the movie *Stormy Weather*, the jungle dances. We always thought we were doing African dancing. It was off. But, as long as I can remember, we thought we were doing African dance. Darlene made me and other dancers want to really make sure we were doing some real African dancing.

What was that moment in the sixties like?

We had to get back to Africa as a people. Everybody starting relating to Africa. Everyone wanted to know more about Africa. We wanted to know more about ourselves. This was everyone whether they danced or not. Everyone wanted to know more about Africa, and everyone claimed Africa. Africa is our original home. That's our heritage. And if you were a dancer, then you wanted to know about your African heritage in dance. Here in Chicago, we had a strong African movement. They were teaching African history in the colleges and in the schools. People were demanding it. We were demanding that the children had to know it. I mean we had Phil Cohran on the beach every Sunday. The Affro-Arts Theater every week was teaching all about our heritage. So it was a strong movement here. I was dancing for a living. I *had* to dance for a living. My dancing wasn't a plaything. I did whatever was necessary for me to earn a living. If people wanted to dance African dance, I had to teach it. Because I was teaching, I had to make myself knowledgeable. This is why I studied so hard. I studied Afro-Cuban with Jimmy Payne. I knew Afro-Cuban. I knew the history behind it. I knew the steps. I knew how to separate that from calypso. I knew how to separate Bahamian dance from calypso because there's a difference. I had to learn history, and the difference between the West Indian Islands and the Caribbean Islands. It made me be more serious about all of it and what I was telling people and what I was showing people. Before I could just teach dance, but somehow now people wanted information. When people want[ed] information, I had to give it to them. It made me study. It went on like that until I looked up thirty years later, I've studied a lot. I went to Africa. I studied in different parts of Africa: Senegal, Ivory Coast, Liberian dance, and Nigerian dance. I had a good Nigerian teacher, [Babatunde] Olatunji, who was from Nigeria. I did and still do a lot of his dance technique. He used to teach at his school in New York. He used to teach different styles of African dance.

And Darlene Blackburn's trip was important for changing African dance practices in Chicago?

Like we always say, she did it. Everybody might have talked about it or wanted to, but she did it. She made it happen. Everybody loved it. It was just so wonderful, and she was such a beautiful dancer—tall and willowy and doing movements so strong and graceful.

When things were shifting, you were starting to work with Julian Swain and his company?

Well, I was working, right. I was working with him anyway, always. He formed the company. I think it was formed in probably '68 or something like that. I was his assistant artistic director and choreographer. I worked more or less in the company as a principal dancer, and I did choreography. I had to do a lot of performing myself because I was at my peak with my solo act at that time.

And this was the fire act?

Yes, I was in demand for my solo act.

What were some of the pieces that the [Julian Swain Inner City Dance Theatre] performed?

With Julian, we had a big fire ritual. It was about a half-hour-long suite, and that was real popular. He incorporated my act into it with him. We were a duo anyway. I performed solo, I performed with him, and then I performed with the company. Before he formed the company, we were doing our act. I always have to say that I worked with Julian over fifty years, on and off. In the end, I don't know when Julian Swain Inner City Theatre stopped functioning, but I worked with Julian over the past fifty years.

Where were some of the places that you were teaching?

We were teaching downtown in the Fine Arts Building. I was teaching at St. Columbanus School, Better Boys Foundation, and the Johnson School. The big classes we were teaching were downtown in the Fine Art Building.

When was your first trip to Africa?

Well, my first trip to Africa was with FESTAC '77 [Second World Black and African Festival of Arts and Culture]. We didn't get a chance to study that much there. We saw a lot, but we didn't get a chance to really study. The only thing I had to go on were the things that I had learned at [Babatunde] Olatunji's school and from—I can't think of his name—another guy in New York. I just saw a lot, and we were able to get together and do movements and stuff with other people over there. It was just fun. But as far as really separating and really getting it together, I wasn't able to do it there [in Africa].

What did you perform at FESTAC? What dances did you perform?

Fire Dance and Gula Matari, those that I mentioned to you. We did both at different times. We did something else. I can't remember. We performed it with Sun Ra. He was there at that time. Darlene went then too. Julian Swain Dance Theater. I think Kuumba. That was a theater group. It used to be in Chicago. There were three groups from here: Kuumba, Julian Swain Dance Theater, and Darlene Blackburn. I think that was the three.

You went with Julian Swain?

Yes, and when I got back I worked on a master's degree at Governors State University.

Where did you do your undergraduate degree?

At the University of Massachusetts in education. In the seventies, I did it here. Here and there. I danced all that time and went back school to get a bachelor's degree. Then, I went to Governors State for a master's degree. Dancing through it all. Students and dancers today, they're all in school. You have to finish school before you can dance, and that's wonderful! I tell them all to go to school, finish school. You can take dance classes while you're in school. You can dance while you're in college, and when you come out then you can really do it. You can still dance all the way through and still train your body all the way. You can still find work to do as a dancer while you're in college. But, you've got to go to school. I wouldn't tell a child coming out of high school right now you can just go into dancing. You're going to make a living. No, I wouldn't take that chance. We were always taught to have something to fall back on. I give them the example of these big artists out here now that's making tons of money. Beyoncé [Knowles] and what's her husband's name? Jay-Z. What do they have? They sing and then they have their clothing company. All that's so they can make sure that they can make it. When you decide that you don't want to hear their kind of music no more or you don't like them, you like somebody [else] and would rather buy their records, they still got something to fall back on. You're no different. You got to have something to fall back on too. I always danced and taught. I used to do a lot of things. I would dance and in between I would teach. I had a clothing store, a boutique. You have to think about what you're into and use those guys as an example—Jay-Z and all of them. What's the other one that makes all the money? The preacher's brother, his brother is a preacher, the rapping preacher. Kimora's ex-husband. He was with Run DMC.

Russell Simmons.

Look at their industries. Look at Oprah. She didn't just sit up on her TV show. She had so many things going on it's unbelievable. She's very, very wealthy.

What made you decide to start your own company?

When I was teaching at the Better Boys Foundation, I had a lot of dancers coming to class. They wanted to have a dance group. I said no because I had seen all that Julian had gone through, and I didn't want to go through that. I was working and still dancing myself. They said, "We want to do some of the dances and styles you told us about." They wanted the dance experiences I had. I told them I would teach them a chorus line dance, and they just loved it. They kept asking me about forming a company, so I suggested we workshop the group for a year. I informed them that if everyone was still there and we still had something good going, then we would start the company. They stayed and worked really hard. We started the workshop around '77. By the time we had almost finished that year, Red Saunders was doing his fifty-year anniversary. He was a famous bandleader here in Chicago. He had been at the Club DeLisa for years, and he had a famous big band. It was his fiftieth anniversary, and Count Basie was headlining the show. They said they wanted a chorus line. It was at the Auditorium Theater downtown. That was in '78. We had almost finished our workshop year with the group, and then we had the opportunity to work with Count Basie. Billy Eckstine was also a headliner. We didn't even have a name. The group wanted something

with my name in it. I didn't want to use my name. We couldn't find anything to go with Najwa. I think Red Saunders or somebody said, "You're
dancers. Just be Najwa Dance Team." We said, "OK, we have to go with
whatever right now." But later, Mineral Bramletta, a calligrapher, came
by my house one day, and I told him that we were trying to get a name
for our company. I don't know how they came up with it, but him and
his wife, Cheri, came up with Corps. I said, "That's it! I like that. That's
it! Go no further." I liked Corps, like the Army Air Corps. The dancers
said we would like to use Najwa Dance Corps. We had to go with Najwa
Dance Team at that time because we were already in production at the
Auditorium Theater. It was our very first gig as a company. We had some
beautiful white costumes, and we were very happy and ready to go. I have
the picture. That is what happened. I had all these young ladies in college saying they would do this and do that because they wanted to use
their skills to make the company work. They also had in mind the promise they made to me about not putting all the work on me. They said they
wanted me to be the artistic director, and they would do the rest to make
the company work. I looked up, and one was busy with medical school,
another one was getting married, one was moving out of town, and one
was in law school. Everyone was busy with their lives and still wanted
to dance with the company. They did well for a length of time, and then
it got to be a lot. If you are in medical school or if you're a lawyer, how
much time do you have to really do extra work and dance too? We had
big ideas too. We said that we were starting a company and we were our
own everything, and that is how Najwa Dance Corps got its start.

What do you mean by "we were our own everything"?

We can do it. It's ten of us. There were ten women. We were going to be
big women. We were our own board. The dancers were strong, and they
were good. But then they had their own lives.

Who were some of these original people who started out with you?

Well, one is Sheila Walker Wilkens. She's still with us. She's our executive director now. LaQuietta, she's Judge LaQuietta Hardy[-Campbell]
now, and she is the chair of our board. Andrea Vinson is presently the

associate artistic director of the company and is about to move into my position of artistic director. Brenda Malika Moore is the associate artistic director of Najwa Junior Corps.

What were some of the early dances you did?

They wanted to learn about the chorus [line]. I taught them the kicks, the tiller. It's one of our signature pieces today. I taught them a chorus production piece. That's with traditional jazz, swing. A lot of people think when you say swing that you're talking about jitterbug. But, when we say jazz, we're talking about swing jazz. We're talking about traditional jazz dancing. We're talking about dancing to Count Basie and Duke Ellington and Lionel Hamilton. We're talking about being able to dance to that music, the big band sound. We got little bitty babies five years old or six that can do it because we passed the tradition on, even if [we] just teach them our dance history from all different areas. They can dance Charleston. That is what Najwa Dance Corps is about. We are a company of dancers that's about the preservation of different dance styles and techniques as it relates to the African American heritage dance experience.

What are some of the other dances that you do in your company?

Well, in our company, we do African dance and Caribbean. We do modern—I mean contemporary—and traditional and contemporary jazz. We do some modern dances. When we are interpreting some stories, we use modern. We are fortunate enough to have people in our company that are very good in certain areas. We got a couple of people who are really good in ballet. They studied ballet all the years they've been studying with us and before. So they're really good there. We have people who are really good in modern. Now while all the company members might not be at the same level with that, they still can function.

How do you define African dance? How do you define black dance?

African dance is dance from Africa. Dance that originated in Africa, developed in Africa. African American dance is dance that originated in this country, was developed and originated in this country. But, I still think it all started in Africa. And that basic beat is underlined in all of our dancing. I know where it came from. When you ask where is it from, I know where that rhythm came from. I know where that beat came from.

When people come to a Najwa Dance Corps performance, what are some things that you hope they learn from the performance?

When we do our performances, we perform a dance concert, first of all we hope you're going to enjoy the concert. We hope you're going to get something out of it. People get different things out of it. We tell stories. We talk about our lives through our performances, maybe talk about the lives of African Americans through our performances, and hope you see something and feel something. We're trying to get stronger every day. I hope you can see the progress in us. I hope you see progress in the quality of our performances, see progress in the dancers and their technique, can [appreciate] the significance of history in it, and understand more about our culture and some positive things from our cultures. We aim to entertain and to add a little educational component to your lives.

DARLENE BLACKBURN

Darlene Blackburn, originally from Chicago's Englewood neighborhood, began dancing by learning social dances from her family members and in local night-clubs. She started her formal dance training in her twenties at a number of the dance studios located in downtown Chicago. After Blackburn began dancing with Kelan Phil Cohran and the Artistic Heritage Ensemble as an interpretive dancer, she formed a professional dance company, the Darlene Blackburn Dance Troupe, which lasted until the 1980s. Blackburn has taught at Kennedy-King College, Columbia College Chicago, and Purdue University. She is the recipient of a number of awards and honors, including the Phenomenal Women Award at V-103's Expo for Today's Black Woman and the Alyo Award from Muntu Dance Theatre of Chicago.

In interviews conducted in May and August 2011, Darlene Blackburn reflects on the social dance scene in Chicago in the 1960s and 1970s, and her perfor-mances as an interpretive dancer during the Black Arts Movement. Blackburn also discusses her extensive travels to Africa, which helped her to understand the connection between African dance and African American social dances, and her efforts to bring African dance forms to Chicago.

My name is Darlene Blackburn. I was born July 12, 1942. I'll be sixty-nine this year [2011], and that's a blessing. I work at Dunbar High School. I'm a physical education teacher. I've only been there five years. Before that

I was working at Calumet High School, which [became] Perspectives [Charter School]. I was there for twenty years.

How did you begin dancing?

Everybody in my family could dance, so it wasn't a big deal. They all could dance, and I just marveled at watching my mother and father, at that time, doing the jitterbug. That's what they called it. I used to say, "Oooh, y'all gotta teach me how to do that!" My uncle and auntie would be doing it, and I just loved the way they danced. They just seemed to be so good at it. They taught me, but they never wanted me to really be a dancer. At that time, you didn't see any black dancers on TV, and everybody that was dancing was in the nightclubs and stuff. My mom didn't want me doing all that.

What were some of the nightclubs at that time that people were dancing in?

At Club DeLisa, you had the chorus line. At the Regal [Theater], you had a chorus line. They would bring in the entertainers.

Was that, basically, the only option for black women or black dancers?

Mmmm-hmmm . . . and exotic dancing. It wasn't looked on as something that you would want your child to be a part of. As I started getting older, they had a place called Budland, and I loved Budland. If you wanted to learn any social dance, you would go down to Budland. If you wanted to learn any of the Latin dances—like the cha-cha, the mambo, the meringue—you would go to Basin Street. They were all on 63rd and Cottage Grove. We're talking about the sixties, the seventies, and probably eighties. Then, across the street, if you wanted to get dressed and look sharp, you went to the Grand Ballroom. If you were into jazz, right across the street was a jazz club where all the great jazz musicians would come. Budland was downstairs [in the basement of the Pershing Hotel], and upstairs was the Pershing Ballroom. People like Jackie Wilson performed there. It's unbelievable we don't have places like that now.

What kind of dances were you doing? Jitterbug?

Well, no, that's what my parents did. In my day, it was called the bop. You see, that's how it went. It went from the jitterbug to the bop, and now it's called steppin'. [*Laughing*] I was doing the bop during that time and all the different social dances. At Budland, they would have dance contests to see who could do those social dances the best—Uncle Willie, the jerk, snake, all of these here—and I used to win all the contests. I'm not going to say I just won them because I was one of the better dancers. I won them because I didn't drink. [*Laughing*] The crowd, my buddies, they would cheer for me so they'd get that fifth of whiskey. I'd say, "You all ain't cheering for me just because I can dance and my partner can dance." Me and my partner—he was a basketball player—we didn't drink. They were cheering for us so that they got the bottle [given to the winner]. [*Laughing*] So, I thought that was interesting. At first it looked good, until I started winning too much.

What was your partner's name?

His name was George Moore. He got a scholarship to go away to college playing basketball and stuff.

So this was when you were about seventeen and eighteen?

Mmmm-hmmm. Exactly. I was dancing at all these clubs, and I would go down the street and do my little Latin dances because I really wanted to learn that too. I just loved all forms of dance. Then I met a friend down at Basin Street. His name was Master Henry [Gibson]. He would be down there, and he was playing the Timbales. I was dancing in front of the Timbales, and he said, "Oooh, you got the groove. You really can do this." I said, "Oh, thank you." Then he said, "I'm working with a band, and they're having auditions. They need a dancer to interpret their music. Why don't you audition for it?" I said, "I don't know nothing about no real dancing. I'm just having fun." He said, "Oh no, this is exactly what the composer wants. He just wants somebody that can just listen to the music and do whatever they feel. So come on, go to the audition." He took me to the audition, and it was for Kelan Phil Cohran—at that time, Phil

Cohran and the Artistic Heritage Ensemble. I auditioned. He [Kelan Phil Cohran] said, "I just want you to listen to this music, and I'll come back and then you can show me what you have decided to do on this music." So I listened to the music, and I started feeling some of the movements I would do. Then I showed him. I danced, and he said, "Well, let's try another one," another piece of his compositions. He said, "Yeah, that's what I'm looking for. I like the way you dance, sister." [*Laughing*] That's the way he would talk. He was very serious. He scared me to death. He said, "We're getting ready to open up this club called the Sultan, and we need just one dancer only that is willing to dance." Well, at that time I wasn't wearing no natural, even though the so-called blacks were wearing naturals. He said, "Only thing is, I need you to get your ears pierced." I hadn't had my ears pierced then. He said, "And I need you to wear a natural because that's what you're representing. You're representing black women and so you have to look like the real black, natural woman." So, I went home and told my mom. I said, "Wow, I got this thing. They want me to dance, but they want me to wear an Afro. They want me to get my ears pierced. It seems like it's a little bit too much." She said, "Well, that's up to you." My mom was very liberal with me. She said, "It's up to you to make that decision."

By that time, I had dropped out of school, out of college, and I had decided that I wanted to pursue dance. That's what I was doing. I was taking some dance classes at that time, and I was working downtown at Illinois Bell [phone company]. I was taking [classes with] Jimmy Payne, Afro-Cuban and calypso, and I was doing pretty good in that. Then I was taking modern dancing from Neville Black, and I was doing good in that. But my ballet, which I was taking from Stone and Camryn, I would be the only black in the classes. That class was killing me and making me feel very inferior. I was feeling very self-conscious and feeling that I couldn't dance, that I had so much to learn. I didn't realize until later on that I hadn't been taking ballet since I was five, so why was I coming in there at [the age of] twenty-one thinking that I'm going to be able to keep up with them? But being that I thought I was a dancer, I thought I could do it and all I needed to do was practice hard. I really wasn't—that's why I didn't want to audition because I really wasn't secure as a dancer, or what I call a real dancer, after seeing these ladies put their leg up to their forehead, point their feet, and all of that. What made me even go to

Stone and Camryn, because I didn't know about them, was Julian Swain, one of our great dancers that just passed. He was at Club DeLisa with a group of dancers, which Najwa, Arnell Pugh, was in. That's how I met Arnell Pugh. I went and saw them doing the chorus line. I told you that was all that was going on then. I said, "Oh, I want to be in that chorus line." Here I am about twenty, twenty-one, and I said, "This is what I want to do. I want to parade across the stage and look good, too." [*Laughing*] And he told me—and I was so hurt—he said, "No, I don't think this is for you." Julian Swain told me, "I think that you need to just go and take some classes and learn some real dancing." He asked me if I had ever taken any classes. I said, "No, just social dancing." He said, "No, you go ahead." He [Julian Swain] is the one that recommended Stone and Camryn, and he told me to take some modern classes, ballet, jazz, [and] tap. I was working, like I told you, at a telephone company [Illinois Bell]. He said, "Just take the gamut of classes since you're working downtown where you can walk to these classes." All the classes were downtown. I would get off of work and go—we had respect for our elders. He was an elder dancer telling me, as a young dancer, what I should do instead of [me] just jumping into a chorus line, so I thought he should know. I was hurt. I wanted to be in that chorus line, but since he said that's what I should do, I said, "OK, I'll pursue it that way, then." So that's who really got me to take classes, and, like I said, I started doing just that. Tommy Sutton was downtown. I took some jazz classes and tap classes from him. I took, from Jimmy Payne, Afro-Cuban and calypso. I took, from Stone and Camryn, ballet. I took from Neville Black—the Jamaican—modern and contemporary dance. I just took the gamut. At that time, what it was all about was that, if you called yourself a dancer, you should be able to do any form of dance. I wanted to call myself a dancer, so that was the reason I went that route with that guidance. Arnell said the same thing, she said, "Well, if that's what he told you to do," because I came to her and them [the other chorus line dancers]. They thought I was going to make the audition, but I didn't make the audition. I was so hurt, and she told me, "Nah, don't feel like that! You're young." She said, "Just go ahead and do what he tells you to do." I went on and did it, and I would still come [and] watch them perform. I would ask, "When y'all performing next?" because I'm following them around just watching them perform.

What was it about the chorus line that made you so . . .

Just the pretty idea. Just grand. Just looking grand, and putting on the big feathers and the clothing. You would see that kind of thing on whites doing it on TV, the Las Vegas look and all that, but you never saw any blacks. In New York, you would see the Rockettes, but back then there weren't any black Rockettes. I thought, "I got the figure. I look like that. Why can't I do that? I can't understand why I can't do that."

So this was your opportunity to do that.

Mmmm-hmmm. Yes.

How many years did you take all of these classes?

I continued taking those classes for a long, long period of time, maybe ten to fifteen years. I never stopped taking classes until I got older. I was always taking class. I learned that it just keeps you growing as long as you're studying. And now I am with Phil Cohran and the Artistic Heritage Ensemble, and I was choreographing this music, so I gotta come up with different ideas. I gotta get a vocabulary of dance to fit whatever the dance happens to represent. That even made me want to take classes more whereas Phil Cohran was into, "Go into yourself, lady. Go into yourself." So then I started taking yoga to go into myself. Me and Asar Ha-pi hooked up and before we knew it another brother named Yirser [Ra Hotep hooked up with us]. We were just beginning and getting involved in these things. They would just come over here, and we wouldn't start doing yoga until ten, eleven, twelve at night, when it was really quiet and peaceful. We were serious, serious about our diet, fasting and stuff. Asar, he wanted to totally be spiritual, and he had it in his mind that all of these hieroglyphics and all the movements of yoga came from Egypt, so he started the Egyptian yoga. Everybody was really serious about learning it and seeing how you could really meditate, not eat, and take yourself someplace else where you could spiritually come up with more creations from The Creator—see from *The Creator*—not from yourself really but putting yourself in such a spiritual state. It definitely has happened. I remember when I did a dance called Black Beauty on the beach.

It was close to the end of the sixties, about '69 or so—'68 or '69. We used to have a thing out at Jackson Park Beach where I used to do workshops out there [with] Brother Phil [Kelan Phil Cohran]. In the evenings, we did performances. One Sunday we were doing a performance, and we had everybody performing. Oscar Brown Jr. was performing. I was performing. At that time the Blackstone Rangers had a singing group, and they would perform. It was all walks of life. Everybody was out there. The place was so packed. It was unbelievable. I got up there, and I had been fasting for about three days trying to prepare myself for this performance. Brother Phillip's wife used to make all my clothes. She was extraordinary in fashion design.

What was her name?

Sister Delores [Cohran] and then later on she changed her name to Rahel. She's passed on too. She made me this Black Beauty outfit that had the chiffon black skirt and just a top and a bottom. When I got on that stage, I felt like I was floating. I don't know if I was floating because I hadn't eaten either. [*Laughing*] But at that time, all them people, and everything it felt like magic was happening on that stage. I felt like I was totally in a different world. I was the representation of the black woman. I just did my interpretation of the dance, but there wasn't no fear on me—"Oh, look at all these thousands of people," none of that. "I'm representing you. I'm not showing you. I'm representing you. Do you understand that?" That's the vibe I had on me. "Do you understand that I'm representing you?" So we really felt that what we were doing was something that was a contribution to blackness. People really treated us grand during those times too. They knew that we were really serious about being as good a representation of what you should be like that's possible and what you should be trying to do, taking yourself to a higher stage.

Why was that important to you at that moment?

Well, I think the sixties were a time when black people finally started saying, "Hey, it's all right for my hair to be nappy, and I still look good." We would flaunt it. We would go into the universities, and we'd be performing. We'd go into the washroom, and then we'd just really pick our hair out. [*Laughing*] I remember one time I was dancing at the Natural History Museum, and I was walking around all grand in my African garb. This little white girl said to her father, she said, "Why is she walking around like that?" She had a good father, and her father said, "Oh, she just feels good about herself, that's all." He said that, he said, "She's just feeling good about herself. She likes her African heritage." I never forgot that because I thought that was very respectful of him.

That really, really was. Did that event at Jackson Park beach happen every year or was it a one-time event?

I don't remember it happening more than two years. That's it. Because then, after that, it became so big and so huge that we decided, "What are we going to do in the winter?" We decided that we needed a theater of our own, and that's how we started the Affro-Arts Theater. From that beginning on the beach, we met at one of the lodges—I think at about 74th and Ingleside. We came together and said that we wanted to raise this money to try to open up the Affro-Arts Theater. And we did. That was on 39th and Drexel.

At this time, were you still dancing by yourself?

No, I started working at Englewood Urban Progress Center right here on 64th and Green, and I was teaching dancing there. A bunch of the students from Englewood High School and Simeon [Vocational High School] started taking classes from me. At that particular time, those were times they were giving out all these grants. They had given the Englewood Urban Progress Center a grant, so, that summer, the kids could come [and participate] in an apprentice program under me. Other kids would just take dance classes for free. I had about fifteen students that were in the apprenticeship program that I had auditioned, and they could dance real good. Then I had all the little preteens taking classes, and I would teach the big group how to teach the little ones. I had them every day. They would have the time where they would teach the kids, and then they would have the time that they would have to be with me and learn the techniques. That is really how I developed a dance troupe.

This was in the summer. They worked eight hours, ten to six or something like that. We even had the adult class if you wanted to lose weight or change your diet. They would come in the evenings. Sometimes my girls would just stay there all day with me.

That's really awesome. What kind of dances were you doing then?

It was a lot of modern. With African, it was just our feelings of what African dance was. It was our interpretations at that time because I hadn't gone to Africa yet. So in 1967, I was working at the Englewood Progress Center, and I worked dancing at night at the Sultan Club with Phil Cohran and the Artistic Heritage Ensemble. Then in '68 we did the beach and got ready to open up the Affro-Arts Theater. Then in 1969, I met Dr. Margaret Burroughs. At that time, she was still working at the DuSable Museum. I did a performance there, and she said, "How'd you learn to do that African dancing like that?" I said, "Oh, that's just my interpretation." She said, "You ain't never been to Africa?" I said, "No, I never been to Africa." She said, "You got to go." I said, "Well, I would like to." She said, "Do you want to go?" I said, "Yeah, I would love to go. I don't have no money to go. I'm just working at this progress center teaching dance." She said, "Well, do you *want* to go?" I said, "Yes." She said, "Well, I have a group that I'm involved with called the American Forum that is going this summer," and that was in 1969. She said, "The American Forum is going to go to Ghana." It [the American Forum] was a group of teachers from all over the United States that were getting ready to start African studies programs in their universities and schools. She says, "And they're going over there to study in Legon at the University there." I said, "Oh yeah, I would love to do that." She said, "Yeah, because that's where the Ghana Dance Ensemble works." I said, "Oh, OK." She said, "So we just have to raise you some money. But what I want you to do is I want you to every day make affirmations that I am going to Ghana. I want you to start your affirmations." Well, I didn't know nothing about no affirmations. [*Laughing*] I don't know nothing about none of that. But here's an elder again telling me what to do, and I'm good at following instructions. I said, "OK, I'll do it." So I started making my affirmations, "I am going to Ghana. I will get the funds that I need to go." Girl, I went to Ghana.

How long did it take you to raise those funds? And what did you do to raise those funds?

Well, remember we had started the Affro-Arts Theater then. So Dr. Burroughs took me down to this stockbroker. I'll never forget his name, Mr. Wieczorkowski. She said, "This girl needs some money to go to Ghana with me this summer, so what can we do?" And he said, "Well, what does she do that she deserves some money to go?" She said, "She's a dancer." He said, "Oh, she's a dancer, huh? Well, I need to see her dance to see if she can dance. When you gonna dance again?" I said, "Well, I'll be dancing this weekend down at the Affro-Arts Theater down on 39th and Drexel." He said, "OK, I'm going to bring my whole family to see you dance." So he brought his children, his wife, and they all sat there, and this is *black theater,* you know? [*Laughing*] I told them that I got these people coming because I want to go to Ghana this summer. Dr. Burroughs was there, of course, and I danced. At that time, I had this thing where I would do this dance where I would come out in Egyptian poses and stuff and then I would do a backward somersault and make like I'm going to pass out, and then I would do a kip up and do a forward roll into a handstand. I don't know if you know what a kip is, but when you bring your legs back and then you end up standing on your feet. I would stand on my feet and then do a forward roll into a handstand.

Oh my goodness.

That's right! Then I would come around, twist where I was really only on one leg, and ask the audience to give it up. [*Laughing*] I knew that that would get it, and sure enough it did. He said, "Yeah, you can dance." He gave me the rest of the money I needed. Yeah, that was something. I went to Ghana that summer with all these people from all over the United States. I hung with Victor Clottey, he was there at that time. Mr. Wieczorkowski had helped him a little and had sent a message to him to make sure that he helped me, so I was in the click. By then I could dance too. One time a girl was up on the stage dancing at rehearsal, and I was just all into what she was doing because she wasn't doing nothing but the mashed potatoes. I jumped right onstage with her [*Laughing*] because I was never scared, and I started dancing with her. We were doing African highlife. At that time, that's what it was called. The traditional name was called the Kpanlogo. They just marveled, and the Ghana Dance Ensemble just took me in because I could do their dances. I took classes, and you couldn't move on to the next class until you were able to listen to the drummer and follow directions of the drummer. During my stay there, I met their lead dancer, who also came to Chicago, [Kofi] Jantuah, and we became close friends. I became really tight with the Ghana Dance Ensemble, and then when they came here I traveled around with them. They were out of Northwestern. I was with the Ghana Dance Ensemble, and I was with a few other dancers. We gave programs at the university. I performed in the clubs while I was there in the evenings. I didn't have no money, don't forget, so I had to make some money. [*Laughing*] Yeah, I got pictures of me "the African American has come to Ghana." So Victor and them, they were around collecting the money for me because they throw you money. [*Laughing*] Right. So I can buy some souvenirs and take some things back.

So you would dance at the nightclubs in the evening and during the day you would take classes . . .

And going with the Ghana Dance Ensemble, and watching them perform all over. When you take some classes you [would] go from one class to the other, maybe two or three hours. I think that the main thing that I liked was going into the village with them. These are young dancers too, so when they go into the village they are learning. So that was the pride, being able to go into that Kumasi village of the Ashanti people and learn from the elders how to do the Adowa. It was not so much learning from them, but being able to be there firsthand with them in that village and learn the same time they learned from the elders. That was the key that I learned.

How long were you in Ghana?

I was only in Ghana for that summer, but it sparked up a thing in me that made me want to go back. Not to Ghana, but want to go back to Africa. I felt that as much as I had brought back by myself, then—that's where I was at that time—suppose I took some dancers with me. When I came back in '69, I choreographed a dance called *From Africa to America.*

When I went to Ghana and saw that girl doing the mashed potatoes, it clicked to me right then that our social dances were just like we had amnesia. We didn't know that we were doing African movements. All those social dances that we were doing were African movements. The music was going back and forth from Africa to America, whereas now I do it with just a drummer doing eight bars of America and eight bars of African dance.

So then my next trip was to Nigeria in 1971. I thought this was so great, what I had done, let me take some dancers. We raised the money again. Oscar Brown Jr. and Jean Pace, all of them helped us raise some money. Herb Kent was our DJ. I did an African fashion show *Moods of Blackness*. This took place at—at that time it was called the Colonial House, which was on 79th right off of Cottage Grove. It used to be a place where kids used to go and dance and eat. They used to have Steppers Sets there, but now it's a motel.

How many dancers did you take to Nigeria?

I took eight dancers and two drummers. I wanted to make sure that the drummers knew the rhythms. At that time, his name was Black Harold [Murray]. Now his name is Brother Atu. He was one of the master drummers that ended up teaching all of the drummers that were here. I'm sure you heard them talk about him. He was my main drummer at that time and Kewu, another one of the drummers. I took him, Kewu, because the rest of them couldn't go at that particular time, and he wanted to go. I took Alyo Tolbert who later on became Muntu's director. I took him with me as my lead male dancer.

Who was your lead female dancer?

Melveda Blackman. She ended up being a nurse and moved to Oregon, but she was my lead dancer.

So how did you arrange this trip? So you said that you . . .

Just making them affirmations, and we were well respected by then. I didn't go until 1971, my second trip, and we had been performing around with Brother Phil at the different universities. People had seen us before, so I thought about it, I said, "I'm going to do some performances of my own." I talked to different people at different universities and told them that when we came back we would do a performance, just give us the money. They agreed. They gave us money. All these different universities gave us money because they had all these black studies programs. Then the last monies that we needed, we had a couple of donations from—see, somebody else handled that, but I remember it was some kind of sausage company. Some black company on Wabash or State Street. I can't remember the name of that place, but that was one of the black companies that gave us some money and then the Colonial House—we really raised a lot of money there at that performance and everybody did everything free. And all the money went to our trip.

. . . to get everybody there. Were the universities local?

No, they weren't. I was in residence at Purdue University. No, it wasn't local.

Who were your contacts in Nigeria? How did you initiate contact in Nigeria?

That was interesting too because the reason why we decided to go to Nigeria was because at that particular time, in '71, some of the Nigerians were over here. They said that they knew this hotel that wanted some performers. So that's how we could have our room and board paid if we were willing to perform. I said, "Well, we're definitely willing to perform, if y'all want to give us our room and board free." That's how we first started out when we got there. They met us at the airport and took us to the hotel. It was a hotel in Nigeria in Akoka, it was one of the suburbs of Lagos. I know it was close to Lagos, I do know that for sure.

How long did you stay in Nigeria at that time?

Same thing. Maybe about six weeks. That's all. We started performing in the evenings, and they started taking us around and seeing the different dances. We were learning—a little bit—we ain't really learning that much, and I'm really angry because this is the real reason why I came. I said, "Don't y'all have some dance companies? I need to meet some dance companies because I ain't learning what I want to learn. Y'all are teaching me these little social dances, but it's not enough. I need to meet some companies." I hate to tell the truth on that one, it never did occur. I said, "This is not working for us because we're not interested in just coming here sightseeing and being tourists. We want to meet with some dancers." So we spaced from that hotel because I wasn't learning nothing and hooked up with some college students. I hate to say it, but the college kids were not into the culture. You have to go into the villages and meet the real dancers. They [the students] were just not in tune. We finally met an Afro-American named Oliver, and he had a big place. He was a basketball coach, and he said, "I can house all of y'all," because we weren't splitting up. He housed all of us, and we met Fela [Kuti]. We were going to his club, and he liked the way we danced. I was still trying to find out where we could get to some dance companies before we left. I hate to say that never did really happen.

And then you came back and you brought some stuff back, but not exactly . . .

Not what I wanted to. We made our next show really cool, which means very good, and taught the Juju, which is one of their social dances I learned there. I choreographed that. It just made me want to go back and really learn some stuff and know that that wasn't the area that I wanted to go in—I hate to say, where the Yorubas were—because Nigeria is huge and there's so many ethnic groups there. I said, "No, this was the wrong one." Then what happened, in '77, FESTAC occurred [in Nigeria]. That's when Julian Swain dancers, which Najwa was a part of at that time, and my troupe were voted, more or less, by our peers to go. Between that time of '71 and '77, I had gone and studied in New York and had been with another African dance company, Titos Sompa Congolese Dance [Company, then called Tanawa Dance Company]. I had really gone, as usual, to study modern—the Lester Horton technique—and heard them drums and went in the studio at Clark Center. Titos had just come there, and he was teaching the class. I just looked and marveled because I had never seen this Congolese style of dancing. I said, "I gotta come back and take that class." I came back, took that class, and, before you knew it, he was asking me to join the company. I joined the company while I was there in New York.

So what year was this that you first saw him? You said you were going back and forth to New York.

Right. Back and forth. Well, my uncle started that. That would be my Christmas present. I'd always go there for the holidays and study. It was two weeks at a time. Once in a while, maybe a month, but mostly just two weeks because I was working. [Then] *Purlie* came to Chicago. Purlie is a Broadway musical, and it comes out of the play *Purlie Victorious* by Ossie Davis. They had a Broadway musical called *Purlie*. I auditioned for it, and I made it. It closed in New York on Broadway, and that's how I got to stay in New York again. We traveled all around the United States and then we just came back to Broadway. We had gone from here to Baltimore to Pittsburgh, and I think I was only in New York about a month. That was fabulous being on the road with that because that was something I always wanted to do. I took advantage of that. I think what happened about that time was that my mom knew I was so sad about not taking that other opportunity [joining Katherine Dunham's dance company]—letting that go by—that she pushed me on this opportunity. This time she pushed me instead of just leaving it up to me to decide. She said, "Yeah, you ain't got no reason why you can't do it. Go on down there and audition." I was just telling her about it. [She said,] "No, go on down there. Audition." Then the next day, I said, "I think I made it." [She said,] "Well, then, let's get ready to get packin'." [*Laughing*] She changed her vibe on dance with me.

So you stayed in New York and danced with Titos Sompa and his company. Where was that company performing? Just places in New York or was that traveling around?

Yes, just places in New York. We became real close friends, and I told him I had a company here in Chicago. He said, "I don't have a lot of money. I'm making little chump change." I said, "I don't want the money. I just want your permission to use the choreography. That's all I want. I have a company here in Chicago, and I would really love to teach them these dances and different movements you have taught me. I would like to make up some dances from them." He said, "Sure, but you don't want to keep the money. [*Laughing*] Fine." You know how people are. Girl, I used that material over and over and my company was in awe with that material.

Was your company suspended while you were gone?

No, that's the beauty of having good people like Alyo Tolbert who became the first director and choreographer of Muntu Dance Theatre of Chicago. Alyo, I tell you, he was my lead dancer, and I had male dancers at that time that worked downtown at the TV studios. They kept the company going while I was gone. They were performing while I was gone. They would send me money.

Oh, wow! [Laughing] *Really good people. So you came back with all this new material and taught it to them. What was the reaction?*

They were just flabbergasted. It was just awesome. That was how we got the standing ovation. That's how we got a standing ovation to go to FESTAC because I taught them that material and nobody had seen that material.

Right. Because people weren't doing Congolese dance then.

That's right. That's right. They couldn't believe that material. I'll never forget Don L. Lee, which is Haki R. Madhubuti, one of the ones in charge, kidding me. He said, "Y'all already been"—teasing us—"so why should you go back to Nigeria?" I said, "Did you see them stand up for us? That's why we should represent. That's why. [*Laughing*] It's that simple. We should represent." Any time your peers stand up for you and your elders—Tommy Gomez from the Katherine Dunham Dance Company was still alive then, Lucille Ellis, who I studied with also—stood up and said, "Y'all are just . . . That was just awesome."

What were some of the dances you choreographed with this material?

The main one that I choreographed that marveled me was—because my great grandmother had passed and she lived out in Robbins, Illinois—

this piece called "Mama Delé." I have a lot of artist friends. I told one of the AACM [Association for the Advancement of Creative Musicians] people—I can't remember his name right now—that I had this song that I wanted him to make up about Mama Delé being sad because nobody was coming and visiting her, and it was making her sick. I felt that that was the reason why my great grandmother had passed because she would not come and live with any of us. She was out there in that house by herself. Her husband had died, and she didn't come into the city. We didn't come out there enough to see her. So that was the feeling that I had choreographing this piece. I told it to him, and he wrote the song, lyrics and music, to it. I had another friend, and I asked her to sing it. They taught it to my dance company, the song, "Woka. Woka. Woe is Mama Delé." I choreographed it where I played Mama Delé and Alyo [Tolbert] would be the native doctor. He would come and try to heal Mama Delé. Before he came, all of them would come back and they would try to dance in front of her, try to show, "We love you, Mama Delé," and dance and try to get her to move to get her to feel better. But they finally had to call the native doctor in. He puts some stuff on her, and she starts moving. Then she starts dancing with everybody and that's how—it's a crescendo thing.

And that's how she kind of got healed?

Mmmm-hmmm.

So you took that movement and then you turned it into something that was speaking to what was happening in this community here when you came here?

Yeah, I just felt that his stuff was fun, and I just had a little more serious—I didn't mind doing that stuff because I became popular from Bouché. Bouché got to be one of my numbers. Mama Delé was my serious pieces because, like I said, it wasn't about trying to entertain nobody. It was a crying number. It was sad for me, even choreographing it, because it was close to me.

Do you know who organized that competition?

I remember [that] it was at Malcolm X College. They had a FESTAC [committee]. Abena [Joan Brown], Don L. Lee, Jeff Donaldson—he was the head of the Midwest. When we went to FESTAC, they [the groups] were from all over the United States, but they were in charge of who was going to go. They—Lerone Bennett was another one that was in there—knew they couldn't just say, "You go. You go." They couldn't have done that. They couldn't have gotten away with it. They would have to let the people choose who they wanted to go.

How many companies or how many groups competed at this competition?

Oh, maybe about five or six companies.

So it was Darlene Blackburn Dancers, Najwa . . .

There wasn't no Najwa [Dance Corps] then.

Julian Swain . . .

Julian Swain Dancers. We really were the two main, big companies in there. There was a lot of other companies trying to start up and stuff. It was almost like just giving them a chance. That's why Haki joked that, "You've been there before. Why you need to go back." But it really wasn't a lot of companies that had put in the work. It was just that simple. That's why I didn't go along with none of that mess. If you put in the time, you deserve to go. We had put in the work. We had put in the time. Julian Swain and them—the same thing—they put in the work and put in the time. We would perform—all of us—would perform without getting paid a lot of times all over the city. That's because we thought it was the right thing to do, to let black kids see us out there.

So you went to FESTAC in '77. How long were you there?

I'd say probably about two weeks because they kept filtering different companies in. It was really big fun. When we were coming in, Val Gray Ward and them were leaving out and telling us how awesome it was. [They said,] "You're going to enjoy yourself!" It was so awesome, and they had this FESTAC Village where we all stayed. At nighttime, all the different companies—different *African companies*—would be performing also. It wasn't just the African Americans. We had the African American village. The Cameroonians had their village, the Congolese had their village, Sudanese . . . they were from all over Africa.

So you could mingle and meet . . .

Mmmm-hmmm. And meet all these different ethnic groups. It was just fantastic.

What kinds of exchanges did you have? In my mind, there must have been huge jam sessions.

Yeah, the drummers did. The drummers had a whole lot of that. The different companies would have dance workshops. That was really great.

Did you teach workshops yourself there?

No, I didn't. We were performing. When we weren't performing, we were traveling around because then I really knew I needed to get close to the villagers. I needed to get out of the tourist life and get where I could meet with the people.

So during this trip, at FESTAC, is where you met folks from Calabar University?

Cross River State [in southeastern Nigeria].

And they're the ones that brought you back?

No. Yeah, they're the ones that brought me back, but that's not how I got back. OK, we performed in Nigeria, and we were all in the newspaper. We got standing ovations and a fellow told me, he said, "We are looking to start a dance company at Calabar University, and would you be interested in being interviewed for the position?" I said, "Sure." Well, I didn't expect to hear from none of them. I came on back to Chicago, and, a couple months later, I heard from them. They said, "We're having interviews in Atlanta. Can you come to Atlanta for the interview?" I said,

"I don't have no money to be coming [to Atlanta]. I don't got no money to be doing none of this stuff." They said, "We'll send for you. That's not a problem." So I went to Atlanta, and I can't even remember the university. I went to the university and interviewed for the job. It was a circle of Nigerians and professors that worked at the Calabar University. They said, "Oh yeah, we heard about your company and how good it was. Would you be willing to leave them to teach in Nigeria?" I said, "Of course, because that's just going to just give me more knowledge." They said, "Well, we are looking for someone." He [one of the professors] asked me a whole lot of questions that I personally don't even remember now. I just remember that the main thing they wanted to know was would I be willing to leave, and I said I would. They called me back and sent me that plane ticket, and there I was. That's when I told you I called [Kofi] Jantuah because he had just gotten here. I said, "I'm going to Nigeria. If you really need someplace to stay, you can stay here while I'm gone."

He was just coming here because he was moving to Chicago?

Yeah. He had come with the Ghana Dance Ensemble and decided he wanted to stay here. He liked the people here and people liked him. He liked the Ghanaians because the Ghanaians were what was happening at that time. That was the same thing that happened to the Senegalese companies, some of them, that came here.

They decided that they wanted to stay.

Mmmm-hmmm. [*Laughing*]

What were some of the dances you were performing at FESTAC when you were there?

Again, we were doing our own thing. We did *From Africa to America.* You know that genre. Then the dance that got the standing ovation was this calypso number that was in fluorescent costume. We had that. We put that altar light on it, and, when we came out, all you see is blackness and the costumes. And they *screamed*! They had never seen nothing like that. That just knocked 'em out. That's the one that took over because all of us—and we were all tall—had on our costumes and head wrapped. After that, we came back with *Afro*. Afro's the one where I flip and stand on my head. I got another girl that does walking splits and does the Chinese split. In Afro, we did all these gymnastics. They probably had never seen women doing gymnastics like that because they called us Amazon women. [*Laughing*] The boys did a lot of push-up things and all the acrobatics too, but I know what it was. Before you knew it, we were all in the newspapers. "Girl splits in the air." I said, "Girl splits in the air?" [The company members said,] "They're talking about you when you stood on your head and opened your legs." I was wondering what . . . "Split in the air?" It was so funny. They got one picture of one of my dancers, who lives in New York now, doing the Chinese split, and like you see her legs out like that.

Oh yeah. So they hadn't seen women doing those kinds of acrobatics.

Mmmm-hmmm. That's what it was.

So you interviewed for this job, you got the job at Calabar University, and you left. So this was the end of '77?

Mmmm-hmmm. And I stayed there until '80.

What was that like? Tell me a little bit more about that trip.

Awesome, girl. But, like I told you, I got there thinking that these kids can dance. I go there, and they don't know their dances. I'm at this university, and they don't know their dances. Some of them tell me they haven't been home since elementary.

So these are like high-achieving . . .

High-money kids because you gotta have money to go to school in Africa. They had gone to high school in Europe, in Great Britain somewhere, in London. They hadn't been home. They came back now that they're building universities [after Nigeria's independence from the British in 1960]. So I said, "Well then, this is not going to work." I talked to the theater department, I said, "This is not working because I'm not learning no dances. They don't know their dances. I need to go into the interior. I need to go to their villages." They didn't have no problem. They said, "OK. We'll give you whatever you need." They gave me a couple vans—for people to take me because I wasn't getting ready to go there by myself— and told me to choose a couple of the students and take them with me. I asked the students what would be the best time for me to go. We planned this. No more of this just jumping up [and] doing. We planned it. They said, "Well, the New Yam Festival would be a good time because that's when they'll be doing all the dances." I said, "Oh, OK, then. To what village should we go? I want to see it [dance] from all different parts of Nigeria. I want to see the south. I want to see up north." So we planned wherever we were going to go, and then I was supposed to come back and choreograph this big production. We went everywhere, and then we sat down and decided how the stories would go with the dancers because everything was done in story form that I choreographed. We wasn't just doing the dances. I wanted them to tell me the stories.

Behind the dances.

Uh-huh. So we did it all in a story form and the New Yam Festival was the one that I liked more than any that I've done. It tells the whole story of how important those new yams are. If they're big, they're going to have enough food to feed their whole village for the rest of the year. So that's real important for the yams that they bring back to be big. You could tell that when the girls are coming down the hills with the yams on their head, and they're singing and stuff, they must be good. Everything is OK. Everybody's cheering them. At that time, all the little virgin girls are coming out to show off their wares, trying to find a husband. They got the maiden dance. Then you got the bride coming out of the fatten-ing house. She done got all luscious. All the older women been coming in telling her how to cook and take care of a man and all the herbs—if somebody gets sick—because you gonna have plenty of children. They done taught her everything, and so they bring her out of the fatten-ing house. She's got her thing on her head and all the beads around her waistline and on these hips and stuff. Fabulous. Fabulous. Then all the maidens are dancing around her and stuff.

Oh my goodness.

Fabulous. I choreographed all that too. I choreographed it there too for the stage in Nigeria, and it was so good that we [my company] traveled. I started a company there. They asked me to, and we traveled all around Nigeria performing.

Nice. What was the name of the company you started in Nigeria?

We just called it the Calabar University Theatre Company.

So you created this troupe and you stayed there for three years.

I stayed there two years first and then I told them I would come back for another two, but I came home. Of course, when I came home, I did not want to leave home. But I had made my promise that I would come back, so I did come back to get everything in order. I told them that I would only be there a year because I was going to go back home and go back to school and then possibly, after school, I might come back. Never did happen. But I stayed in contact with them.

Did the Nigerian dance troupe continue?

Yeah. I left one of the best dancers, and one they respected in charge. I already had taught them that "you respect him, you respect me, because he's in charge now." I gave him my house.

1980. Your troupe in Chicago still existed, and you had a place where you could teach these dances. What was it like when you came back?

Again, everybody wanted to see what I had. Everybody wanted to see these new dances. Chicago wanted to see what Blackburn had brought back, and I was just happy that I had some dancers to put the choreography on. I started teaching downtown on Wabash again and that worked out well. Then I started dealing with tai chi, which was awesome, with one of my friends, Jabulani Kamau Makalani (Clovis E. Semmes). He used my studio, and I started taking tai chi. Then I started working with

Yirser [Ra Hotep]. Yirser was taking tai chi and teaching yoga in my studio. I told you I had the universal idea by then of seeing all these different
connections, and, with the tai chi and the yoga, I was choreographing a
variety of things that I had in my mind. Plus, I had my dancers then. I was
just trying to expand my growth because I didn't want to just be known
for copying traditional dancing. I never liked that kind of stuff. I'm really
glad I started with Kelan Phil Cohran, as being an interpretive dancer,
because it didn't take away from my creativity. I always tried to keep that
alive—where something came from within me. That's why I always kept
yoga and tai chi and all of that going and kept studying to keep my technique because, like I told you, I didn't want to not be able to move. We
kept performing. I started performing a lot with Urban Gateways.

Where were you rehearsing at this time?

An elder lady, European, let me use her studio downtown on Wabash. It
was around Lake and Wabash. She had a studio downtown, and she was
crippled. See, that's what I'm talking about. She was an elderly dancer—
another one—her hip had gone out. She couldn't teach anymore, and I
was renting from her. She was teaching from a wheelchair, and then that
didn't work out. She had to close her studio, and then I started teaching
at the South Side Community Arts Center, right across the street from
Dr. Burroughs's home on 38th and Michigan. That worked out really
well. Asar was teaching up there too and a photographer was right down
on the next floor. We were on the third floor, the photographers were on
the second floor, and an art gallery was on the first floor. I taught there
for a while. When I say a while, I'm talking about years, several years.
Then from there, Kennedy-King College and, like I said, I decided to go
back to school. I just told them just like that. They didn't believe me. I
said, "I'm going back to school. You're doing good in Urban Gateways." I
told Ravanna [Prince Ravanna Bey] and them, I said, "Y'all got to keep
it going so y'all have some funds. I'm not going to keep doing this. I'm
going on back to school, and then I'm going into the system. I'm getting older." That is exactly what I did. I went on some trips. I went to
Cuba with Dr. Burroughs. I went to Barbados with the DuSable Museum. That's when I started getting into the islands. Gateway sent me to
Trinidad. Barbados turned out so good, the company asked me to come

back there and work with them. I went back to Barbados. I really liked Barbados.

What was that decision to go back to school about?

I had a child. That was really what it was about. I knew that I could do without because I had done it so many times. I never was worried. But I felt, as she was growing up, I didn't want her to say I want this or I want that and I would have to say, "Well I'm not dancing at this time, so I can't get you that. You got to wait until I'm performing." Performing, it's not all the time. That was the reason why I taught all the time because I wasn't performing all the time, but I could teach all the time. And teaching, like I said, there wasn't always money. Most of the times I taught, it was free or I wrote grants, especially when I had a company. I wrote grants because I had to make sure that all the dancers working were getting paid. I never thought that that was a good way to do it because then you got to choreograph things a certain way. I never wanted to do that either, be limited to always choreographing a certain way to please people. That was one of the reasons why I stopped the company because it was just too much work for me. I didn't want to go through just getting grants and trying to please people and choreographing and worrying about my choreography being a certain way. I said, "No, this is too much work. I'm going to let this go." I graduated in 1984 from Northeastern University in physical education. I came out with 4.3. Then I got my Chicago State master's in 1987—master of science in physical education. I guess a lot of dancers don't know I have that. I taught it to all my young dancers, get your education. I taught it to them. When I was with Lucille Ellis, that is something that Lucille taught us. [We would] sit around and talk about the arts and talk about history. So when I was with my dancers, I sat around and talked to them about [getting an education and the dances]. "You need to get an education. You need to know about the dances in case someone comes up to you and asks you what was that dance you did. You don't even know the name of it or where it came from?" I said, "No, we are not going to have none of that. We're going to sit around, and I'm going to teach you, show you where the dances come from, and you're going to try to remember." I taught them that. I have dancers that have come back to me and say, "I didn't listen to you, but I'm doing those

dances now. You think you could give me a little history again?" I remember I used to say to them every day, "You need to know where these
dances come from." In traditional dances, I told them, "They're not my
dances. They're our dances. They're our ancestors' dances. I'm not going
to tell you not to do them dances." Any of the dancers that dance with
me can use any of my material. There's never been a problem with that.
Sometimes they'll call me up and give me that type of respect and say,
"I really would like to teach . . . because I've got some little boys and I
want them to learn this dance." I say, "Fine, yes. Take it to them. Pass it
on." That's what it's all about. When it comes to traditional dances, that
is what you're supposed to do, pass it on.

In 1987, you finished your master's, you started working in the schools?

Yes. I was working at Kennedy-King College. I'd already applied to be a
sub because that's all I thought about doing. I said, "I'm already working
here, I'll just go ahead and sub sometimes and keep some extra money
because I'm still dancing." They called me to be a "cadre" [substitute
teacher] at Sullivan, which means that I don't have to go to different
schools. I just stay at that one school.

Sullivan is a high school?

Yes, up on the North Side. That's where Deidre Dawson was.

What was your dance life like at this time? Where were you dancing?

I also was teaching at Columbia College and now—see, here I am again—
I got another group of dancers. See all these dancers that are coming
through me? Now they're coming out of Columbia College because I'm
teaching there on Saturdays, just part time. I got all these dancers coming to take my African dance class, and I'm getting some good dancers
because they're already majoring in dance at Columbia College.

You were teaching the dances you learned from Nigeria, Ghana, and the Con-
golese dances?

Yes. Calypso. Caribbean dances.

That was very diasporic.

Right. Who was there? [Shirley] Mordine was there at that time, and I knew her very well. Mordine Dance Company. She was the director at the dance center. We were up north, 4700 North Sheridan. They started off right on the lake. I started with them when they started teaching classes for Shirley Mordine. That was where the dance center was.

How long did you stay there?

I stayed there about seven years—five, six, seven years—something like that. It went off and on at Columbia. I had a company of dancers there. We were performing all over.

What are some of the dances that you were creating at this point?

We kept *African Highlights* active because that was something that everybody liked. I always dealt with that theme of *From Africa to America.* We would do maybe about four or five African dances, and then we'd turn around and do four or five American dances. We actually would go from *Calypso* into *RAW, Raw Soul,* and then we would end up with *From Africa to America.*

Why is that theme important for you?

That theme, *From Africa to America*, is very important for me because I believe everything comes out of Africa. No doubt about it. Now I'm telling everybody. They thought I was very arrogant at Columbia, but they took my class. Everything comes out of Africa, the second largest continent in the world. I made them learn the history. They had to learn at least five black dancers. How can you not know five black dancers? It's like saying you play the trumpet and you don't know Miles Davis. How can you not know Miles Davis and call yourself a trumpet player? So I don't know how you can be a black dancer and can't name me five black dancers. So that was the kind of teacher I was, and I was allowed to be that kind of teacher or I would've never stayed there that long. It was a great time, though, because I got a couple grants while I was at Columbia College to choreograph stuff.

This generation, they are such a challenge. That's the only reason why I still try to—I used to want to try to reach everybody when I was a young teacher. Now if I reach one black pearl, I am so happy. If I could reach one or two of them and keep them on the right path, it is to me a miracle because it is so hard. It is so hard to keep them steadfast.

We were at '87 [1987], after I graduated and went into the school system. I went to Sullivan and then I came to Calumet because they called me and asked me to come over there. How they persuaded me, they said, "We got a full-time sub [substitute teacher] position over here and you'll be able to have your benefits." So the benefit word got me. So I came on over to Calumet High School at 81st and May, and they were wide open. Of course, they had heard about me. I was still teaching at Columbia College and started teaching dance under P.E. I just was having a good time over there. I started a dance company over there, and they were open to it. They were open to it. That's what I'm talking about. Now, we're in '87, '88, '89, '90, and they were just open. A couple of my dancers that graduated from there are teaching dancing now. Some of them are teaching in their church, one of them is coming over here now and teaches in her church. She wants to show the students when she danced.

She's coming to get videos from you.

Right. We had groups like Mostly Music started helping us over at Calumet, and they gave us grants and stuff and helped some of the kids go to college. After that, like I said, then I went to South Shore for just a couple of years, tried to get some dancing going there, and did shows there for them.

This was at the South Shore Cultural Center?

No. South Shore High School. So I was at South Shore High School for two years. They were broken up [into] all these little bitty small schools competing against each other. I said, "Oh no, this is horrible." I'm working at one school over here, then in the evening I'm working over here at another school. They're competing against each other, and they don't want to work with each other. I'm working with everybody because I'm a choreographer. I'm working with the theater department downstairs. I'm working in the tech department—that's where I'm supposed to be. Up here is tech, down here is theater arts, across the street is entrepreneurship. I'm working at all these different schools in the big circle of South Shore. I'm working with three different small schools that are competing with each other. That's nonsense.

And this is around funding and stability?

Yes. They're not getting along with each other. I said, "Oh, let me out of this. Ain't nothing black in this." I went to one of the teachers' fairs, and that's where I met Dr. Hall. She was looking for a P.E. teacher and said that I could probably get dance going strong there and that's why I went on over to Dunbar [High School].

But she left?

Yes. And their focus now is on academics only. They don't understand. You can get more done with the children by giving them something [where] they can learn discipline, learn how to listen, learn how to think, memorize. I try to tell them.

To this question of using performance to teach, what are some other things that you hope audiences learn when they come to a performance?

The main thing is to understand others' cultures. That's the reason why I think using media of any kind in the arts educates. That's one of the things I always liked about Katherine Dunham is that she would always make that statement, too, that she was just using the medium of dance. She was just using dance to educate about African American culture, and I always wanted my choreography to do the same thing. People would have more respect for African culture and more appreciation for it by seeing us perform. I think people have a better appreciation of African dance from seeing Muntu [Dance Theatre of Chicago] and Najwa [Dance Corps], all of us performing through the ages. They have a better appreciation of [African dance]—I think that's what we brought to Chicago to places that have a respect for it—than just some people jumping up and down. That's the main thing. Every time I teach, I say, "They're not just jumping up and down. Everything has a meaning. Every movement has a meaning. You think that because you just don't know the meaning."

What's something that you found rewarding about being a dancer?

Travels. I can look back and sit back and just think of all the places I've traveled and all the people I've encountered, adventures I've had. [*Laughing*] I feel blessed that I'm still here too.

GERALDINE WILLIAMS

Geraldine Williams (Mama Gerri) started studying dance in 1974. She is a certified Katherine Dunham Dance Technique instructor who studied under Lenwood Morris, Archie Savage, Talley Beatty, Vanoye Aikens, Pearl Reynolds, and Norman Davis. She has also studied alongside Lucille Ellis, Tommy Gomez, and Wilbert Bradley. Ms. Williams has taught dance at the Abraham Lincoln Center, eta Creative Arts Foundation, and in the Chicago Public School system for over twenty-five years. Her choreography has been seen in eta Theatre's youth productions and mainstage productions, including Eyes *and* Hip Hop Aesop.

In this April 20, 2011 interview, Mama Gerri vividly recalls her experiences with master dancers Lucille Ellis, Katherine Dunham, and Alvin Ailey as well as her experiences at the Katherine Dunham Dance Technique Seminar. Williams discusses both the power and importance of dance as a tool for building community and empowering youth.

Right now, I'm teaching dance at eta. I've been there eighteen years. I'm a former schoolteacher. I went into modeling, and modeling was moving me toward dance moves. I started taking some dance classes, and Darlene Blackburn was teaching. Then a friend of mine named Queen Mitchell told me about Ms. Ellis's class. So I started taking dance class with Ms. Ellis, and it was a wrap. I've been there since 1974.

Are those your beginnings in dance?

That was the beginning. I took a little tap with Sadie Bruce here in Chicago. It wasn't my serious interest. I went from that to racing cars. I was going to be the first racecar on U.S. 30. We used to drag race on the lakefront. When I met [my ex-husband], I met him racing. We just kind of hooked up and started racing. We had similar interests because we liked clothes too. He was going to build a race car. We started working on building the race car, and I started modeling. A friend of mine turned me on to modeling. And then from that, like I said, Ms. Ellis—

You said you started taking classes with Darlene Blackburn? Where was she teaching?

Darlene was at 39th and South Michigan. There's a museum there [now].

What was Darlene Blackburn teaching?

African dance. She had a history with Ms. Dunham and Ms. Ellis. There was an African-centered community around here: the Tropical Africa Institute, the Affro-Arts Theater, the Abraham Lincoln Center, Andy Thompson, [Jacob] Carruthers, and all that. They used to teach about Africa on Saturdays. We would all just meet up around those times, just having the same interests. We became friends. Darlene was teaching, and she had her own group. I got into it.

From Darlene you moved to Ms. Ellis?

We were all taking classes. Actually, it was right before Muntu [Dance Theatre of Chicago] started. Some of the dancers, old dancers that were with Muntu started taking classes, and Alyo [Tolbert] took classes with Ms. Ellis.

Where was Ms. Ellis teaching at that time?

Abraham Lincoln Center, on Cottage, right at 38th. [It is] Northeastern now, the Center for Inner City Studies. It used to be the Abraham Lincoln

Center. The university took it over. Like I said, Andy Thompson, [Jacob] Carruthers, and all of them basically had a foothold in that school.

Can you describe Ms. Ellis's class? Can you describe that community?

I can remember it like yesterday. Delia [Tyson] was teaching. Ms. Ellis would teach from her office. She could tell if you were making a mistake. She would be in her office, which was a couple of doors down the hallway, and she would say, "Your leg is not up high enough." And we would say, "How the hell does she [know]." She would come in toward the end, and really give us a kick-butt class. We used to call it boot camp training. She was too much. Too much! Yes! It was wonderful! We all became like family. We stayed together. It evolved into the Katherine Dunham Dance Theatre Studio in 1979 because Ms. Ellis wanted to further the Dunham Technique being taught. We started meeting after our classes on Saturday. We used to meet Tuesdays, Thursdays, and Saturdays, and this used to be for two hours, but Saturday we would be there like from twelve to six or whatever, which included a meeting after class. During that time, the Blackstone Rangers had the fort. When Jeff Fort was a little boy, Ms. Ellis was kind to him. They would send him out of the Center, and she'd say, "Oh, send that boy back here to me." She didn't tell us for years that he was protecting us. That's why no one ever bothered us down there. He would have his little celebrations on Saturdays. I think once or twice a year where they would come out in garb and they would be in that Center—actually, they've torn it down. It was a little area between 39th and close to Drexel because that's where the Fort was. It was like the mind-set of Ms. Dunham, working with the gang members. That's right. We are working with the community and not being afraid of them, and it worked. We would be down there sometimes late at night. Not many of us had cars, so we would be waiting on the bus. Ms. Ellis's husband was a white guy, and he'd come down there and no one ever harassed him.

Where were you living at that time?

I was living on 32nd and Calumet. I moved to 77th and Honore and then to my family's house on 113th and Wentworth, so I was catching the bus. That's when I went back to school. Actually, I got pregnant when I was taking classes with Ms. Ellis, and I danced with her and took classes until I was like almost eight months.

And there was no issue?

No. Many of us had children. She started a nursery. When you came into dance class, I think you paid like one or two dollars to have them watch your children. Everybody donated toys and things. You didn't have to worry about your kids running up to you, and you took class. It was wonderful.

Do you have a sense of how Ms. Ellis started? How did she get involved with this community?

Looking for a job after she finished performing. She wanted to continue teaching dance. She got some of her old books of the classes that she used to have with the teenagers because the Abraham Lincoln Center basically has always been a community center and worked with the children and stuff. She taught classes there.

What were some of the differences between her approach to dance, culture, and community and the African-centered dance community that was forming at that time?

I don't know if there was as much a difference, but not necessarily knowing how similar they were; she was older, and we were just learning and going to the lectures and things. It just happened to all come together. With Ms. Dunham's history and wanting to know why people of color move the way they do, we all came together. We saw the likeness of mind and stuff because they had been everywhere. They went through the racism. They wore naturals when it was not . . .

Done.

. . . at all because of necessity. Not doing your hair all the time and being in other countries, they just started wearing naturals. Ms. Dunham was always about knowledge, and her dancers were the same way, especially that main company.

Knowledge in terms of learning about the culture? What do you mean by "knowledge"?

Knowledge. Overall knowledge. Not just about the culture, but knowledge period. Also knowing who you are, having a foundation. That's what I teach with Dunham. Ms. Ellis taught us the foundation. That's the floor. Everything is built on something. Something is holding it up. It was started [by] taking the classes and realizing who Ms. Dunham was at the time. Knowing that this was a woman of awesome knowledge. If you went to her lectures, you would be sitting up there—I would!—with my mouth open trying to write down what she's saying and just being in awe. She's soft-spoken, and she is strong in her commitment. That's what I found with Ms. Ellis and all of them. That's what I loved and respected about them. They knew what they were doing, and to see them come together, like I said, I can't describe it. She [Ms. Ellis] introduced us to Café Society . . .

And what was that?

It was, I guess like in New York, where the performers all come, dancers, and you had the stage show. We had, I think, comedians. We had showgirls. We had dance. We had song. People dressed [up] when they came there. It was at this placed called Sawyers, which was down around McCormick Place. It's been torn down.

What year was this?

About '78. It was between '78 and '80 because my youngest daughter, Jamilah, was about three or four. She had my youngest daughter come out of a cake and say, "Hello, everybody. Hello." Ah, girl, it was—I'm telling you, just some of the stuff that we did. [*Laughing*]

What was the point of these Café Societies?

Just to take folk back to the old times to the little clubs in New York where they did swing and stuff and to introduce us back [to that], not to lose our history.

Were there only folks of color at these events? Or did anyone . . .

Anybody. It was integrated. We did a fashion show of old clothes, from the '40s and stuff. We dressed in that time. It was nice. I found an old resale shop on the North Side, and it had antiques and outfits with fur. We came out dressed in the '40s. We did it twice, and each time the same time period.

Who were some of the performers in the Café Society shows?

All the people who were in class with us. We put on the show. We did dances from that time. Mr. Wilbert Bradley worked with a good friend of mine. Roz [Johnson] and I, we were the showgirls. We had on these skimpy clothes, the tall hats, and we just walked around being beautiful and glamorous representing Josephine Baker and Eartha Kitt, and all of them when they were in their prime. Ma Rainey. She had the comedians. It just took you back in time. It was a wonderful experience.

What other kinds of events did you do?

We did a couple of shows at Kennedy-King [College]. Phil Williams was the director of the theater there, and that's when they named the theater at Kennedy-King after Ms. Dunham. We did a couple of shows there. As a matter of fact, it was filmed, but the film was lost some kind of way in transition. It showed Dunham Technique, and, basically, that's my background, Ms. Dunham. I've taken other classes, but not to the extent of Dunham.

Can you describe one of Ms. Ellis's typical classes?

We'd start with breathing to relax our body, and then we'd go into barre work to Wes Montgomery's music. Da, da, da, da, da. It was fast. We went from there to center floor. We did our work at center floor, body conditioning. From body conditioning, we would go into progressions, and it was different Dunham steps. We did steps from some of Ms. Dunham's choreography. When we developed our group, [Ms. Ellis] named it the Katherine Dunham Dance Theatre Studio. Not only did we do dance, but there was theater involved in it too and just keeping the Dunham Technique alive. Dunham was not known to the black community like Graham is to other communities. This was Ms. Ellis's way—and Tommy [Gomez's] and Wilbert's [Bradley] way—of keeping Dunham alive on the South Side. We had Norman Davis who was one of the younger Dunham instructors. He was in East St. Louis, but he would also come to Chicago sometimes and teach.

What was the initial reaction of the black community to your group and to what she was doing?

It was respect. We knew who we were. The ones who were teaching dance, like I said, took classes with Ms. Ellis to learn that technique. Dunham has a foundation of African-Caribbean dance. Those who were into African dance [would] take class with her, and she was an elder in the community.

How about the larger Chicago community?

I think they did too. We were so involved in what we were doing. Ms. Ellis sent me to Jimmy Payne. I even studied with this man, Jimmy King the Limbo King. The Limbo King was a tall man, and he did the limbo all the way down to the floor. We worked with him, Sadie Bruce, Fred Baker, and Ronnie Marshall (Sadie Bruce's nephew). It was just bringing that together, and then you'd branch out.

Why did you continue to do this when you first started?

[There was] something about it, and the respect that I had for Ms. Ellis. She became my other mother. The strength. A lot of the time she was in pain. She had crippling arthritis, and it was something that did not come from dance. It was earlier in her life that she had acquired this. I remember she said that, when it got to the point where she had difficulty moving, the doctor told her that she might not ever walk again. She told him, "Hell, no! I'm going to walk," and she did. I've watched her move and teach and continue on with her life like it was nothing and the pain was not even there. That gave me strength to see the strength in her. She wasn't easy. She and Abena Joan Brown remind me of each other, that old school strength. The Harriet Tubmans and the Zora Neale Hurstons. That strength, that [will to] continue to move. When people say that you can't, "Oh yes, I can!" It was overwhelming. The things that Ms. Ellis introduced me to: going and meeting Ms. Dunham, seeing them coming together, seeing the strength coming out of there, and the knowledge that they had. When they would come together after not seeing each other for so long, they greeted each other, hugged, and you could see that bonding. It was overpowering.

What are some of the messages that you think Ms. Ellis was trying to convey to the Chicago community with the dance?

Knowledge and a foundation. She wanted us to have an understanding of what we were doing and to pass that legacy on. With the knowledge that I have, what am I going to do with that? Having the history and not being afraid of getting the knowledge. Knowledge is power. It's about telling kids everything is built on something. Even the kids I teach dance to, I say, "I'm your foundation. I want you to study other forms of dance, but don't forget, this ground force that you have here." If your foundation is gone, everything tumbles. That's what I want them to know, and have that. Seeking that knowledge. I've always taught children, and I wanted to pass [this knowledge to] them. I even taught Dunham to my special ed [education] students. One of the words that was taken out of my classroom was "can't," can't doesn't exist. I said, "When you say 'can't,' that means you're not going to even try because you can't do it so why try." I would have them do twenty-five push-ups if they said "can't." It wasn't a punishment. It was to make them think about how they spoke because your words have power. Take that [can't] out. That means you can do anything to a certain degree. That's how we worked with it. As a schoolteacher, I played music all day. In the public school system, our kids don't know that much about themselves as a people. They are not being taught it. Some of the teachers don't know, so it's difficult. In my class, that's what we dealt with. If I'm teaching reading, there [would be] black authors. I'd get the black books to let them know that we are—we did not all come from kings and queens, but we have power because those who made it across that water were strong. You had to be strong to survive that far. Your spirit was never broken. It might have taken different forms, but the spirit was never broken. That's one of the things that I found in Dunham Technique. Don't lose your strength. Seek the knowledge. All of that came from studying with Dunham. Ms. Ellis always said that Dunham is not just about dance. It becomes a way of life. It's the way you approach stuff.

How long did the group stay at the Abraham Lincoln Center?

I don't know what happened—[why] we stopped being at the Abraham Lincoln Center—but we moved to 79th and Stony Island. A lady had a dance studio there, and Ms. Ellis taught classes there for a while. Her job might have been closed, her position, and—I think that's what it was—she didn't want to stop the dance classes. So she moved over there and started teaching. Then we moved to Sho'Nuff Studio. Ms. Ellis started teaching classes. We rented the studio, and she started teaching classes there.

And that was on 79th?

That was like 68th and Stony Island. It was on the second floor. I don't think they've torn that building down yet. It was one of the old buildings back in the 60 somethings on the west side of the street, and we were taking classes there.

How long did you stay in that space?

It was just a couple of years. I think that [was] the time when she had—what was it—and they operated. I remember she said before the operation that the only thing she was afraid of was a stroke. We went from there to—now his place was on 79th Street near Jeffrey—Tyehimba. He was a drummer, and he would make drums and different African statutes and stuff. He's an awesome artist. She started teaching there because, during that time, she started trying to find places to teach her classes.

Around what year was this?

Let's see, it was in Hyde Park. So, it was like '86.

Is he still around?

Tyehimba is. As a matter of fact, during the African arts festival, you will find him in the drum section.

When did you yourself start teaching?

That's when she [Ms. Ellis] started moving me into teaching more. She put me in front of folk at the [Dunham] seminar. She'd say, "OK, teach class." And, it was like, "Oh no. Can I really do it?" She didn't want you just to take class and just follow directions. She wanted you to take it in and develop from that, and that's what we did. I taught at the Abraham Lincoln Center. We would have certain days that she would have us teach. When we were teaching, they watched you. They watched me. I had to teach in front of Ms. Ellis and Tommy Gomez. I was taking class with Vanoye Aikens. He's more jazz. I remember at the same time I took class with him, I stumbled through that man's class. He called my name—I remember. I counted—about nineteen times during this one class. So my whole spirit was like this [low], I said, "I'm not going to stop." When the class was over, I thanked him and said, "I'm going to be back tomorrow." I said, "You called my name nineteen times, but it won't be nineteen tomorrow." So, the next day, it was seventeen times. Progress, yes. [*Laughing*] But, I did it. It was a start, and I didn't give up. When we developed into the club or group, there were certain things, certain information, that she [Ms. Ellis] gave to us. We just became family. I remember one of our girls that was working [with us] had a very abusive husband. We all got together, the girls, and we went to some kind of spa or something. Ms. Ellis had a retreat. We went up in the woods for the weekend and had classes, and I remember we had class in a barn. Gwendolyn Brooks's daughter, Nora Brooks Blakely, she took classes. We were at some kind of spa or something, and we started talking to her [this other girl and found out] he was abusive. We got her out of Chicago. She's in California now and has five kids. One night he was gone for something, and we moved her out. When he came home, she was on a plane to California with all the kids. The two weeks that we would spend at the seminar [The Katherine Dunham Technique Seminar], it was almost like you were taken out of this world here. The first time we went was when they opened up the museum [in 1977]. There was all the lectures and the different things. It was a family. They cooked. They laughed. They told old stories, and you could see the joy in them. To know that our people—during that time when it was really difficult because she was not subsidized—how they traveled, performed, and were accepted in other theater companies. They just worked it.

What were the lectures on?

The philosophy of dance, how they started, moved, and continued to grow. It was like around the same time of Josephine Baker. It was just about giving their history and the strength that they gained from it (the things they overcame). [They were about] how they continued to get their information out. [They] wanted folks to have knowledge, to be aware of what they were doing, and to pass it on to keep that foundation growing. When you came from that boy, you were just [strong]. Toward the end, I would bring my daughters down. I took my youngest one to classes. She would stay with me for the two weeks. My oldest one, sometimes I would let her go with her father. But Jamilah, she took the classes, you know. Akon, the rapper, his father was Ms. Dunham's master drummer.

Mor Thiam.

Mor Thiam, yes. He would bring all his kids. It was Ali [Akon], Muhammad, and I think his two other sons. He had a daughter. The baby is the daughter. And after class, we'd get back to the hotel around eight and then the kids would have their little time. The next morning, seven o'clock in the morning, you were up because you had to be out the door by at least 8:30 to get to class.

You said she had three houses at that time?

Right. The corner house was for the students, and that's where we would come in and stay while we were down there to take classes. Then the center house was for costumes and the props. They had the costumes from all the shows that they did when they were performing. At the other end was Ms. Dunham's house. The first time I walked in there, girl, my mouth was hanging wide open, and she came downstairs, and she was like, "Yes?" I was speaking to Ms. Dunham. When we received our certification—Dr. [Albirda] Rose, Ruby [Streate], I forgot who else was there—it was six or seven that stayed in the house. The certification exam had ten questions. By the time you finished typing up the twenty or thirty pages to answer those questions, you then had to justify your answers. [Joyce] Aschenbrenner, she wrote several books on Ms. Dunham, would question your answers to these questions. It was rigorous. Ms. Dunham used to call Ms. Ellis because Ms. Ellis was like the history keeper, and they would talk on different things. She would send us to meet Alvin Ailey or Arthur Mitchell. [If] she couldn't do it, she would send us to meet them and have them look at us and whatever.

So, you traveled to New York?

No, right here in Chicago. Alvin Ailey came here, and he was at the theater on Michigan. Alvin Ailey performed there. Ms. Ellis had sent us down to meet him and talk with him and let him know that we were her children and whatever he needed . . .

What did you do with Alvin Ailey when he came into Chicago?

I think we took him to Tommy Gomez's house because that's where they all were. We just sat down, and [they just started] talking about when they were together when they were younger. To see them enjoying themselves and having that strength, that strength in their bodies, that is something that our children nowadays do not see. They don't get a chance to experience.

They don't get a chance to see dancers or men with that kind of . . .

Right. It wasn't about whether someone—like now, the whole emphasis is on are they gay or are they straight? They were people. They were men and women, and we would come together to watch them enjoy. She [Ms. Ellis] was like the matriarch.

What are some of the other things that have changed from when you first started or from back then?

Most of the master teachers—Vanoye [Aikens], Tommy [Gomez], and Ms. Ellis—they've passed on. Now, it's the certified teachers that came through my generation. That's the only difference. They still try to keep the same basic concept. That's one thing Albirda Rose is trying to keep going.

How about in terms of the larger black dance community? What are some things that are different now than before?

It's different, but yet it's the same. With some of the younger folk—those who really haven't studied but are natural dancers—they think they're doing something new when actually it's just being recycled. It's just to different music. There are some, you find, that are really serious and want to study, not just study the movements but study the dance. [They want to] know the philosophy behind the dance, the knowledge. I had some boys from a grammar school [do] footwork, and I said, "Oh, that's African dance." We were rehearsing for this show at DuSable, and I had my boys with me. I had my son play for him. That was their warm-up, and the only difference was that they didn't have on African clothes. That footwork is the same, and they don't know it. I try and teach my kids that.

Make that connection.

Yes, make that connection. It's all the same. There are so many dance moves, and [you have to] see what you do with [them] and the knowledge you have. You can do it to hip-hop. It's all right. When I started changing my style of clothes, I became less critical of what other people were wearing because I know I dress different. It's all right. It's fine when people have their different styles. I'm still trying to get used to these pants hanging down below the butt, and I say, "That's them expressing themselves. Sometimes, you have to let them do that so they can get where they need to go." Fashion is just an expression, sometimes an expression, of how you feel. How you feel about yourself or what you want to represent. I used to work at 625 N. Michigan, and that's when I had the baldhead. I was like a shock to that area of town. When people see and feel you're insecure, they are going to mess with you. When they see the confidence, then they want to know [more]. I always tell my kids, "Walk proud, even when you're getting on the buses and the gangbangers and all that stuff are there. Hold your head up. Because sometimes they look at you and say, 'Dag, why is he or she so happy?'" Regardless, they are going to do what they're going to do anyway. But sometimes, when they see that power in you, they say, "Well, I'm going to leave them alone." In following Dunham's training, I've worked with gang members. When we used to do talent shows up at Barnes school, I would send word out to the gang members that I wanted peace in the valley. I was going to have a show in the evening, and I wanted people to get there safe, for their cars to be there when they came back, and nobody robbed. They would send messages back to me and say there would be peace. I would walk the kids to school. I figure that's following in that same mind-set of Ms. Dunham because I had the youth interest. I've always had that.

And it's powerful because it's such a completely different story and image than what you get . . .

Going back to Jeff Fort, we didn't know for a long time that we were being protected. We could go to the stores where the gang members were, and they never bothered us. We had gay, straight, [and] we dressed different, but those gang members never, never one time said anything out of the way, were disrespectful, or anything to us. One day, I don't know what we were talking about, but [Ms. Ellis] laughed. She said, "Oh, you want to know why they haven't bothered you," and she told us. So everybody was sitting up there—"Jeff Fort?" She said, "Yeah, when he was little boy, I . . ." She was kind and sometimes that's the difference between being harassed and being protected. A lot of the times these kids, and from working with them, they just want to know that you respect them. You are not looking at them out the side of your face criticizing them. So that's what she did, and I saw that through Ms. Ellis. I keep it going. A lot of the certified instructions at Dunham teach adults. I work with the babies.

What age?

Mine could start at six years old—from six to eighteen.

When did you start your work with youth?

Really seriously teaching? I've been teaching at eta for eighteen years, so I've worked with children there. I've always worked with kids. For twenty-nine years, I was teaching. I would pull them in and have some kind of side something because it interested me. That's where my heart is. So, we'd do the academics. I had one group of kids, and we used to do the fables. We'd read the moral of the fables, and then I would have them re-create that fable and then act it out. I got them into reading. Me and Susan [another teacher at the school] would go by their house and tell them, "Come on, we're going to school. Why are you still in the bed?" The parents got used to it. The principal would say, "Gerri," and I'd say, "I'm going to get so and so," and they would be there watching the class. If you need to buy them clothes, buy them clothes. So, they usually became my family.

Why do you think dance, theater, and the arts are so important and helpful for the youth?

There's more than one way to teach, to enter a person's life. Sometimes we focus so much on academia that we don't see that academia is in every form of life. I speak more so for the kids because that's who I work with more than others. You need to reach them when they are younger, in the grammar schools. My little gangbanging boys, you want to hit something, play the drums. I found sixteen drums in the school, brand new, locked up. I pulled them out, developed a drum line, and those boys worked it. There were certain things that they had to adhere to be in the group, and they did it. Sometimes we just have to be creative in how we reach them. Let them know that you love them [and] that you respect them because a lot of kids don't have love or they don't have food or they don't know or want somebody to touch them.

You show them love?

Yes. A lot of that came from studying Ms. Dunham's philosophy and putting that into practice. Like she said, it's not just about dance, it becomes a way of life.

How did you start working at eta Creative Arts Foundation?

Bobby [Andrews], he was doing a play, and they were going to go on the road. I was working at Boulevard Arts Center teaching dance, and he said, "Well, come on over to eta." I went on over there, and I've been there ever since.

You said you teach Dunham Technique there with the . . .

From six to eighteen. We have a good play going on now. It's called *Ama & the Magic Toy Box* (2011), and the kids are from ages of six to eighteen. They sing, dance, and act. They dress up like toys and each is a creator. They are creative because it's part of my curriculum. At a certain time, the kids have to choreograph the dance, choose their own music, and costume it out of what they have at home. I tell the parents, "Don't buy a thing. Let them create out of what they have at the house." They've done swing, and then I give them the history of swing. I try to teach them to have knowledge of what you're doing because when you have knowledge then you *know*. We did the Black Panthers. We studied the Black Panthers, so when they did the Black Power [fist], they knew what it meant. One of the old Black Panthers, his daughter was in our program, so I had him come in and talk to them. [Kelan] Phil Cohran, African Skys at the Planetarium—he did the music. Girl, it was an awesome piece. It was so much knowledge. You would have to go umpteen times just to get it.

What are some things that you would say stayed the same in the larger black dance/arts community here in Chicago?

I think committed teachers. People who want to teach that traditional [way]. Uncle [Runako] Jahi, I've been working for him the eighteen years. I call him my theater husband. Sometimes you're happy with your husband, and sometimes you're not. But the bottom line to him is that he is an awesome instructor. As a matter of fact, he prepared Jennifer Hudson for her piece when she auditioned for *Dream Girls*.

Wow!

I got high respect for him. I have that respect because I see what he does. We do have some consistent parents who are there for their children. I always tell the kids, "Your parents are trying to enhance your life. You don't even have to want to be an actor, dancer, or singer, but all the stuff that you learn here you use every day." We've had kids call us back that have gone on and thanked us for exposing them and giving them the confidence to go on, especially when you leave Chicago and go to New York. That's a whole new world, and how they've survived it!

From your stories of how Ms. Ellis and Mr. Gomez continued to dance through pain and illness, it seems like they were redefining the dancing body and/or revaluing a disabled body. A disabled body is no longer just discarded. It's just a body that you need to work with and you need to find a way to do . . .

Find a way to do it. Especially, as we get older and different things happen to our bodies. You get a crook and wonder where did that pain come from, but you find a way to take care of it and try to heal it. If you cannot heal it, you don't have to give in to it. That's what I saw them do. I saw them be the master, not give into it, and continue going. Ms. Ellis had crippling arthritis, but she didn't give into it. I remember Ms. Dunham was teaching. There was a movement she wanted us to do with our hips, and we weren't doing it right. Ms. Dunham was in her wheelchair. She got out of her wheelchair. I said, "Oh my God!" She stood up, and she showed us the movement because she was the woman with the hip movements. Tommy Gomez had a leg amputated. He had gone to the doctor for something, and I don't know if it was during the operation that something went wrong. He was having one kind of pain, and when he came out of the hospital, they had amputated his leg. He came back from that. He got that prosthesis and continued to teach dance. I have a saying, "Life is only for the living," so you've got to live this life that you have. We have choices. You can give in—just [be] weak—to it and be pitiful, or you can say, "I don't have this now. I got this to work with. What am I going to do with it? I'm going to put this best foot forward. If the best foot is only a tenth, that's my best foot today."

I've been blessed with awesome friends with talents beyond belief. I always tell Amaniyea [Payne]—because I just have such a high regard for her—I look at her and say, "You can do anything!" I mean, the girl, she done built a stove in the backyard, an outside grill, with bricks and stuff. She can cook! Can dance! And the ideas she comes up with! I remember a guy said, "Wow, so-and-so is fine." I said, "You haven't met the rest of my friends. All my friends are fine." All of them! To be able to look at your good friend and say, "Girl, you know you really look good today!" or "What's wrong with you? You better get it together!" or "Come on, now," because that's what friendship is about. It's accepting someone for who they are and just encouraging them to be their best. That's just like in the theater community.

IDELLA REED-DAVIS

Idella Reed-Davis began training at one of the oldest theatrical institutions in the Chicagoland area, The Sammy Dyer School of the Theatre. Under the tutelage of Ms. Shirley Hall Bass, Ms. Muriel Wilson Foster, and Mr. Ted L. Levy, she was exposed to a repository of theatrical knowledge that spans the school's sixty-eight years of operation. A founding member and the artistic director of Rhythm ISS, a female tap trio, Ms. Reed is recognized as both a skillful artist and one of Chicago's most sought-after tap instructors.

In this February 2011 interview, Idella Reed-Davis remembers her nearly lifelong relationship with the Sammy Dyer School of the Theatre, reveals how the history of dance is transmitted person to person, and talks about the dance competition circuit in Chicago. Reed-Davis also discusses how she developed her own identity within tap dance as well as some of the gender norms she has negotiated throughout her career.

What events or circumstances led to you becoming a tap dancer?

When I was about twelve or thirteen years old, my mom had taken me to see *A Chorus Line.* As a result of seeing *A Chorus Line*—actually, it was that "One" number at the very end, in the finale, when the dancers realized that they were going to be a part of this chorus line. They walked off stage, and it seemed to me how miraculously they had changed into these gold costumes and came out and did "One." That just spoke to me. I told my mom at that time that I wanted to dance. When we got home, she immediately pulled out the Yellow Pages. She just thumbed through the Yellow Pages, and she came up with the dance school, Sammy Dyer. She said, "Well, maybe we'll start here." She sent me to Sammy Dyer's school, and that's where it all started. I had never had a formal dance class of any kind. At the dance school, you took all genres of dance. There was ballet, tap, jazz, and acrobatics. She signed me up—I didn't take jazz—for ballet, tap, and acrobatics. As I recollect, I started with the beginner's group. I started out with Mrs. [Shirley] Bass's daughter, Joanne. She taught the beginner's class. She was my very first tap dance instructor. The following year I was placed in the advanced group for two years. I left her and went to Ted Levy, who I just attached myself to. He had become my best friend for life. By age sixteen—I think I have the math correct—I was student teaching in tap dance. I had a natural ability for the art form of tap, and that's how my dancing started. That's how my formal training started. I was student teaching under Muriel Foster, who's now the director of the school, and she taught me a lot about being a lady in the dance. I got all of my technical training from Mr. Ted Levy who was my mentor. Everything that I know about tap dancing came from his instruction, and everything I know about being a lady tap dancer came from Muriel Foster. I actually dance a lot like he did, like a man, and she would always be that person in my ear saying, "You are not a man. You're a lady. Lighten up. You're a lady." But I wanted to dance like Teddy, and so that's how my career started.

As a child, did you attend many dance performances? Was A Chorus Line *the first?*

A Chorus Line was the very first time I had seen professional dance on-stage, and I hadn't seen anything after that until, actually, I had become an adult and a professional dancer. So it was *A Chorus Line* that sparked my interest. Once tap had become a part of my life, every single New Year's Eve I used to watch Fred Astaire and Ginger Rogers movies on television all night long. That just drove my passion for wanting to dance, for wanting to tap dance, but I had not ventured out and gone to any other performances. I didn't know anything about anybody other than Fred Astaire and Ginger Rogers.

Where did you grow up in Chicago?

On the West Side. It was the Near West Side. No specific neighborhood [name] was placed on the area in which I grew up. Just the Near West Side near the United Center.

Was there much dancing in your family when you were growing up?

Not at all. No one in the family danced. No one in the family expressed an interest in dance but me at the time. My parents have always been, "Whatever you want to do, just do it." They were always there to support me. At the very same time, I was taking piano lessons, private piano lessons, when I was dancing. I actually started piano lessons when I was six. My sister was taking piano lessons first, and then I would get on the piano behind her, after she'd do her practicing, and I would play what she was playing. I would play by ear. When my mom saw that I had that gift for playing piano, she signed me up for piano lessons at that time. But as far as dance was concerned, there was none in the house.

What did your parents do as professions?

My dad was a pipe fitter for General Electric, and my mom worked at the Veterans Hospital. She was an Army veteran, and, when she finished with the Army, she worked for the hospital. She was supervising benefits.

What did your mother do in the Army?

I don't really know. She has pictures of her playing baseball. That's all I know. [*Laughing*]

What were your parents' reactions to your decision to become a professional dancer?

My dad was against it. He wanted me to have a career with insurance, and he didn't like the fact that I was traveling out of the state to perform. He was very timid about it. Even when I started traveling to Europe, he was vocally not happy. I think that was just more out of concern. My mom has always been, "Whatever you want to do, do it to the best of your ability."

What year was it that you began dance lessons at the Sammy Dyer School?

I want to say it was about 1977.

What was the Sammy Dyer School like in 1977?

It was completely African American. When I started Sammy Dyer in the seventies, it was located on 22nd and Cermak Road. It was a small studio, but there were hundreds of students. I want to say about 300 families of students were represented at the school at that time. It ran only on Saturday from nine until like six/seven in the evening. Classes lasted all day, and I was there all day trying to absorb everything that I could absorb on a Saturday. It was strictly African American. It's still African American owned and operated until this day.

Did your mother ever tell you why it was that she picked the Sammy Dyer School?

I never asked her why, but I remember sitting next to her and she was going through the phone book. I don't think she had any experience with Sammy Dyer, the performer, the man as a choreographer, or the Dyer-ettes as a dance group. She didn't know anything. It was strictly out of ignorance. I want to say it was godly divine picking. That's what I want to say because there were many—well not many—but there were a few in the Chicagoland area during the time.

And how many dance schools do you think there were in terms of tap that were in Chicago at that time?

Well, I know that there was the Sadie Bruce Dance School, Mayfair had already been established, I believe Jimmy Payne had a school—at least those. That's four.

How are those four different than Sammy Dyer in terms of training and approach?

I believe it's the rhythm that comes from each of the communities, and a lot of this comes from Miss Foster who does an oral history. She likes talking about the different dance companies. I know she always speaks of Sadie Bruce and how it was more—rhythmically—to the floor [than] what comes out of Sammy Dyer's. She was recently speaking to me about Jimmy Payne. He had some Cuban roots or some Latin kind of roots, so his dance style was a little different in where the rhythm would hit.

What did you learn from Ted Levy?

The heart of the dance is what I learned from him. Not only the advanced movement, but shuffling and dynamics and the marriage of the rhythm with the music. He took me to jazz clubs, different nightclubs, where we would listen to music and we would listen to the scatting of vocal performance, jazz performance, [and] artists. We'd talk about how we scat with our feet, the same kind of scatting that jazz vocalists would do. As percussionists, we did that same kind of thing with our feet. We'd just listen to music all the time, and we'd spend night after night watching videos, old footage, of tap dancers and just being inundated with the whole tap culture. That transferred to the studio, and we would have some reference point when we were creating or when he was teaching. We spent a lot of time [together]. The legacy of the dance is generally taught from person to person: the oral history and that spent time. He was the person with whom I spent a lot of time learning.

Did you ever watch him perform professionally?

Always, after our relationship became a true friendship and when he became "the tap dance kid." They did a local audition, and he went out for the audition. I was with him there when he won *The Tap Dance Kid*, and then he had an opportunity to perform when the musical actually came to Chicago. I was with him there and watched him perform. When he got his break in New York City for *Black and Blue* (1989) and *Jelly's Last Jam* (1992), I was with him there. When he did a show that Gregory

Hines actually produced, I was there just soaking it all up. He kept me there. I was like his right-hand woman, right-hand man. [*Laughing*]

You said that he taught you how to dance like a man. What does that mean?

I became him. You know how there's some dancers who are sponges—or artists who are sponges—where they not only watch. I not only watched his feet, [but also] I watched his mannerisms. Still today, when I create and I choreograph, there are moments where I feel his spirit. I feel like him. I felt like I have become one with this person. So whenever I would execute, I executed like he would execute without my own little feminine flair. I executed as Ted Levy would execute. When we would dance on-stage, I think that we were pretty much the same height, same kind of build—for a man, I guess he's small or for a woman, I guess I'm a little large. In any case, I think if we had on the same costume and our faces were covered, I don't think you would be able to tell one from the other. I was that closely a part of who he was. I liked what I felt like when I danced. I liked how I looked when I danced, manly or not. I wore the low oxford tap shoes. I liked what that felt like, but I did understand eventually. As I grew older, I guess you grow wiser as well. I needed to find my own identity, and finding my own identity as a tap dancer meant that I needed to stand up a little more. I can still hit just as any man can hit, just as hard, but soften up as well. I took on the philosophy: OK, I can compete with any given man, but I can still breathe like a woman in the dance. If I wanted to get down, I'll do that. But as a performing artist, I wanted you to still realize that I was a lady not trying to be a man. It was Muriel Foster who helped me come to that realization that it can be both ways. She comes from a chorus line of women who were hitting but still women. So I really do, today, believe that she was breathing that into me. I don't have to be a man to be accepted in the dance world. I could still be who I am. Who I am.

How would you describe Miss Foster's style?

She is so cool. She's eighty years old today, and last year, at age seventy-nine, she performed a piece of choreography that I set on our adult class at the dance school. She still is clear. She still is cool. She still is beautiful as any performing artist that is out there, and she amazes me. I so aspire to be that clear—the clarity in her sound, in her articulation, and the way that she reaches for steps and the beauty makes her a pleasure to look at. I contrast it to, now, when I look at some of our women now who still are hitting like men but not necessarily standing up as women. I see the difference or I understand. I'm attracted more to a hitting lady as opposed to—and I'm not sure if this even makes really good sense—a student who is hitting and trying to be hard and want to be fast and try to show off every skill that they have without personality, without paying respect to the dance. It's hard for me to really receive what they're doing. I'm impressed by their technique. I'm impressed by the clarity of the sound, but that element—what I like to call the "it" factor—that makes them individuals, that makes women true to being women, is missing in the dance.

That makes sense. How old were you when you first worked with Muriel Foster?

I want to say I was about fifteen turning sixteen.

It was just before you began teaching, because you were student teaching?

Right. I was student teaching under her.

How long did you student teach under her?

Until I was a senior in high school, eighteen, and I left the school for four years to go off to college. When I came back, I was asked to teach. I became an instructor at the dance school because Teddy went off to the Navy, and I assumed his classes after that.

In the early eighties, when you were student teaching for Muriel Foster, she would have been in her fifties. Were there stories that she might've told you about her early experiences in the city working as a dancer?

No. Not at that time. No. Actually, I didn't start hearing her stories until I was an adult, once I started a professional career. That's when she spoke, or started reminiscing, about when she was a Dyerette and her experiences.

Is there anything that stands out to you in terms of a story she told about her time as a Dyerette?

Well, not major stories, but she spoke often of when she danced with the band, Duke Ellington's [band]. I can't remember anything other than just comments about her tap teacher Cholly Atkins and how he would work them really hard. She talked about performing onstage and opening for Sammy Davis Jr. and with Sarah Vaughan. She talked a lot about not actual performance but things that they would do. At the time she was a Dyerette, she was like sixteen, seventeen years old. After the shows, they would have to be escorted back to their hotel rooms because the men would get after them. [*Laughing*] Those kinds of stories, and how they would try to sneak out and hang out after hours but they were too young. But I guess that doesn't relate to the dance other than just the whole life experience of growing up on the road with musicians and performing artists. I'm probably going to have to come back to you with that one.

When you were student teaching, were there other artists who were working in Chicago who influenced you? Not directly as a mentor, but as a person whose style or approach you liked and then thought maybe I want to borrow some of this or that?

Not in the city of Chicago. What's interesting is—and I know that you're not from Chicago—that we are a city—and really back then—a city that was completely segregated. Even within our own community. It wasn't until I was doing an industrial show at the Merchandise Mart that I even knew that other dance schools were out there. It wasn't until I did that industrial [show]. Then we started a performing arts team at our dance school, and we would take them to competitions. That's when I realized that there was a FieldCrest and other dance schools that were in our community. It's sad, but that is so much the story. When I did this industrial, that was the first time I knew that Mayfair was out there. I come from the West Side of Chicago. Mayfair was on the South Side of Chicago and—you know what? As I speak with you, I'm going back to, maybe, why Sammy Dyer was the school of choice for my mother. We lived on the Near West Side, and Sammy Dyer was right downtown. It was closer to our home than these South Side schools that were in existence. So, now I'd have to ask my mom, but I wonder if that played into her decision to choose Sammy Dyer because it wasn't so far away from our neighborhood. You know what I'm saying? So these South Side schools—the Mayfair Academy, FieldCrest, and Jimmy Payne's school—they all were doing their thing on the South Side while we're doing our thing where we're located. There was never any interaction. I said before, I didn't go to any other professional dance shows, let alone any dance school shows, because I wasn't aware of any of them. My only experience was the Sammy Dyer experience and the video footage of Cholly Atkins, the Four Step Brothers, all these different—I had no idea that these schools existed. What did happen, though, as Ted Levy was growing in his experience, the director at the school, Shirley Hall at the time, she would pull in people who she worked with to help further train Teddy. But as Teddy was being trained, so were the advanced dancers that he was training. So everything that I had at the time, all of my development, came through Sammy Dyer's school and Ted Levy. I was very segregated.

What were these dance competitions like? Where did they take place? How large were they in terms of numbers of people who participated?

The dance competition scene is huge, and it still is today, attended by hundreds and hundreds of dance schools and dancers who come in and compete. The competitions are designed, I guess, to have professional feedback given to the performances and they were scored. Your number of points, your score, determined whether you came in first, second, or third place at this particular dance competition. In the tap category, we had a group of students who performed both tap and jazz. There were different categories set aside for different types of performances [and age groups]. Then our category, in tap, that's when we would go up against these other dance schools. I'm really biased . . . actually, the numbers [and] the awards speak for themselves. We killed them . . . [in] the kids' language. They didn't dance as strongly as our students did, and we would win the competitions every time we would go. As a result of that, too, we were pulling students from other dance schools who wanted to attend Sammy Dyer so they could get the tap dance training that our students were receiving.

And how often were these competitions?

We would probably go out maybe twice a year. Then if you won the regional, you were invited to attend the national. We went to about four national competitions.

How big were the regional competitions? Was it primarily Greater Chicago, or did it pull from St. Louis?

It was the Chicagoland area.

In terms of the tap division, how many schools do you think participated in these competitions?

Hundreds.

Hundreds of dance schools? Hundreds of tap dance schools?

Yes, hundreds of [groups] from all around. The suburban area. Like you said, the Greater Chicagoland region, all suburban areas, they were all at these dance competitions.

In the early 1980s, in the larger Chicago area, how many tap dance schools do you think there were at that time?

Now, understand, they're not tap dance schools. The dance schools that—tap was a part of the curriculum. There had to be many. It's difficult for me to put a number on the number of dance studios. But in reference to a competition, the competitions may start at ten in the morning and they would run through three in the evening. Then you'd have your awards ceremony at four. Mind you, the dance numbers are between two to four minutes, and they run constantly. So, just in that respect, the number of entries . . . Now, mind you, there could've been two or three entries per dance school. But for a competition to run that long, there were a number of schools being represented.

How has that changed in terms of numbers from the early eighties to today?

I think there are more dance schools out there, primarily because artists are trying to make a living in the dance and the dance community, especially the tap dance community, in finding work. It's not easy to stay working as a tap dancer, so you have to create your own work. From that, many dance schools have crept up.

In your experience teaching dance, from when you were sixteen to today, how has the enrollment changed, if at all, in terms of number or makeup of classes? The types of students whom you encounter?

When I started, when I was in the school, there were 300 or so students. It peaked, I would say, in about the early '90s. We had a lot of student dancers from everywhere. And then just slowly over the years, enrollment has been falling. I think it's primarily because of the economy. It's playing a great deal in whether or not parents have that luxury money because dancing and dance classes are a luxury. They're not a necessity today. And so the enrollment is falling I think because of that. Now what I am finding, though, is that the students that we have, a great deal of the students, are children of alumni. So parents today who have been a part of the school and know the rich history of the school they're keeping the legacy moving. They're keeping it going. I now teach a lot of children of students I had when I was just a kid teaching, which is great. They find the value in the dance experience.

How large is your average class?

My average class now is about twelve students, twelve to fifteen students. That's average. And there are some classes that have, like, five or six students in them.

Are the smaller classes the more advanced ones?

Yes, they are.

For the beginner ones or the earlier ones that are larger, twelve to fifteen, what's the gender breakdown there in that class? How many men versus women or girls versus boys?

The majority of the classes are primarily girls. I can tell you there are actually nine boys.

Nine boys . . .

Nine boys in our entire dance school.

How many, just comparatively, girls are there, would you say? If you just had to guess the number?

So there are, there were the nine boys, there are about a hundred girls.

Has that changed at all? When you first started teaching, were there more boys or men taking classes or has that been consistent?

Not too much more. The ratio has definitely always probably been ten to one.

Why is it that whenever you think of the public face of tap dance, it tends to be a man dancing as opposed to a woman?

Isn't that interesting? Isn't that interesting? I've had this conversation before that there are a lot of men dancing, but the majority of them have been taught by women in the dance school setting. We have a tendency—and I know I still do today—to want to push the boys. I have to always check myself. Because there's such a low enrollment in the dance school, the tendency is to push the boys more. Just because men sort of take the leadership role in society, we still sort of, women, perpetuate that be-cause—and this is my Christendom coming out now, too. As men being the head of the household, to be the speakers, and the providers, and the priests of the family, you want to push them to the forefront. So I don't know if just subconsciously women do that, even in the dance school setting. Once they show a knack or a love or a drive or an innate ability to be good, that is nurtured in our male student dancers. They take that confidence, and they move it on out. They take it beyond the studio walls. While women, we are really just satisfied at being the educators, being the nurturers, [and] being the ones who pour into the students. That's satisfying for a lot of women. You know? That same thing now is happening with my son who's one of the nine in dance school. He has been grabbed a hold of, even by our one male jazz teacher, and I mean he is being pushed and poured into and nurtured so much. Where there are some girls in the school who dance just as well as him but because, I think because, he's a guy—and we like seeing male performers who dance like men—he's being pushed.

What do parents tell you in terms of why they enroll their children for dance lessons?

To be honest, and in the community that I'm in, it's to keep them off the streets. To keep their minds productive. Once you provide opportunities for them that they need to—one parent even said that I want my child to know that there's more out here than playing basketball, more out here than being in the streets, and getting involved in things that will either end them up in jail or dead. So dance is being used as an outlet.

You said you left the Dyer school when you were eighteen and you went away to college. Where did you go?

I went to Illinois State.

Were you a dance major there?

I was not. I majored in industrial technology, with electronics as my concentration. I took two dance classes while I was there. One was a tap class and one was a jazz class. I didn't pursue the classes because by the time I was in school, I was teaching the teacher. I wasn't being fed, I guess. I didn't learn anything.

That makes sense because you came in with more experience and more knowledge than the person who was teaching the class.

Right.

Would you walk me through the events that led to the creation of Rhythm ISS?

So, I came back [from Illinois State], and I was teaching. Lane Alexander invited the dance school—actually, he invited Ted Levy. Teddy was back from the Navy. He invited Ted to come out and do a workshop. No, it wasn't Lane, it was a woman, in Evanston, but I can't recall her name at this very moment. [She] called Teddy up to do a workshop. Ted asks that I assist him, so as he was teaching [and] I was assisting, helping students with the choreography [and] with the steps. Out of that, the lady who invited Teddy asked if I would come back and teach a workshop because she noticed that I did a lot of breaking down of steps, and she thought that I would be a good teacher. So out of that, I went to teach these classes. That was the following year. I taught these classes with her, and that's how this school, the name Sammy Dyer, the school, was starting to be recognized. Lane found out that I had a group of dancers, which was my performing arts group. He invited them to a performance, and, based on the number that they did in this performance, he asked that I dance with him with am/FM, which was at the time alexander michaels / Future Movement. I danced with Lane's company for a little while and then I was still teaching master classes. Lane had started the Chicago Human Rhythm Project. At its inception, Lane had me there as one of the master teachers. From teaching, I met this guy from St. Louis, his name was Robert Reid, and he invited me to St. Louis to teach. alexander michaels—we were performing there frequently—and Robert said, "You should form a company." I said, "You really think so?" [*Laughing*] He told me, "Yes, do it!" I was in class. This young lady Sharon Rushing was in my class, and that was always in the back of my mind. She was a good dancer. She's African American. At the time, I'm thinking, African American company. Black women dancers. So we talked a little while. Someone else had said something to this woman named Nila Barnes, and then Nila Barnes approached me. We were thinking about it, having a performing company, at the same time Nila Barnes approached me. She was also at the festivals that I was teaching at. She was opening up a dance studio of her own, and she wanted to put together a performing company, too, that represented her dance school. So we talked about forming a company, and it was Rhythm Women. So, when I first became an artistic director, it was with Rhythm Women. That's the way it first started. The company was women. Out of Rhythm Women, Nila Barnes, there was—I don't even know how to say it—but you know how sometimes women don't get along very well? There was some tension with Nila and the other women in the company. At the time, it was Nila, Sharon, myself, and Sarah Savelli, who was a sixteen-year-old at the time. [Sarah] was coming in and out of Chicago from a suburban area of Cleveland, Ohio, [and] wanted to dance. We would rehearse at Nila's studio. There was some tension, and we decided to disband the company. Nila was going to go her own way and do her own thing, and so that left Sarah, Sharon, and I not dancing with Nila anymore. I sat down with the girls, and we decided that we wanted to continue to dance. Since I was setting most of the choreography, we decided to form Rhythm ISS to keep Rhythm Women going with a different name. Rhythm ISS stands for Idella, Sharon, and Sarah. We just continued together with the company. We actually cofounded the company, but I was the artistic director because I happened to be the visionary at the time and did the choreography for the company.

How did your vision change when it went from the original plans for an all–African American–female company to one that was more multicultural?

That happened out of a conversation that I had with Teddy and—who was it, there was another person and just throwing around the idea of—and Nila, actually Nila, too. Nila would say, just from a business aspect, that it should be multicultural so that we didn't appear to be as if we wanted to segregate ourselves. If we wanted to reach the wider audience, if we wanted to appeal to a portion of society who would pay to see us dance, they had to see themselves. Sarah had attached herself so much so, like I attached to Teddy, to me, and she was the likely choice. She was good, and she had a heart. She danced very well, so she was an easy choice. She was an easy choice. So, yeah, the multicultural thing happened out of trying to be real with working as an artist, as a performing artist.

Could you contrast your experiences involved with the Sammy Dyer School and the Chicago Human Rhythm Project? They seem to be two different entities, two dynamic powerhouses, with different missions.

Yes, OK, so the dance school [is] where all of the foundation and all of the training takes place. We pride ourselves on being an educational institution, not one who tries to promote—let me find the word—Sammy Dyer's School is a theater, setting a foundation for dancers. We're trying to educate the whole dancer to prepare them for what the Chicago Rhythm Project will have to offer. So, if you will, we provide that foundational training. We're not promoting or trying to push the students into the limelight or groom them—I don't want to say it incorrectly—for their professional career. We are providing the foundation for a professional career, but we don't promote that part of performance. We do have a performing arts group that we will take out to showcase what the Sammy Dyer School has to offer children. We—and I guess that's the word I should say—our instruction is geared primarily to children. We're trying to raise up children to be dancers. We don't have a clientele of adults who are pursuing dance as a career. Does that make sense? That's what we do at Sammy Dyer? Now, the Chicago Human Rhythm Project, on the other hand, although they have a kids' program, they are providing opportunities for the more serious dancer. Those who want to pursue dance as a career, those who are taking dance courses in college, and really those who are looking to preserve the artistry and history of the dance. While the dance school is providing that foundation, and it's only in a dance school setting, the Sammy Dyer setting, there's only a handful in every generation who move to the next level. The Chicago Human Rhythm Project provides the experiences for that next level.

How long have you been involved with the Chicago Human Rhythm Project?

I've been involved—I want to say—for the twenty years that it's been in existence. I was a part of its inception. There was a moment when I retired as a performing artist that I also retired from being a master teacher with the Chicago Human Rhythm Project. That was a time in which I just needed to find myself. I had so much going on: the husband and the children, family and career. [I had] all of that going on at the very same time, and trying to manage a company and the practicing that goes into perfecting company routines and creating . . . It was just . . . it was a lot. So there was a period of time that I stepped off the scene, but, at that same time, I was still yet producing children and sending them to that scene. So I really wasn't gone, I just wasn't an integral part of the actual program. Just recently I've been brought back, like full speed ahead, like I never left.

I wanted to address that whole men thing. In thinking [about] the question that you had asked, why men dominate the field? A lot of it has to do with the responsibility of home that women have. I had this conversation with Dianne Walker. We call her the Princess Diana of tap dance. [*Laughing*] She's a lady of dance, and when we got on the scene she was always the one who would just pour into Rhythm ISS, just being women and the dance field. I know one conversation we had in the dressing room, she had even told me that there was going to be a point in time where it was going to be hard for me traveling out of the country and having little children at home and a husband at home. The struggle that she had when she was raising her children, trying to manage home and being a performing artist, and how it was so much different for women than for men. There were just going to be extra things [and] that I would need to do them both effectively—take care of home and . . . So I think when men venture off like that, they don't have that maternal instinct of home to worry about . . . Most of them don't because their counterpart's at home taking care of home. But they're providers, you know? That could be it; the reason why men go forth and women don't, unless they're single women who don't have those obligations.

That makes sense. When was Rhythm Women founded?

I can give you a ballpark date. As I get older, I just lose all track of time. So this is how I can pinpoint it. My middle son was born in '96, I became pregnant . . . 1995.

How long did it last?

Two years.

Two years, so '95 or thereabouts?

Rhythm ISS started in '95. Yes, as Rhythm ISS was getting off the floor, I became pregnant with my second child and he was born in '96. Yes, that timeframe is good. In 2001, I left the company.

Why did you leave the company?

I left the company because I was on a three-week tour of Europe, pregnant, and that's when it really fell on me that this was too much. This was too much. I was pregnant with my third child, trying to be a performing artist, traveling and carrying luggage, and performing with child. Everyone thought it was cute, but it didn't feel good. When I came home from Europe, I decided that that would be it, that I needed a break. Sarah then assumed the reins of artistic director of the company.

And was someone brought in to replace you?

It was the three of us, and then we had students who were really good. We were training them up as well. Rhythm ISS actually, at one point, performed with about five, six women. It started as a trio. It was conceptualized as a trio, but then, keeping the young blood and trying to keep it going and thriving, we would audition and other women joined the company. It evolved from the trio.

When did Rhythm ISS fold as a company? Or, did it never actually formally fold and just pause or stop for a little while?

It's funny that you were saying that because I've been running this through my mind for at least a month now of bringing together women again just to have another voice out there and trying to give performing artists work, someplace to go and hone their skills because there are very few opportunities. In any case, it sort of disbanded itself because the woman thing happened. Women do what women do. They become catty. Sarah could no longer manage some of the cattiness that was happening within the company, and she disbanded it. She went on and pursued her solo career.

Whatever became of Sharon Rushing?

Sharon now lives in Texas. She's no longer dancing. She got married, remarried, and moved to Texas. She's doing her thing.

You mentioned that you watched videos of Cholly Atkins, of the Four Step Brothers and others. I'm just curious to know, where did you find these videos? Were they part of a library at the Sammy Dyer School?

My collection came from Teddy. I'm telling you, he's like the life and breath of my dance. He had this footage. Now I believe he got the footage from Finis Henderson, who probably got the footage from somewhere else. Again, these kinds of things are passed down, like person to person. It's such an intimate legacy. It's almost—if you're not in the fold—hard to get the rich history. So he gave me the video footage, and he even put together some footage of himself and that's what we would watch: the Nicholas Brothers, Peg Leg Bates, all the oldies, Bunny Briggs, Chuck Green, a lot of that. Even when he went to New York and he was working with Gregory Hines and Savion Glover, they all had footage. They would record the footage and listen to it all night and steal steps. That's what we do. [*Laughing*] It's amazing how we think that we create, even today in the studio. I think I'm creating something, I go back and look at that footage [and] I done stole it from somebody. You know? [*Laughing*] That's what it was about. Now that footage . . . I sit in my son's room with him and we watch the footage. That's how it's done. That's how it's done.

If you were to write the history of tap dance in Chicago, who are the people who you would include? Who are the pillars in the history and the development of tap dance in Chicago?

If we start with today, that would be Bril Barrett, Trey Dumas, Jumaane Taylor. There's a new kind of thing happening too with Lane Alexander. He has brought the dance community together. He has connected the dots so that we can see who is doing what around the Chicagoland area. I would say Lane Alexander, as well. And then going down, my mentor and friend, Ted Levy, Finis Henderson, the Suttons from out of Mayfair.

There's Reggio the Hoofer. [You have] the Jimmy Payne family who are pillars in the community. I ran into Jimmy [Jr.], but I'm not sure what Jimmy's doing. I haven't seen the fruit of his labor—talking about legacies of people that have come from him, so I'm not quite sure. I know he has teaching jobs in the community, but his name—I guess just based on his dad—should be mentioned. Then there was Bruce Stegmann, who no longer is in Chicago, but he had a company, especially tap, that was phenomenal. He poured a lot into students, especially tap. Julie Cartier, who was actually a part of Especially Tap Company with Bruce Stegmann, spoke volumes in the Chicagoland area. There's Jay Fagan. Yes. Jay was great. He's out of one of the suburban areas. That has been really the extent. I'm trying to—yeah—who have poured back—who have kept the fire of tap dance in Chicago burning. And if I've missed anybody, you'll have to charge that to my head, not my heart. [*Laughing*] Yeah.

BABU ATIBA

Babu Atiba (Herbert Walker) is one of the founding members of Muntu Dance Theatre of Chicago. Atiba has traveled throughout the United States, Mexico, Canada, West Africa, Europe, and the Caribbean Islands playing various musical instruments.

In interviews conducted in May 2010 and August 2011, Babu Atiba discusses the origins of Muntu Dance Theatre of Chicago and his role in the development of Chicago's West African drumming community. Babu Atiba talks about the healing power of the drum and his involvement in groups, like the Sun Drummer, that sought to use the drums to build and empower their communities.

I was born in Chicago at 49th and Forestville and raised in the housing development called Dearborn Homes on 29th and Federal and then State Street. In 1971, when I was living on Cermak and 22nd Street in Harold Ickes Homes, I started to seriously study. In the late sixties, I was into the drums and playing in the hood. It was an attractive force that was powerful beyond my imagination, and the youth really were gathering around it. We had an opportunity to talk about issues that were happening. This was the time after Malcolm and King had gotten killed, so there was a lot of disruptive energy going on. The COINTEL [FBI Counterintelligence Program] program was going on, and a lot of people were being snatched off the streets and jailed and all kinds of things. I was very into that revolutionary mind. I worked at Standard Oil Company for a minute, and I had been told on numerous occasions by some of my white coworkers when I spoke about black people's plight here in America, "Go back to Africa." Go back to Africa. So I did. I have a cousin named Michael Hawkins. He played drums for years during family gatherings. I had him teach me the fundamentals of the hand drum, and from then on I was going to classes. That's where I met Darlene Blackburn, who's one of the pioneer dancers of Chicago. He [Michael Hawkins] played for her classes. He would take me there to accompany those classes sometimes, and that's when I got turned on to dance and its significance and the value of dance because before that I was just into the drumming. I wanted to learn the drumming. I learned the fundamentals, the hand patterns, and the hand techniques, and I just wanted to play. When I met Darlene Blackburn, her mind-set was so clear about delivering a message through the dance that it made me investigate it more. And I met Alyo Tolbert, who was one of the male dancers with the Darlene Blackburn Dance Troupe. This was actually in '71 when I met them working out of a social center on 64th and Green Street. It's one block west of Halsted. That's where we had our drum classes, so it was very easy to go from the drum class to the dance class. After about a year of doing that, I was asked to perform with Darlene Blackburn along with my cousin and a few other drummers who were with an organization called the Sun Drummer, who I also happened to hook up with. The Sun Drummer is a group of musicians in Chicago. One of the requirements for being a Sun Drummer was to make your own drum. The Sun Drummer was coming from an African frame of reference, so they wanted to have that relationship with the drum as opposed to just buying a drum and playing. What is it that gives you a more intimate relation? So we made drums. I'm talking about carving them out of tree trunks from scratch or taking old pickle barrels—because they were real big and wide—and breaking down the slats. Then, we'd have to plane the edge and be able to fit them into a smaller barrel and then make some rims or bands for them out of old tie rods. It was a lot of work involved.

What did you do for the head [of the drum]?

Well, after we got the band on there to make sure the drum was solid, we used cow skin. We were getting cow skin from a tanning factory out north of Chicago, 2222 N. Weber, if I'm not mistaken. We were getting skins there, and the skins were fresh. Fat on them. Hair on them. Everything. Stanking. And we had to get it, soak it, get the hair off, pull the fat off, cut the fat off, and then put the skin [over the drum]. We had two systems. We had the tacking system where you put the skin on, stretch each side, tack, tack, tack, tack, tack, tack, tack, all the way around. That was one system. We had a rope system where you had to have a tension rod at the top, and a tension rod at the bottom, pull the rope through it, holding the skin, lace it, lace it, lace it, lace it, and then pull it. And that's the way we got the tension.

At that time, I was at Malcolm X Community College on the West Side. I was studying to be a criminal lawyer. The Sun Drummer would play outside sometimes along with wordsmiths or people doing recitations, poetry, or what have you. It was so dynamic. The Sun Drummer was talking about universal law, and that's when I decided I was gonna really get into this drumming real seriously and check it from an African frame of reference. Go back to Africa. One of the lead drummers was Harold Murray. We called him Atu. He asked me to come and join the Sun Drummer. And all of this is, mind you, in late '71. So early '72, I think it was, when he really asked me to do that, I joined the Sun Drummer. My cousin was working with a group of Hebrew Israelites at the African Flea Market, which is on 79th and Essex, between Essex and Kingston in Chicago. They were studying the black presence in the Bible, but they would have cultural events like dance classes. And one of the most intriguing things about that was they spoke about how many times Ethiopia was mentioned in the King James Version of the Bible. And we were wondering, "What is that all about?" Because at that time all the images out of the Bible were all European, all white, no black nothing. But then we started researching the information. That led us into studying Africa's connection to religion, to spirituality. All that we were taught about Africa's whole spiritual thing was that they were backwards, crazy, savage, and had no real relationship to higher forms of spirituality. But as we investigated and talked with various people who came from Africa at that time—a brother named Kofi Jantuah from Ghana, some other people from Nigeria, I can't think of their names—we would have interesting dialogues. They talked about the Yoruba religion and the spiritual practices of the Akan people. And all of these things dealt with a lot of respect for all life—not just humanity but all life. It was about a connectedness to all life, so all of that was just the tip of it. When I say, "I'm going into universal law, forget criminal law." I left criminal law alone. [*Laughing*] I went in deeper and deeper into the drum.

That's when we were traveling around with the brother that was one of the lecturers at the flea market, Baba Daniel, to universities in Michigan and around in the Midwest here mostly. We played behind him as he did his lectures. The response from the people was always so positive that we decided to go ahead and form a dance group with the dancers that we had and the musicians. It wasn't Muntu then. It was originally called UHCC, which stood for Unifying Humanity through Cultural Creativity. And that was our aim. Not only black people, [but] we definitely wanted to bring black people out of this misconception that we were backward and primitive and out of touch and had nothing to do with reality. We understood that primitive meant first, so it took us to another respect for that [idea of primitiveness]. We decided to delve deeper into African studies and understand the origins of why they deal the way they deal [African culture]. That's what got us into promoting Unifying Humanity through Cultural Creativity. We saw black people gravitate to it, but we also saw the European people [and] Asian people that were in the audiences at those times gravitate to it at the same time. We started having open classes at Washington Park Field House, I'd say around 1973. And that's when Alyo Tolbert, who was one of the principal dancers of Darlene Blackburn Dance Troupe, came to us. My cousin was a good friend of his and invited him to come teach a class. He taught a class for us at UHCC and enjoyed our energy so much that he wanted to do regular sessions and even be a part of UHCC when he could because he was still with Darlene Blackburn. So, '74–'75, we had drawn such a large following at Washington Park Field House, we decided to go on and not just be UHCC. We decided to take this company to another level and get a little bit more serious about presenting African dance and music for the community and the world. Now, Alyo was a mathematician, right? So he was always thinking about ways of bringing these lines together, bringing these steps and dances together, and bringing out the functional qualities of the dances. He used to say, these are his words, "We're gonna sophisticate the art, Atiba. We're gonna sophisticate it. If we're gonna take it to the stage, we have to sophisticate it and take it to another level. We can't just bring bush to the people. People don't want to just see bush. We're gonna sophisticate it so they can enjoy the art." So that's when we went into costuming. We went into the props that we would use on the stage [and] the whole script. Theater is what came to our minds. That's when, during '74–'75, we decided to change our name to Muntu Dance Theatre. *Muntu* is a word from the Bantu dialect that means "human being," but there is another spiritual meaning of it that is "the essence of humanity." And that's what we took from that, the essence of humanity, because we wanted to deal with the connections. What makes us connected? Forget all of this stuff. We know we're separate. We know our differences. But what connects us? One of our mentors, Baba Duke Jenkins, he used to teach at Northwestern University. I don't know if you know him. Duke Jenkins taught an African history or Afro-American history course. He did something with the history program here at Northwestern University, and he was one of our mentors. And one thing he said that stuck is that in the first place is spirit. In the first place is spirit, and that, as far as essence is concerned, was a very moving and telling statement because it made me have to investigate. I just couldn't readily grasp that. I had to dig deep. But muntu being the essence of humanity, it was beautiful linkage for us. We started rolling with that, and Muntu started growing. It started to grow.

For a while, there was a major controversy in terms of Europeans coming to the dance class. Some of us were still so revolutionary. We didn't like that. We were like, "Hey, wait, what they want? Now they want to take this from us." No, we couldn't go with that. But we had to begin to understand that the African culture is a unifying factor for all life. That's the one thing we learned about Africa. The continent itself is the origin of civilization. It was real heavy, and it took us back into Egypt, into ancient Kemet.* We didn't know it as Kemet then. We were just under Egypt, and many of us were under the impression that Egypt wasn't even a part of Africa. I mean, we, many of us, had been taught that Egypt was somewhere in what they call the Middle East, and it was separate from Africa. We knew being pro-black was not anti-white, so

---

* Kemet is the name that ancient Egyptians used to refer to Egypt. Its usage is connected to Kemiticism or the Kemitic faith, which is a spiritual practice that developed in the United States around the 1970s that tries to reconstruct the religious and cultural practices of ancient Egypt.

we continued to study, do our research, and find out about Egypt. As we dug into it—the Akan culture, the Yoruba culture—they all had ties with the Egyptian customs and ancient ways of living. We were dealing mostly with dances out of Ghana [and] Nigeria during the first part, and a lot of Senegalese started coming over [and] Guinea[ns]. Mor Thiam, a Jembe drummer from Senegal, came over with Katherine Dunham back in 1968. She brought him because he was one of those drummers over there that could mark and catch her moves without her saying a word. They were in sync. When he came in, we went down South to East St. Louis to take classes where Mor Thiam was teaching. That's where Katherine Dunham's center was. We traveled back and forth studying with him.

You said you had this image of Africa being backward. And that was coming out of . . . ?

That was coming out of school. That was out of Daniel Hale Williams School. At Daniel Hale Williams School, they would teach us that Africa really was meaningless. It was meaningful in that the missionaries went on down there and brought the African people over here to civilize them. That's what slavery was supposed to have been about. I was learning that in school. We were brought over to be civilized, and anything African we did not like. I had a friend. We used to call him Midnight, [and] that was the greatest, um—what's the word they use when they denigrate you? I guess denigrate. But that was the greatest put-down you could [use]. Calling somebody black was like fighting. And so Midnight was really fighting [words], but that's what we called him because he was. He had kept the same complexion as any of the brothers and sisters that are born there [in Africa] to this day, but I loved that brother. We were real tight. And after I got into Africa and understanding [it], I began to compliment him more and let him know what that was really about. We told him he should be thankful for that name. He dug it, but not quite. He couldn't really get into it because he didn't get into understanding the culture. Now, mind you, I got in the culture.

I was working with Darlene Blackburn. In 1977, we went to FESTAC, which was held in Lagos, Nigeria. [It] was a festival of the arts of all African people. I mean from all over the world, all over the continent of Africa, from Asia, from Europe, from North America here, South America, the Caribbean. People converged on Nigeria. I'm still riding that energy now because I could get up at two or three in the morning, walk out into the compound that we were living in during that time, and people, different groups, were out rehearsing, two or three in the morning. It was crazy to me. I just couldn't believe this. I would sit there and just be mesmerized watching them rehearse as if it were the last time they were gonna do this.

Was that your first trip to Africa?

That was my first trip to Africa.

And you've been back many times since?

No, not many, but I've been back twice since. I went back. We, Muntu Dance Theatre, were invited to perform at Panafest I: The Reemergence of African Civilization in Ghana in 1992. That was the first time we went as a group, and then we were called back to perform at Panafest II: The Reunification of the African Family in 1994. Those were the three times that I've been to Africa.

So were the African drummers, musicians, and dancers that you were meeting members of visiting dance companies who had stayed here in Chicago? Or were there African students who'd come to Malcolm X to study? When did you first start meeting Africans who'd come to the U.S.?

Well, I started paying attention to it when I met Mor Thiam. That's why I spoke of when he came in. That was the first djembe drummer here in the Midwest. But there were Africans who were here who had come to study that weren't musicians, weren't dancers. They had various import/export shops that were doing a little business there, and we'd have our discussions there. I would discuss with a lot of Yoruba brothers I knew from Nigeria, [and] that really was giving me the insight to what was happening spiritually. That was my contact with the African-born Africans and those of us who were here because we still have a great misunderstanding about our connectedness to Africa. The blood is a very heavy thing, very heavy thing. I'm just finding this out now. You know about this word *djeli*, which is where they get the word *griot*. *Griot* is a French terminology for the [African] oral historian, but the *djeli* is what the [West African] Mandingue call it. The *djeli* means "blood." Just like the blood circulates throughout the entire body, the djeli circulates throughout the entire land telling the stories and the histories of the people so they can remember and not forget who they were and how they all are connected. That's the beauty of that oral history. The oral history and the written history are very linked, but right now they're not. They're clashing. People wouldn't even think that Africa had such a great literary history—I mean, it's tremendous—starting with the hieroglyphs, the languages coming out of ancient Kemet and ancient Egypt. So the oral historians and the scribes of that time, they were very linked and they were keeping the memory of the people alive.

Can you talk a little bit more about those early years of the company of Muntu? What were some of the challenges that you faced [while] getting the company going?

Challenges were keeping people involved enough to keep doing it [while] feeling some sense of worth. It wasn't a lot of pay. We had to establish a payroll system. In the early days when we started going out doing gigs, we'd do the gigs, get the money, [and] split the money up. Our first payroll system was whatever gigs we did, we kept the money in one lump sum and paid everybody who would be there regularly. I think it was $12.50 a week or every other week. Then it moved up to $25 every other week or something to that effect. I believe it was the biweekly thing we were dealing with. But all of us were working other gigs and doing other things. It wasn't until 1973–74 when I left Standard Oil and decided to become a full-fledged artist. I said, "I'm gonna try this. I'm gonna try to survive." Now, mind you, I was raising children at the time. My wife, Kemba—thank God for her. She's a blessing—was of the same mind as I in terms of, "Let's do what we have to do to make this thing happen." I left Standard Oil [and] joined an organization called Urban Gateways, which was a group that took arts into the school system. It's an arts and education program. I started doing quite a few of their residencies then at a lot of schools on the West Side of Chicago and around the Chicago area, but I started getting a lot of exposure to the suburban areas. It was still, [at the time], a racial thing in terms of us being able to understand how do we relate to all the different races? From going to the suburban areas and then in schools where some white children had never seen black people in person, that was an amazing thing to see how they would look at me and wanted to touch you and all kinds of looks. That tripped me out. [*Laughing*] I still had my revolutionary mind. I had to check my anger. Our challenge was that we must not be angry at ignorance. We have to be able to understand and be able to clarify or shed some light. That was the whole reason for going into the culture. Between '77 and '78, we became 501(c)(3) tax exempt. It helped us to do that, and it also helped us to consider structuring our payroll situation even more.

It wasn't until Alyo went to Africa in 1979, to Senegal, and while he was there he met this brother, Abdoulaye Camara. Abdoulaye Camara came back with him ready to work with us and teach us some of the inner workings of the dance and music. His main thing was to make us really understand the elements of music, dance, and costuming, how all three of them have to go together. There's a marriage involved here that we've got to be able to maintain and keep it on the high level. Don't just go out—because remember a lot of times people when they did African performances they would take bedsheets or old curtains or whatever and just wrap it around and come out and "booga booga." That was your African thing, "Ooga booga ah ah ah." We had to raise it from that. We started dealing with the dress codes of the various people as we learned about their traditions. And Abdoulaye Camara, being Mandingo, hooked us up with a lot of the Mandingo tradition. He was out of Casamance, Senegal, in West Africa. But his coming back was a turning point for us. He came back in early '83, and later on during that year Alyo was getting more sick. We didn't know it. He wouldn't let anybody know. He was taken sick and Camara was still with us. In October of '83, Alyo Tolbert passed. He was our original artistic director, first artistic director of Muntu. He passed and Abdoulaye Camara was still with us. At that time we were working on our first full-length African ballet in the Mandingo language. We were right in the flow of that. He, [Abdoulaye Camara], decided rather than leave and go back, he would stay with us and take over the role of artistic director of the company and have us carry through with the project. *Woloba* (The Big Forest) was the name of that project. [It was] the first full-length African ballet that we put on as an African company of those born in the Americas. And that was heavy right there in itself because just learning the phrases and some of the language had us tripping. We still had English on our minds. So to say some of those words the way they were supposed to be, we had to really consciously make an extra effort to do that, but it was good. The whole idea of Muntu [was] to bring peace to the black people first, but also to anybody that wanted to relate to our culture with some respect. A lot of people gravitated to our programs respectfully appreciating what we were bringing, and that was a great thing. So we definitely couldn't be going around hating white people, hating people because of color or religion or any of those differences because [of] the unique thing of what makes us come together and appreciate each other. Then we're having audiences come in and pay for our presentations. We had to develop a clear understanding about what it is we were doing as a socialization program with the world. We developed a council of members of Muntu, to reflect the elders that we didn't have at that time, to be able to sit down and try to arbitrate all the differences and difficulties that we have. That served us well until we began to recognize the elders that we did have. It wasn't that we didn't have them. We didn't recognize them like we needed to, to bring them to us the way we needed to. Like I said, Duke Jenkins was one of our mentors. Another sister by the name of Abena Joan Brown, who was the executive director and the head of eta Creative Arts in Chicago, she was another one of our mentors. The Sun Drummer had a senior brother by the name of Brother Atu. He was another one of our mentors that would come and help us. The brother that was teaching African history classes back in the flea market about the connection of the black people to the Bible, that was another one of my elders. His name was Baba Daniel.

Four years after Camara became artistic director, Amaniyea Payne became artistic director. How did that transition happen?

Abdoulaye was with us after Alyo passed. He stayed with us for those four years, but during that time he was still in the process of working on getting his papers done so he could stay in the country legally and be right. We were having difficulties with our lawyers. I didn't quite understand it. But, anyway, he had a connection in New Orleans, and he was going down there to deal with this lawyer—someone down there that was able to supposedly expedite that situation. But Amaniyea had come and done work with us before, and we had grumblings long before this about having a female direct the company because we had all, from the inception up until that point, it had been male directed. Men were running it. We were doing the lead in what we were doing as a company, but the women were running it in their own way in the positions where they were. So it was a matter of time. Well, let's have a female artistic director. That was a historical occasion when Amaniyea came.

Where is Abdoulaye today?

Abdoulaye got caught up in Hurricane Katrina [in New Orleans, 2005]. He got sick. He passed.

Was he working in another company down there or . . .

He was. I don't even know the name of the organization he was in. He was doing a lot of arts and stuff. He was doing a lot of accessory work for many dance companies throughout the country. He was very good at making the waist beads and the headpieces and chest pieces and all types of accessories for dancers. He was doing a lot of that. He's one of the ancestors. We thank the creator for blessing us with his presence.

Let's see, talk more about the music and more about how the dancers are leading and how the musicians are leading and following the dancers . . .

Let me say this first before I go into my thing. I danced with Muntu during those years earlier. I didn't want to. Reluctantly. Most of us didn't want to get into the dance because we had a negative idea about dance, especially men dancing. We thought, a lot of us thought, it was a sissy thing. That was the thing that was put on us. All we saw were men that looked like they were emulating women a lot, and we really didn't want to do that. So I talked with Alyo about that one day. He asked me, he said, "Are you secure with your sexuality?" I said, "Yeah. I'm secure with my sexuality. What's up with that?" He said, "Well, then why won't you dance, then? What's wrong with you? You think somebody gonna think you funny or something because you dance?" I said, [no answer]. He said, "You know why men dance in Africa?" I said—I tried to say yeah, but I really didn't quite understand it. He said, "Check it out, man, check it out." When I checked that out, I said, "I'm dancing." Let's dance because they dance in Africa to reflect their particular side of whatever it is that's happening. You have the male and the female. The male and the female are complementary. They are not contentious; but they have their spaces, and they both need to be represented. And that was one of our goals was to make sure that we had the male and the female sides of the dance covered. So I danced, and then many of the brothers who were drumming there danced so that we could have a better understanding of our relationships with the dancers even. Because the good, the really good, drummers really know the dance. Good dancers really know the music. It's a mutual thing, and we had to really get into that. So yeah, I just wanted to touch on that in terms of me getting into dance, because I got into it and really dug it. I had to make a choice in terms of whether I am gonna be a dancer or a drummer or a musician. And I wanted to be a musician because I got into it from the whole universal law thing, and it took me into a lot of instrumentations. Not just the drum, the flutes, the Shekere, various percussion instruments. I play a little bit of the bass guitar, matter of fact. But I'm saying—a trumpet, I was messing with the trumpet. All of it took me to the music and understanding why the music is important. It takes us to that language. You know people always talking about the universal language and it's a real thing. There really is a universal language. Various places I've been to around the world as a result of playing this music attest to that for me. I mean, being with people and languages that I knew nothing about, couldn't speak it, but it didn't matter when it came down to appreciating one another and sharing something.

The healing aspect of the music and the dance is a critical concern of mine. And that's what I think we need to pay more attention to when we get it. I don't just drum just to drum. I don't drum for just my own personal enjoyment. I've been playing at funerals a lot. A lot of funerals. It's not for the people who pass. It's for the people who [are] still here trying to make it through the loss that touched them deeply. And the response I get from families makes me keep [doing it]. Anytime somebody asks me, I'll come and I'll do it. Yeah. I've been playing for a lot of the [baby] naming ceremonies, different ceremonies we have too, and I've been invited to do a lot of things that's functional, as opposed to just as an entertainer. Because we used to say we're not just dealing with entertainment, we're dealing with edutainment. We're educating and entertaining at the same time.

How did you come to understand the healing aspects or the djembe as a tool for healing?

Basically, from what it did to me. I would be a stomped-down drug addict right now if I wouldn't have gotten into this. I tried to play my drum one day when I was high, and I could not play. I played the one time when I wasn't, and I was gone. I was in Africa. And when I came back to myself I said, "Woo." It was so therapeutic for me. This has got something to it. Then it got me getting to talk to certain doctors. I was working and doing Egyptian yoga with a naprapath, and we started to understand the power of sound. Then I started talking with other musicians about that, and I said, "Man, this—the drum is healing." And there's a brother here from Mali that wrote a book called *The Healing Drum,* Yaya Diallo. I don't know if you've heard of him. That really put me in touch with the healing properties of the drum. I just knew that it was all a part of the reparation thing, and it was about the self-repair. I knew we had to do that first before anything.

Now, before I play my drum, I want to play this other instrument as a matter of respect and to remind myself of some things. All right. You know this instrument? It's a flute from the northern part of Ghana. It's called the Wiah. It is played to remind the people of the importance of respecting elders and to remember ancestors. So I'll play this before I start drumming. And bear with me as I stop and may throw out a little proverb or something—just thoughts that come to me as I'm playing. Just get what you can out of it.

[*Plays music*] It is not the gaining of knowledge that makes one wise, it is the application of that knowledge. [*Plays music*] Stupid friends can be worse than enemies. [*Plays music*] One does not test the depth of the river by placing both feet in. [*Plays music*] The monkey sees the hind parts of its neighbors, but never its own. [*Plays music*] Seek not to impress, but strive to express the spirit that lies within. For when you strip most people of material goods, behold an empty shell. Ashe. Thank you.

JOEL HALL

Joel Hall was born in Chicago, Illinois. In 1974, Hall and Joseph Ehrenberg cofounded the Chicago City Theatre Company, which later became the Joel Hall Dancers & Center. Hall now serves as the artistic director and principal choreographer for the Joel Hall Dancers, and director and chief instructor of the training studio.

In this August 2011 interview, Joel Hall recounts the origins of his dance company and chronicles his journey from Cabrini–Green to a juvenile detention center to an arts leader in Chicago. Hall also discusses the strategies he used as an artist of color to navigate biases within the Chicago cultural scene and create opportunities for black artists to live and work.

Can you tell me a little about your history?

I was born Joseph Louis Hall. My name is now Joel Hall. I was born in 1949 in Chicago at Cook County Hospital. I grew up here in Chicago on the North Side in Cabrini–Green until the age of thirteen. Then I left home and started living on my own at thirteen.

Currently, you are the director of Joel Hall Dancers and Center, and also an adjunct at Northwestern University in the dance program. Are you teaching anywhere else in the city?

Well, I teach at South Shore Cultural Center on Thursday and Friday nights, and this fall [2011] Joel Hall Jazz Dance Method on Thursday and Fierce Ballet on Friday, 7:30–9:00 P.M. I will be starting a program near the DuSable Museum and Washington Park on 55th and Martin Luther King Drive. They have a little community center there where we'll have classes. I think it is important for us to be able to bring what we know to the community because a lot of times the community is over-whelmed with so many stimuli that are internal. It might be good to present an external stimulus that might encourage them to grow in a different direction or another direction. That is my intention in being at both the South Shore Cultural Center and in this situation at Washington Park Field House. I teach one class a week at the Cultural Center, and I will be teaching a full program for young adults and children at the Washington Park Field House.

How did you begin dancing?

Well, dance was very much a part of my cultural background because in my history—historically my family would dance at parties, would dance around the house, would go to friends' houses and dance—dance was always a part of my life. It wasn't anything that I had to really learn. It was something that we did. So, transitioning from that level of dancing to a more structured level of dance, for me, was a matter of educating myself in other forms of dance. That began really when I was much younger and was following kids around in the neighborhood who were taking a ballet class. There were several boys that were taking a ballet class with a gentleman by the name of Ed Parish. Mr. Parish, what he did was he took in boys from all over the city, and he would train them in classical ballet for nothing, practically. I mean we paid very little for it. A lot of these guys went on to major companies. [Mr. Parish] had a studio on Kedzie Avenue just north of the Ravenswood stop on the North Side. I guess that would be Lawrence, just before Lawrence or something like that.

Do you remember the name of his studio?

It didn't have a name. You would just go and take class. It was a large loft. It was full windows and ballet barres. It was a mixed group of boys and girls, but primarily there were boys. They were from different neighbor-hoods, and Mr. Parish would take us and give us class. Some went on to ABT [American Ballet Theatre], some went on to New York City Bal-

let, some went to dance, [and] one went to Dance Theatre of Harlem. I
went to New York and continued studying later at [Alvin] Ailey's. Then
I came back and danced with a company here called the Chicago Moving Company. That was in my twenties, while I was in school, and then
I started my own company.

Do you remember where he was from, Mr. Parish?

I have no idea. He was just this white guy.

How long did you stay at this studio?

I would say maybe about two years.

Where did you go from there?

Well . . . from there is when I got locked up. I got locked up for running
away from home, and I, from thirteen to seventeen, was in the Illinois
Youth Mission. At seventeen, I was paroled on an independent parole so
that you're not going to anyone, but you're going out on your own. I had
a parole officer, and the parole officer was trying his best to get me back
in there as quickly as possible, but I avoided that. I managed to avoid
that. I managed to get a job at Wimpy's Grill out on 55th and Lake Park
washing dishes and then later at Dr. Scholl's Foot Factory on Well's and
Goethe just south of North Avenue—between North Avenue and Division. Then, at seventeen, I started attending—maybe eighteen—Central
YMCA College for my GED. I graduated with a GED, and that introduced me to a program that I was eligible for at Northeastern Illinois
University because I had a high school diploma. In those days, they were
really recruiting African Americans to go to school, to go to higher education, and I was very fortunate to be able to slip in that window into a
more academic education. I was studying sociology.

What was the name of the man who got you . . . ?

Ed Parish.

No, who got you to go back to get your . . . ?

His name is really William Wandick, but his name was changed during the revolutionary period of the sixties and seventies, late sixties, to Shabazz Perez. Mr. Perez was the person who really took me under his wing and guided me in a direction of formally trying to acquire more education. I think that he saw things in me that were promising and that showed a need and a want and a yearning to know more. He probably picked up on that and really encouraged me to go to school.

How did you meet him?

I met Shabazz through an organization that was a gay group called the Black Philoctetes. The Black Philoctetes was a group of black gay men that came together for intellectual stimulation and conversations on Sundays. We would get together every Sunday and have coffee or whatever and talk about things, talk about community, talk about the world we were living in, or talk about the times we were living in. We talked about what we could do, what we wanted to do, or what our yearnings were to become in life.

Would this happen at someone's house?

Yeah, and it would float to different members' houses. There were about twelve of us.

Were there a lot of other groups like that getting together?

Well, later, there was a black group called the Third World Gay Revolution, which was more a mixture of cultures of black and Hispanic and Asian. At that time, that was gay liberation, an offshoot of the Gay Liberation Front. I was very involved in gay liberation also.

This was still in the late sixties?

Yeah, the late sixties.

And was there a huge gay liberation movement in Chicago?

Oh my God, yes! Actually, on my campus, I was gay liberation [*Laughing*], along with the Black Panther party, SDS [Students for a Democratic Society], and all these other groups. I was encouraged by Dr. William Speller, at that time, who was at Northeastern to be me and discouraged by a lot of brothers and sisters who didn't understand where I was coming from, being a gay man. But they later found out, as we grew together, that we could trust each other and love each other and respect each other. We got to that point of respect. Then things just kind of opened up, and we were able to flow more freely and have more flow between each other in conversations and so forth. During that time, which was the time of differentiation for most people who were black, individuation was not necessarily something that people grasped. I became individuated at that time, Shabazz and I. We were kind of the leading radical gay group on campus. I'd come in my Brown maxi-coat and big hats. It was quite gay, quite fabulous!

You would come into meetings . . . ?

Yeah, I'd go everywhere with it. I was living my life. You have to live your life. You can't live for other people. You have to live for yourself. I learned that very early on when I was incarcerated that I had to live my life. I couldn't live for somebody else.

What was it about being incarcerated that taught you that?

I think that it gave you time [for] reflection [to] look at the possibility of what might the future hold for you. In my case it did that. My future held that I would not go back because that was not going to be a lifestyle that I was going to exist in. I mean, I could have probably chosen to accept that as a normal part of my existence. You have to really go deep within yourself and you have to say, "OK, what is it that I want for me? What do I want to become? Who do I want to be?" And that's where the individuation comes in. That's where you become individuated. That's where you decide who it is you want to be—not who you are, but who you are becoming because we're always becoming. We never just are.

You said you had to do that kind of work when you were incarcerated?

Yes, I had to do that kind of work in there and especially when I got out. But then [after being incarcerated] I had my brothers to help me. I had brothers. I had a group of gay men that embraced me and said, "OK, you're going to be fine. You're going to be OK. Don't worry. Here's some food. Here's a place to stay. Now what are you going to do? How are you going to live your life? You want to go back there? I don't think so." Then you become the famous Joel L. Hall! [*Laughing*] Or infamous!

How did you get back to dance? You could have gone in a number of different directions.

At Northeastern, when I was there, they had a dance department, and it was headed by Marge Hobley—at first Trina Collins and then Marge Hobbly. I started taking academic classes at Northeastern and walked by the dance department one day, and they were rehearsing. I just kind of popped in and saw what was going on and decided to join their group. And it was kind of an orchesis—not exactly an orchesis, but close to an orchesis. Orchesis is usually the name of a group of students who get together in a university environment and call themselves a group. I joined the orchesis and started taking classes again and then was encouraged to continue taking classes. So, while I was going to school, I was taking classes. Then I ran off to Ailey and started taking classes in New York.

What classes were you taking at Northeastern?

I was taking ballet. I was taking jazz, modern. At that time they did not have tap or flamenco, now they have flamenco. It's their strong point now with Ensemble Español out of Northeastern. I was there pre–Ensemble Español. Dame Libby Fleming went on to develop her group out of, at, Northeastern and remain in residence there. My group performed at Northeastern, and [we] left Northeastern and went out on our own.

And how did this group come together?

It came together by my doing most of the choreography that was being done for the dancers at the school.

What were the pieces you choreographed back then? What were they about?

They were about life being a song worth singing. I remember we did this piece to Johnny Mathis called "Life Is a Song Worth Singing." I did a blues suite there to Billie Holiday. I did a piece called "Changes" there. I think I did "Changes" there. Those were my very early days of probing, putting the pieces of the puzzle together, watching, listening—you know, learning. I went to see everything that came into the city with dance. If it had a D in front of it, I was there watching, learning, and looking at professional companies—from New York City Ballet to Ailey to Dance Theatre of Harlem to absolutely everything that you can possibly imagine plus all of the companies that were here in the city at that time as well. I was there! I was watching, and I knew who those people were. I have a history of—a very knowledgeable history—who was doing what, where, and when because I was there to see it.

What were some of these early companies?

Well, some of the early people were Jewell McLaurin on the South Side. She was doing work. She had a little studio in her basement actually. Betty Taylor was teaching jazz. Lester Goodman and Joseph Holmes were doing modern. Tommy Gomez was doing Dunham. Let's see, Darlene Blackburn was doing work. Let's see, Najwa was doing work. Alyo Tolbert from Muntu was doing work. A woman by the name of Veda Sidney and I danced modern. And Thea Barnes was also in the city at that time.

At that time, had you already decided that this was the path that you were going to take?

Yeah, I kind of always knew it. I knew even when I was teaching sociology. My work was always from a sociological perspective. It's about life. It was about people on the street. It was about homelessness. It was about all of these things related to me and to my culture. The reason I chose jazz as an idiom is because that was related directly to me as a person, as an individual within my culture, so I could come from my cultural perspective in my work as others come from their cultural perspective in their work. Later, I did incorporate contemporary or what is now called contemporary modern dance and classical ballet into my work as well. In order to be competitive, I realized that I had to learn those techniques. So, I studied ballet. I studied Graham. I studied all of those. I studied Cunningham. I studied ballet so that I could have a broader point of view [and] so that more people would listen. As a black man people do not listen to you because you're invisible, so you have to make yourself visible by informing yourself. The more informed you are, the more visible you become even though they don't want to see you.

They can't deny you.

Well . . . they can deny you, but you can't deny you. It's all about you. It's not about them. It's all about what we make it. It's not about what people make it for us. This did not come about by people making anything for me. This came about [because of] the choices that I made to engage myself with people who could understand where it was I was headed and which direction I wanted to go as a vision and wanted to follow that vision. That's why this exists. Without them and without me, this would not exist.

Now I'm looking at a 200-year vision of how the Joel Hall Dancers and Center will look in 200 years when Joel Hall is not here. Do you see what I'm saying? That's when we become an institution. I'm looking at how I will look 200 years from now, historically. What part will I have played? What influence will I have been? What influence to others will I have been? How will I have influenced a movement of dance, an idea or philosophy of movement, or statement of movement? I'm looking at a big large world and not just being a part of it.

Can we go back to this early moment? What was the larger environment like in Chicago at that early moment when you started to dance?

Black dance?

Black dance.

In terms of black dance, it was pretty much ignored and still is for the most part. When I say ignored, I'm talking about the media ignoring [it].

I'm not talking about the community. Of course, the community always recognizes dance, but the media will take a position to clarify what is art. "This is art and this is not art." "This is art and this is not art." What usually has a tendency to be art is not of color, and what is not art is usually of color. What we have to do is we have to again differentiate ourselves and individuate ourselves and create our own environment where we are safe and where we are able to educate others to be safe. Where we're able to educate young artists to come and train in a healthy, nurturing environment to be who they are rather than who someone would hold them to be, which has nothing to do with them. So, art at that time, getting back to that subject, was something that was selective, which it should be carefully [created] but should not be—it is nothing that should be mental. People shouldn't judge it as not being what they want it to be simply because it's different.

Are you talking about trying to take art on its own terms?

Exactly. Art is art. Dance is dance. So what makes one form art and one form not? Nothing.

And when you say media, do you mean TV, newspaper . . . ?

Everything. Anything that writes. Anything that has influence with public opinion. I had to be very careful of that because early on I was criticized very heavily for what I did.

What was the basis of the criticism?

Nothing. It was different. The basis was that it was different. It was not all of these other groups that were rolling around on the floor and walking around with candles in front of their faces in the dark and all that kind of stuff. I mean that's great stuff, great material. It's great art, but so is mine. I have value too. Do you see what I'm saying? I have to believe that. I have to know that I matter. If I don't know that, I'm in trouble. That's when we become less than. That's when we go out of business because we don't think we matter, but I matter a lot. A lot of people depend upon what information I have, and I want to share it with them to make them share it with others so that they become more.

A lot of your choreography has to do with various aspects of life.

Ghetto life.

Ghetto life. Various experiences in ghetto life. Giving voice to that experience, to your experience from your perspective, and that's why you chose jazz as an idiom, right? And then you decided to go to Ailey?

I went to Ailey's for almost two years.

How did you make that decision?

Well, I had been going in the summer and taking classes for two weeks [at a time]. I'd just go in and take two weeks of classes at Ailey's, because Ailey is what I aspired to be. I wanted to be Alvin Ailey. I didn't want to dance in his company. I wanted to be Mr. Ailey himself.

Why?

Because he was so . . . because he was so large and he was so brilliant and he was so . . . He was a black man who was famous. He was someone who I just wanted to be like. I wanted to have a company of fifty dancers that traveled all over the world, was just fierce, and people would scream and throw money at the stage at them. Yeah, that's what I wanted to be. So I went to where I wanted to be, [to] what I wanted to become. I took classes there. I got a job in New York working.

Where were you working?

I was working as a restaurant manager for Zoom Zoom, which was a chain of restaurants that was German owned. I think Let Us Entertain You, [a group of concept restaurants], had something to do with them at that time, and I was the only black manager that they had hired in New York City out of all of their stores. I would work there from nine to five, and then I'd go to evening class. I had spent all the money that I had saved taking day classes when I got there. I had to get a job in order to have a place to live and take class, so I did that. Then after a while I thought, "You know what? I'm not doing what I wanted to do. I'm not taking class all day every day like I want to do. I'm not here to be a manager of a Zoom Zoom." I mean it was a good job. I made good money and everything, you know what I'm saying? But that was not why I was there. I was there to learn dance. So, I spent the money that I had saved working at Zoom Zoom, and I left and came home. I came back to Chicago.

Did you pick up with your dancers where you left off?

Well, during that time, I had ceased. We had ceased. I held auditions and brought in new dancers.

What was the name of your company?

Joel Hall Dancers.

Joel Hall at that time too? This first company of people whom you directed also was called Joel Hall?

Well, they were the Northeastern Dance Ensemble, but the group that I formed there was called the Joel Hall Dancers. I claimed it because I noticed that people in the profession would have [their companies] taken from them by their board of directors. Well, they can take anything from me, but they can't take my name. You can take my school, but I'll go down the street and open another one and still be Joel Hall. I didn't know what I was doing at the time was as wise as it was, but now it makes sense. I think that God kind of lined these things up for me that way to think that way about it so that the outcome would be that I would be in control of my own destiny. It's so very important for a black person of any sex to be in control of our own destiny.

Why?

Other people determining your destiny does not work. I was in prison, and I learned what that was. It doesn't work. You have to be your own person. You have to be your own business. Otherwise, you're working for somebody else as work. They determine when the lights go on and when the lights go off, when you have a job and when you don't have a job, when you're going to eat and when you're not going to eat, [and] when you're going to buy toilet paper and when you're not going to buy toilet paper. It doesn't work.

So, you held auditions when you came back. You got a new group of dancers. Where were you rehearsing and performing?

I got a factory down on South Michigan Avenue, through a person that I knew, to let us come in to rehearse for $15 a day or night on a vacant floor. It was a higher floor, so we would use the lighting from the inside and the windows as mirrors. You couldn't see from the waist down, but we could see from the waist up what we were doing. The reflection of the light against the window and the black at night allowed us to see ourselves in the windows as mirrors. So, that was how I started my first rehearsal space. Then we moved out into the Fine Arts Building at 410 South Michigan Avenue. I was there for fourteen years in the Fine Arts Building. They have a little building right next to it that's a three-, maybe four-story building adjacent to the Fine Arts Building. It was an annex of the Fine Arts Building. I had the second floor or the third floor all the way to the back and my partner, Joseph, had the fourth floor for theater, for the Chicago City Theater Company/Joel Hall Dancers.

What was Joseph's last name?

Ehrenberg. That's him right up there [*pointing to a picture above the door*].

How did you guys meet? Where did you start?

Joseph and I met during a show with a black director by the name of Herb Allen. Herbert introduced Joseph to me, and Herbert was doing something at the Museum of Contemporary Art that was called *Markings*. It was a show that was based around the writings of Dag Hammarskjold, the U.N. guy. Joseph was doing the reading in the show. He was doing the voice, and Herbert asked me if I would create dances around this show. So, I went home, and I thought about it. I read the material, and I came into rehearsal and [*snaps fingers three times*] we were on. It was a very successful run. It was performed at the Museum of Contemporary Art.

And then Joseph and I continued our relationship, which went deeper than our initial relationship. He died in 1995 of congestive heart failure, and he is the person who actually founded this organization with me.

And it was founded as?

It was founded as Chicago City Theater Company/Joel Hall Dancers— Chicago City Theater Company being the parent company and Joel Hall Dancers being a subsidiary of Chicago City Theater. Then it flipped with Joel Hall Dancers becoming the bigger company and Chicago City Theater Company became the lesser company. I don't want to say lesser, but it switched.

The Chicago City Theater Company still exists?

It still exists, yeah. We call ourselves Chicago City Theater Company/ Joel Hall Dancers. I still honor his presence in this organization by keeping that name Chicago City Theater.

Why did both of you start a company?

Because there was not really a place for black people to be able to express our work, and there was no real support behind it. Joseph did classical theater. He would do Ibsen. He would do Shakespeare. He'd do all of these classical pieces using all black actors back in the seventies, which was unheard of because black people were not in major productions downtown at all. So, it was very interesting listening to the conversation that you had [at the "Black Theater Is Black Life" Symposium at Northwestern in June 2011] and listening to people talk about that period and realizing that we were a part of that period too, but we were located downtown doing all black casts instead of mixed casts. Eventually, we went to mixed casts, but the primary purpose was to give African American actors a place to do theater, to do classical theater, and the Joel Hall Dancers the space to have a school. The school was on the third floor and the theater was on the fourth floor.

Was it just convention that people did not cast black actors?

Not in classical works.

Not in classical works. They just thought the role didn't fit.

Very few black actors were cast at all in plays. Along Lincoln Avenue, there was something called Wisdom Bridge Theater, which later moved up to Howard Street. They were doing some, not avant-garde, but seventies period theater with a director by the name of Eleven. I remember Eleven, and I went to see several pieces that they were doing that were very interesting. They did something called *War* that used black actors—young black actors, maybe two—but you didn't see more than two black people or one black person on the stage at that time on the North Side if you saw them at all. And it was in something that was more contemporary to the period of the seventies, which was a revolutionary period where black people were being seen for the first time really in any serious way outside of what had been depicted on television in the fifties with *Amos and Andy* and so forth. Historically, Chicago was not an open city and still is not in a lot of ways. We still have to make [it] ourselves. Most of the work we have to do for ourselves. They'll take all this money and give it to white companies to teach black people how to do stuff. They've got one black person doing recruitment. That's their black employee. They've got maybe one black ballerina in the company.

That's their diversity.

That's their diversity. I don't appreciate it. It makes me very angry because diversity is a full representation of the world. It represents black people. It represents Hispanic people. It represents Native American people. It represents Asian people. It represents white people. It represents everybody. That's diversity. It represents gay people. It represents straight people. It represents any people. [That] is diversity. That's what it is. It's not going out and teaching people of color something. That's not diversity, but that's what they're calling it so that the money keeps going into "diverse" programs that are not diverse. This is a diverse school.

You see some of everybody in this school.

You better. You walk in that door. I hope you see yourself at some point walking in that door because they do. That's what it is, and that's the way I feel the world is. I live the world the way I see it being. I don't live the world the way I see it wanting to be.

When you and Joseph were doing all-black-casted classical plays, did you get a lot of push back?

We got some good reviews. There was no push back. People were coming to the theater because they wanted to see it. Everybody was coming to see it, so it wasn't that it was doing badly but at one point the company, my company, took more of a priority. All of the focus started going to our going to Europe and performing there and getting out of the city of Chicago. Chicago was saying where they wanted us to be, and I was saying where I wanted to be. And they were two different places. I had to—not go out and prove myself but—get out of here because it was not helping me to only hear negative things. I had to go someplace. I had to go test myself to see if this was true what I was hearing these people saying. You know what I'm saying? If you hear something for so long, you begin to believe it. I had to find out, "Is this true?" And I went to New York. I took my company to the Joyce Theater, and we got rave reviews. They loved us. I took my company to Europe to the Glasgow Festival called Mayfest. Four people in the audience came up afterwards. One, from London, said, "Would you come next week to a festival in London that we're doing?" And I said, "Well . . . no, we have tickets to go back to Chicago. We've got to go back to Chicago, so we can't stay here for another week." And they said, "OK. Well, would you come back next year?" So, we went to the Bloomsbury Theater in London. No, we started at the—here's how that happened. We were at the Mitchell Theater in Glasgow. This guy came up from London. He invited us down to participate in the festival. We said that we could not, but we did participate in part of the festival in a place called Deptford. Deptford was like this little area of London that was black. It was ghetto. We went and did a full show in a nightclub kind of setting in Deptford, and it was fabulous. The next thing we knew, they were asking us to come back the next year to do the Bloomsbury Theater in London. From the Bloomsbury, we got bookings like that [*snapping fingers*]. They just kept coming. We'd be over there like twice a year for like two months. We went to England. We went to Scotland. We went to Germany. Then we went to Holland. Then we went to Norway and Russia and all of these places just out of that. It just kind of snowballed.

You said you went to the Joyce first. What year was that?

I went to the Joyce in maybe the late eighties, early '90s . . . late eighties. It was the late eighties.

And you took that first trip to Europe in . . . ?

We took that first trip to Europe in the early '90s. No, because that sign out there is from Russia in '89. Our first night staying in Moscow, I remember being in this huge hotel, and I could hear these tanks. The night we arrived there you could hear these tanks rumbling down the streets, these Russian tanks. They were practicing for their revolution day [parade] the next day. We went to Lenin's tomb. They treated us like royalty. I mean, it was really stunning. It was really something. It was really back in the day.

When you got out of this environment, what were you able to see?

I was able to see what the truth was. You see, people will not tell you the truth. You have to find it out for yourself because people will lie to you. They don't want you to know the truth because, if you know the truth, you might become successful in what you're doing. You know what I'm saying? If you know what the truth is. If you believe the lie, you will go out of business because you are listening to something that's not true.

You've continued to go back and do tours every year?

Every year, we were doing festivals every year. The company has had some really interesting challenges and changes and wonderful, wonderful, wonderful opportunities to meet all of these people in the world that

I never would have dreamt of meeting. I mean this little black child from Cabrini–Green. Never would I have dreamed in my wildest dream ever that I would have been able to move around the world as much, meet as many interesting people, and be treated with such influence and respect as I have been. I've had a very fortunate, beautiful life, still today.

What would you say is the philosophy behind your choreography?

I'm trying to tell the truth. I'm trying to be truthful. I'm trying to be meaningful. I want people, when they come to my work, to get in touch with what they're feeling. I want people to experience their experience through my experience. When they're looking at that stage, they're identifying themselves with what they're seeing rather than the dancer that they are seeing—the relationships, the choreography that takes place, [and] the feelings that transpire. I want people to come away with an experience that they have never had before from any place they've ever been or ever seen. That's my philosophy. I want them to take that and hold on to it and have it add meaning to their lives in some way.

Is it hard to train dancers to get to that point where they can convey that?

It is, especially now. Dancers are younger now, and they don't want to— we live in an instant world where I can go online and I can be in China in less than a minute, OK? I'm asking people to come in and train for five years before I put them onstage. They don't want to do that. They want it now, but the art form itself is so important. The discipline of the art form—the discipline of being in class regularly on an everyday basis two or three times a day in class, learning the craft, and learning the technique—is so very important. And to get people to really connect with that—that's a twentieth-century thing. Now, I've got to take that twentieth-century thing and move it into a twenty-first-century mode and figure out what are the dynamics that can get people engaged to the point that they need to be to take class at the level to become what they need to become and they want to become. I've had some lovely children come in here, really beautiful, halfway there. Their bodies just do it, but they're not willing to fall into the discipline of what it really takes to become a professional dancer. It's really hard work. It's a lot of time, a lot of sacrifice, and a lot of pain. I mean in terms of being in class when you could be at home sitting watching your favorite TV program *So You Think You Can Dance.* But you've got to be in class. People are not interested in that.

Do you think that people don't see the rewards that it can have?

No, they don't see the benefit. They don't realize the sequence that that takes. It's like learning your ABCs—what comes after what? It's like there's a sequence to that. You don't come in and learn your alphabet the first time your parents sit down with you at the table. That's a process that they go through with you over and over and over again until you just do it. Then you know your ABCs. Well, this is applicable to anything that we want in life. We have to learn to sit down and do it over and over and over and over and over again until we get it. Then, all of a sudden, we have it. Then that stays with us forever. It never leaves. It belongs to you. Your ABCs belong to you alone. It's not my ABCs. It's yours because you learned them. Right? That means, OK, now we can put together a word. Now we can put together a sentence. Now we can put together a paragraph. Now we can read a book.

The fundamentals are consistently taught every class—the beginning ballet classes and the advanced ballet classes—same exercises just done with variation. What you learn—simple positions, those five positions— once you learn what each step is, a tendu becomes a degage, battement becomes a grand battement. It all is sequential. It all fits together. So it's not anything that they're going to get like that.

It's almost like you're training the body how to think and how to speak in a particular language.

It's also training the body how to think. It's also training the body how to act, how to respect. OK? It's also giving the art form a place of respect, rather than something that they're doing. OK? When I was growing up and I came into class, if my teacher walked into class, we were all at the barre waiting for the teacher to come. You would never see a dancer sitting on the floor stretching . . . ever. Never. Ever. When the teacher walked in, that was the focal point. Back in the day, whether our instructors were smoking a cigarette or drinking a nip, that was your focus.

That was your mentor. That was your person that you were learning to be—not the alcoholic or the cigarette smoker, necessarily, but what they were doing. So, I teach my students when the teacher walks in, you're standing ready. When I walk into my class, all of my students are standing. If they're sitting, they stand up until I say, "Good morning. It is very good to have you in class this morning. Let's begin." Boom. I start my class. You see, there's a respect and there's a protocol there that I feel is essential to old-school standards that is missing somehow in relationships. That way you always can separate church from state also. That way the student never becomes familiar with you to the point where they go, "Joel, let's go out and have a drink." You're the student, and I'm the teacher. Now, when you're the teacher, you'll be the teacher and they'll be the student. But that's what they're learning. I'm teaching that. They don't know until you teach them.

I know you also mentor choreographers, also teachers . . .

Anyone related to the art form of black dance particularly, of dance generally, but I think without mentoring there is no [continuation]. It stops. If I want to suck it all up, there's nothing there. I need to share what information it is that I have so that it's not all sucked up so that it can grow because that young man might set a piece that might change someone's life. My sharing of information with him or her is so very, very, very important for me at my age now because I'm at an age where I have to look at those things. I have to look at what it is that I'm doing and my purpose. I have to be purposeful. I have to be responsible, and in being responsible I have to mentor. It's very important because otherwise we lose the form. We lose the art form. We lose the initiative or the interest because it's not there.

It's not there in terms of the larger public?

Exactly. Exactly. Something is missing. There's some missing link. Something is gone. Something is less. You don't see it. That's part of the 200-year vision—mentoring—so that 200 years from now, there'll be mentoring. That information will still be transitional through whatever process of time it leads to.

And it seems like now the financial situation for dancers is even more . . .

It's direr. It's pretty scary, actually.

What is scary about it?

Well . . . business does not understand the importance of art to their stability and their sustainability. They don't understand the importance of
not-for-profit to support business and business to support not-for-profit.
One really does not happen without the other in this culture. They don't
really understand that relationship. Business thinks that not-for-profit is
something that they give to, rather than not-for-profit being something
that services them as well as they service it. It's an equal exchange. Business doesn't understand that when a not-for-profit moves into a neighborhood, they establish a business: the Joel Hall Dancers and Center.
There's nothing on the block that way. There's nothing on the block
that way but a hair salon and store. Then, two years later, there's a business that's opened as a restaurant. There's a business that's opened as a
corner store. There's a business that's opened that's a karate school as the
result of a not-for-profit being visible. They see all these people coming
in and out of here every day. Maybe I should open up someplace in that
place right there. They don't connect the dots. It's really very simple. It's
not complicated. Really. But they don't want to touch that. It's all about
them. Well, it's got to be about everybody, otherwise it fails. It does not
work when it's only about one thing.

*Why is such a thing as black dance still important? Why is it still important to
have something called black dance? Or is it still important to have something
called black dance?*

Well, it is important because black people are not equal. Until we are at
the table with everybody else, then we can start calling it dance. As long
as you have black people, you have to have black dance because we're
black. Now when we have people, then we call it dance. They're people
so you can call what they're doing dance, but we're not people.

We are still dealing with all that inequality?

Well, it has to do with equality for me, and we're still not free. We're not free as black people. We're not free as gay people. I'm not free as a gay person. We're not free as Americans. I'm still fighting for the right to marry my other half. Why shouldn't I have that right? That's an inalienable right. That's equality. That's being equal. That's not being more than or less than but the same as. Equal is the same as. You see what I'm saying?

Discrimination at any level to me is an absolute . . . [*long pause*] . . . pain in the butt. I refuse to accept that as a way of my life being. I don't want [to]. So, I carry myself in a way that is very specific to equality—in terms of business, in terms of who I am and how I carry myself and what I think and what I do and who I am and who I am becoming. I am becoming equal. I am not there yet. You're not there yet. Nobody is. They're not there yet, really. They just think they are. That's an illusion. That's a television thing. That's Rupert Murdoch stuff. That equality is nonexistent, because now equality is all-rich. That's equal but that's not the reality. Reality of the world is rich and poor, middle class, black and white, people of color, everything. That's the reality, but what is becoming reality is a show.

The other question your story brought me to is that on the panel [at Northwestern], we had a dancer who said that she was frustrated because of the kind of discrimination and the kind of abuse that she has experienced from black people themselves. Part of her question was how do you expect me to be exclusively black, or deal only with black people, when my own people have abused me and my own people have done this or that to me?

My argument with that is that you must stand out and be different and be a leader. Show them that this is the way things must be and not succumb to what they've done to you. Succumb to what you are doing and what you are becoming as opposed to what other people are doing. Other people are always going to do that [discriminate]. That's not going to change, but you have to change. So, I understand what the sister is saying, because all of us receive that discrimination. We receive it in terms of educated versus noneducated. We receive it in terms of male–female. We receive it in terms of gay–straight. We receive it in terms of black–white. Every possible range of the gamut, somebody is not going to like you. But, you have to be a leader. And when you're transformational, you become someone that changes other people's behavior [and] other patterns of thinking. That's when you become a transformational leader. I am becoming a transformational leader. Barack Obama is a transformational leader. Gandhi was a transformational leader. Martin Luther King was a transformational leader. These are people who change culture, change the world. Those are my aspirations as a dance choreographer and leader. I want to do it on a larger scale on, a global scale. To be able to change lives by what I'm doing, that's my work. That's my work on myself.

ALFRED (FRED) BAKER

Born in Montego Bay, Jamaica, Alfred (Fred) Baker has taught and performed Afro-Caribbean dance forms internationally as well as in various U.S. cities. In 1971, Mr. Baker founded and served as the artistic director of the Western Jamaica Folk Dance Company, which became the West Indian Folk Dance Company. Baker was honored by Malcolm X College at their 2011 Kwanzaa celebration for his artistic contributions and achievements.

In this April 2011 interview, Fred Baker fondly remembers his early years as a preteen dancing in Jamaica, his international touring career, and the events that led to his arrival in the United States. Baker's interview touches on his experiences as an immigrant artist in the United States and the strategies he used to reestablish his company in Chicago.

I was born in Jamaica, and I've been in Chicago for the past twenty-five to thirty years. I started dancing when I was a child in Jamaica. I really didn't want to dance, but, unfortunately, it happened. Originally, it was my brother who started dancing—my big brother. I was the last child, so I used to go there and watch him all the time. People used to keep throwing money and give it to him when he danced. He didn't show up [for a couple of weeks] because he was getting [older]. He was about thirteen [or] fourteen, [so] he was getting to that age and he had a girlfriend. He didn't want his girlfriend to see him dancing in the street. We waited around to look for him for two Saturdays [when he would dance], but he wasn't there. I realized that people were asking, "What happened to this kid that was dancing?" I used to go and watch him because every time he was dancing [and] he'd get money, he would give me something nice to eat. [*Laughing*] So, I was one of his favorite fans. He didn't show up, and the lady would ask about him. I said to myself, "Well, they didn't know he was my brother, right? And they don't know who he is, so, if I go out there and dance, maybe they would do the same thing to me." So I got out there and start[ed] dancing. I wanted to do it because I wanted to run and buy sweets. [*Laughing*] It was really a knockout for me. I started getting so good that people were really asking me to participate in the functions that were happening out there. By the time I get to about nine years old, I really realize that I could dance. It was something I wanted to do. I was invited to a performance by a gentleman they called Mr. Chambers. He had a show. We used to call it Showboat. He used to go into the lighter—it's a big old boat, [a transfer barge], that used to carry banana[s]—dress it up like a stage, and people would go in there and dance.

Inside the boat?

Inside the boat. They used to call it the Showboat, but it was a lighter. The ship could not come into the dock, so they had to fill the lighter with banana[s] to take it to the boat. So it was a big ol' lighter, very big. What he used to do is that he used to rent lighters, and he dressed it up and put it out to the sea. It was beautiful. It was something that actually was unique. That's number one. I was so young, and I wanted to be in the boat. The boat was interesting for me. I did that for quite a while, almost [until I was] ten, when I got my first experience [as a] professional dancer. I made it into Alan Ivanhoe's company. He was a student of Ms. Ivy Baxter, and I know Ms. Ivy Baxter also. But at the time what they called dance to me was . . . it was ridiculous! It was not dance.

What was it?

It was dance. Well, to me, what I was doing was dance, but what they were doing was not dance because, you see, they were trained. My dance was just something that comes natural to me. I was doing the jitterbug and the jubie, and they were doing dances that were trained—modern and contemporary. I was like, "What's that?" I was like, "Huh?" [*Laughing*] That was so stupid for them to do [those dances], but I was doing all the jitterbugs and all these things and the flips and the carrying on. It was livelier to me than what they were doing, and to me what they were doing was stupid. What I was doing was *the* dance. I thought I was the hottest thing in town. I thought I was really into what dancing was all about at the time. [At] about ten, I started wondering about my future. "Am I going to go to school to be a lawyer? Am I going to go to school and, after school [is] finish[ed], go into dancing?" I didn't get a chance to sort of work that out because my father died. I was nine years old, going [on] ten. I was nine and a half, anyway, and my father died. I think he died about three months before my birthday, and I had to become a man at nine. I started taking over everything and started working for the family, and I was the last one. Everybody was dumbstruck [when my father died] and didn't know where they were going. My bigger brother was supposed to be the one who took over, but he was hopeless. I knew everything. I knew everything [that] was supposed to be in place. I knew how to bury my father. I knew how to go to ask about the church, to ask about the coffin, find [out] about the burial spot, what to pick . . . everything. That came from dancing. That came from the money that I was getting in the showboat. The dancing took over, and I said, "Well, this is what I—my father is passed away and nobody else has to do it." So, I had to do it. I went straight into dancing at that time. Bertie King asked me if I wanted to go to Cayman, and that was my first experience leaving the island. I was about ten at that time. Then, all of a sudden, when I came back from Cayman, Mr. Deans, Eric Deans, asked me if I wanted to go to Belize. So it seemed like there was a blessing that started to follow me right after that. When I went to Belize, I start[ed] seeing trained dancers in Belize. There was a fellow that was dancing in a club called De Savoy, and he was a trained dancer. I wanted to dance like how he danced because his arms were good, his motion was good, and people were just going crazy over him.

They were trained in what kind of dance?

He was a Latin dancer, but he was good. When I came back from Belize, Alan Ivanhoe started asking me again about joining his company. He took me to one of Ms. Ivy Baxter's classes up in MoBay High School for Girls. In the third month, he wanted me to go to America with him. I came to America with him—I think in 1959—and I went to New York. When I got to New York, Alan Ivanhoe started training me, but we didn't have training too long because his brother left the group and I had to learn the routines. In New York, I saw these kids running down to the basements in these little black tights. When I saw that I said to myself, "What on earth is that? Is it a funeral house?" It wasn't because it was a dance room. I thought it was a funeral house because I never saw people in black tights. People were dancing in black tights. So, anyway, I got curious to the point where I said, "I'm going to look." I went down, and I saw a boy turn on his toe eighteen times. He did a pirouette. It was so fast, I was in half a daze. And I went to the lady and said, "Excuse me, you see what he did? I can do that in two weeks . . ." Miss Ashkin she was. [*Laughing*] Yes, she was Miss Ashkin. I said, "Excuse me, miss, I'm a dancer from Jamaica and you know what? I can do it in two weeks." She laughed. That was the reason why she took me in because she had never seen a guy so bold. [I] started dancing in Jamaica, [and I] didn't know that I would have to go through all of these positions: turn out, jetés and pliés. I didn't have no idea of all of that. So I had my first teacher. My first real teacher teaching me to do dance—teaching me twelve positions, five positions, and the turnouts and the jetés, and the plié, and the balance, and the brisé. All those things that I learned in school were from Miss Ashkin, but the gentleman that led me through the door was Alan Ivanhoe. He was first because he had taken classical dance from Ms. Ivy Baxter. So I started there, and I went to Europe with [him]. We went to Paris and got stranded. [*Laughing*]

What year was this?

I think that was '60. We were in '60, because Jamaica got independence in '62. We were in Canada when Jamaica got its independence.

So you were traveling and staying here as a young boy?

Yes, and then Jamaica got independence in August, on the 6th of August, and I was so sorry that I wasn't home. I was crying when I saw the whole thing. Then my mother took sick again, so I went home in 1964. What happened was that she keep saying to me, "Don't go back." And I said, "I have to go back because I have a job." My next contract was going to be in Nassau [Bahamas]. And she said, "No, no, no, no, no, no. We have a lot of kids over here. Why don't you just form something down here. Help these kids out." I said, "I can't do that. I have to go back." So anyhow, in '64, my mother kept saying to come back, so I went back to Jamaica just after my birthday. It was in October. My mother asked me if I was going to go again, and I said, "Yes, I'm still leaving. I have to meet the company in Santo Domingo [Dominican Republic]." I said to myself, "Well, OK, what if I start this dance school? When I go to Santo Domingo I can't go nowhere, so I'll go back in May."

What happened in Santo Domingo that . . .

I saw a group in Santo Domingo where this woman was trying to teach some young kids [to dance], and they were very good. When I spoke to her—she could speak English and also Spanish—she said the reason she had started a group was because she had [gone] to Cuba and saw Alicia Alonso dancing. She was talking about the effort [Alicia Alonso was] putting out to have Cubans to do their culture, their art, and thing[s] like that. So I went back to Jamaica. Starting a company was an opportunity for me to please my mother and to see if I had it in me because I studied choreography, too.

By the time I got to Jamaica, and we started the company, we were a group of seven people: the Watsons, a family of four boys and one girl; Ms. Fay Lawrince; and myself. I said to myself, "What are we going to do? How are we going to do this?" Fay Lawrince and I talked, and she said, "Let's start a dance school." I said, "We've got to give it a name." She said that she did not have a name. I said, "Well, by tomorrow I'll find a name for it." The next morning, I got up, and I went to see her. She asked me if I had a name, and I said, "Yes, I do. We are going to call it The School of Creative Dance and Music, and I'll do creative dance [and] you do music." So it was named the Modern Day School of Creative Dance and Music—[we called] it the School of Creative Dance and Music. In the first two months, we had almost ninety people join the school. After three months, we had 350. I've never seen a school grow so fast in my life, and the reason for that was that we had no competition. The only other school [in Jamaica] was in Kingston. There was nothing in Montego Bay. There was no other dance school. If you wanted a school, if you wanted classical [dance], you had to go to Kingston, [ninety miles away]. People were getting very tired of it. So when the school started out, everybody was just all behind us. It was one of the most beautiful things for us. We did it for seven years straight, and, in the seventh year, they asked us to enter [the] Jamaican Festival. At this time, Joyce Campbell asked me to be the commissioner for the Western side of Jamaica, which is from Ocho Rios all the way down to Negril. I was the director for the whole area. I thought it was a very big demand on me, but when they told me what I had to do, I thought it was an ideal thing for me to do because I was researching past dances of Jamaica. I thought it was absolutely ideal for me, so I jumped at the opportunity. The first time we entered [the Jamaican Festival] in 1970, we did a dance called *Sophisticated Reggae* and won the parish [competition]. We went on to Kingston for the International Competition with all the parishes, because each parish that wins has to go to Kingston for the gold and silver and bronze medal. We went to Kingston, and we won the gold medal for *Sophisticated Reggae.* When we came back down, we said, "OK, we gonna enter again next year." Next year, we won the gold medal for *Kuminia,* silver for *Mother-in-Law,* bronze for *Village Dance,* and we decided it was time for us to form a company. We formed the Western Jamaican Dance Theatre Company, which combined dance, drama, and music. We did our first performance on the 18th of November, 1971. It was called *Triplet 1.* It rocked! It was fantastic!

During '78, we were having a problem in Jamaica and—what's his name?—President Carter went into power in the U.S. The government wanted Carter to lend them the money—Jamaica was bankrupt—so they came to America to ask for a loan. We came with the government officials and did four performances in Washington D.C.—one for President Carter in the White House, one for the Jamaican Ambassador to America Mr. Rattray, one for Baltimore Brotherhood Association, and one for Mayor Schafer [Baltimore's mayor at the time]. They talked to Carter, and Carter asked the ambassador to put together a program for a loan that focused on the Ministry of Tourism, Ministry of Health, and the Ministry of Youth, Communication, and Development. The program focused on food, dance, health, and investments. So I was the dance ambassador. I got here [in] the U.S., and the person who was in charge of us saw an opportunity to run with the money. [*Laughing*] So he actually ran off with the money and left us. I was stranded in Baltimore. He stole $30,000 from us. The only thing I could do [was] to get in touch with people I knew like Jimmy Payne and Tony Smith. We had done two shows: one in Philadelphia and one in New Jersey. When Felix Grey got the money, he didn't give it to us. It was a cultural exchange, so people were giving money for the cultural exchange program to take care of food and clothes. After the last show in New Jersey, we didn't see Felix again. And we haven't seen him up until now.

There was nobody to complain to?

We complained to Mr. Radcliffe, who was the ambassador in New York, Mr. John Radcliffe. He found out that Mr. Felix Grey was in Canada, and he got back the passports for us . . . after ten years of waiting for it. We couldn't leave. If we left there was two things that [would] happen. If we were brought back to Jamaica, we couldn't come back to the United States for a long time because they would actually deport us. We didn't want that to happen. We were one of the best companies out there, and we'd have to go back to Jamaica by being deported. Who would want to be deported? They find us and deport us? So we didn't want to do that. So what we did was we asked Mr. Radcliffe if he would speak to the U.S. commissioner and immigration officer and ask them to give us enough time for us to get our passport. They extended our visas for two years. Then we heard it through the grapevine that if you got married to a lady from America, you would be able to stay. So everybody was trying to get hooked up. They got married and started raising families. Others started to find their own way of getting their papers. So things worked out for those that stayed in the United States and remained with the company.

In the United States we started to [have] so many different West Indian people within our company. All of us were Jamaican when we first came here. The first person that joined us was Rudy Johnson who came from Trinidad. Rudy has been with us thirty years. A female dancer that joined us was Marily Bauck. She's the oldest member that we have dancing. She came from Belize. Buster Marley from the Bahamas was the third person. The fourth person that joined us was Ika President from St. Croix. Then Mandingo Moses from Montserrat. Elita Bennet from Belize. Then two more girls from Belize knew her, and they came in and joined us. Then we have Mark Vaughn and Danny Hines, who came from Barbados. We have Felicia, who was German, and Marise Campos from Mexico. Irma Miller was from Nassau. Delia Spencer, Jackie Ross, and Beverly Perkins were the Americans in the company. We had Esther Long, who was sixty-five when she came into the company. She was a golden-age dancer, which was fantastic! We did some things with that we would not believe she could have done, but she kept up and made our audience wonder if she was really sixty-five years [old]. Me, Clifton Robinson, Harry Detry, Jenise McKinzie, Horace Brown, Michelle Jarrett, Rose Watson, Margo Murre, Audry Blacke, Valroy Dawkins, Patrick Paysle, and Peter Richards were Jamaican. So we had to change the name from the Western Jamaican Dance Theatre to the West Indian Folk Dance Company because we were all West Indian. That's where that name comes from.

So, to go back, you connected with Jimmy Payne, and he hooked you up with . . .

Tony Smith.

Tony Smith. And they brought you to a club out here [in Chicago].

Yes, it was called the Four Kings Club. It was on Mannheim Road.

What kind of dance were you doing there?

When we came here, we came with three types of dancing: One was traditional West Indian dance, two was modern, and three was the cabaret dance. Now the traditional dances were the quadrille and mento. The modern dances were ballet, jazz, and modern. The cabaret dancers would dance the fire dance, limbo—those things that we do—and bottle dance. We used to break up the bottle and dance on top of it, we used to do the limbo, and we used to do the fire dance with people. So that was the cabaret side of it. Then we had the contemporary side of it, which was the modern dance. We do things like *Saints and Sinners,* and we do things

like *Son of Sultan*. We do beautiful dances. Then we would go back to doing things like quadrille. Then we found out that we were making more
money out of cabaret and not with the rest of the dancing. I'm thinking because of the name they did not associate us with being modern or
contemporary. What we did was that we decided that, "OK, we'd do the
show—which was at [the Four Kings Club]—and combine modern and
cabaret together." And that's what we did, and that's what we're doing
now, dancing cabaret and ballet. [Audiences] can see the contemporary,
and they can see the cabaret now. We do the folk songs and dances, fire
dance, and dance limbo and do contemporary dances together. That's
how we make that work.

How long did you stay at the Four Kings Club?

We were there six [years]. We came in '78. I think we left Baltimore the
middle of '79, and we came there. We were here from '79 until like '80,
'81, '82, '83, '84, '85. Yeah, '85 we left. My daughter was born in '88. When
my daughter was born, we weren't working there anymore.

So why did you leave that club?

OK, what happened was that the guy who was the original bar owner
when we went there, he was a very old man, but he was so nice. When [the
original owner's son] started taking over the bar, everything was just messed
up. He didn't have no business [skills], and he didn't know how to talk to
people. He was losing customers. Tony was supposed to get 50 percent of
the club, and he would pay all the entertainment. Tony was taking care of
the music, taking care of the dancers, and thinking that 50 percent of the
club was his. Tony didn't make anything. He got fed up, and Tony left.

Where were you staying? Where were you rehearsing?

Delia's friend, Margo, had an aunt that had a house on 63rd and Wood-
lawn Street, [which] had six available rooms, and we moved over there.
We did not have a place to rehearse. Margo knew Jimmy Payne and told
me that he had a studio, and I went down to see him, and he invited us
to rehearse at his studio. I met Mr. Moses, Cory Moses, at a function

that Jimmy Payne and I did. We were having a concert in Jimmy Payne's studio. He did the first half and we did the second half. He liked the company and he wanted us to work with him, and he wanted us to come to Gill Park on Sheridan Road. He introduced us to the park system. We stayed there for two years, and we moved with him when he left to Austin Town Hall. After two years, he was going to retire. He wanted to find us a space that we were comfortable working with, and he introduced us to Mr. Walter, the supervisor for Columbus Park. He said that he liked the dance company and he was going to move. "Come and look at Columbus Park." So we went to Columbus Park, and we said, "OK, this is it." He gave it to us, and it was such a beautiful [studio]. We have not moved from that place. We have done some fantastic work over there. We've done some very good productions at that place. It was made *for* us. It was the right size. He was 100 percent into the arts. I stayed there [and] this is the fourth supervisor that I've worked under. Walter left, and then Mr. Moses took over. After Mr. Moses left, there was Mr. Turner. Now Mr. Turner [is] gone, [and Jeanette Stoval is] there. So I'm getting four supervisors, but it was a very nice place.

Where was Jimmy Payne teaching?

It was 218 S. Wabash. We were at Jimmy Payne's studio in '81, '82, and '83. Yeah. We were there that time. Jimmy Payne had that studio, I think it was '76, '75. I think he had it in the seventies, and we came down here in '79. So we were there '79 until like '80, '81, '82. The whole idea of teaching dance and being around kids is my life. I can look [at] a person, right, and tell if the person can dance. I find dancers that turn out to be absolutely fantastic. When I first met Horace Brown, I looked at him in Jamaica. He was sixteen—I think fifteen or sixteen—and he told me that he was a weight lifter. I said, "No, you're not. You're a dancer." He said, "No way I'm gonna do that." I said, "Yes, you are." And I wasn't wrong. He is fantastic.

What do you think the kids get from dancing, music, and theater?

Some kids go to the theater and dance because they want to be famous. They don't necessarily have to be able to dance. They dance because they think it's a way to become famous, but, if you look at the discipline part of it, it's all lacking in the way they do dancing. They will be very good dancers, but they haven't got any discipline. Later on down the line, they lose all of what they learn because they decide to drink or they'll start to smoke or they get lazy. It's not something they want to get into. You find kids that will dance [or] that go into theater dance, really serious, and put their mind to it. [At] twenty to thirty years old, they still have that same discipline, that same input that they had when they were younger, that same charisma and all of that. Everything that comes—all the energy—will change as you grow older, but it's still the same pace: going to class, being on time, taking class, that can't change. You also dance, some people go to the theater because [they are] dramatic—the way they are in their whole life. They're so dramatic. The actors that we have, they don't even have to be onstage to be dramatic. They'll sit down in a chair, and there's a highlight. They can sit down and they can light up a whole room because that energy [and] that creativity that they have there. Some kids learn singing not because of the money—they know the money's going to come—but it's the way in which to express themselves. They don't want to be a one-time singer. They want to be a singer that goes on for a long time, so they fashion themselves after people like Luther Vandross or Nat King Cole or some of the great singers that prolong their singing and not just one record and you don't hear any more from them. They are kids that go onstage for different reasons. I'll see the kids that really have the right reasons to be onstage, and that's what happens.

So as a director, a teacher, you're just bringing that kind of stuff out in the student and molding them?

Yes. We mold them because you can have fifty kids out there, and, out of those fifty, five will be really interested. That won't mean all of them can't dance. What you do as a director is try to have a standard direction in which you want them to go or you're telling them to go. You are showing them where you want them to go because they sometimes know where they want to go, they just don't know how to get there. The director or dance teacher, that's your job to show them out there. Everybody [told] me when I was small that I was going to be a dancer. I wasn't interested in [it], but my body was calling for it. So I need[ed] to decide what I wanted to do for myself. And when I got it, it was like something happened. It was a day for the Lord, it happened. I started doing it and doing it, and people were saying that I was good. I stepped right in those shoes, and I would never give it up. I will always dance.

Has your repertoire shifted since coming to Chicago?

My repertoire made a switch. Not extremely, but it made a switch. We found out that there was other things in dancing that was really not something that we wanted to get into, but it was something that was called for because of the young kids that we have around us. We try to go into reggae music, which is a really good form of cultural awareness. If you listen to some of the artists that sing reggae music that coming from a deep-rooted point, or place—Bob Marley's one of them and Peter Tosh is one of them—it's not that they are fighting against the system; they're fighting to *change* the system. By listening to that, you get ideas about how to really implement dance and dance steps and movement by just listening to those words and listening to that. So it has changed a lot, but not too much. I know the basic influence that we have still remains within the modern and cabaret, because cabaret, in a sense, has a very strong, vibrant movement that's contemporary. It makes the movement more energetic and pleasurable. The repertoire we do now, we're taking the slight movements away from that to go ahead to doing reggae music and go into theatrical music. We went into hip-hop—not all too much of the hip-hop, but [it is] something that we do to show how versatile we are. Crunking is a dance that we used to do in Jamaica. When I first looked at [it], I call[ed] it "yacking." I said, "Our parents used to tell us that we couldn't do this." The reason why we couldn't do it [was] because it would jerk our back out of the socket, and people were saying that it was too hard. If you look closely, it looked like you were doing the jerk. I saw it now, and they call it crunk. I said, "That's yacking. That's the same dance." So when you look at it, you find that if you do cabaret and take cabaret to its full length, to its full study, Yacking is a part of cabaret. There's nothing different about it. Even the one we call butterfly, people call it tootsie roll. It comes out of cabaret. People must understand it is like that [with] a lot of things that we do. If you go through the whole of cabaret, you will understand that they're the same thing.

When you came, was there a huge community from Jamaica or from the Caribbean here that you were able to get in touch with? Was there an existing community here?

Yeah, when I came here, there were two groups of people in terms of what we're doing. We have the Jamaican-American Association that has Jamaicans, Belizeans, and Barbadians. It was not a very big association because everybody was sort of trying to get into a group of people. The next one was called West Indian American Association, which was a group of people that were in Milwaukee and here in Chicago. But my involvement came out of Evanston because Evanston had a very large West Indian population. I started to meet a lot of people who were a part of the two groups. For instance, Mr. Lopez, who was the president of the Jamaican-Caribbean Association, and Gene Martin, who was the president of the Jamaican-American Association. There were a lot of people that were [here], but the company never really involved itself totally with the Jamaican group until the '90s when we did the Black USA Dance. We were on the West Side, and most of the West Indian population was on the South Side and [in] Evanston, and people were scared to come to the West Side. That Dance USA was an opening because people were very excited about the company. They said we did such a good job. We not only got the publicity, but we were able to start travel[ing] around to other parts of the city working in the schools. We started to connect with folks.

This year [2011], we are doing a thing, which is called the Caribbean-American Heritage Month Gala. We are working hard on that. We are trying to do it on the 18th of July, [2011]. The Gala is trying to get all the West Indians together to let them understand that we are not different. We are from the same region. We may be from different islands, but we are from the same region. We should celebrate our month just like the Mexicans celebrate their month, the Irish celebrate their month, [and] the Chinese celebrate their month. We think it is good for us to do this. So, we are here and we are trying to keep the Caribbean culture, the West Indian culture, alive.

AMANIYEA PAYNE

Amaniyea Payne is the artistic director of Muntu Dance Theatre of Chicago. She is a versatile artist who has studied, performed, and toured extensively in the United States and globally. Amaniyea provides professional instruction and artistic support to numerous schools, arts organizations, and dance artists in the United States, Africa, Europe, and the Caribbean Islands. She has received numerous recognitions and awards, including the Ruth Page Award in 1994 for Dance Achievement and 2001 for Lifetime Service and the 2012 Lifetime Achievement Award from the African American Arts Alliance of Chicago.

In this January 2011 interview, Amaniyea Payne discusses her training in Baltimore and New York City and her search to learn more about Africana cultural practices and dance forms. Payne's interview details the circumstances that led to her becoming the artistic director of Muntu Dance Theatre of Chicago as well as Muntu's artistic collaborations and international work since she began working with the company.

How did you begin dancing?

I started in Baltimore, Maryland. That's where I was born: Baltimore, Maryland. As a young child during elementary school, my parents, like most parents during that time, sent me to ballet school. That was not an interest for me at that point because I was a little rough around the edges. I liked climbing fences, trees, and jumping off the rocks with my uncles and friends. In 1964, I had the opportunity to go to the World's

Fair in New York, where they had many different aspects [of cultural or ethnic dance]. The Guinea Ballet was there. The Burundians and the Watutsi were there. There were so many aspects, which I had really never seen before, because the only aspect of any ethnic or cultural dance coming from Africa was seen on *Tarzan*. That was quite intriguing and something that made an imprint on my mind and my heart. In Baltimore, being right there at the Mason–Dixon Line, dance was not as accessible to the young people in our community. You had the YWCA or recreational centers during the time—say about 1968. During that time, I think that was like the birth, to my knowledge, of CETA-type [Comprehensive Employment Training Act] programs, where young people were engaged in the arts and looking at it for potential careers and/or opportunities that they could access in life. So, at this particular recreation center, the Schroeder Recreation Center, our dynamic visual artist, Mr. Ernest Kromer,[1] had the opportunity to have many different artists in place: Mr. Orville Johnson,[2] who was the dance director there, and Dr. Lonnetta Gaines,[3] who was based in New York, a dynamic dancer, revo-

1. Ernest Kromer was born in Baltimore in 1939. A celebrated visual artist and chef, he and his wife, Gail, opened Kromah Gallery, Inc., in 1978 as both an art gallery and cultural arts center. See Isaac Rehert, "Gallery Exists to Show, and Inspire, Black Art," *The Sun*, September 19, 1981, and Awanda Roberts, "A Black Art Gallery, Aimed at Blacks," *The Sun*, July 22, 1979.

2. Orville Johnson earned a BA in theater from Columbia College Chicago and an MA in dance education from Northwestern University. He studies with a number of different artists in New York, including Martha Graham, Alvin Ailey, Eleo Pomare, and Babatunde Olatunji. He came to Baltimore in 1971 to be a guest choreographer for the Urban Musical Theatre at Morgan State College. In 1975, he started the Baltimore Dance Theatre in 1975 as a community arts program at Dunbar High School sponsored by Urban Service's Cultural Arts Project. Before starting this company, he traveled to Nigeria for two years teaching and studying dance. Upon his return, he set choreographed pieces using the material he learned from his travel. For more information on Orville Johnson, see Harriet Jackson Scarupa, "Modern Dancers with Ancient Themes," *The Sun*, February 15, 1976.

3. Dr. Lonnetta Gaines is a highly respected educator, performance artist, and author. She received her BA from Fisk University, her MA from Bank Street College, and her PhD in early childhood development from Union Institute in Ohio. She performed nationally and internationally with a number of prominent artists and companies in New York, including Eleo Pomare, Dianne McIntyre, George Faison, Mickey Davidson, and Abdel Salaam. She was the vice president of the Lorraine Monroe Leadership Institute before the company dissolved in 2011. For more information on Dr. Gaines, see Charmaine Patricia Warren, "The Metamorphoses of Dr. Lonnetta Taylor-Gaines," *Black Masks*. Vol. 12.2; and Erica Newport, "Dance Legend Visits Newtown," *Herald Tribune*, May 8, 2012.

lutionary type dancer. At that time black dance was called interpretative dance. That's how we told our stories of our political, spiritual, and social aspects. During the late sixties, I was doing interpretative dance, evolving, and being around; going to the Community College of Baltimore; going to Morgan State as a theater major. At that time, you learned more out of school than you learned in school, especially with the African arts and culture. Being a person with a revolutionary mind, I couldn't find what I wanted inside of the school in terms of dance and politics. So the search was on.

In Baltimore, at Antioch College, a dear friend of mine, now by the name of Aissatou Bey-Grecia, actually came from New York, and she was teaching the style that came from the Olatunji School of Dance. [This] is the school, which was run by our beloved brother who has passed away now, Dr. Michael Olatunji. We learned some dances from the repertoire from West Africa, and that was the impetus for starting [to learn] West African dance. Continuing the studies, Chuck Davis[4] came to Baltimore and presented another aspect of the West African interpretative dance. I became hungry. But I think my real first opportunity to know that I wanted to do this style of dance, in terms of West African style, was in 1972. Les Ballet Africains, the national dance company from Guinea, West Africa, came to Baltimore to the Playhouse Theatre. I remember vaguely sitting in the back of the theater and watching these artists fly.

---

4. Chuck Davis is a highly regarded and respected educator, dancer, and choreographer. Originally from Raleigh, North Carolina, Davis attended Howard University, where he majored in theater and dance. In 1968, Davis founded the Chuck Davis Dance Company in the Bronx, New York. In 1977, his company traveled to Lagos, Nigeria, to participate in FESTAC, and he founded the annual African dance festival DanceAfrica. He began working with the American Dance Festival in Durham, North Carolina, in 1980, and he relocated to Durham, North Carolina, in 1984 to start the African American Dance Ensemble. Still in existence, the company travels nationally and internationally teaching about and performing African and African American dance traditions with the hopes of increasing cross-cultural respect and understanding. See the website of the African American Dance Ensemble: http://www.africanamericandanceensemble.org. See also Zita Allen, "Chuck Davis DanceAfrica's Architect on Flying Carpet," *New York Amsterdam News,* May 5, 1984; Hazziezah, "Chuck Davis' Dance Company: Touring at Home and Abroad," *New York Amsterdam News,* January 29, 1977; David Earl Jackson, "Chuck Davis and the African American Dance Ensemble," *Tri-State Defender,* January 21, 1998; Richard Long, *The Black Tradition in American Dance.* (New York: Rizzoli International Publications, Inc., 1989); and Mark Pinsky, "The Pied Piper of Durham Chuck Davis' African American Dance Ensemble Keeps Faith with the Community," *Los Angeles Times,* July 15, 1990.

They were flying, and all I said was, "Whoa!" I'd never seen nothing like that, and I wanted to do this. So the search was on.

I then moved to Washington D.C., and I worked with a dynamic man by the name of Mr. Melvin Deal, who had the African Heritage Center and a company called the African Heritage Dancers and Drummers. Mr. Deal was a wealth of knowledge. He helped to really give me a firm foundation in informed teachings of African dance where you're told historical aspects. He had a library that was beyond compare. I was about nineteen years old then. [I was] commuting at that time back and forth from Baltimore to D.C. and then later moved to D.C. to engage myself in the company on a full-time basis—not full-time where as you're being paid as a full-time artist, but just the commitment and the passion in the dance. I'm really thankful for that time because I had the opportunity, as a striving young artist, to be able to teach at the Duke Ellington High School of Performing Arts, which was a rarity for young people my age. [I was] working as an assistant with Mr. Deal and then taking over his classes when he went away to do his studies in Africa. I later, in 1976, moved to New York. I winded up working with a company called International Afrikan American Ballet, which I truly give thanks for being a part of that dynamic company. I think it served as a catalyst and inspiration for many African groups throughout North America. I'm going to use slang, it "upped the ante," and that means that it made other companies look at how to really take dances from the village and put it on the stage in a western concept, which is so important in the realm of African dance.

Yes, just a clarification about that part. What were people doing normally? In other words, how did it "up the ante"?

In terms of costuming. In terms of precision. In terms of learning about the dance. In terms of the spirituality. In terms of igniting and engaging audiences. In terms of really studying particulars, and that's very important in the realm of any ethnic dance form because you don't want to deal with the bastardization of anyone's culture. [You want to be] politically correct and spiritually correct inside of this. It also helped to ignite another spirit within me, from a cultural and spiritual perspective. During that time, we performed all over. I spent thirteen to fourteen years in

New York doing West African dances but also working in the realm of Lindy. I had the opportunity to work with the icons in swing dance: Mama Lu Parks, Al Minns, Sugar Sullivan, Norma Miller, Charles Young, Frankie Manning, C. Scoby Stroman. If you look up "Lindy-hop," "swing dance," and etc., you'll see these are pioneers in the field. Throughout that time—having the opportunity to be on tour with Cab Calloway, Ruth Brown, Stevie Wonder, and other major artists in the field who deal with show biz and show dancing—I worked with Jon Hendricks, Redd Foxx, and a list of others. In New York, being a major melting pot, you had the opportunity to have so many different facets of the arts, especially within the African, African American, contemporary, and technical classic realms. You had all of that at your feet and at your hands—from ballet to contemporary to [Katherine] Dunham to [Pearl] Primus to the Brazilian forms to Thelma Hill Performing Arts Center to Pat Hall. That's why I say it was just such a blessing to be a part of that era of black dance. To be there when Eleo Pomare said, "This is black dance." It was education on another level that was not in the schools. So, being with the vanguards and being included now as also being a vanguard myself, I give thanks. While in New York, I met the wonderful director of Muntu Dance Theatre, may his soul rest in peace, Mr. Alyo Tolbert. Alyo would come to New York, and he was such a beautiful spirit. He worked with almost every company and every genre of dance that he was interested in. He made another family so that when the company, Muntu, came to New York, they were welcomed and cherished as part of the dance family there. Through that relationship that was taking place, I had the opportunity to come to Chicago to work as a guest teacher and to share in the family circle of Muntu and the artists there.

What year was this?

Oh my goodness, what year was that? That was back in the early eighties . . . '83, '84, '85, '86, and then I was accepted to come to Chicago in 1987. I moved to Chicago in 1988, and the rest is history. Being here in Chicago has allowed me to be able to stretch my wings as a director, because I had not been a director of a large group like Muntu Dance Theatre, always a smaller entity that dealt with run outs, performances, and etc. I directed children, and I'd been the dance director for different programs off Broadway. It's been a tremendous growth. I've had the opportunity to work with some dynamic artists, collaborate, bring other artists to continue within the mission and legacy of Muntu and the legacy of black dance, and to be able to work with and strive to present programs that tell our stories in many various forms.

Can you talk about those early years in Muntu? What were some of your goals? What was the climate like in the dance world in general? What were some of your goals as an artistic director?

Coming to Chicago back in the late eighties, at that time, Chicago, in the dance field, was almost like virgin territory. There was a lot—my perception, OK—that could happen because, unlike New York, where you have so many companies and so many people that are striving to be funded by this little money that is there, the dance community was not as full as it is now. There has been major growth over the years. It allowed us to be able to grow and to take on the initiatives that were there, especially in the funding world through NEA [National Endowment for the Arts]. Actually, I came here through the Challenge III grant that was happening at that time for dance organizations to organizationally put themselves in place so that you could have staff—administrative staff and artistic staff—and you could build and hopefully go into having your artists as salaried artists—especially first the artistic staff and then the administrative staff. It [the grant] allowed us that opportunity to go for that, and we did. It's been major growing pains, but wonderful growing pains because Muntu has done something that many companies strive to do. We had the opportunity to have an array of artists on salary with insurance benefits, and, for African dance companies or companies of our type, that was almost unheard of in the field. It ignited a spark into many companies across the nation to strive to be able to get to that point. In the economic climate of things, of course there's a struggle to be able to maintain that. But, I'm so happy to be able to say that we've had the opportunity to be able to build upon that and maintain it. What was the climate like during that time you said? I didn't answer that, did I?

Well, you talked about it being really open.

It was open.

There was a lot of opportunity and a lot of space for growth.

A lot of opportunities. During that time, I think that Chicago was opening itself up to deal with diversity in all aspects: in the performing venues, in a lot of other programs, in collaborations, in this, that, and the other. So, it allowed Muntu to take advantage of that. In the mid-'90s or early '90s, we had the opportunity to actually have our annual concert at the Shubert Theater. It had been nineteen years since an African-oriented company had actually performed there, so it allowed us to break ground. It allowed us to be vanguards to a certain degree. It allowed us to be able to grow and sustain ourselves, to become viable in the field of the arts, and to be able to, once again, put African dance in the category of an art form. Many don't know that back in the seventies and eighties, African dance companies could not apply for major dance grants. It was always a folk art. Then during the time of the different changes that the National Endowment of the Arts was going through, and other funding programs, they changed the guidelines. They saw the growth that was taking place and the groundwork that had taken place to be able to open it up and now have African dance included as part of the dance world.

Around what year do you think that changed?

Yes, late eighties, early '90s. I came here and moved in '88, and I was on the panel for National Endowment of the Arts when they were doing the reconstruction of their guidelines. For a very long time, African dance was [misunderstood as evidenced by nicknames accorded to the form]: the Ooga Booga, jungle dance, and the bunny dance. As we grow and become educated and mature in the field, it's important to correct the wrong projections and to really try to be able to put [African dance history] in a place where it can be studied. It can be preserved. It can create legacies for people. And it can serve all communities as well.

Can you talk about some of the collaborations with national or international artists that you've participated in through Muntu?

Yes, I'd like to speak about the one with Papa Chief James Hawthorne Bey who was an icon in the field of African arts and sciences. We had an opportunity to do a collaboration with him. He came to put a piece on us that was called "Old Time Religion," and it dealt with the old spirituals that we dealt with as African Americans—being baptized in their pool and going into the whole transformation of African spiritual realm. Both are the old time religions, but let us not forgot and let us not be afraid of [them]. That was absolutely wonderful, and it was thought provoking for our artists as well as [for] myself and the community. We had the opportunity to work with another icon in the dance that was based in Philadelphia, Mr. Arthur Hall. Mr. Arthur Hall was the director of the Arthur Hall Afro-American Dance Ensemble, and he was the director of the African center called the House of Culture. I can't remember the name right now because that was a while ago. But in the early '90s, I think, we re-created and reconstructed his wonderful piece called "Fat Tuesday and All That Jazz." It was depicting an age-old fable that stemmed out of New Orleans during Mardi Gras time. Most of the time we see Mardi Gras from the commercial aspect, but then there is also a little black Mardi Gras that happens from the community standpoint. Working with Mr. Hall also gave us the opportunity to work with one of the most dynamic jazz bands out of New Orleans with Mr. Milton Batiste and the Preservation Hall Jazz Band. Oh god, that was so much fun and historical, and it brought another realm of history to the artists and also to the community. Oh my goodness, Chuck Davis, who, as we know, is an icon in the field and, God bless him, is still alive and still sharing. We had the opportunity to work with a group from Costa Rica, which was absolutely dynamic in traveling to Jacob's Pillow to do a residency there during the summer. That was a part of this whole facet that was called the International Round Table. During the International Round Table, it allowed many groups from America, North America here, to collaborate with groups across the world. The group that was selected to work with us was the Curubande group, or Metacumba from Costa Rica. That was a wonderful collaborative. We had the opportunity to work in Colorado and then bring them here to Chicago to also work with them. We just finished a Ron Brown work. When we are talking about collaborations, I am talking about the ability to come and work with my artists and [choreograph] a piece [with] them as well. Mr. Theo Jamison, who was one of the Katherine Dunham assistants and working at SIU [Southern Illinois University]. We did some wonderful work with him. Then we had one with Bobby Changó Rascoe. When I say, "Ibiye," that means that may their soul rest in peace. They're in the ancestral realm. One of the icons that I dealt with [was] the whole aspect of masquerading and setting up the altars. Oh my goodness, there's just so many that we worked with, but that's to name a few. I'm just very happy to say that coming up in the near future, we have Mr. Reggie Wilson to be able to collaborate and to do work with. Diedre Dawkins, fabulous dancer and her husband, Kwame Opare, did a wonderful piece on us.

Was this the Sweet Nina piece?

Sweet Nina piece. Then the artists in the company . . . they are so diversified and many are great choreographers. I also use my artist to work and collaborate with the company, and, then, sometimes we do a collaborative piece together where I will engage the artist to be able to work in it. Miss Kim Bears, who just left us not too long ago from working with us, she is the assistant director at Philadanco in Philadelphia. She was actually the person who was the conduit for Dr. Pearl Primus, and Dr. Pearl Primus put her work on Kim. Kim was left with the mission and the responsibility to carry on the traditions of Dr. Pearl Primus. I've been on it and Muntu has been on it, throughout the years, to have had a wonderful array of many different artists from different facets. To be able to work with them, and to study, and to learn, and to grow, and then also to . . . preserve the legacy.

It seems like, from what you've talked about, the repertoire is very diasporic, and you have a mixture of pieces that are being reconstructed and new works set on the company?

Yes, it's very diverse, but it's African-centered in its diversity. I want to say that—because sometimes I've been asked—we do a lot of traditional works; that is our major forte. From that, we believe that our story—when I talk about "our," I'm talking about African people of the world—can be told through so many facets. Through the realm of studying and research and developing, we hope that we can be the ones that can present the stories in their many diverse ways.

What are some of the images of African culture and/or black culture that you think Muntu brings to audiences?

I think Muntu brings a spiritual culture to our audiences. It brings a celebratory culture to our audience. It shows the social ramifications or the secular aspects of it. It shows community. In the engagement, our community is always involved in what we're doing. So, all those little proverbs that we hear—"takes a village to raise a child"—the village is involved. The village is our audience. The village is you. We are all students, or, as my assistant artistic director always says, "It's important to keep a student's mind as we pursue on our path." So, family, culture, spiritual realms, enlightenment, entertainment, edutainment—because we have to, as we entertain, constantly educate, not from a grueling manner but from a spectacular manner. An energy and a feeling is invoked, and it grabs onto our audience and/or those [who] are engaged and are close to us.

One of the things I notice when I watch the company perform is that it is very intergenerational. You have newer members and you have members who have been there for a long time. Can you talk a little bit about the intergenerational nature of the company?

One of the beauties of Muntu is that we have families dancing together—father and daughter, mother and daughter, mother and son. It continues as we speak now. It's still happening. We have from age twenty—and maybe sometimes teenagers or our minors, the young ones—up to maybe over sixty that participate and perform. There is something for everyone to do. When I spoke about community, that was one of the beautiful aspects that I saw when I first came here. It is one of the beautiful aspects that I still see and that I'm engaged with now. That sometimes is a rarity, but it's not a rarity in African dance. African dance, they say, is a dance that you can participate in from your cradle to the grave, and there's a dance for that—when you come into the world and when you transition to the next one. It's a beauty. Coming up, there was a whole thing, "shut up and dance." Dancers didn't talk; dancers just danced. I remember back at one of the NEA [panels], when they went to the reconstruction of "what is necessary now," that's when arts education became very prevalent. Now it was time for the artists to start talking, and I had to raise my hand because they said, "Well, Amaniyea, what do you think?" I said, "Well, it's kind of interesting to me because what's being asked of us now in the field is what we always had to do to be able to survive." Do you understand what I'm saying? We always had to teach in our communities.

"We" being . . .

"We" being African Americans in the field of black dance. We had to engage in the schools. We had to engage with community organizations. We had to engage with our spiritual organizations, the churches, and etc. At that time, we weren't in the main venues. We weren't performing onstage. It wasn't dance. So, when the change came around, I snickered but then I also said, "Hmm, there's less money in the field in the funding." But it's OK because it means that more people are being educated now in all realms and in all facets, and I believe in the aspect that each one [should] teach one [person].

Can you talk a little bit about Muntu's programs that they do in the schools?

Yes. I had mentioned before that Muntu has a variety of school programs. They fall under the category of what we call the ACE programs, A-C-E, Arts for Community Empowerment. When we talk about community empowerment, the only way we can empower our community is through our young people. It's through knowledge, and it's through participation and engagement of life-worthy things. So our program is an educational format that stems from the foundation and the basis of African arts and science and culture. We have our artists who are very prolific and profound and passionate about sharing what it is that they have learned. We engage our young people—yes, in the schools! Yes!—with the programs for our children who are homeless, DCFS [Department of Child and Family Services] programs, the park programs of course, the programs that exist now, and After School Matters. At that time, we had the Gallery 37 as well, and they all deal with the arts education format. As Muntu artists, [we] still keep ourselves updated in how the Chicago Public Schools and/or educational institutions are gearing themselves toward putting arts in the school. We constantly have to keep ourselves updated with the standards that the public schools [set]. You have to teach and make sure that your arts program is implemented in the schools that deal with those standards. You're dealing with history, language, math, and science, and how that applies to life. It's a life-learning, a give-and-take situation with our young people. Sometimes it engages them in performing also, which teaches the lessons of discipline, focus, social studies, and how we work together. In these days, distraction, desolation, temptation, and "-isms" that take us so far away from the natural rhythmic movement, just in terms of life itself, are very prevalent. That's why we instill and ignite in our artists the importance of arts education. Trust me, it's challenging in more ways than one. I was speaking the other day about how teaching the arts have now turned into babysitting. For performing artists that are now engaged in teaching the arts, you really have to have that passion, which makes you find another sense of patience within yourself because it's a terrible thing to give away your jewels to those who don't appreciate it. We're trying to be able to ignite that aspect of appreciation, the aspect of reciprocation, because as we give—you too—as you're getting what we're giving, you too have to give. The aspect of respect [is important] because you have to respect what it is that you are doing in order to be able to give of it wholesomely. It goes a long way. The other aspect is performing, where we take different programs to many different schools and have a lecture demonstration-type hands-on engagement with our young people. That can be from preschool to primary school to middle school to our high schools and, of course, in our major higher educational institutions as well as senior citizen homes too.

What would you say the impact of your company is on Chicago and the larger West African or black dance community?

In 2012, Muntu Dance Theatre will be forty years old. That's a long time for the survival of a not-for-profit organization. So, the impact has been great—fulfilling to many, devastating to some, challenging to many, and rewarding to most. It has opened up the realm for other companies to evolve, be born, to strive to higher heights, to engage in educating themselves or reeducating themselves, because sometimes we've been educated but we have to reeducate ourselves. It's been infectious. When I say that, I'm not talking about an oozing sore. I'm talking about something that has grabbed onto people. [*Laughing*] It has made individuals soar, s-o-a-r, to be able to find new ways to create themselves and to find new ways to continue to take classes. It has opened realms of spirituality for people. It has opened up realms of creativity for people. It has been on the forefront. Muntu, I'd say is a vanguard for many companies right here in Chicago in the field of African dance, and I would say across the nation. It's not just a Chicago name. It has ignited seeds of thought and opportunity for other companies to try to follow in that path. It's not easy. It's been a great impact in the field. It's been a great impact for our community. It's been a great impact for us as artists, ourselves.

Can you talk about some of the international travel that the company has done and some of those festivals?

Sure. We had the opportunity to go Europe. Let's go there first. We went to the Edinburgh Festival, which was in Scotland. We've also performed in England in one of the big tops. That was fun. We had a great time that day.

Are these invites that you received?

These are invites, yes. We've been to Mexico several times. Muntu had the opportunity to work with the Mexican Fine Arts Museum. At the time before the exhibit came up,[5] there was an initiative that took place for the partnering organizations—Mexican Fine Arts, eta, Muntu, and others—to go to Mexico, the south part, to Veracruz. In Veracruz, there's a festival called the Afrocaribeño Festival, which brings groups from all over, African-oriented groups from all over to be able to participate and perform inside of it.

Because Veracruz has a huge African descent . . .

Veracruz has a very huge African descendent population. That's what Muntu was there to do—to look at the African presence inside of Mexican folklore. At that time, we were also studying about the African war-

---

5. Exhibit on the African presence in Mexico at the Mexican Fine Arts Museum.

rior Yanga that was very influential in the whole revolutionary aspect of freeing those that were in bondage. With the mixture of the indigenous groups along with the Africans, a wonderful mixed culture or subculture came out of that. We had the opportunity to do that and perform within the festival. That gave us the opportunity to meet different people, from a historical perspective, to go to the different villages and just live and breathe; to go to the pyramids there in Mexico; and to go up into the mountains with the indigenous people just to watch some of the cultural nuances that were there. The company had the opportunity to go to Ghana, which was fabulous. Well, as a matter of fact, all of our trips to me were fabulous. They were different, but fabulous. I will never forget the first time we went to Panafest [in Ghana]. That was a festival that invited African-oriented groups from all over the world to participate. It was a takeoff from another festival that took place in the seventies called FESTAC. At Panafest, we performed for the presidents and all the dignitaries there. We went to the different villages. We went to the slave castles that were there. One of the performances was at one of the slave castles, and, oh man, I'll never forget it. The company went on the little tour, and it was very heartfelt and very sad and it made you full—not angry, but full—because tears and so forth—and not just us, even the people from various parts of Africa and Europe. For those who have not been to some of the slave dungeons, they are in the western coast of Africa, [and] there are many. Take that opportunity to go there, and take that opportunity to pass back through that door that was called "the door of no return." That time in Africa—visiting that and engaging in historical aspects; working with the PanAfrican Orchestra; going to the site where W. E. B. DuBois Center and all of his archives are; and learning about the work that his wife did and many other aspects, which is not what's always taught here in North America—was a spiritual uplift for the company. The show that we did that particular night—we did many in different regions, but I want to talk about that particular night—the stage was full of water. It was as if all the ancestors or many ancestors' tears was on the stage. We had just come out of the slave castle, so we were like a wreck. Seriously, it's like don't put a camera in my face. But anyway, I don't even know how we danced on that stage because it was just so slippery, but it was one of the most beautiful shows that we had ever done. Even the people in the audience, they said it was so heartfelt.

The one that we did for the president and the dignitaries, that played on the TV in Ghana for two or three years. Then we were invited back again to be able to perform at the second Panafest. Then the company went again to Mexico to one of the major festivals in Mexico City this time, which gave us the opportunity to, from an international perspective, to work with other groups. Wonderful! The company also went to Brazil, South America, on our research tour. We had the opportunity to first take the artistic staff to do the research on the African presence in South America, especially in the region of Bahia. While we were there, we acquired a letter of invitation from the fabulous group Olodum. For those who don't know Olodum, if you saw the Michael Jackson video [*They Don't Care About Us*], they're playing the drums in Brazil with that group. We performed on a major festival that was a drum festival. From there—you never can tell what might happen—the dynamic artist Ben Harper was there in Bahia, and we [wound] up roping the company to perform with him. You are talking about 50,000–70,000 people watching the show. Once again, another spiritual uplift for the company, and TBC—to be continued. We look forward to many other trips for these profound entities and the opportunity to share with our younger artists and to open up doors of opportunities for them as well.

Is there anything else that you would like to share?

Well, I'd just like to say that Muntu is ever evolving and ever growing. We, like all companies and all arts organization, have [our] challenges, but one of the most beautiful things is that we are willing to work through our challenges. What do they say? "Two steps backward and ten steps forward." For all of those who may not know Muntu Dance Theatre, we'd ask you all to please check us out. Come to our performances. Come to our classes. Engage yourself in a conversation with our artists. There is so much to share. There is so much to gain. And on that note, I'd like to thank all of our constituents and all of those communities, diverse, all across the Chicagoland and the nation. I say thank you, thank you, thank you.

IDY CISS

Idy Ciss is assistant artistic director of Muntu Dance Theatre of Chicago. He teaches at various locations around the city, including the Old Town School of Folk Music, Rast Ballet, and Columbia College Chicago. Originally from Senegal, Idy has traveled nationally and internationally teaching and performing in such locations as New York, Ohio, Germany, Brazil, and Mexico, to name a few. His choreography can be seen on Muntu Dance Theatre of Chicago and other dance companies in the United States. In 2007, the Black Theater Alliance, Inc., awarded Ciss the Katherine Dunham and Alvin Ailey Award for Best Choreography in a Music/Dance Program for the piece Dekkal Thiossane (Rebirth of Culture), *which he choreographed for Muntu Dance Theatre of Chicago.*

In interviews conducted in February and March 2011, Idy Ciss reflects on his experience as a professional dance artist in Senegal and the circumstances that led him to migrate to Chicago with a dance company called Silimbo. Ciss discusses the strategies that he used to survive in the city as an immigrant artist, the circumstances that led him to start working with Muntu, and his current practices with the company.

First, my name is Idy Ciss. I'm from Senegal. I've always lived in Chicago. Even though I traveled around the world, Chicago is my hometown. You could call it that. I work with Muntu Dance Theatre of Chicago. Before Muntu, I was working with a group called Silimbo D'Adeane. Silimbo means sunrise in Mandingo. We came from Senegal to Chicago. That's how we got here.

Can you tell me a little bit more about your history? Where did you grow up?

Well, I was born in Senegal in a village called Diass. My ethnic group is called Serer. As you know, in Senegal they have several different ethnic groups: Serer, Wolof, Jola, Mandingue, Toucouleur, Bambara, Sarakhole, Mandingo, Baynouk, and many more. There are a lot, but I was born in Diass. That's where I grew up and went to school. Then, in my twenties, I went to Dakar. Dakar is the capital of Senegal, and that's where I pretty much started my professional dancing. When I was growing up we were dancing. We pretty much didn't learn it. You grow up with it. After school, my guys would get together and dance just to have fun, but in Dakar, that's where I start my professional dancing. First, I was with the group called Kolam. That's a Serer group, Kolam Serer. That means "inherited" in the Serer language. I was with Kolam, then, after Kolam, that's when I joined Silimbo. After joining Silimbo, we came to the United States. So pretty much that's how I became a professional dancer. And I love dancing. That's what made me want to come to professional dancing. Some other people dance, but they just dance when they want to dance. Others know how to dance, but they don't wanna dance. In my case, it's different. I love to dance. That's how I earn my living, and I live for dancing. So yes, that's how I became a dancer.

What kind of dances were you doing when you were younger?

When I was younger, we were doing Serer dances.

Was it what people would call traditional dance?

Yes, it was traditional Serer dance. That's all we were doing when I was growing up in the village. When I came to Dakar and joined the group, we were including other dances from other ethnic groups, like Wolof, Jola, Mandingue, and Malinke. When you perform—like an hour or hour and a half [show]—you need more than just one dance. Also, there are other ethnic groups who are coming to the performance too. So to include those people in the performance, you have to have a variety of different ethnic groups' dances where everybody can enjoy the different dances.

Was this company in existence before you came to Dakar? Were you part of a group of people who started this dance company?

Before I came to Dakar both dance companies were already established.

Did you have to try out to get in? How did you join?

No, I didn't try out. It's funny because I was doing carpentry, and the guys I worked with always commented on how good I could sing. I always loved to sing, so I would sing when I was working. One coworker told me one day, "I think you need to come to this group." [*Laughing*] I was like, "Nah." I was shy during that time. He said, "No, really," and he convinced me. So I went and talked to the director of Kolam, Abdoulaye Faye, about joining the group. When we met, the drummers in the group played for me, and I danced. Well, it might be trying out. Well, you can call it that. I already knew how to dance. So when Abdoulaye and his staff saw me dance, they said, "Yeah, you're in." That's how I joined the group. In other groups, like the National Ballet of Senegal or other local groups, you have to try out or get in by recommendation. In my case, that's how I got into Kolam. Once you get in the groups you can develop and build your skills and knowledge of the dances of other ethnic groups. With Silimbo, I didn't do a tryout because our two groups were friends. When Silimbo had a performance, they would select me and two of my cousins to perform with them. Every other weekend they selected us for a performance.

Where were you performing?

We were performing in hotels, restaurants, and clubs—stuff like that— or at the receptions and the galas when the presidents came from other countries. We performed at different occasions.

Was it mostly foreign audiences or both foreign and Senegalese audiences?

It depends. For example, when a president from another country comes, the audience is pretty much the people who came with the president and the government officials in Senegal. If we perform in a club, the audience is more like the foreign people, the tourists, who come to the club in Senegal. We barely did weddings or a baby naming ceremony because these are done by invitation. Those are not performances. That's just a party. It's kind of like either somebody you know or I know, who is organizing that event, extends an invitation, and everybody goes to that baby naming ceremony or wedding. That's a good time.

When you went to that kind of a party, was the dancing more improvisational and freestyle?

Yes. You freestyle. It's not really instructed, staged, or choreographed—none of that. But at the hotels and clubs, those are performances. And the soirée, gala, that was the performance time also.

What was the choreographic process like in those groups?

There is always a director. The director usually doesn't choreograph; the director does the businesslike booking performances. The choreographer, we call it *mettre en scène,* and dance captain are two different people. *Mettre en scène* is the one who does the choreography. The dance captain is under the choreographer, and they help the dancers rehearse the steps and remember the choreography. They get the dancers to be wherever they need to be for the performance. But the choreographer, his or her job is to do choreography. Sometimes, he or she dances, sometime the person doesn't dance anymore, but they know how to do the choreography.

What did your family think when you decided you wanted to be a professional artist?

I'm going to generalize this, and it's true. A lotta times, your family doesn't agree with you becoming a professional artist. There is a family called Griot in Senegal. In Mandingo, they call it Jali. In Wolof, they call it Géwël. They're the ones who usually sing, dance, and play drums professionally [from] a long time ago. If you're not in that Griot family, it was a terrible thing to be a professional artist, especially to play drums. Your family wouldn't allow you to do it, so you often had to work as an artist in secret until your family found out. When they found out, you had to convince them that this is what you wanted to do. Even Youssou N'Dour, the singer in Senegal, his father didn't want him to sing, and that's what he wanted to do. On his mother's side, they are Gaulo. His mother's a Griot, but his father's not Griot. You just have to stick to what do you wanna do and prove to them this is what you wanna do. Then they will agree with you or not, but you want them to agree with what you are doing. I'm telling you, everybody pretty much is not gonna tell you, "My family liked when I started." But, in the end, your family will say, "That's what he wanna do so let him do it." Now it is different, both Griot and not-Griot, everybody is becoming a professional artist and playing, singing, and drumming. You see people who are not-Griot—we call them Géér* in Wolof—they'll play instruments better than the Griot people. So, it's just the love. If you wanna do it and you love it, you do it.

What do you think caused that change?

The change happens because you become an artist, and you're taking care of a family good. When you're not there you travel, so you prove the people wrong because they think that if you are an artist you won't be worth nothing. It is a good thing. You prove it to them by showing them this is what I do, this is how I earn my living, and I'm taking care of everybody because of this. And you don't have to say it. People see what you do for the family. I think that is part of what made the change. The other thing that made the change is that you become famous and you start to educate other people about your culture. When your family sees what you are doing, they know you are doing something worthy.

---

* A Wolof dictionary, *Ay Baati Wolof: A Wolof dictionary*, defines Géér as "member of the highest Senegalese caste (originally, a member of the nobility or a peasant)." Pamela Munro and Dieynaba Gaye, *Ay Baati Wolof: A Wolof Dictionary* (UCLA Occasional Papers in Linguistics. 1997: 67–68).

Would you say that the existence of dance companies helps people to be able to make a living off of dancing?

Yes, because before—this is another different thing—people who were not Griot were dancing and singing because they just love to do it. It was a lot of fun. They enjoyed doing it, getting together, and dancing without making any money. But now, people are trying to be an artist to earn a living, to have it be their career, and to make it their regular job. That's all they do—traveling and taking care of the family like somebody who is working nine to five.

When did you come to Chicago?

I came to Chicago in 1991. When Silimbo was ready to come to United States, Fatou N'Diaye, the director, was like, "I need those three guys who used to join us to be part of our group to go do the tour in the United States." So, we were lucky to get in. That's how we got to the United States.

And you just came for a performance?

Yes. We were invited by the Chicago Cultural Center during Black History Month. We came on February 1st. The snow was so high.

A lot of times when I talk to other immigrants from warm-climate countries about coming here in the winter, they often are not ready for the cold. People do not prepare them for the cold . . .

Because they don't know! We were so excited to get here, but we didn't even think of the seasons. We didn't even think of the weather. In Senegal, you only have two seasons: a rainy season and a dry season. But when we came here, man, it was so cold. It was cold. We got off the plane in New York, and then we caught the bus to Chicago. We did a couple performances at the Cultural Center and others around the city. We did schools. We also did churches during that Black History Month. After that, we were traveling to different states, but we always came back to Chicago. Chicago was our home. The people who brought us here also found us jobs in different cities. We went to Philadelphia, New York, and Detroit. We were touring around the country.

Where did you stay when you first came to Chicago?

When we were first in Chicago, we went to a place on the South Side on 68th and May Street. It was a church, but they had a community center attached to the church. We didn't see anybody outside on the street. We were looking in the windows like, "We don't see nobody . . . in America?!" When we saw someone, we were like, "Come over! We see one." [*Laughing*] It was funny. Everybody would run over to the window like, "Where? Where? Where?" Man, it was funny! [*Laughing*] After this, we lived in a bunch of different places around the city. We didn't speak any English when we first came. None of us spoke a word in English.

So, how did you manage? Did you just work with translators?

We had a translator because we had some brothers here who'd been in the United States before us, like Cheikh Samb, N'goumba Dioum, Baye Niang, Jo, and Karim. So they're the ones—Prince also—that usually helped. When we were going out, they went with us. I think that one of the ladies who brought us here was Sally Johnson. It's funny. When we were going to the store, we all went together. To buy a chicken, you would make a sound like a chicken.

And people would understand?

[*Laughing*] Yeah! And you just point to whatever you wanna buy. It was funny man. It was good, though. What made it good is that it has to be like that for you to say [that's] where you started. That's what makes the story good for me. If that didn't happen, I wouldn't be telling it to you and laughing about it, see what I'm saying?

Yes.

So I think it was good. [*Laughing*] *Now* it's good. Back then it wasn't at all.

How many performances did you do at the Cultural Center?

Two performances.

Was the audience pretty mixed?

Yeah, it was pretty mixed, and it was good. *Man!* At the end during the Sabar we had, people jumped on the stage. They were dancing in the hall. It was one of the best performances.

Was that surprising to you?

Pretty much, because we usually don't have people come on the stage and dance like that. Usually people are cool, and they sit there and watch. After you perform, they clap. That was the first time people were dancing. I didn't know there were that many African dancers in Chicago—Najwa [Dance Corps] was there, Minianka [Afrikan Drum and Dance Ensemble], Muntu, and Alyo's Children Dance Company. Pretty much everybody was at that performance. That's when we met a lot of those groups.

Did you teach any classes based off those connections? Or was it mostly just the performance at that time?

I don't think that the classes we did were through the people who brought us here. Madame Cissé, she did have connections that we used to go teach some classes. We also taught classes from the connections we made with the audience. Don Jackson had a company called Kopano. We taught dance class there. We also taught a class for Najwa.

How would you describe the dance scene when you first came? What were some of your first impressions?

Oh, I remember this. When we performed, after we finish, there is the thing they do, like, "Whoo-whoo-whoo." I thought they were booing us. [*Laughing*] I'm like, "Dang, they don't like it. They're booing us." One of the older Senegalese brothers who was helping and translating for us, said, "No, this is what they do because they're telling you they like it. That's why they're like, whoo-whoo-whoo."

Because it was in the '90s and people were doing that. [Laughing]

I am never gonna forget that. So that's one of the things I was kind of disappointed about, but overall I really enjoyed it. I was thinking I'm going to see a Caucasian audience, but it was pretty much different. It was the dance, the African American dance, community, and we were so happy too. They were on top of their feet clapping, screaming, and it was great. I will never forget *those performances.* Never.

What did you perform?

For our opening, we had ensemble instrumental. That's like singing. In that time, Nelson Mandela was just released from prison, so we opened with Soweto. We did Balanta. We did Kutiro. They also had Kora and Balafon for the interlude. We did Sabar. We did pretty much all of it in those two days.

So . . . a variety of dances.

Yes.

And you opened with Soweto because of Nelson Mandela being released . . .

Yeah, we'd been having that. Even in Senegal, we used to open with Soweto. That was our program. We would sing and there was a poem about Nelson Mandela. It was in French.

What made you decide to perform that poem about Nelson Mandela in Senegal and in the United States?

It was to educate people. This was happening in South Africa, and it could happen in Senegal too. It could happen somewhere else, but it was a history people needed to know along with Senegal's history. We also had some stories to tell about the kings and queens in Senegal and the role that they played in Senegal's History. The art form is very vast. During that time, people needed to know what he [Nelson Mandela] was going through along with other people in South Africa. That was the story to tell during that time because it was happening at that time. We were educating people in Senegal and the United States. We thought it was important to educate people in both places.

Did people really respond to that performance?

Yes. You saw the expression on people's faces. Some people were crying along with us on the stage. Mandela's story takes you there because of his struggle, the love he had for his country, and all that he was going through by being locked up. When you perform it, you feel it, the emotions, so the audience will feel it just like you.

You did that performance, and you performed in different places around the city, state, and country. Then, you decided you wanted to try to stay here? How long did the group stay together after you came here?

Three good years.

Did you go back to Senegal at all during that time?

No, we didn't go back. We all stayed in one house. It was like twenty of us, something like that, in one house.

How did it end?

The people who brought us here really didn't find us any more jobs. It was hard for them to find jobs, and they decided it was time to move on. Mère N'Diaye, the director, didn't have that connection, and we had to start over trying to make new connections. This was difficult to do in that short amount of time and with our limited English. Some went back to Senegal, some went to Europe, and some stayed. Mary Mane, Sibo Keita, Yassin N'Diaye, they went back. Lanssana also went back. Some people got married and moved on. Mami got married and moved to Europe. That's how people separated. Mary Mane's still dancing. Sibo's still dancing. She's teaching in Spain. Mary's still dancing in Senegal, they have a group called Senemewe now. Allassane Sarr, he's in Buffalo, New York. Morikeba [Kouyate] is in Louisiana, but he comes here often. He is the one who plays Kora. Mère N'Diaye is in Cincinnati. She doesn't dance any more. Fatou Gueye is here. She don't dance anymore. Yancouba [Mane] is in Ohio now with his wife and children. It's just me, Ali M'Baye, and Assane Seck in Chicago.

How did you get connected to Muntu?

After Silimbo fell apart, I was working two jobs. I was working at Soul by the Pound, a restaurant. That's how I know how to cook soul food. It was on the South Side on 84th and Cottage Grove. I also was working at Subway in Hyde Park on 53rd and Kenwood. Amaniyea Payne, the director of Muntu, passed in the window. She saw me. She was like, "Is that Idy?" to whoever she was with. Then Amaniyea came in, and she was like, "Idy, you work here?" I'm like, "Yeah." So she said, "OK, I need to talk to Joan [Gray]." Then she went and talked to Joan. She was like, "Idy works at Subway. We want him to come dance with us." So that's how I came to Muntu. Through Amaniyea seeing me working at Subway . . . not like I don't wanna work at the Subway. I love Subway sandwiches. [*Laughing*] That's how.

You got to get back into the thing that you love to do. Were you teaching at that time? Were you doing anything related to dancing?

No, unless we had a performance. Every now and then some people would find a performance, but it was not regular like we used to do.

What was your schedule like when you first joined the group?

The schedule was pretty much performing and teaching. Muntu had a program where they sent artists to teach at the schools. This was '95. When I joined Muntu, everything was already established. Muntu had a lot of pieces, which they could do forever. They had Alyo's pieces. They had Papa [Abdoulaye] Camara's, may his soul rest in peace, choreography, along with other choreographers like Yousouff Koumbassa and Djibril Traore, may his soul rest in peace. They also had pieces from Mickey Davis, and they had Amaniyea's choreography as well.

So when you joined the group, it was a process of really trying to learn this existing repertoire. What was that process like for you?

It wasn't hard. I pretty much didn't struggle. I'm a fast learner. That's the meaning of my name. So I pretty much nailed it pretty good. My way of learning is that when I see dance moves or choreography and I hear the music, it doesn't take me long to pick up the moves. That's how I pretty much learn. During this time, I went to school at Kennedy-King College to learn English. That also helped me to write. I already know how to write in French, but it helped me also to develop my English writing. I have my high school diploma. This guy named Brutus, he said, "You guys gotta go to school." Some other people didn't wanna go. Me and M'biaye Ciss, we are the ones who were going to school, which I didn't regret. I should've kept on doing it, but I didn't regret it at all.

So you came to the company. You had to learn the existing repertoire. I know you also choreographed some pieces for the company. When you're choreographing, what are you trying to convey to audiences? What are you thinking about when you decide to choreograph?

Sometimes I tell a story. For example, Fangama was about a young boy who didn't want to join the army, and he ran to the forest. They went to look for him, and they found him. They convinced him to not just go fight, but to fight for, to defend, the city, his culture, and his family. So, I tell a story through the dance and choreography even if I am not saying it out loud.

What do you think people learn by going to a show? What do they learn about Africa by going to a show?

People learn different things. First of all, some people still think Africa's backward. When they learn that the first civilization started in Africa, how Africa is connected to America, or about the culture itself, do you know what it does to people? In a lot of different ways, it heals people. It helps people to understand their history and helps to release anger and bitterness because some of that can be about misunderstanding what happened. It makes you wanna be the nicest you can to the other people.

It makes you be proud of yourself. On the other side, this dance form can heal people spiritually. This dance form has two sides: the social side and the spiritual side. Watching a performance can heal audiences because of what they see and feel, but when you get sick certain dances can be performed to heal those spiritual sicknesses.

What is something you find rewarding about being an artist?

The people, the respect I get from people, and the teaching. I love to teach people and to share my knowledge of the culture. I also love to travel. I've been to Europe and South America. So this is what I chose to do, and I enjoy doing it. I love it. I think that this is my purpose in life.

KEVIN IEGA JEFF

Kevin "Iega" Jeff cofounded Deeply Rooted Productions in 1995. Iega's choreography has been presented by a number of companies around the country, including Alvin Ailey American Dance Theater, River North Dance Company, Dallas Black Dance Theater, the Cleveland Contemporary Dance Theatre, Cleo Parker Robinson Dance Ensemble, and the Wylliams/Henry Contemporary Dance Company. Iega was recognized as one of the Juilliard School's 100 Outstanding Alumni in 2005. He also received choreography awards from the National Endowment for the Arts, the National Council for Culture and Arts, and the Black Theater Alliance.

In this August 2011 interview, Kevin Iega Jeff discusses his training and career in New York City before moving to Chicago to become the artistic director of the Joseph Holmes Dance Theatre, which he transformed into Deeply Rooted Dance Theater. Iega's interview explores issues of race and racism within the dance world and the strategies that he uses to navigate the Chicago environment and build a supportive community around his work and company.

Can you tell me a little bit about your current life?

Essentially, I am the artistic director of Deeply Rooted Dance Theater. We have Deeply Rooted Dance Theater, which is the professional dance company. We also have training components that serve matriculation into the company, which include Deeply Rooted Dance Theater 2; Deeply

Rooted Dance Theater 3, which is the apprentice company to Deeply Rooted Dance Theater 2; [and] then Deeply Rooted Dance Theater 4, which is an evening study program for dancers interested in the professional track [that] feeds usually into Deeply Rooted Dance Theater 2. I want to say too that not only do we train dancers for our company, but we train dancers basically for the vision they want to pursue. Sometimes dancers will come to us and they love what we do, but they may want to work with another company. So we provide training that gives them a broad base to keep them on track with whatever goals they are looking to achieve. That is really important to our mission as well. We have community training classes. We have a program called Mature H.O.T. Women, which is for Healthy, Optimistic, and Triumphant Women. We have a program called Brothers Sharing, which premieres this spring. That's a program where brothers come together and talk about issues that men face, using dance as a catalyst for discussion. We have a youth program, which is an ad hoc program, because we target it to specific communities at times during the year to teach youth professional dance and/or help enhance their lives with dance. That's what we do. We, of course, do outreach programming here in the Chicago public schools as well as community-based organizations and churches. We tour nationally and internationally, and we produce two seasons annually here in Chicago. We are at the Harris Theater for Music and Dance. We recently began producing at Kennedy-King College so that we have a downtown venue, I should say a Chicago Loop venue, and then we also have a Chicago South Side venue. It's very important to our mission as well.

Why is that important?

Because we want to be in underserved communities and communities that reflect who we are. We serve everyone in terms of humanity. People love what we do. If they love what we do and they connect to it, they are welcome to come and enjoy it. What we do is basically African American dance aesthetics, so it's important that we are rooted in African communities as well, black communities. Especially since our mission is not only to get people onstage in the performing arts, but also to give them access to behind-the-scenes and management opportunities as well. Being in those communities helps people become aware of the arts as a profession.

I think in our communities—meaning communities of color, particularly black communities—we have been socialized that art is an elitist thing that doesn't always relate to us. Even though we are very artistic people and very creative people. If you look in the antiquity of our culture, we were progenitors of the importance of the arts. We knew the importance of the arts. I think our socialization in America has—that knowledge has fallen, has receded because people are inclined to be more focused on education. People are inclined to be more focused on professions where they are seeking more security because we have had to survive in this country. We have had to rely on the church for survival. We had to rely on education to pull ourselves up from slavery. So I think our socialization is that the arts is a nebulous career, and it's not something that we really, really, really need, which I totally disagree with completely. Obviously, because I'm an artist!

Right, right. [Laughing]

So I advocate for arts professionals and, particularly, arts professionals of color because if you look at the industry, there are very, very, very, very few of us behind the scenes, particularly working at the higher-end level of the field. You might find us in start-ups because we are there helping the organization start it up, and not necessarily having the skill set or training to do it, but we just get in there and we do it. Some of us will pursue a career out of that experience. Many of us will not. But if you get into the organizations where they have national and/or international profiles, you don't find many African Americans. That's really, really tragic to me. It becomes an issue of access. We all know that when you have diversity in the room, access becomes more attainable. When you walk into a room and the people that you are seeking to receive funding from—if you walk into a room and walk into an office, those are lovely people, but [if] none of them look like you and understand your experience or value your cultural perspective, then you have a lot more to kind of work through. I think that artists don't always communicate that because they are looking to be beholden so they can say the right things to get what they want. I think we have to be a lot more courageous than that. I think we have to be willing to sacrifice some of the immediate visioning and growth that we might seek if it is going to delay our true and authentic voice or suppress our true and authentic voices. Bottom line is if you really want to be artists with voices that are authentic and really helpful to humanity, then it has to [reflect] who we are in creation specifically. If we are not offering our true essence, then we are not going to be helpful to humanity.

When you say the African American aesthetic, does that mean those works and cultural productions and expression based on the African American experience, the African experience, and/or experience of people from the Africa Diaspora?

I think that, yes. It's the African Diaspora and the experiences thereof. It's literally the aesthetics. I've made some trips to Africa, specifically Kemet. I've gone to Kemet, Egypt, four times. Egypt, if you understand, is an African civilization. In its origins, and in its years of establishing itself as a world magnet. It was an African civilization. It gave to the world, just like America gave the world [values]—different values than America, but it gave the world. It was an essential place of focus for the world to kind of test its values and its visioning and what not. So looking at Kemet and looking at the aesthetics of Kemet, those aesthetics also are a part of what we look to sustain in our work or any work that is African. It's cultural. It's physical aesthetics. It's all of that. For instance, the African American also includes people who might be of European heritage like Martha Graham, whose work I adore. Now, Martha Graham, in creating the Graham technique, freed herself from ballet, traditional ballet, because she wanted to express her movement through another idiom. So she looked east to what I call root cultures to really start developing Graham technique. If you know anything about kemetic yoga and you know Graham technique, then you know that they are connected. [Graham] looked and was inspired by African movement and Eastern cultures to create Graham technique, which is an American technique. So the African and American aesthetic is a combination of all of the influences within the diaspora.

How did you come to that understanding of the African American aesthetic?

Just by training and being exposed. I started training at Bernice Johnson Dance Studio, which was a school that serviced primarily the black community because it was rooted in the black community in Jamaica, Queens, New York. I was a little boy, about thirteen years old, and I wanted to do dance. She gave me a scholarship, and she prepared me for my audition for Performing Arts High School, which is the school in the movie *Fame*. I went to both of those schools at the same time. At Bernice Johnson, I got not only good dance training, but I got the cultural importance of who I am and who I am in creation. She helped me to understand my spiritual mission and the challenges that we probably needed to consider with regard to business. When I would go downtown to Performing Arts High School, it was more of a Eurocentric approach to dance and the values were based in that. I was able to appreciate the best of both worlds, and I was also able to examine the inappropriateness of both worlds, perhaps.

What do you mean by that?

I remember I would go to Performing Arts High School, and, from the Eurocentric perspective, they would say, "Don't study African dance." I would say, "Why?" They would say, "Because it's going to hurt your back. It's going to develop your body incorrectly." Yet when I would go to Bernice Johnson Dance Studio, all of the students who were excelling at Performing Arts High School were coming from Bernice Johnson Dance Studio. We were doing gang gang. We called it gang gang. We were doing—

What's that?

Gang gang is the bell in Africa[n drumming]. That's gang gang. Yeah, it's very New York. We called it gang gang. We would study it on Wednesday, Friday, and Saturday nights, and we'd go to class. First thing in the morning at Performing Arts High School, we would be at the barre doing ballet. The kids were beautiful and excelling, but in their minds, inside of the school's minds and the values inside of their aesthetic, they thought that African dance was damaging. They would try to have us not do it, and we, of course, ignored them. [*Laughing*] And these were the kids, again, who were graduating at the top of the class, but that conversation went on the whole four years while I was at Performing Arts High School.

But there was something about that kind of cultural rootedness that helped you navigate that kind of understanding . . .

Absolutely.

. . . the kind of incorrectness of that thinking.

Absolutely. I loved going to Performing Arts High School. There were some great teachers there. I had some great experiences and made great friends. I was grateful because I was exposed to the brilliance and exposed to the ignorance, and I had to discern where my values would lie. I think it's very important for African, or people of color, to define their own value system because we are so often defined by value systems that keep us weak and keep us not focused on the brilliance of who we are. We can embrace everyone else's brilliance. I have been trained inside the European aesthetic, so I can embrace that because I have been trained and informed by it. But, by that same token, I don't see equity necessarily inside of that exchange.

What was it at thirteen that made you want to dance?

Just intuitive spirit. I just knew it.

Intuitive spirit?

Yeah. I think dance was very—when you're young and you're physical—dance was just right there for me. I loved it all to be honest with you. I loved music. I loved acting. I loved all of those things. Dance was right there for me. We (P.S. 52 in Springfield Gardens, Queens, New York) had an elementary school dance festival, and that's how I started dancing, by doing that dance festival and making up African dances to [Babatunde] Olatunji. I wasn't trained or anything like that, but I loved Olatunji. I loved movement, and so I would just start making up dances. The way kids do all the time. Then one thing leads to another. Somebody sees you dance, and they say, oh my God, you have some talent there. You should study. You should go take part—this is what they actually said, I should take part in this program that Mayor Lindsay, the mayor of

New York at the time, instituted called Performing Arts Workshop. The Performing Arts Workshop was a musical theater workshop. You could go there and work with Broadway professionals who were hired to put up a show in communities around New York City. We literally got some really wonderful training, direction, and leadership. It was really top draw. What I loved about the program [was that] they didn't cut corners. I am sure they had a budget that they had to manage like everybody else, but it felt like you were doing a Broadway show. What I am always troubled by right now with arts and education is that the standards are lower than I experienced when I was training. The standards are almost—I call it babysitting or policing. I'm sure there are some great programs out there, but a lot of the programs, particularly in underserved communities, I think it's really based on keep the kids occupied, babysit them. They don't always get the standards that point to a career opportunity. What moved me was that when I saw these professionals coming in and they had standards about their work. They talked to me about a career—a possible career path—that opened up a whole new possibility.

From there you went into the Bernice—

To Bernice Johnson Dance Studio. Someone at the Performing Arts Workshop said, "You need to go to Bernice Johnson." To give you an idea of BJ, BJ Studio basically, at its peak, had about anywhere between 800 and 1,000 kids from the surrounding community. This was a black woman who used to dance at the Apollo Theater. Her mother was a Cotton Club dancer. OK?

She started this school because she wanted, as a hobby really, to expose kids to the business of art and to the business of being an artist. She was in the field, and she felt like kids didn't know enough about that. I came to her about, probably about, twenty-five years into her school, maybe twenty-five to thirty years into her school. She's not a sung hero. People don't know about her because she didn't have a big marketing office. She just did her work, and she became a millionaire through that school [by] just being a good businesswoman. She wasn't trying, but she did go out in her community. I did learn from her that we have a very powerful community. We don't have to exclusively focus on our community, but we must focus on our community. We must see its value.

That's so powerful because that's a different story than the one that you some-
times hear about dancers opening up schools. You hear the story of them going
bankrupt and the schools failing. But, it seems like, like you said, she was a good
businesswoman.

She was a really good businesswoman. I think that what made the school
work was that she was building lives. I know that because I am working
to codify, inside of my own visioning, what it was that we received at
the Bernice Johnson Dance Studio. In other words, I've taken the best
of what I've learned there and [applied] that to my own intuitive nature
about what I want to contribute in my lifetime and what I want to contribute with my colleagues at Deeply Rooted. They are also contributing
to codifying the communication around not only teaching the dance and
the arts, but the mind-set that keeps one strong and centered in their
genius as they are working in the arts.

Earlier, you talked about equity within the cultural exchange, between—I think
this is what you are saying, so please correct me if I am wrong—European-
derived and African-derived dance forms. What did you mean by that? Did
you just mean equally valued?

The simplest way without—I don't want to sound like I am complaining because I'm really not because I understand what is happening in
creation [and] what's happening in the world—but the simplest way is
that this country was not founded on equitable ground. OK? We have
not—though we obviously have made some accomplishments—we are
not on equitable ground to this day. That ground has been shaped in race.
And that ground has been shaped in culture. Whose culture and whose
race is more prominent or more dominant than the others, and who deserves more. We camouflage it now politically. I think people say a lot of
great things for the camera, but the underpinnings of things are still very
much influenced by that culture. And we are not able to have a straight
conversation about it. When you look at Chicago, OK? Chicago has a
Joffrey, and we should, that came to Chicago with multimillion dollars of debt. How does it go from coming to a city where it doesn't have
roots, being in multimillion dollars of debt, to having a beautiful building, which they deserve, on State Street? Well, what happens with the

Joffrey is they have a community around that says that they are important enough to be here and exist and thrive in Chicago. That community has access, and that community looks like the Joffrey. OK? And then you have companies like Joel Hall. You have companies like eta. You have companies like Joseph Holmes Chicago Dance Theatre. You have companies—before even those people. I am talking about these are Chicago people, OK—that have been here working, that have been here building artists and dancers and everything, and they are doing good work. They are—I often hear the word used—surviving. I think that there's no equity in, "This company is thriving and these companies are surviving." Now you could say, what we often get is, "Well, they don't know how to manage themselves." Well, we have a company that came to Chicago that was millions of dollars in debt. They didn't seem to know how to manage themselves. They were able to get the community that had value for what they were doing and said they were important enough to thrive. We don't have that in Chicago. Chicago is an international city. We have the Joffrey. We have the Goodman Theatre. We have Steppenwolf. We have Hubbard Street Dance Chicago. Now, I mention those four because those, and I could go on, but let's talk about those four. Those four have national and, in many cases, international profiles. The companies that I mentioned to you that are from the African American aesthetic or companies of color, they do not have national profiles per se. They may be noted—people may know that they exist—just like they know that we exist, but we don't have a national profile like the companies that I mentioned. This is an international city. That's a problem. That tells me something. It tells me that it's not about the intelligence of black people or Latino people, you know, or whatever. It tells me that there is a problem in the politics of Chicago. There is a problem in equity. Whether people want to face that or not, I am going to talk about it. There're a lot of layers there, but equity goes back to the founding of this country. Until we have a real conversation about that, until we are able to mature into real conversations about that, we are just slowly commenting, slowly happening.

Can you talk a little bit more about Joseph Holmes and what he was doing with dance? How you met him?

Well, I never met Joseph Holmes.

Oh.

Here's the deal. Joseph Holmes died before I took over Joseph Holmes Chicago Dance Theatre. The person who was appointed after Joseph was Randy Duncan. I am not sure exactly how many years Randy served, but he served for several years. There was something internal that happened inside of the organization where Randy left Joseph Holmes, and they were looking for an artistic director. They did a national search. I had a company in New York for many years, which was at a pinnacle to go to a whole other level, then we ran smack into the AIDS epidemic. We were about to go "boom" because we had built the infrastructure within the hearts of our people. We had built the infrastructure within the organization. We were about to go—we were touring internationally. ABT would load out of the theater, American Ballet Theatre, and then we would load in. Twyla Tharp would come in after us, that type of thing. We were really doing quite well, and then we ran smack into the AIDS epidemic. I ended up, slowing, kind of adjusting, my visioning because my, literally, whole team had passed away. And I said I really couldn't continue the same way. So I ended up doing freelance work and more community-based work for a period. And it was during that period that Joseph Holmes approached me about becoming artistic director for Joseph Holmes Chicago Dance Theatre. OK?

OK.

I came to Chicago from New York by invitation to take over Joseph Holmes with a very specific plan, well defined, which I insisted on defining. They gave me the job without me defining it specifically. I said wait until I define it specifically, and I did. Then they asked me to take over the position. What I know about Joseph is that he was very much inspired by Alvin. I know that he went to New York and studied at the Ailey school. I know that he came back to Chicago and said that he wanted to do what Alvin was doing here in Chicago in his own way. I know that he inspired the community. They really believed in him. He was a force of personality. The community was very inspired by him. I know that he died early. He was also an AIDS victim. I do know that he was en route to igniting some interest inside of the Chicago community, having a diversified base as well, and then he died prematurely. I know that Randy is also some-one whom Chicago loved. He is a very gifted choreographer, and they really appreciate his work as well. I don't know what happened for him to leave the company. I know when I inherited the company and I began to act upon the plan that I said that I would do, I ran into some tensions and things like [that]. I remember getting off the plane and there was an article—and I won't say who wrote it at this point—in the paper about how I was going to turn the company and make it an all-black dance company. Now, I had never said one word to anyone about anything. I never even met anybody, but I was getting off the plane and there was an article in the paper that had already shaped my words and said what I was going to do, which was extremely far from the truth. The company that I founded here under Joseph Holmes, or that I instituted here under Joseph Holmes, was integrated. It was integrated because the talent in the company was people I liked working with. I am not interested in in-tegrating the company for any other reasons except for it works and that these people really belong here. So, I ran into a lot of conversations about race. I'd walk into a funder's office and the funder would say how many white people do you have in the company?

Outright?

Yeah, outright. I would say, well, how many white people does Hubbard Street have in their [company]? How many black people does Hubbard Street have in their company? How many people of color?

Wow.

It was that kind of an environment. I just, frankly, had to make some de-cisions about who I was. That's when I really had to pull into, "Well, who am I? And, what am I to do here?" And I love Chicago. I love the diver-sity of Chicago when it is diverse. I love its potential inside of all of that diversity. But, this is a city that really hasn't come to terms yet with the fact that Dr. King could say, "I've been in the bowels of the racist South, and I've never been in a place more racist than Chicago." We want to act like that just disappeared. There is an elite that governs this city, and it filters into the arts where the impact of it is what I just shared with you.

How did you navigate that?

I made some mistakes in that I think what I . . . I made some mistakes. Let me start there. I made some mistakes. What I learned is the best thing to do regardless of all of that is to meet people where they are and to come into this city and get to know people, good, bad, or indifferent. Sit down across from them. Just don't be in judgment of their judgment. Just kind of try to find out where the human connection is, and, if there is a common ground for humanity—a human connection—you can definitely build on that over time. So that's what I began to do. I was thirty-four at the time that I came here, and there wasn't a large community around that understood those values. I was really stepping into an environment where I had to begin to teach values and teach perspectives that I had grown up inside of, and I was very fearful. I had no reason to be fearful of it, but I was very fearful because I come from great stock and could see through things. I am educated. I'm exposed. So the things they were [saying], they could say them to other people that had less knowledge but they couldn't say them to me. It made for a slower process, a slower build. It made for maturation, me being more committed to my evolution and maturation as a man than immediate results.

On the other side of it, I can tell you I feel very happy and primed where I am at right now. I think I am more ready than ever for the next level because now we're primed. Deeply Rooted is now primed to go to our next level, and that's because we've built a community around the work that is diverse. It is rooted in people of color, but it is also rooted in humanity's diversity because we all connect. We work to connect and/or connect spiritually. We understand that work is an art of spirit. OK. Whether you are working in the office as a businessperson or you're working on the board or you are working in the studio, there is an art to how we need to interface with each other. There's a way, a reason that we are doing this and it has to get beyond not just the academic or the criteria for success that would have us not be fully who we are.

I like how you put that. I want to go back. I skipped over what happened and what you did with your life and your career after Performing Arts High School. I want to go back to that.

OK. So, Performing Arts High School and Bernice Johnson Dance Studio. When I graduated from Performing Arts High School, I went into the Juilliard School. While at Juilliard, I danced on Broadway in the show called *The Wiz,* which is really special for me. I saw *The Wiz* opening night because there were dancers from Bernice Johnson Dance Studio in the original cast of *The Wiz.* I had to go see my teachers, and I was so moved. I fell in love with Stephanie Mills, and I said I want to do that show. When I graduated at seventeen, I auditioned for that show, and I got that show. I did that show while going to Juilliard, which is like going to school and then to school again. It was just phenomenal to have—again, I've always had this juxtaposition of theory in training and reality in execution. I've always had the two together. What a gift.

That's awesome.

Awesome. After Juilliard, I did another Broadway show called *Coming Uptown*—still at Juilliard, I should say. That show stared Gregory Hines and Loretta Devine. Once I did the second Broadway show, that's when I started working behind the scenes. Then I started Jubil[ation]. I did Jubilation first as a show. I worked on it for a year. We had three performances, and it was an incredible learning experience. Then I decided I was going to focus on the choreography, and I was going to focus on developing a company that could do my work. That's what I did. I worked for thirteen years as artistic director of Jubilation Dance Company, and we toured. We started with nothing and ended up touring nationally. They did ten national tours within that thirteen-year period and seven international tours. We were right at a precipice to go to the next level, and we lost our board chair. We lost my artistic partner. We lost our booking agent. By the way, that was a diverse team. My board chair was Latino. He was Puerto Rican. My artistic partner was African American. My booking agent was white. OK? And they were all lovely people. We had those candid conversations that built the organization to where it was, and we had an infrastructure within the hearts of those people. Each of those folks was designated to take care of an area, and when they died within three years of each other . . . completely devastating.

That's when I had a life shift, and I decided that I would not try to continue doing what I was doing because by then it was big and needed those people to guide it. I was one person working with people I didn't know. I tried it for three years. Through that three-year period while they were sick and passing. I even opened a studio. I even renovated and opened the studio during that period in New York, but it just didn't feel right. Then I closed it, and I said, "OK." I humbled myself. "What do I really need to do?" I started freelancing, and Jubilation, the corporate structure, started working in communities. There was one place, Mount Sinai Baptist Church, was having issues with their youth, and they asked us to come in. They asked me to come in and design a program that would help them save their youth. I did that with my sister managing it for about four or five years.

What kind of program did you design?

I designed a dance program where they would come take class on Saturdays, a community-based dance program. Not only, of course, would they dance, but there were conversations around the work that would help give them a different perspective on life. I instituted that during that period and did it for about five years. It was during that period that I was approached by Joseph Holmes and asked if I would come to Chicago. At first I didn't—you know how spirit speaks to you, and that's what got me here. I didn't really have all the pieces together. Spirit spoke to me, and I came. I am really glad that I did. It's very challenging, very lonely at times as well because I had to learn Chicago. I am a person who loves people no matter who they are. If people are lovely people, I love people. I do think New York has its issues as well, and I didn't need to be in New York. I was blessed to come here to see the depth of racism, to really experience it and to see it. To see its impact and to begin to create a way, in my methodology, to deal with it through the arts to really have that enhance the work that I want to do. So Chicago has been a gift to me, and a challenge, for all of that, for all of those reasons. Then beyond race, and beyond—like when you get to the people that are beyond it—there's so much beauty here. There's just so much potential and so much beauty. I'm into that. I am into that phase now where I understand it well enough now to be enjoying it. [*Laughing*]

Let's talk more about Deeply Rooted as a company and your process. You said that you've been to Kemet a number of times, and I want to talk about that kind of connection and how you got on that path.

That was intuitive, and I was blessed. When you are intuitive and you are in flow with your flow—there are times I haven't been in flow, and I know the difference—you are drawn to the people that give you access. Bernice Johnson was one of those people that gave me access. At Bernice Johnson Dance Studio, there was a man named Lee Aca Thompson, who is my mentor, and he used to go to Kemet every year. I always had an affinity. I would be sitting in church, and I would be like, "Some of what they are saying doesn't make sense to me." I am not into fear. If it doesn't make sense intuitively, I think God gave us that understanding for a reason. I don't need to let what I am hearing from the pulpit distort what my instincts are telling me. As a boy, I would just know that something . . . I need to look further than what I am hearing. Some of the values I am hearing in church are great, but some of them don't make sense to me. When I got to Bernice Johnson Dance Studio, I realized I had this affinity with Kemet. Then, Aca, we started talking about Kemet, and he would go to Kemet. He said, "You should go to Kemet." I went to Kemet because he fronted the money for me to go. He said, "You need to pay me back, but I want you to go, and I will front this money for you." I remember working all summer to make sure I paid him back, but I went to Kemet, and that's when I chose my name actually, Iega. That's my chosen name.

What does Iega mean?

"Messenger." I chose it when I was at the pyramids of Giza. It just was intuitive. It came to me, and I said, "I am going to trust this." I kept the name, and it's there to remind me that what I put onstage or put in front of people or communicate to people is going to have a message, period. I need to be responsible about that. It's not that I am a messenger, but it is that I need to be responsible about what it is I am communicating. That's what Iega means.

But, Kemet is . . . oh, I will explain it this way. On the American seal, the front of the American seal is the eagle with talons and all of that stuff. On the back of the American seal is the Great Pyramid of Giza with the all-seeing eye with the words underneath it "New World Order" in Latin. OK? There's a reason for that. OK? This country was founded on those principles that are African.

Like what? What do you mean?

Basically, the African constitution and just understanding, when you understand why the Pyramid of Giza is there, that connection. Now, we don't know about that. We are asleep on that, and the reason that we are asleep on that is because we are powerful people. We are better asleep because they can manipulate us to build capitalism if you are asleep. You can't build capitalism if you are awake to what is going on. That's why countries around the world that are waking, they've awoke, their countries are waking up to the challenge of capitalism. Now, however they decide to pursue that, they are looking out for their own best interest. Whereas there was a time where America could just dictate what's going to happen. That's not going to happen anymore because different people around the globe are saying we matter and we are going to do it our way so fall in line with everybody else. That's evolution. America says we want America back. You are not going to get it. You are not going to get it back. You can get it forward. [*Laughing*]

[Laughing] *Right.*

Back is over.

It's done.

It [the present moment] reminds me of the post-Reconstruction period. Slavery is over. You see some black faces in office. People had a stroke. The country had a stroke, and they wanted their country back then. What was born out of that? The Ku Klux Klan and Jim Crow. OK? That's what we are dealing with again. We are dealing with fears, inequity, and people wanting something back so they can have more. Why can't we talk about what it is? Because we want to go backwards. You see? As an artist I have to—I chose to—live a fruitful and wonderful and happy life on behalf of everyone. Let's reincite some authentic conversations and put some authentic work up there.

It seems like this is what you do with your company. It completely informs your process.

It does. Our company is diverse. When we're in the room, it's important that everybody has the space to speak into the work what they need to bring to the work. I take that very seriously because I remember being a black boy in a room that didn't have the space or the black boy in the room that wouldn't take the space because he wasn't courageous enough at the time. Because they can say Dr. King didn't have the space. Malcolm X didn't have the space. They took the space. They were courageous, and I admire them. I admire Mahatma Gandhi. I admire Akhenaten. I admire Hatshepsut. I can go on and on about people who take the space and make things possible. We are living in a time where it's scary. There are times I am scared like everybody else for sure, but I am more scared about living a life that's not true. That really scares me. This company is about that. Our work speaks on behalf of all humanity through the African American aesthetic and perspective. That aesthetic and perspective is not necessarily defined by skin color or genealogy. It's defined by a continuum, a diaspora of informed people throughout history and humanity that speak art to power. That's what this is about.

What do you think is necessary for the black dance community and black dance artists in Chicago to succeed?

I was thinking about that recently. Honestly, I was thinking about that recently. I think we are so consumed by making our organizations work that we don't, and I am definitely a part of this, reach out to each other in a way that we're building a consortium. We're learning from each other, and we're building trust with each other so that we can [do this]. Recently I've been thinking about how it would be wonderful to have a Chicago African American dance center, or not even dance center, but cultural art center. There's a center in Minneapolis called Hennepin Center for the Arts. I love that building because that's where several arts organizations have come together and they are housed inside of this building, which is

a beautiful building that is supported by the city. And it just makes sense.
I just feel like if we could [do that], I'd love to find the time. I think that,
as I was saying, we're consumed by the work of keeping our organizations
going with little access and less support and less of all those different
things. We are consumed by that, and it doesn't afford us the opportunity to come together and talk about how we can work more effectively
together. We are going to have to come together and build trust and not
be inside a competitive, negatively competitive, conversation. I think that
I am in a space where I am capable of doing that. I think that certainly
there are other people as well. We might all find challenges in the process, but I think that we would be stronger together . . . of course we
would be stronger together. We also need to understand that we've been
conditioned to feel like, because the system has shown us that, we are going to raise one person up, and everybody is trying to be that one person.
OK? So, who is going to be the top dog that's going to get the funding
or whatever? Sometimes that comes in the mix, just that subliminal fear.
Foundations may fund all of us, which in some cases they do, but there's
ceiling of funding. They have this whole rate where if your budget size is
this much then you can only ask for this much. There's a whole structure
there [and] companies of color don't get past a certain ceiling. The funders
can say, well, we are funding everybody. We are funding diversity. But
if you add up what we are being funded, that may total what one larger
organization is being funded. We're afraid sometimes to break the mold
that protects that particular funding that we're getting because we are so
dependent upon it. It doesn't allow us to be as free and authentic in our
needs—or not even free and authentic. It doesn't allow us to come and
gather and examine that [issue] to propose something that foundations
might be ready for, because some foundations are in it for the good game.
They're in it for a greater good. Some of them are questionable to me.
Some of them are leaders of control. Jay-Z wrote a wonderful comment
about how—in his experience of being a poor person to a very, very, very,
very, very wealthy person and being able to intermix with philanthropy
and the mind-sets thereof—his conclusion is that a lot of philanthropy
support is there so that people who are receiving it feel beholden. If you
feel beholden, and I agree, if you feel beholden, you are not going to be
free to be inside of your authentic voice. He was talking about how he is
discovering that his mission, as he matures as a man, is about access. He

[Jay-Z] said, "I have access now, and my job is to provide access to other people." That's how I feel about it. That's what I think our challenge is. We'll have to have those conversations so we can come to a place of unity. We're diverse, and we're not monolithic. We're going to come. Because we come to a table doesn't mean we all gotta like what's at the table, but we need to come to the table. We need to be disciplined enough to come to the table and come to a place of common ground if we're going to talk about building Chicago's black theater and dance community.

TOSHA ALSTON

Tosha Alston is artistic director of Ayodele Drum & Dance and a principle dancer with Muntu Dance Theatre of Chicago. Alston teaches in various public schools and community centers throughout Chicago, and she has traveled both nationally and internationally—to places including Brazil, Mexico, Guinea, Canada, and England—performing and studying dance.

In this January 2011 interview, Tosha Alston discusses her training in West African dance in New York and her decision to relocate to Chicago to work with Muntu Dance Theatre of Chicago. Alston's interview also reveals the circumstances that led her to create a multicultural West African dance group in the city, Ayodele Drum & Dance, and her efforts at creating a more inclusive West African dance community.

My name is Tosha. A lot of people call me Ayo. *Ayo* means "joy" in the Yoruba language. People used to call me Sunshine, Joy, [because] I was always smiling onstage. Just being a friendly person, it was always a nickname that tagged along. The more I got into African culture and learning about different languages, I decided to recognize that childhood name as a nickname for myself in the African aspect. I'm from Brooklyn, New York. I have been in Chicago for nine years this May [2011]. I moved here to dance with Muntu Dance Theatre of Chicago. I came in as a full-time company member and, later, moved up to become dance captain/assistant to Amaniyea Payne, my artistic director. I've been dancing for at least twenty-seven years. I started very young. I started in dance school about six or seven. After my mother passed away when I was fourteen years old, I got more serious with the dancing because it was more of an outlet for me.

Did your mom put you in your first dance class?

Yep.

And did she dance herself?

No, she always wanted to be a can-can girl. She always said that. She was a singer. My mother sang with a gospel group. I started dancing more professionally right out of high school. I had some issues after my mother died—just not focusing and not really having guidance or support. I was getting into a lot of trouble. I saw a program in the school, an after-school program, and they were offering several art forms. People asked me, "Well, what are you interested in?" I actually took a part in the singing after-school program. I saw African dance there, and I was like, "Oh, I want to do that! That's what I want to do." I'd only done a little bit of it [African dance] in middle school. My first drummer—*Ibiye*—was Baba Olukose Wiles. This is Marie Basse's late husband. That was my very first drummer when I was in the tenth grade.

What was the name of your high school program?

The Carter G. Woodson Cultural Literacy Project. It was led by Stanley Kinard and his wife—she's kind of popular—Tulani. It was a very African-grounded organization. The brother—he has a Yoruba background—would have the room [in Boys and Girls High School in Brooklyn, New York] where you saw all the African print and stuff up on the door.

So you knew where you were going.

So you knew where you were going. They offered everything. I took part in the vocal chorus as well as the dance part, and I've been doing it ever since. I started teaching for him when I got out of high school.

I went to Florida to start college. Well, I started college in the city—in New York—then I went to Florida to try to do a transfer there. That fell through, so I moved back to the city. I went back to school in the city. When I came back I needed work, and Mr. Kinard hired me as a teacher for one of the elementary schools where he was at because I pretty much was one of his prizewinners. I ended up becoming one of his prizewinners by my senior year in school. He called me back to teach for his programs, and I've been teaching ever since then.

You were teaching West African dance?

Yes.

Who was your first dance teacher?

West African? Her name was Tanya Gray. We were in high school, like sixteen. She had to be one of those teachers who were nineteen/twenty, like when I started teaching in the elementary school. She was in the high school, but she had been dancing since two/three/four years old. She grew up with one of the dance companies that was studying with Baba Olukose and other companies. We started with her, and then it moved to different teachers that they had at the school, who came to work with the program. Tanya actually was one of the teachers that started taking us out and encouraging us to go to other companies to take classes.

You started out in New York, and you moved to Chicago about nine years ago to dance with Muntu Dance Theatre of Chicago. How did you learn about that position? What made you come to dance with Muntu?

Diedre Dawkins, who is one of the codirectors of DishiBem Dance Company.

She danced with Ron Brown, right?

She danced with Ron Brown. She's very versatile. She is someone whom I admired. I met her dancing with the first dance company that I danced with. She was a teacher for that company.

What company was that?

Indoda Entsha Society, and she came to teach us. We did a dance to the Jones Girls' "Nights Over Egypt." It was my first time tapping back into contemporary modern-style dance since early high school because in the [Carter G. Woodson] program, we had African dance on certain days and modern dance on other days. She danced with Muntu for a year. She had come back to New York, and I saw her at a Yoruba gathering. They were having these Yoruba meeting/ceremonies, kind of like church, once a month for the Yoruba community, where we all got together and congregated. We talked about the Orisha and danced and drummed the music and stuff like that. I saw her there. I had known that she was into the Orisha studies. We hugged. I was always so bashful around her because she was just an amazing dancer, and she was beautiful. So, being one of her students, every time I was around her, it was just like that humbling, "Hi," you know. [*Laughing*] She said, "Are you interested in relocating?" I said, "What do you mean?" She said, "I think I know a position that you would be good for. I think I know somewhere you might want to look into if you want to continue with your dancing." 'Cause I was working at a law firm, and I was dancing. I wasn't doing it full-time like I did when I moved to Chicago. She says, "I'm going to give you some information." At the time, things were going horribly in the city. I was an outcast in the city with my family and a lot of other stuff. I think I kind of used it as a way to get away and just do something independent and daring because I knew nobody in Illinois. I'd never been to Chicago in my life before, and I was, what, twenty-two? I was twenty-two going on twenty-three—I think—when I moved here. I hadn't finished college. It was just stepping out on a limb. So she called. She gave me the information, so I inquired about the audition. She had already called Amaniyea and told her that she knew a girl that would be good to come work for her. Muntu flew me there for the audition. I was applying for a full-time position because to relocate I needed a job. If I'm going there for you, you gotta be paying me. Their intentions of getting somebody from out of town was to know that [that person] was going to be at a certain level, so they paid for me to come. I auditioned. The panel liked me. Vaune [Charles], she didn't know which girl was from [New York]. She said, "Don't point her out." She was telling them don't point me out to her so she can be fair. She studied in New York, so that whole—"Oh, you from New York! She can dance!"—thing.

When you applied for the audition, was it clear that it was going to be Guinean dance?

Yes, that was clear. It was about traditional African dance, and that's what I knew. That's what I did. I know contemporary modern. I can make it fit my body, but my forte is African. Muntu was an African dance company. I wanted to go ahead and see what it would be like to be an artist without other side jobs, see how that felt. I did it for nine years. I've been able to travel off of my little salary like I'm making those big bucks, but I've seen how to make this life work. I could still be happy with where I am and growing and helping other people to grow.

Are you primarily teaching classes in the city now? Do you take classes also?

Well, I haven't been doing much because of my injury. I had an injury last year. Tomorrow marks a year from my surgery. I actually have my last doctor's appointment on Tuesday morning, so I haven't been on the dance scene. Right before I injured myself, I had actually started taking classes at Joel Hall before they moved further up north.

These were what kind of classes?

Ballet.

How did you injure yourself?

It was something that has taught me a very valuable lesson. We did a show, Muntu, which is why my insurance covered [it] and I was able to get medical attention. Thank God for insurance, and that Muntu was able to provide insurance at that time. [*Sighs*] We were outside dancing, and there were other companies. It was raining outside. It was wet. It was cold. The other dance companies had on long-sleeved stuff underneath their little African attire. We noticed and watched, and some of us complained. We were trying to keep warm. We were jogging trying to keep warm. We get onstage. The energy was so high. I wasn't in my body 'cause I didn't even know I hurt myself, and I was *dancing.* Everybody was dancing. It was just a high [energy]. You could tell it was just some real intimate, from the heart, movement, and it was like, "Yes!" Well, I went out there, and it felt so good. I came back and go to lift my arm to do a "time step" and couldn't move it at all. I got scared. My eyes got big. I looked at Amaniyea. I was about to start crying. Because there were other solos and stuff going on, I was able to kind of slide to the back of the stage and say, "Amaniyea, I can't move my arm." [*Sighs*] I had all kind of people jerking on my arm. "Oh, it was just the cold got in it." I got back home paranoid and upset because I couldn't move it still. I went to the doctor, and because I'm not a sports player, they didn't think it was torn. They treated it with physical therapy, thinking it would get better. One of the motions wasn't getting better, so that was a longer period of time. I guess whatever stretching exercises I did, I feel like that stuff ripped it more. It probably wasn't even as bad of a rip, but that was it. It's like either you have surgery or you don't dance with this arm at its full potential. Yep. So all last year, when I say emotional . . . it was like, "Hmm, I can't do this no more," the artist thing. I was like, "This is not gonna work."

What made you feel like that? Was it other people saying that to you, or was that something that you thought yourself?

It was just me. It was me thinking about what I wanted to accomplish in a certain timeframe. In certain careers, age matters. I was really trying to hone in on what I was gonna be doing and working toward. Right at the cusp of me about to do that, I hurt myself. Going through a lot of the spiritual things that I ended up having to go through this year just to try to keep my mind sane, I was in a bad depression. People wouldn't know that at all because when I step outside, I have to let God be through me. There's so much negativity and chaos in the world. If I'm walking out with all this negative [energy], visible especially, I'm asking for it.

It would attract more negativity?

Yes. I'm asking for it. I took a two-week leave of absence from Muntu, went to New York, and got some spiritual work done. I came back ready, a little bit more confident, and a little bit more prepared for whatever God has in store for me. No matter how well or not my arm becomes— whether it's 100 percent or 95 percent or 60 percent—I'm still gonna do what I'm supposed to do, what I'm meant to do.

I have a question about that age thing because it seems like, within West African dance, you have a lot of older dancers still dancing. I thought the age thing was not an issue in the way it is in other dance forms like ballet. Am I wrong with that? Is it an issue or not?

Well, you know, I agree to a certain extent about the art. The elders are kicking butt. You know they do. But how much are they doing it? Are they doing it at the capacity of the people my age? Or, are they just teaching classes? Teaching classes and performing, you're exerting a whole 'nother kind of energy. The energy you can exert and maintain during an hour-and-a-half-long class or a two-hour workshop [is one thing]. [But] to get onstage and do a two-hour show, I can't say that I've seen any of my teachers do that for a long time unless they're a drummer. Dance-wise, I haven't seen no teacher do a concert. Usually they're just featured. So, yes, they do, but how much and how involved are they? And for me, I feel like I'm too young for my body to be wearing out or giving out like that. But then, at the same time, I'm old enough to where I'm responsible for the longevity of my career to a degree to where I can make the executive decisions to say I'm not gonna dance in the rain. African dance is a warm climate kind of dance if you haven't noticed. All of that stuff just kind of depends on who, where, how, and what they're doing. So at thirty-two, I don't want to be just some old mediocre person just doing dance for a company because of prestige or their name. I do want to be groomed into what can be the continuation of Muntu or whoever—just this art, this music, what I've learned, what I've gained, and how I could continue to make it work for our people. I have the group Ayodele Drum & Dance, which started out just as a hobby thing for a couple of the other dancers that I worked with at Muntu. We had spent so much time together, I thought it would be wise to start utilizing that time to really help make us a lot more skillful in our art and just start doing more studying in the music. Things started to grow from there. When I started Ayodele, I targeted most of the companies I knew because I wanted the study group to show that we could study together and are all doing the same thing with our own flavor.

To be united.

Yeah! But some of the forces in the community didn't want to see that happen, and these are our people. They're spewing negativity because of things that they don't agree with about people's personal lives. We always get wrapped up into that same thing over and over again, but I continue to share my passion. I am thankful for the other part of this community, and the other communities that I work with, that embraced me despite the labels and stereotypes that society has given people like me. I've been beat down a bit by parts of this community because of how some people chose to view me, and [my] being open to white people dancing with me has made things even more difficult.

Talk a little bit more about that what that decision was about for you?

Having white people in my group? I don't even know. We were a study group so we were just drumming and dancing. I was working on some stunts and different things with the drumming. I'm trying to remember. There was this one white girl, every time she came and took my class, she would drive three hours every week because she liked my style. She liked the way I danced, and, not only that, she was a badass dancer. She was a good dancer. She was good. I asked her, "You interested in learning some drum stuff?" That's where it started. It was just like, "The work that I have to do, I think your body would look good doing it." It had nothing to do with what color her skin was because apparently she's in an African dance class. Somebody else had to teach her this before I got to her, as good as she was. She was dancing with an all-white African dance company in Madison, and her commitment and dedication to Ayodele blew me away. It just made me feel like she loves doing this. This is where we are right now, these are people that just love doing this. I was an outcast in my community because of preferences of mine. It made me feel like I'm taking in all the people that don't get taken in. If they want to grow, learn, and do, I'm going to help them do that. At that point, we weren't even thinking about becoming a performing company, it was just about being a study group.

You said you were outcast because of preferences?

Girl, I'm not into labels. I used to always think that the dance community was a home for outcasted gay men and people that were gay. But the African community here did not accept that fact about me when I moved here right away. It was something that took them a hard time to deal with. They associated homosexuality immediately with pedophilia and tried to put labels on me. As I got older, I realized I was twenty-two. If I was too flamboyant and boisterous for them or anybody else, that was where an elder was supposed to step in and say, "Look, I don't agree with your decision, but, if this is who you're going to be, you have to hold a certain amount of class with yourself." Anything! I had to learn all that stuff on my own. I had to learn how to be a little bit more mature about not being so open and free—place and time for everything. Instead of them taking me in to groom me—as a black African girl from the states who you can see knows this artistic material, is doing this work, and is taking it seriously—they chose to damage my reputation based on assumptions and uninformed opinions before I could even begin. So before I got started, people in the community—"Oh, that gay girl from New York." Then it was, "Oh, Muntu is turning into a gay company." Then everybody that hung out with me was gay. People never got the chance to know me, they just heard the gossip and that was it. It's funny how, in life, people can make you or break you if you let them. The gay thing has been a hard thing for people in the African community to suck up, but over time people saw past that. Some people were able to see past that and see what I really wanted to offer, my artistry. I've been in a relationship for five years, and people can think what they want at this point. I just feel like the African community, we were made to be against each other for the color of our [skin]—like who's light skinned and who's dark skinned, who's fat and who's skinny. That was something that was positioned to keep the slaves under control. Why can't we get nowhere? 'Cause we still in that same control mentality, like in order for me to be somebody I got to . . .

Put my foot on somebody else's neck.

Yeah. People gonna always find a way to attack. I didn't grow up spending time attacking people. So being in an arena of work where some people are cutthroat a little bit, I've learned how to have a tough skin. At the same time, I'm so mushy inside because I have a true heart for what the real meaning of it is—community building—and this is outside of the racial thing. My thing is . . . I went to Guinea for two weeks. When we got in that dance circle [at a Dundunba in Conakry], did any of those African girls come dance with me? No. When that white girl got in that dance circle, they all got out there and danced with her. Do you remember that?

I remember that.

Do you know that messed me up for a little while?

Are you serious?

Mmmm-hmmm. I wrote about it. I wrote a poem about it. How we're trying so hard to be African when most Africans won't even accept us. We try so hard to prove this whole community thing when a community is made up of different people. Like I say, you have some people that are born African that are white. It's not their fault. I had to start really just looking at it like, "OK, there are people that are born on the continent that are not black." How would we feel, as people born in America, about any one of those white people coming to us to tell us, "You ain't African," and have every right to because they are, no matter what their roots. That's what we're living off of. We're living off of what our roots are. Some people that's in this pro-black thing, if they really search their roots, they probably from Polish people somewhere because we're mixed up by now. We're all mixed up, but because we do know we got this . . . [*slapping skin on arm*] . . . we know we come from some kind of African descent. Second example: We [Ayodele] danced at the Shrine. When the girls came out, Imania [Detry] got onstage—this was at Afro-beat night, African night. One of the Nigerian girls looked at Imania and said, "Oh, whatever"—her little friends were standing there—"Uh-uh, well, they not African. They just know how to African dance."

Ayodele has been thinking about what this thing is supposed to be about: change. Nobody can take something from me that is mine. So all of that, "Oh, the white people, they gonna just be in your group and take all your stuff." Even with the traditional stuff, if I'm gonna do tradition, I'm gonna imitate exactly what I learned, and I'm gonna do that. I'm a creator. I'm an artist. I do the tradition, and I also create off of it by [asking] why people do a dance, where the people come from, what dances are being done, and really finding the similarities in the dances. Coming into this whole new stage of performing and getting into the whole artistry thing, that community is more than just black people. You know what I'm saying? It's more than black people. It's weird because when you're dealing with the cultural community, it seems like it always goes back to race issues. I mean I have my opinions about certain things. They ain't going nowhere just because I'm cool with the white people that's in my group. I have my limits, but I set those for myself. All these other people, if you feel like somebody, like some white person, came in and took something that belonged to you, that means you must not have been doing what you were supposed to be doing to keep that thing. I just feel like all that passing the blame [and] passing the buck why people can't get ahead, I'm done with. That's not my era of where I am. I'll leave that for the elders. I understand it. I understand some of the elders that really just feel like, "No, we can't have white people doing it." Like I spoke to an elder that's so hard on that. He said, "They can take class, but to perform it?" And I'm like, "What's the difference? If they're doing it, they're doing it." And really, really the Asians are *DOING IT*. They're the ones doing [it]. We just watched on YouTube [one Asian group] was on a Senegalese tour somewhere. That's why I say, right now people, we damage our own stuff sometimes. We damage our own communities and not even consciously. Our communities are gonna have blacks, gonna have whites, might have a Latino in there somewhere. So now do we just isolate whoever's [different]? I was isolated. Do I claim to not be African because I was isolated by my community? But now this same community that isolated me wants me to isolate someone else? Treat others how you want to be treated. Somebody come in here say, "I love your work. I want to study with you." That's where I am with it.

What are the images that you think you're bringing to audiences through your performances?

When people see Ayodele, they see multicultural. That's the first thing people see image-wise. They see that there are white people with us. That's always the first thing that people see usually. I'm thinking that that image is setting—for some who are receptive of it—that idea that Ayodele is trying to make a change in what the standard community, African community, should look like. When people see Ayodele, at this point of where we are, the imagery is becoming this is not just a traditional African dance company. They know that this is not just that. When people see us they see, I think, what they know is tradition, and then they get the chance to see what certain artists are doing creatively with the tradition. It is giving them a sense of 2010/2011, and how times evolve, how things change, and how, "Whoa! There was a white person onstage at Kwanzaa." So change. I think trendsetting changes. And trust me, I'm not the first African company that has white people in it, not by a long shot. But in Chicago, oh yeah. Chicago is very, very, very stern on that kind of thing. I think some see the tradition, and they see the creativity in what I'm trying to do with the tradition.

Do you do think your company's presence is impacting that segregation?

Mmmm-hmmm. I think that it is reaching and targeting people that would . . . like this sister. I love her. She sat me down and had a long talk with me. In the cusp of me crying last year when I was going through a lot, and she was just talking to me. She's like, you know, "Ayo, don't leave. White people need to know this too. Everybody needs to know the richness of who we are and where we come from." Why do we have to . . . "It's a secret." You know, "It's mine." They don't want anybody to have it. And she said, "I'll be honest with you, I am not fo' the h————[white people]." OK, she went there, OK. "I'm not for the h————, but what you all did out there was beautiful." And that's how she spoke, but she was just like it was a beautiful show. It wasn't about the color. It was just about the show. It was people that normally probably would despise it, or if they had a buddy to talk about it with, were able to kind of adjust to it and almost say, "That didn't hurt me too bad to see her doing that dance up there. It didn't hurt too bad." I definitely have spoken to several people that it is impacting in a very positive way. Very positive.

When I think about your show last year [2010], there was so much about women's empowerment in the show. I loved the part of your show when you had the older girls dancing onstage, they were dancing in a really seductive way, and then you had the young girls put the signs around their neck asking for help. It was just, like, brilliant, powerful, and awesome. You don't see that kind of political message—at least I don't—in a lot of African dance. So what is it about women's issues and women's rights that you're trying to deal with in the company?

Because I have been outcasted for being a lesbian, I think with the group, when it came to the women thing, started out as, "Hmm, there's not too many women drumming. I got this piece, hey, you know, let's do this." The idea in working with the other group that I was with, Seneke West African Percussion Ensemble, choreographing for them was just to be able to give me the hands on [experience and] to be able to get the women trained. What we wanted to do was to have Seneke be the male drummers, [and] Ayodele be the dancers for Seneke and the female drumming company. We kind of travel like that. That's how it started till we ended up having to branch off and just become Ayodele Drum & Dance. Because of what I've gone through with women, not only just being in relationships with them, but just the ridicule, the cattiness, the judgment, the playing down on our sisters, and just all of that stuff—being a victim of it, seeing it done—I was just feeling like, "Uh-uh, it's not necessary." It just made me feel geared more toward trying to get the females together. So, like I said, I invited people from other dance companies. [I was] like we need to get together because—guess what?—when the women get it together and we hold strong, we can take care of our children and our men, like back before [Willie] Lynch[–like practices impacted] us and before the men were stripped. That's where the whole women thing came into play. Nobody groomed me when I was at an [early] age. I probably could have been at where I am a little earlier. I may even have had the time to go to school because someone saw where I was, never really officially having a rites-of-passage ceremony for myself. All of that stuff started gearing me toward wanting to get my sisters strong because just the fact of me having to do it by myself. I couldn't think of continuing to do it by myself. Some of the stuff that I had to go through, I just feel like when people feel as if they have a support system—and that's with any organization, anything—you can get through [the fire]. You know what I'm saying? Sometimes women just need that camaraderie and that support from a group of women, another group of women. I instigated the sister circles. Me and a friend, Joy Conway, started those a few years back. We were interested in getting together, talking, and trying to figure out how we could work through our issues [and] stuff that we (women) deal with every day. It's hard on us. We're strong creatures. What can we do to keep ourselves from going off the deep end? What can we do to help encourage each other? I know my sister does XYZ, and I'll pay her to do this instead of probably having to search somewhere [else]. All of that stuff influenced my decision about really going toward the women focus. I'm a woman, and I think it's something that's important.

Ayodele, what will make it different is the stories. The storyline last year was about the girl going back to trace her roots of mothers—what she learned, what she went through, and how times change. In that show there was a lot of stuff I wanted to say, and it was just like, "Uh, no time." I didn't know I was going to continue because after that show last year I was actually gonna let it go. I got tired of people harassing [me]. This woman put a blog up to support our show in May, and the nasty comments . . .

Are you serious?

. . . that was on that blog. "I wouldn't waste my money to go see them. They're just this. Oh, they're horrible. They're just trying to be like so-and-so." I'm sure these are people in the community that know us that have issues with some of us. There are but so many people that can really get that personal to really say, "Oh, they're trying to be like so . . ." No. No, not with some of the stuff I have seen on [that blog]. We're a group of sisters! Or the blog got into the white people. Somebody put on there, "If this is Tosha from Muntu, you must be confused and something-something-something . . ." It was real nasty. "You need to go back and get some schooling having white people on your stage with you and dah-dah-dah-dah-dah." People were eating me alive. I cried a lot. I cried a lot, but I don't feel like what I'm doing is so wrong for people to really react this way.

I want to ask you about Africa and African identity. What is Africa to you?

Africa to me is . . . a continent. Africa for me is life. It's life. It's life just as much as the air I breathe. I say that because African dance saved me from suicide. Just my mother . . . All that stuff in high school . . . I was getting into being a part of an African dance program. Being a part of that program gave me love. It showed me a love first for myself and for what I never knew about so far as where I came from. Growing up, all I knew was a little Ethiopia commercial—"Sponsor a Child." Because my family was Christian, they had African Sundays some days. So going into junior high school, that's when I started learning more about a lot of Caribbean cultures and African cultures. For me, when I think of Africa, it saved my life—African dance, the music, the culture, and the richness of knowing that my people came from a place of this caliber [and] wealth. Everything. The love from [that knowledge]. That's just how it empowered me because of the way it [Africa] was introduced to me.

When did you begin to think of yourself as African?

I started thinking about myself more as an African and not an African American, or referring to myself as that, around the time Muntu did *Sweet Nina*. I did the drum piece, [and] there was a lot of choreography going on. It was, of course, then the talk about the Africans and the white people in the company. One of the elder brothers said, "I'm an African because it wasn't by choice that my people came over here." You understand? That made a lot of sense for me. You have Africans that come over here that are African. They have children, and their children still consider themselves to be African. They don't call themselves African American even though they were born in America. You understand? So like that stuff is what made me feel like, you came over here on your own. We were forced from our home, our parents, whatever. So we're the result of a situation that was beyond our control, so why does that make me less African because I was born in America? After that point,

I just felt like I am an African. I am an African. I just was brought to this country through X, Y, and Z. The same thing as any person that was born on the continent who comes over here and they have children. When their children go to school, they have an African name. Other kids will identify them as "the African girl," but that girl was born in '89 in the same hospital you were born in. Same thing. My parents are here. My parents are from the South, so I don't get anal about it. I don't make a big deal about it. But, I do like to be recognized as an African, not just an African American girl that knows how to do African dance.

Can I just ask you about one thing in a Muntu show that I saw? In 2010, you were doing the show at the space right around here, the Gary Comer Center. It was the piece where you were talking about—I think it was Kakilambe—the cowives. And you pulled out a rainbow flag.

Yes. Did you see the flag?

I did! Did you consciously decide to bring out the rainbow flag?

You know I did. Part of it is because I haven't been able to express myself. Through my company, I'm able to express myself. When we have the freedom to add, nine times out of ten I'm adding something to make a message known. It is not even the fact about me being me, but about the fact that you could go to Africa right now and somebody will have a rainbow thing, but does that mean they're gay? We are in the village. We are doing laundry. This is something that would be in my laundry, my big 'ol rainbow [flag]. I remember that I shook it too. Held it up. Then, of course, my character was the character that was telling the other girl, "I'm just sick of these men bossing me around and telling me what to do. Cook this! Clean that! Do that! Finish this! I don't want to do it no more. I'm tired. I just want to chill out and relax." I had that demeanor and that attitude. I just figured I'm beefin', people know me and I'm like beefin' about the dudes, so let me go ahead and tell you about, "Yep, I'm the gay one in the group." [*Laughing*] Yeah, that's me. It was to put that message that—guess what?—I'm in an African village, but we count too. There are plenty of gay Africans. We're African too.

Did anybody say anything to you about that?

About the flag? Oh no. Nobody. I think that during that point people had gotten over the gay hump with me. They just knew I was gonna be me. No. People that probably noticed probably cracked jokes or something like, "Did you see that big rainbow lappa? Tosha . . . ?" I'm sure. Nobody said anything at all about it to me. That's kind of funny. You so precious! Intentional. Oh, yeah, that was very intentional. I said, "Yeah, I know. I'm about to bring a big rainbow lappa."

Is there anything that I didn't ask you about—your experience, your life, about African dance in general—that you want to tell me about?

I think African dance should be done by everybody. Why? Because of what African dance does for you. It's healing. It's stress relieving. The music is penetrating. It feels good. I feel like in this life with all the bad things and the good things that are out here, feeling good is what's important. The color of anybody's skin, somebody's sexual preference, or any of that stuff shouldn't deprive them of being able to experience African dance. You can definitely quote that. For real! African dance is what it is. It should be shared. It's great. It's beautiful. It's life saving. If I see some old white person dying and think that African dance can save their life, I'm gonna do it. That's all I have to say.

DANIEL "BRAVE MONK" HAYWOOD

Daniel Haywood, known as Brave Monk in the hip-hop community, has dedi-cated his energy toward mastering the origins, concepts, and foundations of hip-hop's cultural dance form known as b-boying/breaking while also putting a focus into other aspects such as freestyle, house, hip-hop, fitness, movement, and choreography. He is a member of Chicago's legendary and internationally rec-ognized breaking crew Phaze II—Crosstown Crew (established in 1982). He is also a founding member, active leader, mentor, and performer for Awesome Style Konnection (A.S.K.), as well as F.E.W. Collective, an artist collective.

In this May 2010 interview, Brave Monk talks about his entry into the world of b-boying/breaking and his development as an artist researching this cultural dance form. Using freestyling as a metaphor for navigating the unpredictable turns in one's life, he highlights some of the fundamental elements of b-boying/breaking as well as the development of hip-hop and house music and dance in Chicago.

I grew up the youngest of four kids about two-and-a-half hours south of Chicago in a town called Normal, Illinois. Bloomington–Normal, there's a college campus [there]. A lot of people are like it's nothing but corn-fields down there. My first experience with movement would probably be in a church—seeing the elders catch what we call the "Holy Ghost" or the "Holy Spirit." That was my first intake. If you've never been to an African American church [and seen] the kind of stuff that happens in those churches, the music is really intense. There's the speaking of the tongues—you don't necessarily know what those words are, but the words have a vibration, they have a feeling. They emit a certain emotion. The movement reflects that as well. That whole losing yourself, breaking, letting go and being free, being one with the spirit, being one with the universe, being one with God, being one with life, being one with existence, that's really the only way I've known dance. I haven't known it from a material perspective; it's always been spiritual.

I was born in 1981 and my brother—my eldest brother—is six years older than me. I guess it started off with my older brother—he showed me a couple moves. I can distinctly remember doing the backspin and the worm for show-and-tell in kindergarten. Other people would be bringing in their parents. I'd be doing the worm or spinning on my back. Afterwards, kids were asking me to show them how to do it. So, I was teaching when I was in kindergarten. My older brother was into martial arts, Taekwondo, because that was what we had available to us in our area. When I was four, I got put into martial arts. My brother used to make me and my other brother—this is the second oldest now, he's three years older than me—battle each other. He'd put on the music and freestyle—wasn't no set anything, everything was just improv. We would freestyle battle against each other for like two hours straight. When you're a little kid, you have energy to burn and you do it. That wasn't enough. He then called his friends over and would have all his friends around us. Then it became a battle. We were freestyle battling. I just remember it being hours and hours—must have seemed like about five or six hours—just doing this.

In hip-hop, style is very important. The way you develop style is by finding who you are. You do that through freestyling. It's like calibration, right? It's like GPS. GPS always has to find out where you are—in this position—on the globe. Freestyling is like finding your energy, finding what motivates you, what pushes you, what kinds of movements and what kind of sounds stimulate what emotion, and what kinds of movements feel pleasing to your body or feel natural to your body. It's also your intent. What is your purpose? Why are you dancing? Where is your strength? Where is your weakness? In freestyling, you experience all of those questions. It's an awareness thing, and that's really what it is. It's just being aware of the energy around you and being able to manipulate the energy around you. If you haven't experienced it, it is a quest that everyone should experience. It doesn't necessarily have to be through the forms that I practice. You can get that through other forms.

My mom raised us. My father passed three months before I was born. He somehow knew I was gonna be a boy. He already [had given] me my name, Daniel Joseph. And my mom was like, "But you don't even know if it's gonna be a boy or a girl." He was like, "His name is going to be Daniel Joseph." He passed three months before I was born in a car accident. I was left with my mom working and raising four kids—one sister who's the oldest and three guys. I'm not gonna say my mom wasn't there—she was definitely there—but it left a lot of creative time for me. I filled that creative time with martial arts, dance, and comic books.

A lot of people think that they can just go in the studio, watch a video, do some choreography, and call it hip-hop dance. Hip-hop has distinct roots that have been developing for over thirty-five years. It's kind of a slap in the face when you do that, [do not appreciate the history of hip-hop]. If you do it in the spirit of hip-hop, it's a little bit more understandable. You need to know the spirit of hip-hop, and you need to understand it before you can just feel like you're a hip-hop dancer, because hip-hop is not a product. That's the later term [form] of hip-hop. Hip-hop is a culture. It's a name to describe this energy that was coming at that time from majority African American, but also Latino and Afro-Caribbean, brothers and sisters in the ghetto in New York. I'm not saying that [it] wasn't happening anywhere else, because it was happening on the West Coast. It was a funk movement, and that's where styles like popping and locking and strutting and boogalooing and waving and all that are from. In New York it was rocking. Then it was breaking—b-boying and b-girling. You know what I mean? In Chicago, it was house. It went from blues to jazz and swing and then to rock-'n'-roll. Look at the terms. Rock-'n'-roll, that's a description of motion. It's describing an energy. Funk, you get in a funk. It's so potent you can smell it. You know what I mean? Again, it's multidimensional. You find these other ways to stimulate the senses. Soul, it hits you so hard you feel it. It actually, literally touches your heart. You can feel it touch your heart. You're describing a feeling. Hip-hop, again, we're back to motion. Hip meaning to be aware, to know, and hop is actually a physical motion, a movement. They used to call it rocking in '73/'74. Rocking, like I said, is just another energy.

I use the term "street dance," and I use the term "hip-hop." When you say hip-hop dance, what the majority of people are gonna think is the way people dance in music videos. I'm not saying that's not hip-hop dance—if you can connect with it. Street dance, a term that is kind of general, means dance that was developed in the community and that kind of space. There are some dances that were developed in the clubs. There are some dances that were developed literally on the streets. There are some dances that were developed in the studios. Now, when we take it to the studio, it then becomes a little bit more commercial. I'm not knocking it, but you just have to understand the environment. What does having a mirror do? You're constantly evaluating yourself in the mirror or fixing your form to adjust to whomever is showing you that technique verses no mirror—you're in a circle. Feel my energy and interpret the energy. If I say I want you to hit it this way with your arm this way, you have to use your own mind to calibrate. You don't have a mirror to adjust. It's all internal. When you have the mirror, it then becomes physical. You can still be internal, but—you understand what I'm saying?—it is external.

The majority of these dances started [in] the early seventies—contrary to what people think when they're like "Yo, man, breaking was the eighties." Eighties was the exploitation era of hip-hop. Especially, I would say, '83–'84. That's when the cameras finally penetrated the inner city. That was when they, actually, someone said, "You know what? I'm gonna document this. I'm gonna put it on film." The films that you hear talked about the most are *Wild Style* [1983], *Flashdance* [1983], *Beat Street* [1984], and *Breakin'* [1984]. Hip-hop has a lot of different layers to it. It's deep. You even deal with the gender thing and the machismo and the bravado and the testosterone because, again, this is a dance coming out of the hood and, unless you have that kind of warrior spirit, you might not survive. That's just the truth because there was a lot of crazy stuff going on in the seventies, a lot of gangs. I'm not saying gangs are bad. The foundation of hip-hop, a lot of it comes from that grouping, whether it was a style coming from the gangs or just the idea of this territorial competition and the aspect of battling. So, if I say "hip-hop dance," there's two things I would say: freestyling and battling. Those two aspects are pivotal to hip-hop dance.

I would say my whole life is a freestyle and basically that means that I don't necessarily know what's gonna happen every [second or minute] or what's gonna happen in the coming months or coming years. I can have a direction. I can pick a focus of where I want to be and try to get there. But I'm aware that there are also outside influences and an outside energy that may affect that. And I must—if I want to achieve—be able to adapt to whatever. Change. I need to be able to do that at a moment's notice. To me that's the art of freestyling. Freestyling does not just embody dance, it's also a mind state. I'll just take it back to slavery. Some slaves revolted and said, "You know what? I just know we need to be free. I'm tired of these conditions," and they snuck off or did whatever they had to do to get away from that plantation, from that slave master. There's this whole big mass of land, and they don't know what's out there other than the area that they've been working in, but they're now on a journey to get free. They have stories that have been passed on, "We heard to go up north or follow this star at this point at this time of the night." Certain tips, "Don't go near the city, stay to the—wherever you see a lot of trees, that's where you should be." Things like that, and I think that that condition of becoming free was a freestyle. You know what I mean? Like you didn't know what was gonna happen, and you just had to be ready for whatever came.

Up until I was about seventeen, I literally wanted to be a master martial artist. At seventeen, I realized that wasn't gonna happen. I had an older brother living in Chicago. He was in school in Chicago. I'd come up with him a couple summers to stay with him. One of my brother's friends, one of our friends, brought one of his boys back from Chicago. This dude was Jamaican. I used to hear stories about this guy. And the dude came down one day and he was running up walls flipping. He did this move called the 1990, which is where he goes up on his hand and he spins and he does rotation. Seeing it on TV and seeing it in person are two different [things]. I've seen it on TV. When I saw it in person, it was just like wow. I started practicing the 1990. Started practicing it over and over. I didn't really start physically breaking until '98. I say that because, when I was young, doing the backspin and the worm didn't mean I was a b-boy. That just meant I could do a move. But like truly understanding, like piecing it in, top rock, transition drops, footwork, leg steps, groundwork, ground moves, back rocks, freezes, stalls, hesitations, power moves, air moves, like the whole vocabulary, the vernacular of what these moves were, and the categories that make up this full art—that's why I say like in '98 I just started breaking. I started b-boying. I started on my quest to become a b-boy. While I was in school, I started doing research papers on breaking. Obviously, a lot of information points to the Rock Steady Crew. They're the ones who kind of put b-boying out there for the world on a commercial level. A lot of people like to use that as a starting point. There's so much more information other than that.

When I got America Online [the internet], that was my chance to have access to whatever kind of information I wanted. The first thing I did was create a [user]name. I'm gonna get into the name now so that you can understand my name. The first name that I tried was Golden Monk. "Denied. Sorry, that name has been taken. Damn!" My mom's [standing] right over me. She's got to punch in her credit card. I'm like, OK, I feel it. "Brave Monk." "Confirmed. Now choose your password." When I came up with the name, first off, I wanted to have a name that was like a call sign. A call sign basically being like when you see the Batman signal in the air, you know what it is. The name I chose to enter into the Internet, or into the matrix, was Brave Monk. That was the name I chose. My whole thing was to connect with like-minded individuals, share information and build. I jumped on the information superhighway and learned. I used to host these underground chat, hip-hop, rooms. It was an invitation to find out [the culture and history of hip-hop and street dance]. You could do what I'm doing now—interview, ask questions. Whatever you wanted to know, you could ask. You could ask Joe-Joe (one of the original founders of Rock Steady Crew for whom I searched and found online) or whoever else.

When did you move to Chicago?

I moved to the Chicago area in '99 going into 2000. I stayed in the burbs, but I was going to school in the city. At that time it was the International Academy of Merchandising and Design, which has gone through three name changes. Now it is the School or the Academy of Design Technology on One North State Street. I was going there, and I was staying in the city with people who lived in the city. On the weekends, I would just go home, wash the gear, and I'm back in the city. But, again, my brother was up here, and I came up here a couple summers before. Let me talk about the styles that I found out while I was questing. During the period, a little bit before breaking, I found out there was a style in Chicago called flexing. At least that's what they called it. They called it flexing. I hadn't seen house, at least back then. I knew it was house music. The footworking and juking, that's what I knew it as. We had a lot of people who were transported from Chicago to our town. Like there were people from Cabrini–Green in our town. Basically, it was like, "We're trying to get rid of a problem, so we're gonna move them somewhere. We're gonna move them to a small town." They would have these development programs in our town. There would be parties and people would be doing footwork and juking. Because I never had someone to teach me the foundations, per se, extensively in those styles, it was my interpretation. It was me freestyling footwork. I learned certain basic moves like, at that time, what was called "the skateboard." I began to find out there's this whole debate between New York and Chicago, like who started house music and whatnot.

When I say house music, house music is taken from funk/soul/gospel, and basically, imagine, adding a 4/4 beat to that. A 4/4 beat just being . . . [*Clapping hands*] That gives house its feel. They call it house because the music was being played at this place called the Warehouse in Chicago. So when they would be trying to describe [it], "Do you play the music they play at the Warehouse? Oh yeah, we play house music." It just went from warehouse to "house." But also, too, symbolically there's a reason why it's called house. In the space of house, it's peace, it's love, it's unity. In a home, there is love, right? Hip-hop and house are brother and sister. One was the guy who was a little machismo, sometimes really hard-headed and a rebel. The other was the sister who had the kind and loving mother-like qualities. House was very embracive. Gay culture played a huge influence in [its] foundation. Off of that 4/4 beat the foundation for house became this movement that was known as jack. And jack is the groove basically. There's a song, "Jack Had a Groove,"[1] and it basically breaks down the philosophy of what jack is. It personifies jack and talks about how Jack had a groove, and the evolution of his groove gave birth to house. The movement of jack is like a connection to your core, to your

---

1. "Jack Had a Groove" refers to a spoken word recording by Chuck Roberts, which first appeared in the song "Our House," by a group called Rhythm Control. Catch A Beat Records produced it in 1987.

being. Your being is giving birth to this movement. This movement giving birth to this music. This music is this culture. This culture is what we do, is what we live, you know what I mean? And that's house. Starting with jack in Chicago, it progresses in New York. There were DJs going back and forth from New York. New York grabs a hold of it as well, and a lot of different styles start to get integrated in it. Some salsa steps, modern jazz, capoeira. Even now, b-boys are turning to house, too. There are sub-styles, like voguing and waacking. Those are sub-styles of house, but, in their own right, they're their own style. You could say, "I dance to house music," but the style you dance would be voguing or waacking. You could say, "I dance to house music," and the style you dance might be footworking. House to me is still being modified. It's still evolving just like the way b-boying is, just like the way popping and locking are. The dance styles are not stagnant. They're all underground cultures.

You've got to look at the elements that [gave] hip-hop exposure—you had graffiti and you had DJs and b-boys. If I go to New York, and I see a big [graffiti] piece from top to bottom on a train with bright colors, whether I like it or not, it's gonna catch my attention. I'm going to wonder how did that get there, who did that, and where did it come from. I think that piqued the interest, and the cameras went to follow where those trains were coming from. Through graffiti—that was like a promotion—they found the b-boys. The b-boys were like the embodiment of hip-hop. When they saw them, they heard the music they were dancing to. They saw the people who were creating the music, who were emceeing. [Hip-hop] allowed so many different channels. You didn't have to just be a b-boy, you could write graffiti, beatbox, and just dress and just hang around cats. People, like myself, took pilgrimages and went to New York, found and trained with them, hung around them, and went to the places where the competitions were happening. Others took it back to Europe or to Australia with them and to Japan and Korea and . . . It's just crazy.

Can you talk a little bit about the work that you do with, like, the University of Hip-Hop?

Basically gang intervention or pulling kids from the street, giving them an outlet to channel their creativity, to channel their anger or sadness or even happiness, whatever they feel. Just giving them a channel. I've done a lot of that, and I'm always gonna do that wherever I go. I'm always gonna do that, whether it's doing it [for a] not-for-profit or whether I'm just doing it out of my own love. I think it's important. It's each one teach one. The way that you survive—and this movement continues—is by that person-to-person interaction. If everyone starts to just learn to dance off of DVDs or YouTube, I think there's a lot that's still being missed. There's something about the rites of passage of having a teacher or educator or a guide, someone to lead you. That's very important. It'll save you a lot of wasted energy, a lot of misguided energy. Sometimes, you need to go through it to find yourself or to find your purpose.

I'm trying to dance as long as I can, and I understand that my career (a lot of times) is based on what I can do physically. If I injure myself or a break a leg, I'm out of work. So, I better have some other skills to utilize—you know what I mean?—or I better be able to talk, hold a conversation, and give you this insight that I'm giving you now, because there's other things that have value. As an artist it's in your best interest to learn as much as you can about your art and to be able to transfer those into other outlets. It's very hard for artists, in general, to survive unless you somehow get the right break or connect with the right people. It's livable. You've just got to have drive.

APPENDIX A

PEOPLE MENTIONED IN INTERVIEWS

This appendix provides information about individuals mentioned in the preceding interviews. These are dancers, theater makers, journalists, and politicians who either directly or indirectly, through their influence on the artists interviewed in this book, contributed to the development of theater and dance in Chicago.

Hope Abelson was a theater producer, patron of Chicago's off-Loop theater movement, and major benefactor to the Goodman Theatre and Steppenwolf Theatre. Abelson died in 2006 at the age of ninety-five.

Vanoye Aikens joined Katherine Dunham's dance company in 1943. He eventually became Dunham's principal partner until 1963, when the company was dissolved.

Alvin Ailey was a choreographer and the founder of Alvin Ailey American Dance Theater, an internationally touring company that performs annually in Chicago. Ailey died in 1989 at the age of fifty-eight.

Lane Alexander is Chicago Human Rhythm Project's cofounder (with Kelly Michaels) and current artistic director. He has a performing career spanning over thirty years that includes work on the concert stage and television and in musical theater and film.

Herbert Allen is a playwright and currently works as a director of advertising studies at Columbia College Chicago.

Alicia Alonso is a Cuban ballerina who danced in New York for Ballet Theatre (later, American Ballet Theatre) in the 1930s and 1940s. She returned to Cuba in 1948 and founded Ballet Alicia Alonso, which was renamed Ballet Nacional de Cuba when it became the national ballet after the Cuban Revolution in 1959.

Alana Arenas is an actress and an ensemble member of the Steppenwolf Theatre Company. Notable roles include Pecola in Lydia Diamond's adaptation of Toni Morrison's *The Bluest Eye*.

Joyce Aschenbrenner is a renowned Katherine Dunham scholar, professor emerita of anthropology at Southern Illinois University at Edwardsville, and former curator of the Katherine Dunham Museum in East Saint Louis, Illinois.

Charles "Cholly" Atkins is a former vaudeville star, Tony Award–winning choreographer, and choreographer for Motown Records. He died in 2003 at the age of eighty-nine.

Thea Barnes is a modern dancer and choreographer who performed with the Julian Swain Inner City Dance Theater before moving to New York and joining the Alvin Ailey American Dance Theater and the Martha Graham Dance Company. Recently, she has worked as the resident dance supervisor for the musical *The Lion King* in London's West End.

Bril Barrett is a tap dancer, dance instructor, choreographer, and founder and co-artistic director of M.A.D.D. Rhythms.

Count Basie was a composer, pianist, and bandleader who first recorded in Chicago in 1936, and subsequently returned to the city with his big band on annual tours for decades. He died in 1984 at the age of seventy-nine.

Shirley Hall Bass was a Dyerette who founded the Bahamas Dance Theatre. In 1968, as director of the Sammy Dyer School and the Bahamas Dance Theatre, Bass initiated a series of international dance exchanges. Bass died in 1998 at the age of sixty-two.

Marie Basse Wiles is a Senegalese dancer who lives in New York City and directs the Maimouna Keita School of African Dance, which she cofounded with her late husband, Olukose Wiles, in 1983. Her international touring experience includes performances with the National Ballet of Senegal and Koumpo Dance Company, under the direction of Ibrahim Camara.

Daniel Beaty is a contemporary solo performer and playwright who wrote and performed *Emergence-See!* (later retitled *Emergency*) and *Mt. Joy.*

Talley Beatty was a leading modern dance choreographer who was raised in Chicago and made his professional debut, at the age of twelve, at the Chicago Civic Opera. A former student of Katherine Dunham, Beatty was a member of and choreographer for Katherine Dunham's dance company. Beatty died in 1995 at the age of seventy-six.

Blackstone Rangers were a Chicago gang originally founded as the Black P. Stone Nation in the late 1950s/early 1960s by Jeff Fort and Eugene Hairston.

Arthur Braggs produced and created the *Idlewild Revue,* a variety show that ran during the 1950s and 1960s and showcased a number of top entertainers. The *Idlewild Revue* was performed at Idlewild, Michigan, an African American resort town founded in 1912.

Abena Joan Brown is the cofounder and former president of eta Creative Arts Foundation, an African American theater and art museum in Chicago, led by Brown for forty years. A pillar of Chicago's arts scene, Brown has touched almost every aspect of theater and dance in the city. Numerous interviews with Brown, including an extensive "History Makers" archival interview, are available online and in print.

Horace Brown is a choreographer, a dancer, and the artistic director of Pocomania Jamaican Dance Company, which he started in Chicago in 1990. Originally from Jamaica, Brown came to the United States in 1978 as one of the members of Fred Baker's Western Jamaica Folk Dance Company.

Oscar Brown Jr. was a prolific songwriter, occasional political candidate, and creator of theatrical musicals. In 1969, Brown wrote and directed the Broadway musical, *Big Time Buck White,* starring Muhammad Ali. He died in 2005 at the age of seventy-eight.

Cheryl Lynn Bruce is a Chicago-based actress and director who has performed on stages across the country, on Broadway, and in London. She currently serves on the board of the African American Arts Alliance of Chicago.

Sadie Bruce was a professional dancer who performed at such Chicago nightclubs as the Golden Lily, the Regal Theater, and the Ritz. Bruce operated her own dance school from 1929 until 1985. She died in 1993 at the age of eighty-five.

Margaret Burroughs moved to Chicago at the age of five in 1920. She actively participated in the South Side Community Art Center, cofounded the DuSable Museum of African American History in 1961, and taught at numerous Chicago institutions, including Kennedy-King College. She died in 2010 at the age of ninety-five.

Jerry Butler, currently a Cook County (Chicago) Commissioner, was raised in the Cabrini–Green public housing development and, eventually, achieved international celebrity as the lead singer of The Impressions, a 1950s and 1960s R&B group. He was inducted into the Rock and Roll Hall of Fame in 1991.

Aboubacar "Papa" Camara is a Guinean dancer, djembe player, and founder of the musical group Doundounba. As a dancer, he studied at the Provincial Ballet School and joined the National Ballet Soleil d'Afrique de Guinea, where he studied under Djibril Camara. He lives in Vancouver, Canada.

Abdoulaye "Papa" Camara was the artistic director of Muntu Dance Theatre of Chicago from 1983–1986. Originally from the Casamance region of Senegal, Camara was the régisseur général de spectacle of the National Ballet of Senegal before coming to Chicago to work with

Muntu. Camara moved to New Orleans where he worked with a number of African dance companies, including Culu Children's Traditonal African Dance Company, which he helped to establish in 1988. Camara died in 2005, shortly after Hurricane Katrina.

Walter Camryn was a dancer with the Chicago Civic Opera Company and cofounder of the Stone-Camryn School of Ballet, which operated from 1941 to 1981. Camryn died in 1984 at the age of eighty-one.

Darren Canady is a playwright whose works include *Brothers of the Dust* and *You're Invited!* He is currently an assistant professor at the University of Kansas in Lawrence.

Jacob Carruthers was a professor at Northeastern Illinois University (NEU) and an authority on classical African civilizations. NEU's Carruthers Center for Inner City Studies is named after him. He died in 2004 at the age of seventy-three.

Steve Carter is the recipient of the 2001 Living Legend Award from the National Black Theatre Festival, an original member of Victory Gardens' Playwrights Ensemble, and the author of numerous works, including *Eden, House of Shadows,* and *Pecong.*

Julie Cartier, artistic director of Especially Tap Chicago (ETC) has performed and choreographed on both the jazz and tap concert stages for over fifteen years with some of Chicago's finest dance companies, including River North Chicago Dance Co., the Lynda Martha Dance Company, and Chi-Town Jazz Dance, for which she served as associate director.

Gene Chandler (born Eugene Dixon) is an R&B and soul singer who was raised in the Cabrini–Green public housing development. His song "The Duke of Earl" reached number one on the pop and R&B charts in 1962.

Eileen Cherry is an author, playwright, solo performer, and assistant professor at Bowling Green State University in Ohio. As a student at

Northwestern University, she cofounded Northwestern Community Ensemble and the African American Theatre Workshop (formerly Black Folks Theater).

Richard Christiansen was a longtime senior theater critic for the *Chicago Tribune* and is an unflagging supporter of Chicago's performing arts scene. He retired from the *Tribune* in 2002, after heading the arts and entertainment division for thirty-four years.

Victor Clottey was a founding member of the Ghana Dance Ensemble, the national dance company of Ghana, West Africa. He moved to Chicago in 1975 where he taught African and Caribbean dance and established the Victor Clottey African Dance Ensemble.

Kelan Phil Cohran is a jazz musician who moved to Chicago in 1961 as a member of Sun Ra's Arkestra. Cohran cofounded the Artistic Heritage Ensemble, which would later evolve into The Pharaohs and then into the popular recording group Earth, Wind & Fire (without Cohran). A cofounder of the Association for the Advancement of Creative Musicians and of the Affro-Arts Theater, he regularly performed in the pit band at the Regal Theater in the 1960s and 1970s.

Joy Conway is an artist, playwright, and educator. Her plays include *FAT.* She also works as the coordinator of Columbia College Chicago's LGBTQ Office of Culture and Community.

Patricia Cox is cofounder of St. Nicholas Theatre Company, former executive director of Chicago Alliance for the Performing Arts, and former chairman of the Goodman Theatre's Board of Trustees.

Arlene Crewdson was founding executive/artistic director of Pegasus Players, a non-Equity theater in Chicago. Crewdson led Pegasus from its founding in 1978 until her retirement in 2008. A former professor at Truman College, she has been honored by the *Chicago Tribune* and the Jeff Awards for her efforts in support of the arts.

Michael Cullen is a former student at the Goodman School of Drama; founder of Travel Light Theatre, an early off-Loop theater company;

cofounder of the Theatre Building Chicago; and owner of the Mercury Theater.

Maggie Daley served as first lady of the city of Chicago for twenty-two years and was an outspoken advocate for the arts. She died in 2011 at the age of sixty-eight.

Richard M. Daley, son of Mayor Richard J. Daley, was also a longtime mayor of Chicago (1989–2011). During his administration, the performing arts flourished in the city in part because of the support of the mayor and his wife, Maggie.

Deidre M. Dawson was a member of the Joseph Holmes Chicago Dance Theatre. She later directed a dance ensemble out of Sullivan High School. She is the director of the Chicago Public Schools' All-City Dance Ensemble and a board member for Muntu Dance Theatre of Chicago.

Aaron Todd Douglas is an actor, a founding ensemble member of Congo Square Theatre Company in Chicago, and an ensemble member of the Cincinnati Shakespeare Festival in Ohio. He has worked at numerous Chicago theaters, including Chicago Shakespeare Theater, eta Creative Arts, Goodman Theatre, Steppenwolf, and Pegasus Players.

Katherine Dunham was a choreographer, dancer, and founder of the Katherine Dunham Dance Company. She died in 2006 at the age of ninety-six. For more information, see the introduction.

Sammy Dyer was a dancer, choreographer, founder of the Sammy Dyer School of the Theatre in 1930, and creator of the Dyerettes, an African American women's dance troupe. He died in 1960. For more information, see the introduction.

Billy Eckstine was a popular singer and big band leader. He died in 1993 at the age of seventy-eight.

Joseph Ehrenberg was a doctoral student in comparative education at the University of Chicago, where he started a theater group called the International Players. In 1974, he cofounded Chicago City Theatre Company/

Joel Hall Dancers with Joel Hall. Ehrenberg died in 1995 at the age of sixty-five.

Lucille Ellis was an original Katherine Dunham dancer, who began working with Dunham in 1929. She died in 1998 at the age of seventy-nine.

Wendell Etherly is a playwright who was born in Chicago in 1979. He started writing at the age of twelve. His plays include *Let No Man Put Asunder, Grace's New Year's Resolution,* and *The Inheritance.*

Jay Fagan is a tap dancer who has worked with numerous dance companies, including CNADM (Chicago National Association of Dance Masters) and the Chicago Human Rhythm Project.

Robert Falls has been a director and artistic director of the Goodman Theatre since 1986. His productions of Arthur Miller's *Death of a Salesman* and Eugene O'Neill's *Long Day's Journey Into Night* received seven Tony Awards and three Drama Desk Awards.

Shirley Jo Finney is an actress and director. Her directing credits include productions at leading regional theaters, including Goodman Theatre, Alabama Shakespeare Festival, the McCarter Theatre, and the Actors Theatre of Louisville Humana Festival of New American Plays.

Muriel Foster was a dancer and then director of the Sammy Dyer School of Dancing. She attended the Dyer School at the age of ten, studied tap with Cholly Atkins, and performed with the Dyerettes in the 1950s. In 2007, she received the JUBA Award from the Chicago Human Rhythm Project, for her lifetime contribution to dance.

Four Step Brothers was a tap group who began in the mid-1920s at the Cotton Club in New York and lasted until 1989. The cast of "Brothers" changed over the years; some of the members included Maceo Anderson, Flash McDonald, Al Williams, Prince Spencer, and Edward Bozeman.

Tommy Gomez was a dancer, member of Katherine Dunham's company, a teacher of Dunham technique, and artistic director of the Body Language Dance Company in Chicago. He taught at Kennedy-King College, Truman College, and the Joel Hall Dance Center. He died in 1998 at the age of seventy-seven.

Lester Goodman was the owner of the Lester Goodman School of Dance and mentor to a number of dancers in Chicago, including Joseph Holmes. In 1998, he was given the Dance Coalition's Ruth Page Award for his lifetime of service to the dance community.

Joan Gray is a dancer and the president of Muntu Dance Theatre of Chicago. Between 1979 and 1991, she danced with the company. She has served on the boards of the African American Arts Alliance of Chicago, Chicago Dance Coalition, and the International Association of Blacks in Dance.

Gary Griffin is a theater director and associate artistic director of Chicago Shakespeare Theater. Twice named a Chicagoan of the Year by the *Chicago Tribune,* he directed *The Color Purple* on Broadway in 2005.

Gary Guidry is chief operations officer of I'm Ready Productions and a producer-playwright in Je'Caryous Johnson's production company.

LaQuietta Hardy, a founding member of Najwa Dance Corps and currently a judge (first elected in 1998) on Cook County's 7th Subcircuit.

Paul Carter Harrison is a playwright, director, and theater professor. His play *The Great MacDaddy* was produced by the Negro Ensemble Company and won an Obie Award in 1973. His plays and scholarship focused on the connections between Africa and African American culture. In 1976, Harrison accepted the position of chair, professor, and writer-in-residence in the theater department of Columbia College Chicago. He became a professor emeritus in 2002.

Patrick Henry was the founder of Free Street Theater of Chicago. He died in 1989 at the age of fifty-three.

Endesha Ida Mae Holland was a playwright and a professor at the University of Southern California in Los Angeles. Her best-known play, *From* *the Mississippi Delta,* was partly financed by Oprah Winfrey, directed by Jonathan Wilson, and starred Cheryl Lynn Bruce. Holland died in 2006 at the age of sixty-one.

Joseph Holmes was the founder, choreographer, and artistic director of the Joseph Holmes Dance Theatre, which was created in 1974. A student of Darlene Blackburn and Alvin Ailey, he died in 1986 at the age of thirty-eight.

Jennifer Hudson is a native Chicago singer and actress. Hudson won an Academy Award for Best Supporting Actress for her portrayal of Effie White in the film musical *Dreamgirls* (2006).

Don Jackson, originally from Chicago, is a cofounder of Kopano Performing Arts Company, which performs West African and South African music, song, and dance. Jackson is the African dance and drum instructor for the Barbara A. Sizemore Academy, a charter school on Chicago's South Side, and he has worked with youth for over forty years.

Runako Jahi is a playwright, painter, and the artistic director of eta Creative Arts Foundation.

Kofi Jantuah is originally from Ghana, West Africa, where he was a principlal dancer with the national dance company of Ghana, the Ghana Dance Ensemble. He moved to Chicago in 1975 and later established the Jantuah Dance Troupe of Chicago.

Bernice Johnson, founder of the Bernice Johnson Dance School (also known as The Bernice Johnson Cultural Arts Center) in New York City, was born in Portsmouth, Virginia in 1911 and was a chorus line dancer who performed at the famed Cotton Club in Harlem. She began teaching in the basement of her house in the late 1940s, and opened her own dance school by the 1950s. She died in 2005 at the age of ninety-three.

Javon Johnson is a founding ensemble member of Congo Square Theatre Company, actor, and playwright.

Je'Caryous Johnson, a Houston native, is a producer-playwright best known for adapting novels to the stage. He is the founder of I'm Ready Productions.

McKinley Johnson is a director and playwright. His plays include *The Nativity* and (with Stephanie Newsom) *Being Beautiful.* As an actor, he has appeared at Black Ensemble Theater, Goodman Theatre, and Remains Theatre Company.

Okoro Harold Johnson was a prominent Chicago actor and was a co-founder and the artistic director of eta Creative Arts Foundation. He died in 2012 at the age of eighty-six.

Chris Jones is a theater critic for the *Chicago Tribune,* where he has worked for two decades. He is an adjunct professor in DePaul University's Theatre School, where he previously served as dean.

Ora Jones is an actress and Steppenwolf ensemble member. Jones has also appeared in productions by the Goodman Theatre and Court Theatre, and received an After Dark Award for her portrayal of the Stage Manager in Writers' Theatre's production of Thornton Wilder's *Our Town.*

Yousouff Koumbassa is a former dancer with Ballet Djoliba, the national ballet company of Guinea, where he studied under Sekouba Camara. Koumbassa travels extensively, teaching and performing in the United States and internationally.

Morikeba Kouyate is a griot and master kora player from Bounkilling in the Casamance region of Senegal. He lives in New Orleans and performs nationally and internationally performing in various venues.

Irv Kupcinet was a popular journalist and gossip columnist for the *Chicago Daily News,* which became the *Chicago Sun-Times.* He began writing "Kup's Column" in 1943 and continued until 2003, when he died at the age of ninety-one.

Major Lance is an R&B singer. Lance was a high-grossing artist for OKeh Records in the 1960s and an important figure in the soul music scene in Chicago. Many of his early songs became hits on both R&B and pop charts, including "The Monkey Time" (1963) and "Um, Um, Um, Um, Um, Um" (1964). Lance died in 1994 at the age of fifty-five.

Harry Lennix is a theater and film actor. A Chicago native, Lennix appeared regularly on the Chicago stage before moving to Los Angeles and primarily working as a film and television actor. His notable film roles include Aaron in *Titus* (1999).

Ted Levy was a tap dancer and choreographer. Levy was trained in Chicago by tap dancer Finis Henderson II and went on to pursue a professional dancing career in theater, television, and film. He received a Tony nomination and an Outer Critics Circle Award for his choreography on the musical *Jelly's Last Jam* (1993), and an Emmy for his role in the PBS Special *Precious Memories*.

Vernell Lillie is a professor emerita of Africana Studies at the University of Pittsburgh and founder of Kuntu Repertory Theatre (Pittsburgh) in 1975.

Douglas Alan Mann was a cofounder and artistic director of Chicago Theatre Company. He died in 2011 at the age of fifty-eight.

Ronnie Marshall is a tap dancer who comes from a lineage of Chicago performers. He studied Katherine Dunham dance technique with Lucille Ellis. He died in 1998.

Curtis Mayfield was an R&B, soul, and funk singer. Mayfield first rose to fame as a member of The Impressions, a popular soul music group in the 1960s. He is remembered for his politically conscious songs such as "Keep on Pushin'" and "People Get Ready," both of which began to feature prominently at civil rights rallies and demonstrations. Mayfield died in 1999 at the age of fifty-seven.

Ali M'Baye comes from a long lineage of griots. Originally from Dakar, Senegal, Ali is a drummer with Muntu Dance Theatre of Chicago. Ali has traveled nationally and internationally teaching West African drum technique and performing.

Marion McClinton is a director best known for interpreting the works of playwright August Wilson. He directed the world premiere of Wilson's *Gem of the Ocean* at the Goodman Theatre and Broadway productions of *King Hedley II* and *Ma Rainey's Black Bottom*, as well as the Broadway production of Regina Taylor's *Drowning Crow* (2004).

Dianne McIntyre is a modern dancer and founder of the dance/music ensemble Sounds in Motion in 1972. She served on the executive board of the Dramatists Guild of America, a professional association of American playwrights.

Jewell McLaurin was owner of the Jewell McLaurin School of Dance in the early 1960s. McLaurin was a professor of physical education at Malcolm X College.

Arthur Mitchell is a dancer, choreographer, and founder of the Dance Theatre of Harlem.

Wes Montgomery was a jazz guitarist who led his own band as well as toured with Lionel Hampton (1948–50) and played in jam sessions with other artists, such as John Coltrane. He died in 1968 at the age of forty-five.

Malika (Brenda) Moore is a dancer and choreographer, former associate artistic director for Najwa Junior Dance Corps, and artistic director for Diamano (Roots) Dancers and Drummers of Chicago.

Charles Michael Moore was a playwright, director, and actor who worked frequently with Black Ensemble Theater, Congo Square Theatre Company, and Chicago Theater Company. His plays include *The Hooch* and *Love's Light in Flight*. He died in 2003 at the age of fifty-four.

Lenwood Morris was a performer with Katherine Dunham Dance Company in the 1940s and 1950s.

Kimosha P. Murphy is the artistic director of Alyo Children's Dance Theatre, which she started in 1985. Murphy was a principal dancer and dance captain with Muntu Dance Theatre of Chicago for over sixteen years, during which she directed the Muntu Young Audiences program and toured nationally and internationally.

Harold "Atu" Murray is a musican, sculpture, and philosopher. He has performed with artists such as Duke Ellington, Chief Bey, Sun Ra, and Dinah Washington. From 1969–1974, Murray moved to Ghana where he performed and studied music, philosophy, and sculpturing. Upon returning to Chicago, he established the Sun Drummer, a society dedicated to traditional African music and philosophy.

Masequa Myers is the former assistant director (1974–79) of the LaMont Zeno Theatre and Cultural Arts Program in Chicago and founder of the Ajabu Children Theatre Company.

Fatou N'Diaye-Davis is the founder and director of the traditional West African dance company Silimbo D'Adeane West African Dance and Drum Company. The company name translates to "Sunrise on Adeane." Fatou was born in the Cassamance region of Senegal in the village of Adeane. Ms. N'Diaye-Davis has danced and acted professionally for over thirty-seven years. She currently resides in Boston.

Stuart Oken began his producing career as managing director of Chicago's Organic Theatre Company in the mid-1970s before cofounding the Apollo Theatre in 1978. He later produced films in Los Angeles before taking the position of executive vice president of Disney Theatrical productions. Credits during his time with Disney include *The Lion King* and *Aida*.

Babatunde Olantunji, born in 1927 in Ajido, Nigeria, West Africa, migrated to the United States in 1950 to attend Morehouse College in Atlanta, Georgia. He recorded his highly regarded album, *Drums of Pas-*

sion, in 1959 and opened the Olantunji Center of African Culture in Harlem in 1967. He died in 2003 at the age of seventy-six.

Ed Parish studied ballet with Mikhail Panieff, Bronsislava Nijinska, and Irene Nijinska. In 1960, he opened a dance studio in Chicago, at 4723 N. Kedzie, where he took in youth off the street and trained them in ballet. The studio, which also became a foster home, closed in 1977 because of an improper zoning permit. Parish reopened the studio in Orangeville, Illinois. He died in 2002 at the age of seventy-seven.

Sheldon Patinkin served as chair in the theater department of Columbia College from 1980 to 2009. He has served as artistic consultant to The Second City and Steppenwolf Theatre, and has written various screenplays, plays, and books on the theater. He is also a prolific director, having directed over thirty operas. Patinkin has received lifetime achievement awards from the Chicago Improv Festival, the Israeli Film Festival, and the League of Chicago Theatres.

Jimmy Payne Jr. is a tap dancer and son of dance legend Jimmy Payne Sr. He has performed at Chicago Blues Festival, the Chicago Jazz Festival, Dance Chicago, and with Chicago Human Rhythm Project.

Jimmy Payne Sr. was born in the Panama Canal Zone in 1905 and moved to New York City with his family in 1917. A master tap dancer, he moved to Chicago in 1947 and eventually opened the Jimmy Payne School of Dance. Jimmy Payne is also credited with introducing Afro-Cuban music and dance, along with other performance traditions from the Caribbean, to a number of artists in the city. He died in 2000 at the age of ninety-five.

Useni Eugene Perkins is a poet and playwright, former executive director of the Better Boys Foundation of Chicago, author of *Home Is a Dirty Street: The Social Oppression of Black Children,* and former interim president of the DuSable Museum of African American History.

Ernest Perry Jr. is a popular and frequently cast actor in Chicago who has worked throughout the city, including Goodman Theatre, Victory

Gardens Theater, Lookingglass Theatre, and Chicago Shakespeare Theater.

Sidney Poitier is an actor, director, and producer. In 1963, Poitier became the first African American to win an Oscar for Best Actor in a Leading Role for his performance in *The Lilies of the Field*. Poitier is often credited with breaking the color barrier in Hollywood, and he would go on to perform in films dealing with race, including *Guess Who's Coming to Dinner* and *In the Heat of the Night* (both in 1967). President Barack Obama awarded Poitier the Presidential Medal of Freedom in 2009.

Will Power is an actor, playwright, and solo performer. His works include *Flow, Seven,* and *Fetch Clay, Make a Man*.

Marie-Christine Dunham Pratt, adopted daughter of Katherine Dunham and John Thomas Pratt. She was adopted in 1952, at the age of four.

Pemon Rami is a former director (1971–72) of the Kuumba Workshop, artistic/managing director (1973–79) of LaMont Zeno Theatre, and casting agent for numerous films, including *Cooley High* and *The Blues Brothers*.

Reggio the Hoofer (Reginald McLaughlin) is a tap dancer and teacher. McLaughlin began his career dancing in Chicago subway stations, until Urban Gateways Centre for Arts Education hired him to teach tap in schools, museums, and libraries. Since then, McLaughlin has performed nationally and internationally, but he remains based in Chicago, where he continues to teach and perform.

Pearl Reynolds is a second-generation member of the Katherine Dunham Dance Company. Based in New York, she taught Dunham Technique at the Dance Theatre of Harlem.

Clifton Robinson is the Musical Director of Muntu Dance Theatre of Chicago. He migrated to the United States in 1978 as a member of Fred Baker's Western Jamaica Folk Dance Company. In 1995, he collaborated with Hannibal Lukumbe and the Chicago Symphony Orchestra, as musical director of the Eye Plus One Percussion Ensemble, in the production of *African Portraits*. In 2011, Robinson received the Rex Nettleford Award for Outstanding Dedication to the Cultural Performing Arts at the First Annual Caribbean American Heritage Month Gala, which was sponsored by the West Indian Folk Dance Company.

Ira Rogers is a singer, actor, and playwright who studied theater at Wilson Junior College. In the 1960s, he was half of Inman and Rogers, a folk duo with LaRoy Inman. Throughout the 1970s, he was a frequently cast actor in Chicago.

Albirda Rose is a professional dancer, actress, singer, and educator. Dr. Rose taught at San Francisco State University, where in 2001 she founded Village Dancers, a company based on Katherine Dunham's teaching philosophy.

Cheikh Samb is the president of the Senegalese community organization in Chicago, Illinois.

Allassane Sarr is a Senegalese griot, dancer, and drummer. Sarr came to the United States in 1991 and remained in the country to perform and teach African dance and drumming, along with other aspects of West African culture.

Red Saunders, born Theodore Dudley Saunders, was a jazz drummer and the bandleader of Club DeLisa in Chicago from 1937 until the mid-1950s. Saunders traveled extensively throughout the United States and internationally performing with many jazz greats. He died in 1981 at the age of sixty-nine.

Archie Savage was a member of the Katherine Dunham Dance Company, an accomplished dancer/actor in numerous films (including uncredited roles in *A Cabin in the Sky* and *La Dolce Vita*), and a longtime youth dance instructor.

Sarah Savelli is a tap dancer and a cofounder and former artistic director of Chicago's all-woman tap-dancing company Rhythm ISS.

Roche Schulfer has been the executive director of the Goodman Theatre since 1979. Under the guidance of Schulfer, the Goodman won the Tony Award for Outstanding Regional Theatre in 1992. Schulfer is also the founder of the League of Chicago Theatres, and teaches in the Theatre School at DePaul University.

Steve Scott is associate producer at the Goodman Theatre, where he has overseen more than 150 productions (and counting). He is a member of the Jeff Committee's Artist and Technical Team, a board member of Season of Concern, and an associate artist with Chicago Dramatists and Colllaboraction theater companies.

Assane Seck is a dancer and drummer from Dakar, Senegal, West Africa. Seck is the artistic director of Groupe Dara Gee, a dancer and drum performance company based in Chicago that specializes in African Diaspora arts and culture. He regularly leads workshops in Chicago's public schools and is an instructor at Loyola University Chicago.

Veda Sidney is a dancer and teacher. Sidney has danced with the Joseph Holmes Chicago Dance Company and the Chicago Moving Company, taught dance in high school and college programs, and worked with Chicago teachers to use movement as an interdisciplinary pedagogical tool.

Charles Smith is head of the Professional Playwriting Program at Ohio University and playwright in residence at the Tony Award–winning Victory Gardens Theater in Chicago.

Mamie Smith was a singer and actress. Smith was a Vaudeville performer and the first African American blues singer to record a song ("Crazy Blues" and "It's Right Here for You" in 1920). Her success paved the way for future black female singers of the era. She also acted in several films in the 1930s and 1940s. She died in 1946, at the age of sixty-three.

Titos Sompa emigrated to the United States from Paris in the 1970s, where he was teaching music and touring with a band called Les Echos Noir. He started his dance company, Tanawa Dance Company, in New York City in 1970.

Larry Steele, born in Chicago in 1913, began his performance career at the Panama Cafe in 1934. His revue, "Smart Affairs," started in 1947 and continued until 1972. A nationally and internationally traveling show, it launched the careers of countless singers, dancers, comedians, and entertainers.

Bruce Stegmann is codirector of Stegmann's School of the Performing Arts in Spring Hill, Tennessee, and founder of Especially Tap Chicago.

Bentley Stone was a dancer with the Chicago Civic Opera Company and cofounder of the Stone-Camryn School of Ballet, which opened in 1941 and closed in 1981. Stone died in 1983.

Rick Stone is a musical theater artist best known for his longtime association (since 1995) with Black Ensemble Theater. An off-and-on resident of Cabrini–Green public housing development for five decades, until 1997, Stone appeared in the film *Cooley High* with BET founder Jackie Taylor.

Sun Ra was a jazz musician. As eccentric as he was influential, Sun Ra began his career in Chicago as the house arranger for the Club DeLisa. By the 1950s, Sun Ra was with the Arkestra, a collective of musicians that shared his commitment to improvisation and his philosophy, a mixture of Egyptian mythology and a pseudo–science fiction fascination with the cosmos. Sun Ra moved from Chicago to New York in 1960, and from New York to Philadelphia in 1968, while band members came and went. He died in 1993, at the age of seventy-nine.

Tommy Sutton founded the Mayfair Academy of Fine Arts in 1957. He taught dance, especially to children, for nearly fifty years. As a performer and choreographer, he toured extensively with Duke Ellington and Count Basie, among others. He died in 1995 at the age of seventy-six.

Renee Sutton-Silas (aka Nahgeree Sutton-Silas) is the artistic director of Minianka Afrikan Drum and Dance Ensemble. Originally a member of Muntu Dance Theatre of Chicago, Sutton-Silas established Minianka with her late husband Meshach Silas in 1994.

Julian Swain was a dancer, choreographer, singer, and actor. Swain spent his early career at the Club DeLisa in Chicago, where he formed a dance trio called the Beige Beaus. The trio subsequently toured under the tutelage of Duke Ellington before breaking up in the 1950s. When Swain finished touring in 1968 and moved back to Chicago, he founded the Julian Swain Inner City Dance Theatre, with the goal of raising awareness of African heritage. The African-American Arts Alliance presented Swain with a Lifetime Achievement award in 1993. He died in 2011, at the age of eighty-six.

Clarence Taylor was an actor and the founding artistic director of the Experimental Black Actors Guild (X-BAG).

Jumaane Taylor is a dancer and artistic director of M.A.D.D. Rhythms, a company dedicated to the art of tap dancing. Taylor also teaches tap at the Sammy Dyer School of the Theatre.

Regina Taylor is a playwright, director, and actress. Taylor has acted for film, theater, and television, and has written several critically acclaimed plays, including the musical *Crowns* (2009). She is currently an artistic associate at Chicago's Goodman Theatre.

Mor Thiam, who was born in Dakar in 1941, is a Senegalese drummer and historian. He came to the United States to work with Katherine Dunham in St. Louis in 1968. He currently lives in the United States where he continues to teach and perform.

Philip Thomas is president and CEO of eta Creative Arts. Between 1996 and 2000, Thomas served as eta Chicago's director of development.

Dr. Anderson (Andy) Thompson is a professor emeritus in the Inner City Studies Educational program, which is housed in the Carruthers Center for Inner City Studies at Northeastern University. Dr. Thompson is a founding member of the Association for the Study of Classical African Civilizations as well as a member of the Kemetic Institute's Councils of Historians and Elders.

Lee Aca Thompson is a performer, choreographer, and fashion designer. He created a dance technique, Piragramac Dance Technique, which is designed to prepare the body for all forms of dance—combining traditional African, South American, and Caribbean dance forms as well as modern, jazz, and tap techniques.

Alyo Tolbert was a choreographer and dancer. Tolbert was a founder and the first artistic director of Muntu Dance Theatre of Chicago, a position he held until his death in 1983.

Tiffany Trent (Rev.) is associate pastor of drama ministry at Trinity United Church of Chicago. She holds a master of divinity from Chicago Theological Seminary and an MFA in directing from Carnegie Mellon University.

Russell Vandenbroucke is a director, playwright, and theater scholar. Vandenbroucke served as Northlight Theatre's artistic director from 1987 to 1997. Vandenbroucke currently serves as professor and chair of Theatre Arts at the University of Louisville.

Andrea Vinson is a dancer, teacher, and the associate artistic director of Najwa Dance Corps. She has taught dance to children and adults in various venues around Chicago, including the Joffrey Ballet, and has performed in theater, film, and television.

Vince Viverito was a veteran Chicago actor who appeared on stages across the city and was especially known for appearing in comic roles. He died in 2005 at the age of sixty-two.

Dianne Walker is a tap dancer and the artistic director of TapDancin, Inc., in Boston.

Theodore Ward was a politically minded playwright whose plays controversially addressed the African American experience in the early twentieth century. He was a member of the Federal Theatre Project, which produced his best-known play, *Big White Fog*, in 1938. Ward went on to found the Negro Playwrights Company in 1940 and continued to write until the early 1970s. Ward died May 8, 1983, at the age of eighty.

Dinah Washington, born Ruth Lee Jones, was a versatile singer of the 1940s and 1950s. She sang gospel, blues, jazz, and R&B, topping both the R&B and pop charts in the height of her popularity. Washington died in 1963, at the age of thirty-nine.

Baba Olukose Wiles was a founding member of the International Afrikan-American Ballet (1974) and an artistic director and music director of the company. He founded the Maimouna Keita School of African Dance with his wife, Marie Basse Wiles in 1983.

Sheila Walker Wilkins has been executive director of Najwa Dance Corps since 1989.

August Wilson was a playwright whose work included his ten-play Pittsburgh Cycle (or Century Cycle), which collectively told the story of the African American experience in the twentieth century by devoting one play to each decade. Two of the cycle plays—*Fences* (1987) and *The Piano Lesson* (1990) won the Pulitzer Prize for Drama. Wilson died October 2, 2005, at the age of sixty.

Oprah Winfrey was host of the monumentally successful, nationally and internationally syndicated talk show *The Oprah Winfrey Show,* which was filmed in Chicago and ran from 1986 to 2011. Winfrey is also the founder of the production company Harpo Productions, cofounder of Oxygen Media, creator of the Oprah Winfrey Network (OWN), and owner of *O: The Oprah Magazine. Forbes Magazine* ranked Winfrey as the wealthiest African American in the twentieth century.

Dennis Zacek was director and artistic director of Victory Gardens Theater from 1977 to 2011. He is responsible for creating the hugely successful fourteen-member playwright ensemble at the Gardens and was at the helm in 2001, when Victory Gardens received the Tony for Outstanding Regional Theatre. He has directed over 250 plays in his career.

DIRECTORY OF CHICAGO'S BLACK PERFORMING ARTS INSTITUTIONS

ASE: Chicago Associate of Black Storytellers
P.O. Box 802834
Chicago, IL 60680
www.aseblackstorytellers.org

Ayodele Drum and Dance Community
7948 S. Paxton Avenue
Chicago, IL 60617
Phone: 773.242.9631; Fax: 773.667.1666
www.ayodeledrumanddance.com

Black Ensemble Theater
4450 N. Clark St.
Chicago, IL 60640
773.769.4451
www.blackensemble.org

Black CouTours, Tours of Black Culture
P.O. Box 201896
Chicago, IL 60620
www.blackcoutours.com

C.A.A.A.P.
The Chicago Alliance of
African-American Photographers
P.O. Box 5284
Chicago, IL 60680
www.caaap.org

Carruther's Center for Inner City Studies
Northeastern Illinois University
700 E. Oakwood
Chicago, IL 60653
773.268.7500
www.neiu.edu/About%20NEIU/Campus%20Locations/Center%20for
%20Inner%20City%20Studies/Center_for_Inner_City_Studies.html

Congo Square Theatre Company
2936 N. Southport Ave.
Suite 210
Chicago, IL 60657
773.296.1108
www.congosquaretheatre.org

Deeply Rooted Dance Theater
17 N. State Street—19th Floor
Chicago, IL 60602
312.795.9777
www.deeplyrootedproductions.org

DuSable Museum of
African American Art
740 E. 56th Place
Chicago, IL 60637
773.947.0600
www.dusablemuseum.org

eta Creative Arts Foundation
7558 S. South Chicago
Chicago, IL 60619
773.752.3955
www.etacreativearts.org

Harold Washington Cultural Center
4701 S. King Drive
Chicago, IL 60653
773.373.1900
www.hwccchicago.org

M.A.D.D. Rhythms
7059 S. Shore Drive
Chicago, IL 60649
773.604.1899
maddrhythms.com

MPAACT Theatre Company
MAAT Production Association of
Afrikan Centered Theatre
P.O. Box 10039
Chicago, IL 60610
312.409.6724
www.mpaact.org

Muntu Dance Theatre of Chicago
7127 S. Ellis Avenue
Suite 2
Chicago, IL 60619
773.241.6080
www.muntu.com

Najwa Dance Corps
Malcolm X College
Bruce K. Hayden Center for the Performing Arts
1900 W. Van Buren Street
Room 0223
Chicago, IL 60612
www.najwadance.org

South Side Community Art Center
3831 S.Michigan Ave
Chicago, IL 60653
773.373.1026
www.southsidecommunityartcenter.com

South Shore Cultural Center
7059 S. South Shore Drive
Chicago, IL 60649
773.256.0149
www.hydepark.org/parks/southshore/sscc1.html

Third World Press
P.O. Box 19730
7822 S. Dobson Ave.
Chicago, IL 60619
773.651.0700
www.thirdworldbooks.com

INDEX